아레테 고전 2
명작 줄거리로 영어 도장깨기

한학선 지음

아레테 고전 2: 명작 줄거리로 영어 도장깨기

발 행 | 2024년 03월 25일
저 자 | 한학선
펴낸이 | 한건희
펴낸곳 | 주식회사 부크크
출판사등록 | 2014.07.15.(제2014-16호)
주 소 | 서울특별시 금천구 가산디지털1로 119 SK트윈타워 A동 305호
전 화 | 1670-8316
이메일 | info@bookk.co.kr

ISBN | 979-11-410-7789-1

www.bookk.co.kr
© 한학선 2024

CONTENTS

Unit 1: The Iliad 일리아드

Unit 2: The Odyssey 오디세이

Unit 3: The Three Kingdoms 삼국지

Unit 4: The Divine Comedy 신곡 (1320)

Unit 5: Decameron 데카메론 (1353)

Unit 6: Canterbury Tales 캔터베리이야기 (1390)

Unit 7: Romeo and Juliet 로미오와 줄리엣 (1597)

Unit 8: Hamlet 햄릿 (1599)

Unit 9: Othello 오셀로 (1603)

Unit 10: King Lear 리어 왕 (1605)

Unit 11: Macbeth 맥베스 (1623)

Unit 12: Don Quixote 돈키호테 (1605)

Unit 13: The Pilgrim's Progress 천로역정 (1678)

Unit 14: Robinson Crusoe 로빈슨 크루소 (1719)

Unit 15: Gulliver's Travels 걸리버 여행기 (1726)

Unit 16: Faust 파우스트 (1808)

Unit 17: Pride and Prejudice 오만과 편견 (1813)

Unit 18: Frankenstein 프랑켄슈타인 (1818)

Unit 19: Oliver Twist 올리버 트위스트 (1838)

Unit 20: The Count of Monte Cristo 몬테 크리스토 백작 (1844)

Unit 21: Jane Eyre 제인 에어 (1847)

Unit 22: Wuthering Heights 폭풍의 언덕 (1847)

Unit 23: Moby-Dick 모비딕 (1851)

Unit 24: Walden 월든 (1854)

Unit 25: Great Expectations 위대한 유산 (1861)

Unit 26: Crime and Punishment 죄와 벌 (1866)

Unit 27: War and Peace 전쟁과 평화 (1869)

Unit 28: 20,000 Leagues Under the Sea 해저 2만 리 (1870)

Unit 29: Anna Karenina 안나 카레니나 (1877)

Unit 30: Treasure Island 보물섬 (1883)

Unit 31: What Men Live By 인간은 무엇으로 사는가? (1885)

Unit 32: The Brothers Karamazov 카라마조프가의 형제들 (1880)

Unit 33: Thus Spoke Zarathustra 차라투스트라는 이렇게 말했다 (1883)

Unit 34: Dr. Jekyll and Mr. Hyde 지킬박사와 하이드 (1886)

Unit 35: Resurrection 부활 (1899)

이 책을 문학과 영어 두 마리의 토끼를 잡고 싶은 분들께 바칩니다.

과학과 문명이 발달하면 할수록 세상은 더욱 각박해져 갑니다.
인간이 동물과 다른 점은 도구를 사용할 지혜가 있음과 동시에
자연과 인간을 사랑할 줄 아는 마음이 있다는 점입니다.
문학은 자연뿐만 아니라 인간을 사랑하고 이해하는 도구입니다.
고전문학에는 현대인들과 맞지 않는 가치관들도 분명 존재 하지만

인간은 어떻게 인간으로 살아가야 하는가?
인간이 왜 자연과 교감해야 하는가?
인간이 왜 낭만과 순수를 유지해야 하는가?
인간은 왜 실패와 좌절을 두려워해서는 안 되는가?
인간은 왜 끊임없이 자기극복을 해야 하는가?
인간은 왜 자신을 사랑해야 하는가?

이러한 질문들에 대한 해답을 찾을 수가 있습니다.
이 책은 이러한 해답을 찾으면서 영어독해, 문법, 영작, 어휘를
아울러 공부할 수 있도록 설계 되었습니다.

1800년대 이전 문학 작품

Unit 1: The Iliad 일리아드

Unit 2: The Odyssey 오디세이

Unit 3: The Three Kingdoms 삼국지

Unit 4: The Divine Comedy 신곡 (1320)

Unit 5: Decameron 데카메론 (1353)

Unit 6: Canterbury Tales 캔터베리이야기 (1390)

Unit 7: Romeo and Juliet 로미오와 줄리엣 (1597)

Unit 8: Hamlet 햄릿 (1599)

Unit 9: Othello 오셀로 (1603)

Unit 10: King Lear 리어 왕 (1605)

Unit 11: Macbeth 맥베스 (1623)

Unit 12: Don Quixote 돈키호테 (1605)

Unit 13: The Pilgrim's Progress 천로역정 (1678)

Unit 14: Robinson Crusoe 로빈슨 크루소 (1719)

Unit 15: Gulliver's Travels 걸리버 여행기 (1726)

Unit 1: Iliad

"Iliad" is an ancient Greek epic poem attributed to the poet Homer. It is one of the most significant works of Western literature and tells the story of the Trojan War. The story is set during the final year of the Trojan War, which is fought between the city of Troy and the Greek city-states, particularly the Achaeans (Greeks). The epic covers a few weeks during the war.

The central character of the poem is Achilles, a great warrior and hero of the Greeks. The conflict begins when Agamemnon, the leader of the Greek forces, takes Achilles' war prize, a girl named Briseis, as his own. This action infuriates Achilles, who withdraws from the battle in anger, causing significant losses for the Greeks. With Achilles refusing to fight, the Trojans, led by Hector (the greatest Trojan warrior), gain the upper hand and begin to win battles against the Greeks. They even breach the Greek defensive walls.

Achilles' close friend Patroclus convinces him to let him lead the Myrmidons (Achilles' soldiers) into battle wearing Achilles' armor, hoping to boost the Greeks' morale. However, Patroclus is killed by Hector, which devastates Achilles. Hearing about Patroclus' death and driven by grief and rage, Achilles decides to rejoin the battle, seeking vengeance for his friend's death. He reconciles with Agamemnon, and the Greeks regain their strength with

Achilles back in action.

In a fierce duel, Achilles confronts Hector outside the walls of Troy. Achilles kills Hector and drags his body back to the Greek camp, showing no mercy and desecrating Hector's corpse. Hector's father, King Priam of Troy, sneaks into the Greek camp and pleads with Achilles to return his son's body for a proper funeral. Touched by the old king's grief, Achilles agrees, showing a brief moment of compassion.

The poem ends with the funeral of Hector, where the Trojans mourn their fallen hero. Despite Hector's death, the war continues, and the poem does not cover the famous Trojan Horse or the fall of Troy, as those events are narrated in the sequel, "The Odyssey."

"The Iliad" explores themes of heroism, honor, pride, and the futility of war. It also delves into the complex emotions and motivations of its characters, particularly Achilles, making it a timeless and enduring work of literature.

[Vocabulary]

ancient 고대의 be attributed to ~의 것으로 추정되다 significant 중요한 literature 문학 summary 요약 main plot 주요 줄거리 set 설정하다 particularly 특히 Achaeans 아키아인 conflict 갈등 significant losses 상당한 손실 refuse 거절하다 convinced 설득된 morale 사기 devastated 파괴된 vengeance 복수 fierce 맹렬한 confront 맞서다 mercy 자비 desecrate 더럽히다 plead 탄원하다 proper funeral 적절한 장례 mourn 애도하다 explore 탐구하다 heroism 영웅적 행위 honor 명예 pride 긍지 futility 무익 delve into 파고들다 motivation 동기 timeless 영원한 enduring 지속되는 sequel 후속 작

[본문 해석] 일리아드

"일리아드"는 시인 호메로스의 작품으로 추정되는 고대 그리스 서사시입니다. 서양 문학의 가장 중요한 작품 중 하나이며 트로이 전쟁에 대한 이야기를 담고 있습니다. 이 이야기는 트로이 도시와 그리스 도시 국가들, 특히 아카이아인들 사이에서 벌어진 트로이 전쟁의 마지막 해를 배경으로 합니다. 이 서사시는 전쟁 중 몇 주를 다루고 있습니다.

이 시의 중심인물은 그리스의 위대한 전사이자 영웅인 아킬레우스입니다. 갈등은 그리스군의 지도자 아가멤논이 아킬레우스가 전쟁의 포상으로 얻은 브리세이스라는 여인을 자신의 것으로 취하면서 시작됩니다. 이 행동은 아킬레우스를 격분시키고, 아킬레우스는 분노하여 전투에서 철수하여 그리스 군에게 큰 손실을 입힙니다. 아킬레우스가 전투를 거부하면서 헥토르(트로이의 가장 위대한 전사)가 이끄는 트로이군이 우위를 점하고 그리스 군에 맞서 전투에서 승리하기 시작합니다. 그들은 심지어 그리스의 방어벽을 부수기도 합니다.

아킬레우스의 절친한 친구 파트로클로스는 그리스인들의 사기를 북돋아 주고자, 자신이 아킬레우스의 갑옷을 입고 미르미돈(아킬레우스의 병사들)을 전투로 이끌게 해달라고 아킬레우스를 설득합니다. 그러나 파트로클로스는 헥토르에게 죽임을 당하는데, 이는 아킬레우스를 망연자실하게 합니다. 파트로클로스의 죽음을 듣고 슬픔과 분노에 휩싸인 아킬레우스는 친구의 죽음에 복수하기 위해 전투에 다시 참가하기로 결심합니다. 그는 아가멤논과 화해하고, 그리스인들은 아킬레우스가 다시 참전하면서 힘을 되찾습니다.

치열한 결투에서 아킬레우스는 트로이 성벽 밖에서 헥토르와 대결합니다. 아킬레우스는 헥토르를 죽이고 그의 시신을 그리스 진영으로 끌고 가 자비를 베풀지 않고 헥토르의 시신을 모독합니다. 헥토르의 아버지 트로이의 왕 프리아모스는 그리스 진영으로 몰래 들어가 아들의 시신을 돌려달라고 아킬레우스에게 간청합니다. 늙은 왕의 슬픔에 감동한 아킬레우스는 동의하며 잠시 애도의 시간을 보냅니다.

시는 헥토르의 장례식을 끝으로 끝나는데, 그곳에서 트로이 인들은 전사한 영웅을 애도합니다. 헥토르가 죽었음에도 불구하고 전쟁은 계속되고, 그 사건들이 속편인 "오디세이"에서 이야기되기 때문에, 유명한 트로이 목마나 트로이의 몰락을 다루지 않습니다.

"일리아드"는 영웅주의, 명예, 자부심, 전쟁의 허무함에 대한 주제를 탐구합니다. 그것은 또한 그것의 등장인물들, 특히 아킬레우스의 복잡한 감정과 동기를 탐구하여, 그것을 시대를 초월하고 지속되는 문학 작품으로 만듭니다.

[Reading Comprehension]

1. Who is the attributed poet of "The Iliad"?
a) Agamemnon   b) Patroclus   c) Hector   d) Homer

2. What is the central conflict in "The Iliad"?
a) The battle between Achilles and Agamemnon
b) The rivalry between Achilles and Hector
c) The Trojan War
d) The conflict between the Greeks and Myrmidons

3. What event causes Achilles to withdraw from the battle?
a) The death of Briseis
b) The death of Patroclus
c) Agamemnon's betrayal
d) The breach of the Greek walls

4. Who is the leader of the Greek forces in the Trojan War?
a) Hector   b) Priam   c) Patroclus   d) Agamemnon

5. How does Achilles react to Patroclus' death?
a) He withdraws from the battle completely.
b) He seeks vengeance against Agamemnon.
c) He reconciles with Hector.
d) He rejoins the battle seeking revenge.

6. What motivates Achilles to rejoin the battle after Patroclus' death?
a) A desire for fame and glory
b) The urging of King Priam
c) His loyalty to Agamemnon
d) Grief and a thirst for revenge

7. Who kills Hector in a fierce duel?
a) Achilles   b) Patroclus   c) Agamemnon   d) Priam

8. How does Achilles treat Hector's body after killing him?
a) He returns it to King Priam immediately.
b) He desecrates it and leaves it on the battlefield.
c) He gives it a proper burial himself.
d) He displays it in front of the Trojan walls.

9. What does King Priam do to retrieve Hector's body?

a) He offers a large ransom to Achilles.

b) He begs the Greek soldiers for mercy.

c) He sneaks into the Greek camp to plead with Achilles.

d) He challenges Achilles to a duel.

10. What emotion does Achilles briefly show when confronted by King Priam?

a) Fear   b) Anger   c) Compassion   d) Indifference

11. In which work are the events of the famous Trojan Horse and the fall of Troy narrated?

a) "The Iliad"   b) "The Odyssey"   c) "The Aeneid"   d) "The Epic of Gilgamesh"

12. What themes does "The Iliad" explore?

a) Romance and adventure

b) Exploration and discovery

c) Heroism, honor, pride, and the futility of war

d) Comedy and satire

13. What role does Briseis play in the story?

a) She is Achilles' close friend.

b) She is Hector's sister.

c) She is King Priam's daughter.

d) She is Achilles' war prize.

14. What is the significance of Patroclus wearing Achilles' armor into battle?

a) It confuses the Greek soldiers.

b) It boosts the Greeks' morale.

c) It intimidates the Trojans.

d) It angers Achilles.

15. Why is Achilles considered a great warrior and hero of the Greeks?

a) He is a master strategist.

b) He is known for his wisdom and wit.

c) He single-handedly defeats the Trojans.

d) He displays exceptional strength and courage.

[Grammar Check-up]

1. "The Iliad" is an ancient Greek epic poem (attributing, attributed) to the poet Homer.
2. It is one of the most (significant, significance) works of Western literature and tells the story of the Trojan War.
3. The story is set during the final year of the Trojan War, which (fights, is fought) between the city of Troy and the Greek city-states, (particularly, particular) the Achaeans (Greeks).
4. The epic (covers, is covered) a few weeks during the war.
5. The central character of the poem is Achilles, a great (war, warrior) and hero of the Greeks.
6. The conflict begins when Agamemnon, the leader of the Greek forces, takes Achilles' war prize, a girl (is named, named) Briseis, as his own.
7. This action infuriates Achilles, who (is withdrawn, withdraws) from the battle in anger, (causing, causes) significant losses for the Greeks.
8. With Achilles refusing to fight, the Trojans, led by Hector (the greatest Trojan warrior), (gains, gain) the upper hand and begin to win battles against the Greeks.
9. Achilles' close friend Patroclus (convinces, is convinced) him to let him lead the Myrmidons (Achilles' soldiers) into battle wearing Achilles' armor, (hoped, hoping) to boost the Greeks' morale.
10. However, Patroclus is killed by Hector, which (devastating, devastates) Achilles.
11. Hearing about Patroclus' death and (driving, driven) by grief and rage, Achilles decides to rejoin the battle, (seeks, seeking) vengeance for his friend's death.
12. He reconciles with Agamemnon, and the Greeks (regain, regaining) their strength with Achilles back in action.
13. In a fierce duel, Achilles (confront, confronts) Hector outside the walls of Troy.
14. Achilles kills Hector and drags his body back to the Greek camp, showing no mercy and (desecrates, desecrating) Hector's corpse.
15. Hector's father, King Priam of Troy, sneaks into the Greek camp and (pleading, pleads) with Achilles to return his son's body for a proper funeral.
16. (Touched by, Touching) the old king's grief, Achilles agrees, showing a brief moment of compassion.
17. The poem ends with the funeral of Hector, (where, who) the Trojans mourn their fallen hero.
18. (In spite, Despite) Hector's death, the war continues, and the poem does not cover the famous Trojan Horse or the fall of Troy, as those events (narrate, are narrated) in the sequel, "The Odyssey."

[Writing Practice]

1. "The Iliad" is _____ and tells the story of the Trojan War.   서양 문학의 가장 중요한 작품 중의 하나이다

2. The story is set during the final year of the Trojan War, _____ _____ the city of Troy *and* the Greek city-states, ~ 사이에서 벌어진(fight) 트로이 전쟁 (관계사)   particularly the Achaeans (Greeks).

3. The central character of the poem is Achilles, _____.
위대한 장수이자 그리스인들의 영웅

4. This action infuriates Achilles, who withdraws from the battle in anger, _____. 그리스인들에게 엄청난 손실을 야기한다 (분사구)

5. _____ the Trojans gain the upper hand and begin to win Achilles가 싸우기를 거절함에 따라 (with 분사)   battles against the Greeks.

6. Achilles' close friend Patroclus _____ the Myrmidons into battle wearing Achilles' armor.   그가 ~를 이끌게 하도록(let) Achilles를 납득시킨다

7. _____,
        Patroclus의 죽음에 관해 *듣고* 슬픔과 분노에 *이끌려*(drive) (두 개의 분사구)
Achilles decides to rejoin the battle, seeking vengeance for his friend's death.

8. _____, Achilles agrees, showing a brief moment of compassion.
늙은 왕의 슬픔에 감동을 받아서 (tough) (분사구)

9. Despite Hector's death, the war continues, and _____ the famous Trojan Horse or the fall of Troy.   그 시는 ~는 다루지 않는다

[Word Quiz]

1. What is the definition of "ancient"?
A) Modern   B) New   C) Old   D) Contemporary

2. The famous epic poem "The Iliad" is believed to ___ Homer.
A) mourn   B) refuse   C) plead   D) be attributed to

3. The battle of Troy had ___ in Greek mythology.
A) significance   B) conflict   C) significant losses   D) morale

4. "Romeo and Juliet" is a renowned piece of ___.
A) summary   B) set   C) literature   D) main plot

5. The ___ of the story involves the protagonist's journey to find the lost treasure.
A) refuse   B) set   C) main plot   D) convinced

6. Odysseus' long journey back home after the Trojan War is a ___ in "The Odyssey."
A) vengeance   B) fierce   C) proper funeral   D) sequel

7. The ___ between the Trojans and Greeks led to the fall of Troy.
A) confront   B) mercy   C) desecrate   D) conflict

8. After the war, the city of Troy was left ___ and in ruins.
A) convinced   B) motivated   C) devastated   D) pleaded

9. The soldiers' ___ was at an all-time low after suffering heavy casualties.
A) pride   B) honor   C) morale   D) heroism

10. Achilles sought ___ for the death of his dear friend Patroclus.
A) delve into   B) explore   C) vengeance   D) plead

11. In the face of danger, some warriors chose to fight with ___ determination.
A) ancient   B) futility   C) timeless   D) fierce

12. Despite the enemy's plea for ___ , the victorious general showed no mercy.

A) summary   B) mourn   C) confront   D) mercy

13. The invaders' act to ___ the sacred temple angered the local community.

A) set   B) refuse   C) desecrate   D) honor

14. The ___ of Hector's body was requested by his family in "The Iliad."

A) convinced   B) proper funeral   C) significant losses   D) refuse

15. The people of the city ___ their fallen king during the somber ceremony.

A) conflict   B) endure   C) plead   D) mourn

16. In "The Odyssey," Odysseus' ___ and bravery are celebrated by his companions.

A) heroism   B) delve into   C) motivation   D) explore

17. The knight's ___ was tarnished after he broke his vow and fled from the battle.

A) ancient   B) honor   C) pride   D) mercy

18. The soldier's death in battle highlighted the ___ of war.

A) significant   B) futility   C) enduring   D) morale

19. The archaeologists plan to ___ the mysteries of the ancient ruins.

A) fierce   B) delve into   C) convinced   D) vengeance

20. Touched by the old king's grief, Achilles agrees, showing a brief moment of ___.

A) expression   B) depression   C) impression   D) compassion

Unit 2: Odyssey

"Odyssey" is an epic poem attributed to the ancient Greek poet Homer. It is one of the two major ancient Greek epic poems, the other being "Iliad." The poem tells the story of the hero Odysseus (also known as Ulysses) and his long journey back home after the Trojan War. The poem is divided into 24 books or chapters, and it encompasses a wide range of adventures and challenges that Odysseus faces during his ten-year voyage.

The story begins with Odysseus' son, Telemachus, who is living with his mother Penelope on the island of Ithaca. Odysseus has been away for twenty years, and his absence has led to the belief that he is dead. Telemachus, feeling frustrated by the suitors who have invaded their home, sets out on a journey to learn about his father's fate.

In the assembly of Ithacan elders, Telemachus calls for the suitors to leave his mother's house, and he declares his intention to search for his father. Inspired by the goddess Athena, he sets sail for Pylos to seek information about Odysseus.

Telemachus arrives in Pylos and meets King Nestor, who fought alongside Odysseus during the Trojan War. Nestor tells him stories of the war and offers some information about his father's whereabouts. Telemachus travels to Sparta and meets King Menelaus and Queen Helen. Menelaus recounts his own journey home from Troy and reveals that Odysseus is being held captive by the nymph Calypso on the island of Ogygia.

The story shifts to the island of Ogygia, where the nymph Calypso has been holding Odysseus as her lover. Hermes, the messenger of the gods, is sent by Zeus to command Calypso to release Odysseus. Reluctantly, Calypso agrees, and Odysseus builds a raft and sets sail.

Odysseus encounters the Phaeacians, who offer him hospitality. He recounts his adventures up to this point and tells them of his desire to return home. The Phaeacian king, Alcinous, offers to help him get back to Ithaca. The Phaeacians host a feast in Odysseus' honor, and during the festivities, the bard Demodocus sings of the Trojan War, bringing tears to Odysseus' eyes.

The next day, the Phaeacians organize games in honor of Odysseus, and he demonstrates his athletic prowess. Later, he requests their assistance to return home, and they provide him with a ship and valuable gifts.

Odysseus begins to narrate his adventures to the Phaeacians. He recounts the story of his encounter with the Cicones, the Lotus-Eaters, and the Cyclops Polyphemus, whom he blinds to escape. Odysseus continues his tale, describing his visit to the island of Aeolus, the god of the winds, who gives him a bag containing all the unfavorable winds to help him sail. However, his crew unwittingly opens the bag, releasing the winds and leading them back to Aeolus' island.

Odysseus speaks of his journey to the Underworld, where he meets the spirit of the blind prophet Tiresias, as well as several other deceased characters from the Trojan War. Odysseus recounts his escape from the sirens, his encounter with Scylla and Charybdis, and his visit to the island of

Thrinacia, where his men eat the sacred cattle of the sun god, Helios, incurring the wrath of the gods. The Phaeacians finally bring Odysseus to Ithaca while he is asleep. They leave him on the shore with the valuable gifts they bestowed upon him.

Athena disguises Odysseus as an old beggar to conceal his identity. He goes to the hut of his loyal swineherd, Eumaeus, who welcomes the stranger and provides him shelter. Athena visits Telemachus again and advises him on how to handle the suitors upon his return to Ithaca. Father and son reunite, and Telemachus hides the weapons in the palace in preparation for the confrontation with the suitors.

Odysseus, still disguised as a beggar, enters his palace to observe the suitors and learns about the state of affairs in his home. Odysseus reveals his true identity to his loyal servant, the nurse Eurycleia. Penelope tests Odysseus by suggesting that she will marry the suitor who can string Odysseus' bow and shoot an arrow through twelve axe heads. Odysseus accomplishes the task, and the suitors' treachery is exposed.

The battle between Odysseus and the suitors begins, with the help of Telemachus, Athena, and Eumaeus. Odysseus, still disguised as a beggar, continues the fight against the suitors, while Penelope remains unaware of his true identity. Odysseus, assisted by Telemachus and loyal allies, defeats the suitors. The disloyal maids who served the suitors are executed for their treachery. Odysseus finally reveals his identity to Penelope, and their reunion is emotional and heartfelt. The families of the slain suitors seek revenge, but Athena intervenes to restore peace. Odysseus reunites with his aging father, Laertes, and order is restored to Ithaca.

In conclusion, "The Odyssey" is a tale of adventure, perseverance, and homecoming, highlighting the hero's trials and tribulations as he navigates through the challenges of life and the wrath of the gods to return to his homeland and loved ones.

[Vocabulary]

attributed 추정되는 epic 서사시적 ancient 고대의 encompass 포괄하다 adventures 모험 challenges 도전 frustration 좌절 invaded 침입당한 intention 의도 assembly 집합 whereabouts 행방 recount 이야기하다 captivity 포로 nymph 물의 요정 reluctantly 마지못해 encounter 마주치다 hospitality 환대 prowess 능력 describe 묘사하다 release 풀어주다 sirens 세이렌 incur 초래하다 confrontation 대립 disguised 위장한 treachery 배반 emotional 감정적인 intervention 개입 perseverance 끈기 navigation 항해 wrath 진노 homeland 조국 tribulations 시련 conclusion 결론 highlight 강조하다

[본문 해석] 오디세이

"오디세이"는 고대 그리스 시인 호머가 쓴 서사시입니다. 그것은 고대의 주요한 그리스 서사시 두 편 중 한편이고, 다른 한 편은 "일리아드"입니다. 그 시는 영웅 오디세우스 (일명 율리시즈)와 트로이 전쟁 후 고향으로 돌아가는 그의 긴 여정에 대한 이야기입니다. 그 시는 24권의 책 또는 장으로 나뉘어져 있고, 오디세우스가 10년간의 항해 동안 직면하는 광범위한 모험과 도전을 포괄합니다.

이야기는 어머니 페넬로페와 함께 이타카 섬에서 살고 있는 오디세우스의 아들 텔레마코스로부터 시작됩니다. 오디세우스는 20년 동안 집을 비웠고, 그의 부재는 그가 죽었다는 믿음으로 이어졌습니다. 그들의 집을 침범한 구혼자들에게 좌절감을 느낀 텔레마코스는 아버지의 운명을 알기 위해 여행을 떠납니다.

이타카의 연장자들의 집회에서, 텔레마코스는 구혼자들에게 그의 어머니의 집을 떠날 것을 요구하고, 아버지를 찾기 위한 그의 의도를 선언합니다. 아테나 여신에게 영감을 받아, 그는 오디세우스에 대한 정보를 찾기 위해 필로스로 출항합니다.

텔레마코스는 필로스에 도착하여 트로이 전쟁 동안 오디세우스와 함께 싸웠던 네스토르 왕을 만납니다. 네스토르는 그에게 전쟁에 대한 이야기를 들려주고 아버지의 행방에 대한 정보를 제공합니다. 텔레마코스는 스파르타로 여행을 떠나 메넬라오스 왕과 헬렌 여왕을 만납니다. 메넬라오스는 트로이에서 집으로 돌아온 자신의 여정을 이야기하고 오디세우스가 오기기아 섬에서 님프 칼립소에게 포로로 잡혀 있음을 밝힙니다.

이야기는 칼립소가 오디세우스를 연인으로 붙잡고 있던 오기기아 섬으로 이동합니다. 신들의 전령 헤르메스는 제우스에 의해 칼립소에게 오디세우스를 풀어달라고 명령하기 위해 보내집니다. 마지못해 칼립소는 동의하고 오디세우스는 뗏목을 만들어 출항합니다.

오디세우스는 파이아키아인들과 마주치게 되고, 그들은 그에게 환대를 제공합니다. 그는 여기까지 자신의 모험을 이야기하고, 집으로 돌아가고자 하는 바람을 이야기합니다. 파이아키아의 왕 알키누스는 그가 이타카로 돌아갈 수 있도록 도와주겠다고 제안합니다. 파이아키아인들은 오디세

우스를 기리기 위해 잔치를 열었고, 축제 기간 동안 음유시인 데모도코스는 트로이 전쟁을 노래하여 오디세우스의 눈에는 눈물이 흐릅니다.

다음 날, 파이아키아인들은 오디세우스를 기리기 위해 경기를 열고, 그는 그의 운동 실력을 보여줍니다. 나중에, 그는 집으로 돌아가기 위해 그들의 도움을 요청하고, 그들은 그에게 배와 귀중한 선물을 제공합니다.

오디세우스는 파이아키아인들에게 그의 모험에 대해 이야기하기 시작합니다. 그는 키코네족, 연꽃을 먹는 사람들, 그리고 그가 탈출을 위해 눈을 멀게 한 키클롭스 폴리페모스를 만난 이야기를 이야기합니다. 오디세우스는 계속해서 바람의 신 아이올로스 섬을 방문한 것을 묘사하는데, 바람의 신은 자신이 항해하는 것을 돕기 위해 모든 불리한 바람이 담긴 주머니를 그에게 줍니다. 그러나 그의 선원들은 우연히 그 주머니를 열게 되자 그 안의 바람이 불어나와 그들을 다시 아이올로스 섬으로 이끕니다.

오디세우스는 지하세계로의 그의 여행에 대해 이야기하는데, 그곳에서 그는 트로이 전쟁에서 죽은 다른 등장인물들뿐만 아니라 맹인 예언자 티레시아스의 영혼을 만나게 됩니다. 오디세우스는 사이렌으로부터 탈출한 것, 스킬라와 카리브디스와의 만남, 그리고 트리나키아 섬을 방문하게 되는데, 그곳에서 그의 부하들이 태양신 헬리오스의 신성한 소를 먹은 것을 이야기합니다. 파이아키아인들은 마침내 오디세우스가 잠든 동안 그를 이타카로 데리고 가, 그들이 그에게 준 귀중한 선물들과 함께 그를 해안에 남겨 둡니다.

아테나는 오디세우스의 신분을 숨기기 위해 그를 늙은 거지로 변장시킵니다. 그는 자신의 충실한 돼지 사육사인 에우마이오스의 오두막으로 갑니다. 에우마이오스는 그 낯선 자를 환영하고 그에게 피난처를 제공합니다. 아테나는 텔레마코스를 다시 방문하여 이타카로 돌아온 그에게 구혼자들을 어떻게 다루어야 할지 조언합니다. 아버지와 아들은 재회하고 텔레마코스는 구혼자들과의 대결에 대비하여 무기를 궁전에 숨깁니다.

여전히 거지로 변장한 오디세우스는 구혼자들을 관찰하기 위해 자신의 궁전으로 들어가 자신의 집 안의 사정을 알게 됩니다. 오디세우스는 자신의 충실한 하인이자 유모인 유리클레이아에게 자신의 진짜 정체를 밝힙니다. 페넬로페는 오디세우스의 활을 당기고 12개의 도끼머리를 통과하여 화살을 쏠 수 있는 구혼자와 결혼할 것이라고 제안하여 오디세우스를 시험합니다. 오디세우스가 임무를 완수하고 구혼자들의 배신은 드러납니다.

텔레마코스, 아테나, 에우마이오스의 도움으로 오디세우스와 구혼자들의 전투가 시작됩니다. 여전히 거지로 변장한 오디세우스는 구혼자들과의 싸움을 계속하고 페넬로페는 오디세우스의 진짜 정체를 알지 못합니다. 텔레마코스와 충성스러운 동맹들의 도움을 받은 오디세우스는 구혼자들을 물리칩니다. 구혼자들을 섬겼던 불충한 하녀들은 그들의 배신으로 인해 처형당합니다. 오디세우스는 마침내 페넬로페에게 자신의 정체를 밝히고, 그들의 감동적이고 진심어린 재회가 이루어집니다. 죽임을 당한 구혼자들의 가족들은 복수를 추구하지만, 아테나는 평화를 회복하기 위해 개입합니다. 오디세우스는 그의 나이든 아버지 레어티스와 재회하고, 이타카의 질서가 회복됩니다.

[Reading Comprehension]

1. Who is the attributed author of "The Odyssey"?
a) Telemachus b) Nestor c) Penelope d) Homer

2. Which other major ancient Greek epic poem is mentioned alongside "The Odyssey"?
a) The Aeneid b) The Epic of Gilgamesh c) Beowulf d) The Iliad

3. What is the central character's name in "The Odyssey"?
a) Nestor b) Achilles c) Odysseus d) Menelaus

4. How long does Odysseus' journey back home take?
a) 5 years b) 20 years c) 10 years d) 2 years

5. Who is Telemachus in relation to Odysseus?
a) Odysseus' father   b) Odysseus' loyal ally
c) Odysseus' son   d) Odysseus' enemy

6. What motivates Telemachus to embark on a journey?
a) To find his lost mother   b) To search for his father
c) To become a great warrior   d) To explore new lands

7. Who inspires Telemachus to set sail and seek information about his father?
a) King Nestor b) Queen Penelope c) Athena d) Hermes

8. Which island is Odysseus held captive on by Calypso?
a) Troy b) Ithaca c) Pylos d) Ogygia

9. Who helps Odysseus by commanding Calypso to release him?
a) Zeus b) Athena c) Poseidon d) Hermes

10. Which king offers to assist Odysseus in returning to Ithaca?
a) Menelaus b) Alcinous c) Nestor d) Polyphemus

11. What is the consequence of Odysseus' crew opening the bag given by Aeolus?
a) The ship is destroyed by a storm.
b) They encounter sirens on their journey.
c) The unfavorable winds are released, leading them astray.
d) Aeolus curses them with eternal wandering.

12. Who does Odysseus meet in the Underworld during his journey?

a) King Nestor

b) Helen of Troy

c) The prophet Tiresias

d) King Menelaus

13. What island's sacred cattle do Odysseus' men eat, angering the gods?

a) Pylos

b) Ogygia

c) Thrinacia

d) Sparta

14. How does Odysseus' true identity remain concealed upon his return to Ithaca?

a) He wears a mask.

b) Athena disguises him as a beggar.

c) He hides in a secret chamber.

d) He changes his name.

15. How is the confrontation with the suitors resolved?

a) The suitors apologize and leave.

b) Athena intervenes to restore peace.

c) Odysseus is defeated in battle.

d) The suitors manage to escape Ithaca.

[Grammar Check-up]

1. "The Odyssey" is an epic poem (attributes, attributed) to the ancient Greek poet Homer.

2. It is one of the two major ancient Greek epic poems, (the other, another) being "The Iliad."

3. The poem (is told, tells) the story of the hero Odysseus and his long journey back home after the Trojan War.

4. The poem is divided into 24 books or chapters, and it (encompasses, is encompassed) a wide range of adventures and challenges that Odysseus (is faced, faces) during his ten-year voyage.

5. The story begins with Odysseus' son, Telemachus, (which, who) is living with his mother Penelope on the island of Ithaca.

6. Odysseus has been away for twenty years, and his absence has led to the belief (which, that) he is dead.

7. Telemachus, (feeling, felt) frustrated by the suitors who have invaded their home, sets out on a journey to learn about his father's fate.

8. In the (assembly, assemble) of Ithacan elders, Telemachus calls for the suitors to leave his mother's house, and he (declares, is declared) his intention to search for his father.

9. (Inspiring, Inspired) by the goddess Athena, he sets sail for Pylos to seek information about Odysseus.

10. Telemachus arrives in Pylos and meets King Nestor, who fought alongside Odysseus (for, during) the Trojan War.

11. Nestor tells him stories of the war and (offering, offers) some information about his father's whereabouts.

12. Menelaus recounts his own journey home from Troy and reveals that Odysseus (is being held, is holding) captive by the nymph Calypso on the island of Ogygia.

13. The story shifts to the island of Ogygia, (which, where) the nymph Calypso has been (held, holding) Odysseus as her lover.

14. Hermes, the messenger of the gods, (sends, is sent by) Zeus to command Calypso to release Odysseus.

15. (Reluctant, Reluctantly), Calypso agrees, and Odysseus builds a raft and sets sail.

16. Odysseus encounters the Phaeacians, who (offers, offer) him hospitality.

17. He (is recounted, recounts) his adventures up to this point and tells them of his desire to return home.

18. The Phaeacian king, Alcinous, (offering, offers) to help him get back to Ithaca.

19. The Phaeacians (are hosted, host) a feast in Odysseus' honor.

20. During the festivities, the bard Demodocus sings of the Trojan War, (brings,

bringing) tears to Odysseus' eyes.

21. The next day, the Phaeacians (organizes, organize) games in honor of Odysseus, and he demonstrates his athletic prowess.

22. Later, he requests their assistance to return home, and they provide him (for, with) a ship and valuable gifts.

23. Odysseus begins (narration, to narrate) his adventures to the Phaeacians.

24. He recounts the story of his encounter with the Cicones, the Lotus-Eaters, and the Cyclops Polyphemus, (where, whom) he blinds to escape.

25. Odysseus continues his tale, (describing, describes) his visit to the island of Aeolus, the god of the winds, who (give, gives) him a bag containing all the unfavorable winds to help him sail.

26. However, his crew unwittingly opens the bag, (releases, releasing) the winds and leading them back to Aeolus' island.

27. Odysseus speaks of his journey to the Underworld, (which, where) he meets the spirit of the blind prophet Tiresias, as well as several other (deceased, deceasing) characters from the Trojan War.

28. Odysseus recounts his visit to the island of Thrinacia, (which, where) his men eat the sacred cattle of the sun god, Helios, (incurs, incurring) the wrath of the gods.

29. The Phaeacians finally (bring, brings) Odysseus to Ithaca while he is asleep.

30. They leave him on the shore with the valuable gifts (them, they) bestowed upon him.

31. Athena (disguises, disguising) Odysseus as an old beggar to conceal his identity.

32. He goes to the hut of his loyal swineherd, Eumaeus, who (welcoming, welcomes) the stranger and provides him shelter.

33. Athena visits Telemachus again and (advices, advises) him on how to handle the suitors upon his return to Ithaca.

34. Father and son reunite, and Telemachus (hide, hides) the weapons in the palace in preparation for the confrontation with the suitors.

35. Odysseus, still (disguising, disguised) as a beggar, enters his palace to observe the suitors and learns about the state of affairs in his home.

36. Odysseus (reveals, is revealed) his true identity to his loyal servant, the nurse Eurycleia.

37. Penelope tests Odysseus by (suggesting, suggestion) that she will marry the suitor (whom, who) can string Odysseus' bow and shoot an arrow through twelve axe heads.

38. Odysseus accomplishes the task, and the suitors' treachery (is exposed, exposes).

39. Odysseus, assisted by Telemachus and loyal allies, (defeat, defeats) the suitors.

40. The disloyal maids who served the suitors (execute, are executed) for their treachery.

[Writing Practice]

1. The poem is divided into 24 books or chapters, and it encompasses a wide range of adventures and challenges _____.

　　　　　　　　　　　　Odysseus가 그의 10년의 항해 동안 직면하는 도전들 (관계사)

2. Odysseus _____, and his absence has led to the belief that he
  20년 동안 멀리 떨어져(away) 있다 (현재완료)　　　　　　　　　　　　　　　　is dead.

3. Telemachus, _____ who have invaded their home, sets
　　　　~한 구애자((suitor)들로 인해 의해 좌절감(frustrate)을 느끼고 (분사구)
out on a journey to learn about his father's fate.

4. Menelaus recounts his own journey home from Troy and reveals that
_____ the nymph Calypso on the island of Ogygia.
Odysseus가 ~에 의해 사로잡혀(captive) 있다는 것을 (진행수동)

5. Hermes, the messenger of the gods, is sent by Zeus _____
.　　　　　　　　　　　　　Calypso에게 Odysseus를 풀어주라고 명령하기 위해서

6. Odysseus encounters the Phaeacians, _____.
　　　　　　　　　　　　　그에게 환대를 제공해주는 페니키아인들 (관계사)

7. He recounts his adventures up to this point and _____.
　　　　　　　　　　　그들에게 집으로 돌아가고 싶다는 그의 욕망에 대해 말한다

8. Odysseus speaks of his journey to the Underworld, _____
the blind prophet Tiresias.　　　　　그리고 그는 그곳에서 ~의 영혼을 만난다 (관계부사)

9. Odysseus recounts his visit to the island of Thrinacia, _____
_____the sun god, Helios, incurring the wrath of the gods.
그리고 그곳에서 그의 부하들(men)이 ~의 신성한 소를 먹는다 (관계부사)

10. Athena _____ to conceal his identity.
　　　　　　　　Odysseus를 늙은 거지로 변장시킨다

[Word Quiz]

1. What is the meaning of the word "ancient"?
a) Modern   b) Recent   c) Old   d) Temporary

2. Which word refers to a long and heroic narrative poem?
a) Encounter   b) Epic   c) Highlight   d) Frustration

3. What is the synonym for "encompass"?
a) Exclude   b) Narrow   c) Include   d) Reduce

4. What is another word for "adventures"?
a) Excursions   b) Disguised   c) Conclusion   d) Hospitality

5. Which term means difficult tasks or situations?
a) Challenges   b) Tribulations   c) Intentions   d) Nymphs

6. If someone is "reluctantly" doing something, what does that mean?
a) Eagerly   b) Happily   c) Unwillingly   d) Swiftly

7. What is the meaning of "captivity"?
a) Freedom   b) Imprisonment   c) Exploration   d) Adventure

8. What are "sirens" in the context of this passage?
a) Mythical creatures   b) Leaders
c) Dangerous animals   d) Hidden treasures

9. What does "confrontation" mean?
a) Agreement   b) Disguise   c) Conflict   d) Release

10. Which word means the ability or skill in doing something?
a) Wrath   b) Emotional   c) Prowess   d) Intervention

11. What is the synonym for "describe"?
a) Encountered   b) Disguised   c) Recount   d) Invaded

12. If someone is showing "hospitality," what are they demonstrating?
a) Treachery   b) Intentions
c) Emotional behavior   d) Welcoming behavior

13. What is the opposite of "release"?
a) Encounter   b) Disguised   c) Captivity   d) Intention

14. What does "tribulations" mean?
a) Triumphs   b) Challenges   c) Intentions   d) Ancient stories

15. What is the synonym for "homeland"?
a) Ancient   b) Encountered   c) Assembly   d) Native land

16. What is the meaning of "intervention"?
a) Evasion   b) Emotional behavior   c) Involvement   d) Release

17. What word refers to the state of being determined and persistent?
a) Navigation   b) Prowess   c) Perseverance   d) Hospitality

18. What does "wrath" indicate?
a) Emotion   b) Intent   c) Anger   d) Encounters

19. What does "treachery" mean?
a) Intention   b) Deception   c) Assembly   d) Prowess

20. What is the opposite of "highlight"?
a) Conclusion   b) Adventures   c) Challenges   d) Disguised

Unit 3: The Three Kingdoms

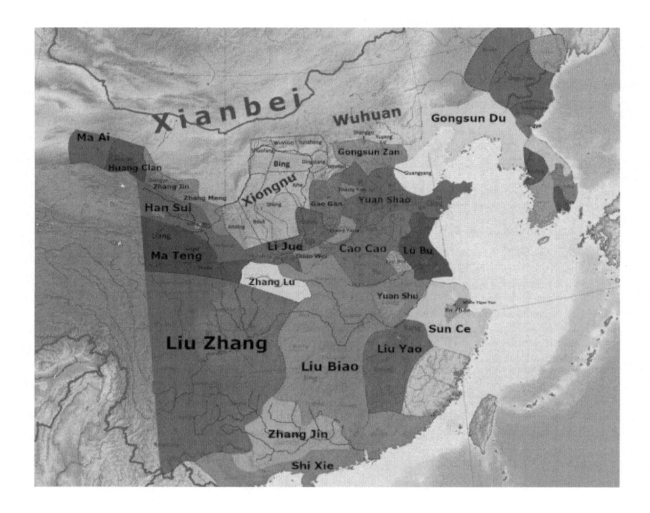

"The Three Kingdoms," also known as "Romance of the Three Kingdoms," is a classic Chinese historical novel attributed to Luo Guanzhong. It is one of the Four Great Classical Novels of Chinese literature and was written during the Ming Dynasty in the 14th century. The novel is a sprawling epic that recounts the tumultuous period of the Three Kingdoms in ancient China (circa 184-280 AD). It primarily follows the lives and adventures of key historical figures as they vie for power, form alliances, engage in military campaigns, and shape the course of Chinese history.

The story begins with the decline of the Han Dynasty, which had ruled China for centuries. The Emperor Ling of Han is a weak and ineffective ruler, and the imperial court is fraught with corruption and internal strife. Various warlords rise to prominence, leading to a fractured empire.

Amid the chaos, three prominent warlords emerge and form their kingdoms. Liu Bei, a virtuous and charismatic leader, establishes the kingdom of Shu in the southwest. Cao Cao, a cunning and ambitious general, founds the kingdom of Wei in the north. Sun Quan, a young and capable ruler, establishes the kingdom of Wu in the southeast.

One of the most famous episodes in the novel is the Battle of the Red Cliffs, where the combined forces of Liu Bei and Sun Quan decisively defeat Cao Cao's much larger army. The battle marks a turning point in the struggle for dominance and solidifies the division of the land into three kingdoms.

The novel follows the power struggles and military campaigns among the three kingdoms. Liu Bei seeks to restore the Han Dynasty and forms alliances with his sworn brothers, Zhang Fei and Guan Yu, as well as the brilliant strategist Zhuge Liang. Cao Cao seeks to unify China under his rule and faces opposition from both Shu and Wu. Sun Quan contends with the ambitions of Wei and engages in strategic battles to defend his kingdom.

Zhuge Liang, one of the central figures in the novel, is renowned for his intelligence and strategic acumen. He serves as the chancellor of Shu and is instrumental in devising military strategies and diplomatic maneuvers to bolster Liu Bei's kingdom.

Guan Yu and Zhang Fei, two of Liu Bei's sworn brothers, are iconic figures known for their loyalty, martial prowess, and unwavering support of their lord. They become legendary heroes in Chinese culture.

As the novel progresses, major historical figures meet their fates. Cao Cao passes away, and his son Cao Pi succeeds him as the ruler of Wei. Liu Bei dies, and his son Liu Shan becomes the ruler of Shu, with Zhuge Liang serving as the regent. In an attempt to unify the land, Zhuge Liang leads a series of Northern Expeditions against Wei, but they meet limited success due to logistical challenges and internal disputes within Shu. After the death of Zhuge Liang, Shu's power declines, and it eventually falls to Wei. Meanwhile, Wu faces internal struggles and is eventually conquered by the Jin Dynasty, which succeeds Wei as the ruling power. The novel concludes with the rise of the Jin Dynasty under the leadership of Sima Yan, who unifies China and brings an end to the era of the Three Kingdoms.

"The Three Kingdoms" is a masterpiece that weaves history, legend, and fictional elements into a compelling narrative. It has inspired countless adaptations in various forms of media and remains an enduring symbol of Chinese culture and history.

[Vocabulary]

Sprawling 방대한/퍼져나간 Tumultuous 뒤얽힌/소란스러운 Prominence 탁월 Charismatic 카리스마 있는 Unify 통일시키다 Strategist 전략가 Decisively 단호하게 Solidify 굳게 하다 Power struggles 권력 다툼 Allegiances 충성 Martial prowess 무술능력 Regent 통치자 Logistical 물류적인 Conquered 정복된 Dynasty 왕조 Compelling 설득력 있는 Inspirations 영감 Enduring 영구적인 Adapations 각색 Decline 쇠퇴(하다) Ineffective 효과 없는 Imperial court 궁정 Fractured 깨어진 Virtuous 덕망 있는 Ambitious 야심적인 Capable 유능한 Strategic battles 전략적 전투 Renowned 유명한 Iconic 상징적인 Succession 계승 Northern Expeditions 북진 Internal disputes 내부 분쟁 Inspire 영감을 주다 narrative 서술 Masterpiece 걸작 Legend 전설 Fictional elements 가상의 요소 Rise 상승 Era 시대 Attributes 귀속하다/탓으로 돌리다 Historical figures 역사적 인물 Military campaigns 군사 작전 Sworn brothers 맹세 형제 Diplomatic maneuvers 외교적 작전

[본문 해석] 삼국지

"삼국지연의"로도 알려진 "삼국지"는 나관중의 것으로 추정되는 중국의 고전 역사 소설입니다. 그것은 중국 문학의 4대 고전 소설 중 하나이고 14세기 명나라 때 쓰여 졌습니다. 그 소설은 고대 중국 삼국 시대의 격동의 시기를 묘사하는 광범위한 서사시입니다. 그것은 주로 그들이 권력을 놓고 경쟁하고 동맹을 맺으며 군사 작전을 벌이고 중국 역사의 흐름을 형성하는 주요 역사 인물들의 삶과 모험을 다루고 있습니다.

이야기는 수세기 동안 중국을 통치했던 한나라의 쇠퇴로부터 시작됩니다. 한의 링(Ling) 황제는 약하고 무능한 통치자이고, 조정은 부패와 내분으로 가득 차 있습니다. 다양한 군벌들이 두각을 나타내면서 제국은 분열되었습니다.

혼란 속에서, 세 명의 뛰어난 군벌들이 나타나 그들의 왕국을 형성합니다. 도덕적이고 카리스마 있는 지도자인 유비는 남서쪽에 촉(Shu)나라를 세웁니다. 교활하고 야심 있는 장군인 조조는 북쪽에 위(Wei)나라를 세웁니다. 젊고 유능한 통치자인 손권은 남동쪽에 오(Wu)나라를 세웁니다.

이 소설에서 가장 유명한 에피소드 중 하나는 유비와 손권의 연합군이 조조의 훨씬 더 큰 군대를 결정적으로 무찌른 적벽 전투입니다. 이 전투는 지배권 다툼의 전환점을 보여주고 국토를 삼국으로 분할하는 것을 공고히 합니다.

소설은 세 나라 사이의 권력 투쟁과 군사 작전을 다루고 있습니다. 유비는 한나라를 회복하려고 하고 그의 맹세한 형제인 장비, 관우뿐만 아니라 뛰어난 전략가 제갈량과 동맹을 맺습니다. 조조는 그의 통치하에 중국을 통일하려고 하고 초와 오 모두의 반대에 직면합니다. 손권은 위의 야망에 맞서고 그의 나라를 지키기 위해 전략적인 전투를 합니다.

소설의 중심인물 중 한 명인 제갈량은 지성과 전략적 혜안으로 유명합니다. 그는 촉의 재상을 역임하고 유비의 왕국을 강화하기 위한 군사 전략과 외교 전략을 고안하는 데 중요한 역할을 합니다. 유비의 맹세한 형제들 중 두 명인 관우와 장비는 그들의 충성심, 무술 실력, 그리고 그들의 주군에 대한 변함없는 지지로 유명한 상징적인 인물들입니다. 그들은 중국 문화에서 전설적인 영웅이 됩니다.

소설이 진행됨에 따라 역사적으로 중요한 인물들이 운명을 맞이합니다. 조조가 세상을 떠나고 그의 아들 조비가 그의 뒤를 이어 위나라의 통치자가 됩니다. 유비가 죽고 그의 아들 유산이 촉나라의 통치자가 되고 제갈량이 섭정을 합니다. 제갈량은 영토를 통일하기 위해 위나라에 대항하는 일련의 북벌을 이끌지만, 병참 문제와 촉의 내부의 분쟁으로 인해 제한적인 성공을 거두게 됩니다. 제갈량이 죽은 후, 촉의 세력은 쇠퇴하고 결국 위나라에게 넘어가고, 한편, 오는 내부 투쟁에 직면하고, 결국 위나라의 뒤를 이은 진나라에게 정복당합니다. 소설은 중국을 통일하고 삼국 시대에 종언을 고하는 사마염(Sima Yan) 지도 아래 진나라의 부상으로 끝이 납니다.

"삼국지"는 역사, 전설, 그리고 허구적인 요소들을 설득력 있는 이야기로 엮어낸 걸작입니다. 그것은 다양한 형태의 매체에서 무수한 각색에 영감을 주었고 중국 문화와 역사의 지속적인 상징으로 남아 있습니다.

[Reading Comprehension]

1. Who is the author of "The Three Kingdoms"?
a) Luo Guanzhong   b) Sun Quan   c) Cao Cao   d) Sima Yan

2. In which dynasty was "The Three Kingdoms" written?
a) Han Dynasty   b) Ming Dynasty   c) Wei Dynasty   d) Jin Dynasty

3. What period does "The Three Kingdoms" depict?
a) Tang Dynasty   b) Three Kingdoms   c) Ming Dynasty   d) Han Dynasty

4. Which of the following is NOT one of the three kingdoms formed in the novel?
a) Shu   b) Wei   c) Han   d) Wu

5. What is the name of the battle where Liu Bei and Sun Quan defeat Cao Cao's army?
a) Battle of Changban   b) Battle of Chibi (Red Cliffs)
c) Battle of Hulao Pass   d) Battle of Guandu

6. Who is the virtuous and charismatic leader who establishes the kingdom of Shu?
a) Cao Cao   b) Sun Quan   c) Liu Bei   d) Guan Yu

7. What is the turning point in the struggle for dominance in the novel?
a) Battle of Hulao Pass   b) Battle of Guandu
c) Battle of Chibi (Red Cliffs)   d) Battle of Wuzhang Plains

8. Who is the brilliant strategist and chancellor of Shu in the novel?
a) Zhang Fei   b) Guan Yu   c) Zhuge Liang   d) Cao Cao

9. Which two characters are known as Liu Bei's sworn brothers in the novel?
a) Zhang Fei and Cao Cao   b) Cao Cao and Guan Yu
c) Zhuge Liang and Zhang Fei   d) Guan Yu and Zhang Fei

10. After the death of Zhuge Liang, which kingdom's power declines, and it eventually falls to Wei?
a) Shu   b) Wei   c) Wu   d) Han

11. Who succeeds Cao Cao as the ruler of Wei?
a) Liu Shan   b) Sun Quan   c) Cao Pi   d) Sima Yan

12. Which dynasty conquers Wu and succeeds Wei as the ruling power?
a) Shu b) Jin c) Wei d) Han

13. What is the conclusion of "The Three Kingdoms"?
a) Rise of the Han Dynasty   b) Rise of the Shu Kingdom
c) Rise of the Jin Dynasty   d) Rise of the Ming Dynasty

14. "The Three Kingdoms" is a classic Chinese historical novel attributed to _____.
a) Cao Cao b) Sun Quan c) Zhang Fei d) Luo Guanzhong

15. What does "The Three Kingdoms" primarily follow in the novel?
a) Adventures of Sun Quan   b) Power struggles among warlords
c) Rise of the Han Dynasty   d) Founding of the Jin Dynasty

[Grammar Check-up]

1. "The Three Kingdoms," also known as "Romance of the Three Kingdoms," is a classic Chinese historical novel (attributed, attributing) to Luo Guanzhong.

2. It is one of the Four Great Classical (Novel, Novels) of Chinese literature and was (writing, written) during the Ming Dynasty in the 14th century.

3. The novel is a sprawling epic that recounts the (tumultuous, tumultuously) period of the Three Kingdoms in ancient China (circa 184-280 AD).

4. It (primary, primarily) follows the lives and adventures of key historical figures as they vie for power, form alliances, engage in military campaigns, and (shaping, shape) the course of Chinese history.

5. The story begins with the decline of the Han Dynasty, which had (ruled, been ruled) China for centuries.

6. The Emperor Ling of Han is a weak and (effective, ineffective) ruler, and the imperial court is fraught with corruption and internal strife.

7. Various warlords (raise, rise) to prominence, leading to a fractured empire.

8. Amid the chaos, three (prominent, prominently) warlords emerge and form their kingdoms.

9. Liu Bei, a virtuous and charismatic leader, (establishes, establishing) the kingdom of Shu in the southwest.

10. Cao Cao, a cunning and ambitious general, (is found, founds) the kingdom of Wei in the north.

11. One of the most famous episodes in the novel (are, is) the Battle of the Red Cliffs, (where, which) the combined forces of Liu Bei and Sun Quan decisively defeat Cao Cao's much larger army.

12. The battle marks a turning point in the struggle for dominance and (solidifies, solidifying) the division of the land into three kingdoms.

13. Liu Bei seeks to restore the Han Dynasty and forms alliances with his (sworn, swearing) brothers, Zhang Fei and Guan Yu, (not only, as well as) the brilliant strategist Zhuge Liang.

14. Cao Cao seeks to unify China under his rule and (faces, is faced) opposition from both Shu and Wu.

15. Sun Quan contends with the (ambitious, ambitions) of Wei and engages in strategic battles to defend his kingdom.

16. Zhuge Liang, one of the central figures in the novel, (are, is) renowned for his intelligence and strategic acumen.

17. He serves as the chancellor of Shu and is (instrumental, instrument) in devising military strategies and diplomatic maneuvers to bolster Liu Bei's kingdom.

18. Guan Yu and Zhang Fei, two of Liu Bei's sworn brothers, are iconic figures (are known, known) for their loyalty, martial prowess, and unwavering support of their lord.

19. They become (legend, legendary) heroes in Chinese culture.

20. As the novel progresses, major historical figures (are met, meet) their fates.

21. Cao Cao passes away, and his son Cao Pi (success, succeeds) him as the ruler of Wei.

22. In an attempt to unify the land, Zhuge Liang (leads, leading) a series of Northern Expeditions against Wei, but they meet (limiting, limited) success due to logistical challenges and internal disputes within Shu.

23. After the death of Zhuge Liang, Shu's power declines, and it eventually (fells, falls) to Wei.

24. Meanwhile, Wu faces (internally, internal) struggles and is (eventually, eventual) conquered by the Jin Dynasty, which succeeds Wei as the ruling power.

25. The novel concludes with the (rise, arise) of the Jin Dynasty under the leadership of Sima Yan, who unifies China and brings an end to the era of the Three Kingdoms.

[Writing Practice]

1. "The Three Kingdoms," also known as "Romance of the Three Kingdoms," is a classic Chinese _____ Luo Guanzhong.
　　　　　　　~의 것으로 생각되는(attribute) 역사 소설

2. It is one of the Four Great Classical Novels of Chinese literature and was written _____.
14세기 명(Ming) 왕조 시기 동안

3. _____ key historical figures as they vie for power. 그것은 주로(pr~) ~의 삶과 모험을 따라 간다

4. The story begins with the decline of the Han Dynasty, _____
_____ 수 세기 동안 중국을 지배했던 (과거완료, 관계사)

5. The Emperor Ling of Han is a weak and ineffective ruler, and the imperial court _____
부패와 내부의 다툼(st~)으로 가득 차 있다

6. _____, leading to a fractured empire.
　　다양한 군벌(warlord)들이 두각(pro~)을 나타내다 *rise, arise 중 선택

7. _____ the Battle of the Red Cliffs.
　　소설에서 가장 유명한 에피소드 중 하나는 ~이다

8. Zhuge Liang, one of the central figures in the novel, _____
_____ 그의 지능과 전략적인 통찰력(ac~)으로 유명하다

9. Cao Cao passes away, and his son Cao Pi _____ Wei.
　　　　　　　　　　위나라의 통치자로서 그의 뒤를 잇는다(su~)

10. _____, Zhuge Liang leads a series of Northern Expeditions against Wei. 땅을 통일하려는 시도(attempt)로 (전치사구)

[Word Quiz]

1. What word describes a vast and extensive landscape?
a) Sprawling   b) Prominence   c) Charismatic   d) Solidify

2. Which term refers to a period of turbulent and chaotic events?
a) Conquered   b) Strategist   c) Tumultuous   d) Inspirations

3. What word means having a remarkable personal charm and appeal?
a) Charismatic   b) Regent   c) Enduring   d) Virtuous

4. Which term means to bring together and make into one?
a) Unify   b) Compelling   c) Iconic   d) Rise

5. Who is a person skilled in planning and implementing strategies?
a) Decisively   b) Dynasty   c) Ambitious   d) Strategist

6. What word means to make something firm or stable?
a) Solidify   b) Decline   c) Fractured   d) Inspire

7. Which phrase refers to conflicts for authority or dominance?
a) Power struggles   b) Northern Expeditions   c) Allegiances   d) Succession

8. What term describes exceptional skills in combat or martial arts?
a) Internal disputes   b) Martial prowess   c) Renowned   d) Era

9. Who is a person appointed to rule in the absence of a monarch?
a) Regent   b) Logistical   c) Inspire   d) Masterpiece

10. What word relates to the management of resources and supplies?
a) Capable   b) Fictional elements   c) Logistical   d) Compelling

11. What does "conquered" mean in the context of a territory?
a) Defeated   b) Inspired   c) Ambitious   d) Diplomatic maneuvers

12. What word means to strengthen or reinforce something?
a) Solidify   b) Fractured   c) Decline   d) Rise

13. Which term describes a sequence of events in a story?
a) Ineffective   b) Prominence   c) Dynasty   d) Narrative

14. What word means capable of lasting for a long time?
a) Enduring b) Iconic c) Diplomatic maneuvers d) Masterpiece

15. Which term refers to modifications to something?
a) Allegiances b) Sprawling c) Adaptations d) Strategic battles

16. What word means lacking the desired effectiveness?
a) Ineffective b) Inspirations c) Northern Expeditions d) Virtuous

17. What is the term for the administrative center of an empire?
a) Sworn brothers b) Imperial court c) Succession d) Dynasty

18. Which word means divided or broken into pieces?
a) Attributes b) Rise c) Fractured d) Conquered

19. What word means having high aspirations or goals?
a) Masterpiece b) Decline c) Logistical d) Ambitious

20. What term refers to military operations or strategies?
a) Military campaigns b) Diplomatic maneuvers c) Renowned d) Inspirations

Unit 4: The Divine Comedy (1320)

The Divine Comedy is an epic poem written by Italian poet Dante Alighieri in the early 14th century. It is widely considered one of the greatest works of Western literature. The poem consists of three parts: Inferno, Purgatorio, and Paradiso, each describing a different realm of the afterlife.

Inferno is the first part and depicts Dante's journey through Hell. Guided by the ancient Roman poet Virgil, Dante descends through nine concentric circles of Hell, encountering various sinners and witnessing their punishments. Each circle represents a different sin, starting with lesser sins like lust and gluttony and progressing to greater sins like violence and treachery. Dante encounters notable historical and mythological figures, as well as contemporary individuals, as he explores the depths of Hell.

Purgatorio is the second part and portrays Dante's ascent up Mount Purgatory. Here, souls are cleansed of their sins and prepared for their eventual entry into Heaven. Dante is guided by Virgil until he reaches the Earthly Paradise, where the spirit of Beatrice, his idealized love and a symbol of divine grace, becomes his guide. Along the way, Dante encounters penitent souls and witnesses their struggles and processes of purification.

Paradiso is the final part and narrates Dante's ascent through the celestial spheres of Heaven. Guided by Beatrice and other heavenly figures, Dante experiences the beauty and wonders of the cosmos. He encounters various saints, theologians, and other blessed souls, who impart wisdom and reveal divine truths. Dante's journey culminates in a vision of the ultimate divine reality, the Beatific Vision, where he attains a glimpse of God's infinite love and wisdom.

Throughout the Divine Comedy, Dante explores themes of sin, redemption, divine justice, and the nature of God's love. The poem combines theological teachings, classical mythology, political allegory, and personal experiences to create a rich and complex tapestry of the afterlife and the human condition. It remains a powerful exploration of the human soul's journey toward salvation and its quest for union with the divine.

[Vocabulary]

afterlife 저승 Inferno 지옥 Purgatorio 연옥 Paradiso 천국 journey 여정 concentric circle 동심원 various sinners 다양한 죄인들 punishment 벌 contemporary 동시대의 ascent up 오르다 Earthly Paradise 지상 낙원 divine grace 신성한 은총 penitent souls 회개하는 영혼들 celestial spheres 천체 구역 ultimate divine reality 궁극적인 신성한 현실 theological teachings 신학적 가르침 classical mythology 고전 신화 political allegory 정치적 우화 personal experiences 개인적 경험들 redemption 구원 divine justice 신성한 정의 nature of God's love 하나님의 사랑의 본질 blessed souls 축복받은 영혼들 theological 신학적인 symbolism 상징주의 spiritual 영적인 allegorical 우화적인 metaphysical 형이상학적인 exploration 탐구 salvation 구원 quest 탐험 complex tapestry 복잡한 비단직물

[본문 해석] 신곡

　　신곡은 이탈리아 시인 단테 알리기에리가 14세기 초에 쓴 서사시입니다. 그것은 서양 문학의 가장 위대한 작품 중 하나로 널리 여겨집니다. 그 시는 각각 사후세계의 다른 영역을 묘사하는 지옥편, 연옥편, 천국편 세 부분으로 구성됩니다.

　　지옥편(Inferno)은 첫 번째 부분이고 지옥을 통한 단테의 여행을 묘사합니다. 고대 로마 시인 버질의 안내로, 단테는 지옥의 9개의 동심원을 통해 내려오며, 다양한 죄인들을 만나고 그들의 처벌을 목격합니다. 각각의 원은 다른 죄를 나타내며, 정욕과 과식과 같은 더 작은 죄에서 시작하여 폭력과 배신과 같은 더 큰 죄로 진행합니다. 단테는 지옥의 깊은 곳을 탐험하면서 동시대의 사람들뿐만 아니라 주목할 만한 역사적이고 신화적인 인물들을 만나게 됩니다.

　　2부는 연옥 산에 오른 단테의 모습을 그린 연옥편(Purgatorio)입니다. 여기서, 영혼들은 자신의 죄로부터 깨끗해지고 결국 천국으로 들어갈 준비가 됩니다. 단테는 지상의 천국에 도달할 때까지 버질의 안내를 받게 됩니다. 그리고 그곳에서 그의 이상화된 사랑이자 신성한 은혜의 상징인 베아트리체의 영혼이 그의 인도자가 됩니다. 그 과정에서, 단테는 참회하는 영혼들을 만나고 그들의 투쟁과 정화 과정을 목격합니다.

　　천국편(Paradiso)은 마지막 부분이고 천국의 천구를 통해 단테의 천국에 오름을 서술합니다. 베아트리체와 다른 천상의 인물들에 의해 인도되는 단테는 우주의 아름다움과 경이로움을 경험합니다. 그는 지혜를 전하고 신성한 진리를 드러내는 다양한 성인들, 신학자들, 그리고 다른 축복받은 영혼들을 만납니다. 단테의 여행은 궁극적인 신성한 실재에 대한 비전인, 지복을 주는 비전으로 정점을 이루고, 거기서 그는 하나님의 무한한 사랑과 지혜를 엿볼 수 있습니다.

　　신곡 전체에서, 단테는 죄, 구원, 신성한 정의, 그리고 신의 사랑의 본질에 대한 주제들을 탐구합니다. 그 시는 사후세계와 인간의 상태에 대한 풍부하고 복잡한 태피스트리를 만들기 위해 신학적인 가르침, 고전 신화, 정치적인 우화, 그리고 개인적인 경험들을 결합합니다. 그 책은 구원을 향한 인간의 영혼의 여행과 신과의 연합에 대한 탐구에 대한 강력한 탐구 대상으로 남아 있습니다.

[Reading Comprehension]

1. Who is the author of "The Divine Comedy"?
a) Virgil b) Dante Alighieri c) Beatrice d) Homer

2. How many parts does "The Divine Comedy" consist of?
a) One b) Two c) Three d) Four

3. Which part of the poem describes Dante's journey through Hell?
a) Inferno b) Purgatorio c) Paradiso d) Celestia

4. Who guides Dante through Hell?
a) Beatrice b) Homer c) Virgil d) Dante's idealized love

5. How many circles of Hell does Dante descend through in "Inferno"?
a) Six b) Eight c) Nine d) Twelve

6. What is the Earthly Paradise in "Purgatorio"?
a) The top of Mount Purgatory
b) The lowest circle of Hell
c) A place where souls are cleansed
d) The final destination of the journey

7. In "Purgatorio," who becomes Dante's guide after Virgil?
a) Homer b) Beatrice c) God d) Dante's friend

8. What does Dante witness in Purgatorio?
a) Punishments of sinners
b) The struggles of the damned
c) Souls being cleansed and purified
d) The celestial spheres of Heaven

9. Which part of "The Divine Comedy" narrates Dante's ascent through Heaven?
a) Inferno b) Purgatorio c) Paradiso d) Celestia

10. Who guides Dante through the celestial spheres of Heaven?

a) Virgil   b) Beatrice   c) Dante's friend   d) God

11. What is the Beatific Vision?

a) Dante's love for Beatrice

b) A glimpse of Hell

c) Dante's ultimate destination in Purgatorio

d) A vision of God's infinite love and wisdom

12. What themes are explored in "The Divine Comedy"?

a) Politics and power

b) Romantic love and friendship

c) Sin, redemption, and divine justice

d) Exploration of the natural world

13. What does the passage combine to create a rich tapestry in "The Divine Comedy"?

a) Contemporary literature and philosophy

b) Personal experiences and political allegory

c) Divine revelation and classical music

d) Theology and astronomy

14. What does Dante's journey toward salvation involve?

a) A quest for earthly treasures

b) A search for historical figures

c) A journey through the celestial spheres

d) A search for union with the divine

15. Why is "The Divine Comedy" considered a powerful exploration of the human condition?

a) It focuses solely on the afterlife

b) It includes extensive political allegory

c) It delves into themes of sin, redemption, and divine love

d) It excludes mythological elements

[Grammar Check-up]

1. The Divine Comedy is an epic poem written by Italian poet Dante Alighieri in the early (14th, 14) century.

2. It is widely (considered, considers) one of the greatest (work, works) of Western literature.

3. The poem (consists, is consisted) of three parts: Inferno, Purgatorio, and Paradiso, each (describes, describing) a different realm of the afterlife.

4. Inferno is the first part and (depicts, depicting) Dante's journey through Hell.

5. (Guided, Guiding) by the ancient Roman poet Virgil, Dante descends through nine concentric circles of Hell, (encounters, encountering) various sinners.

6. (All, Each) circle represents a different sin, starting with lesser sins like lust and gluttony and (progress, progressing) to greater sins like violence and treachery.

7. Dante encounters notable historical and mythological figures, as well as contemporary individuals, (as long as, as) he explores the depths of Hell.

8. Purgatorio is the second part and (portrays, portraying) Dante's ascent up Mount Purgatory.

9. Here, souls are (clean, cleansed) of their sins and prepared for their eventual entry into Heaven.

10. Dante (guides, is guided) by Virgil until he reaches the Earthly Paradise, (where, which) the spirit of Beatrice, his idealized love and a symbol of divine grace, (becoming, becomes) his guide.

11. Along the way, Dante encounters penitent souls and (witnessing, witnesses) their struggles and processes of purification.

12. Paradiso is the final part and (narrating, narrates) Dante's ascent through the celestial spheres of Heaven. Guided by Beatrice and other heavenly figures,

13. He encounters various (saints, saint), theologians, and other blessed (soul, souls), who (impart, imparts) wisdom and reveal divine truths.

14. Dante's journey culminates in a vision of the ultimate divine reality, the Beatific Vision, (which, where) he attains a glimpse of God's infinite love and wisdom.

15. (Throughout, Though) the Divine Comedy, Dante explores themes of sin, redemption, divine justice, and the nature of God's love.

16. The poem (is combined, combines) theological teachings, classical mythology, political allegory, and personal experiences.

17. It (remains, is remained) a powerful exploration of the human soul's journey toward salvation and its quest for union with the divine.

[Writing Practice]

1. The Divine Comedy _____ Italian poet Dante Alighieri in the
early 14th century.   ~에 의해 쓰여 진 서사시이다

2. It _____ of Western literature.
          가장 위대한 작품 중의 하나로 널리 간주 된다

3. The poem _____: Inferno, Purgatorio, and Paradiso, each describing
          3부(part)로 구성되어 있다   a different realm of the afterlife.

4. _____ Virgil, Dante descends through nine concentric
  고대 로마의 시인 버질의 안내를 받아 (분사구)   circles of Hell and encounters various
sinners.

5. _____, starting with lesser sins like lust and gluttony.
  각각의 집단(circle)은 다른 죄를 나타낸다(re~)

6. Dante encounters notable historical and mythological figures, _____
                                                    동시대의 사람들뿐만 아니라

7. Here, souls _____ their eventual entry into Heaven.
          그들의 죄에서 정화(clean)되고 ~를 위한 준비 된다

8. Dante is guided by Virgil until he reaches the Earthly Paradise, _____
_____. 그곳에서는 Beatrice의 영혼이 그의 안내자가 된다 (관계부사)

9. He _____, who impart wisdom and reveal divine truths.
다양한 성인들과 다른 축복받은 영혼들과 만난다(en~)

10. Throughout the Divine Comedy, Dante _____, divine
justice, and the nature of God's love.   죄와 구원이라는 주제를 탐구한다(ex~)

[Word Quiz]

1. What term refers to existence beyond physical death?
a) Afterlife b) Inferno c) Purgatorio d) Paradiso

2. Which word signifies a place of intense punishment or suffering?
a) Afterlife b) Inferno c) Purgatorio d) Paradiso

3. What is the term for a place of purification or temporary suffering before reaching heaven?
a) Afterlife b) Inferno c) Purgatorio d) Paradiso

4. Which term denotes a state of perfect happiness and bliss?
a) Afterlife b) Inferno c) Purgatorio d) Paradiso

5. What word describes a passage or voyage, especially one with significant experiences?
a) Journey b) Concentric c) Sinners d) Punishment

6. Which adjective relates to circles or shapes with a common center?
a) Journey b) Concentric c) Sinners d) Punishment

7. What term refers to individuals who commit wrongful acts or offenses?
a) Journey b) Concentric c) Sinners d) Punishment

8. What is the term for penalties or consequences imposed for wrongdoing?
a) Journey b) Concentric c) Sinners d) Punishment

9. Which word describes something belonging to the present time or era?
a) Contemporary b) Ascent up c) Divine d) Penitent

10. What phrase denotes the act of climbing or moving upward?
a) Contemporary b) Ascent up c) Divine d) Penitent

11. What term pertains to the qualities or attributes of a deity or god?
a) Contemporary b) Ascent up c) Divine d) Penitent

12. Which adjective describes feelings of regret or remorse for one's actions?

a) Contemporary   b) Ascent up   c) Divine   d) Penitent

13. What word refers to heavenly or divine bodies and realms?

a) Celestial   b) Spheres   c) Ultimate   d) Reality

14. What term describes the highest or most fundamental level of something?

a) Celestial   b) Spheres   c) Ultimate   d) Reality

15. Which term relates to the study or doctrines of religion?

a) Theological   b) Mythology   c) Allegory   d) Redemption

16. What word refers to traditional stories or legends often explaining natural or historical events?

a) Theological   b) Mythology   c) Allegory   d) Redemption

17. What term describes a narrative with symbolic meaning, often representing deeper truths or concepts?

a) Theological   b) Mythology   c) Allegory   d) Redemption

18. Which term signifies the act of being saved or rescued from harm or sin?

a) Theological   b) Mythology   c) Allegory   d) Redemption

19. What is the term for the use of symbols to represent ideas or concepts?

a) Symbolism   b) Spiritual   c) Metaphysical   d) Exploration

20. What word relates to the exploration or investigation of abstract concepts or principles?

a) Symbolism   b) Spiritual   c) Metaphysical   d) Redemption

Unit 5: Decameron (1353)

"The Decameron" is a collection of novellas written by the Italian author Giovanni Boccaccio in the 14th century. It consists of 100 tales narrated by a group of young people who have fled Florence to escape the Black Death. The work is considered a masterpiece of Italian literature and an important precursor to the development of the short story genre.

The frame story of "The Decameron" is set in 1348, during the height of the Black Death epidemic in Italy. Ten young people, seven women, and three men, gather at a villa in the countryside near Florence. They come from different social backgrounds and have diverse personalities. To pass the time and distract themselves from the horrors of the plague, they decide to tell stories.

Each day, the group elects a new king or queen, who selects a theme for the day's storytelling. The members then take turns narrating a story that fits the chosen theme. The tales cover a wide range of genres, including romance, comedy, tragedy, and satire. They explore various aspects of human nature, society, and morality.

The stories often feature clever protagonists who use wit, intelligence, and cunning to navigate difficult situations. They showcase the complexities of human relationships, the power of love, and the follies of human behavior. Some tales are humorous and lighthearted, while others are more serious and thought-provoking.

Throughout "The Decameron," Boccaccio addresses social and moral issues of his time, critiquing the church, the nobility, and the societal norms of the day. He also celebrates the vitality and resilience of the human spirit, even in the face of adversity.

One recurring theme in the stories is the transformative power of storytelling itself. The act of sharing tales allows the characters to escape from their immediate reality and find solace in the imaginative world of fiction.

After ten days of storytelling, the group disperses, and the frame story ends with their return to Florence. However, the impact of the stories lingers, as they have not only entertained but also enriched the listeners' understanding of human nature and the world around them.

"The Decameron" is a work that showcases Boccaccio's literary prowess and his ability to capture the essence of the human experience. It remains a timeless classic, celebrated for its artistry, humor, and insightful commentary on life and society.

[Vocabulary]

novellas 소설집 precursor 선구자 narrative 서술 diverse 다양한 distract 산만하게 하다 plague 역병 genres 장르 satire 풍자 morality 도덕성 protagonists 주인공 navigate 탐색하다 complexities 복잡성 lighthearted 명랑한 thought-provoking 생각을 자극하는 critique 비평 nobility 귀족 societal norms 사회적 관습 resilience 회복력 adversity 역경 solace 위로 imaginative 상상력 있는 disperse 흩어지다 artistry 예술성 insightful 통찰력 있는 commentary 주석 literary prowess 문학적 능력 essence 본질 timeless 영구적인 celebrated 유명한 enrich 풍부하게 하다 vitality 생명력

[본문 해석] 데카메론

 "데카메론"은 이탈리아 작가 조반니 보카치오가 14세기에 쓴 소설집입니다. 이 작품은 흑사병을 피해 피렌체를 탈출한 젊은이들이 그린 100편의 이야기로 구성되어 있습니다. 이 작품은 이탈리아 문학의 걸작이자 단편소설 발전의 중요한 선구자로 평가받고 있습니다.

 데카메론의 스토리 프레임은 이탈리아의 흑사병 유행이 가장 심한 1348년을 배경으로 합니다. 7명의 여성과 3명의 남성으로 이루어진 10명의 젊은이들이 피렌체 근교 시골 별장에 모입니다. 그들은 서로 다른 사회적 배경을 가지고 다양한 성격을 지닙니다. 그들은 흑사병의 공포에서 벗어나 시간을 보내기 위해 이야기를 하기로 결정합니다.

 매일, 각 그룹은 새로운 왕 또는 여왕을 선출하고, 그가 그 날의 이야기에 맞는 주제를 선택합니다. 멤버들은 선택된 주제에 맞는 이야기를 번갈아서 설명합니다. 이 소설들은 로맨스, 코미디, 비극 및 풍자 등 다양한 장르를 다루며 인간의 본성, 사회, 도덕 등 다양한 측면을 탐구합니다.

 그 이야기들은 종종 재치, 지성, 그리고 어려운 상황을 헤쳐 나가기 위해 교활함을 사용하는 영리한 주인공들을 등장시킵니다. 그것들은 인간관계의 복잡함, 사랑의 힘, 그리고 인간 행동의 어리석음을 보여줍니다. 어떤 이야기들은 유머러스하고 가벼운 반면, 다른 이야기들은 더 진지하고 생각을 불러일으킵니다.

 "데카메론" 전체를 통해, 보카치오는 그 시대의 사회적 도덕적 문제들을 다루며 교회, 귀족, 그리고 당시 사회적 기준을 비판합니다. 그는 인내와 극복의 인간 정신을 찬양합니다. 이 이야기들에서 반복되는 테마 중 하나는 이야기를 나누는 것 자체의 변화의 힘입니다. 이야기를 나누는 행위는 등장인물들이 그들의 즉각적인 현실에서 벗어나 상상력이 풍부한 허구의 세계에서 위안을 찾을 수 있도록 합니다.

 열흘간의 스토리텔링이 끝나면 집단이 흩어지며, 프레임 스토리는 피렌체로 돌아가는 것으로 끝이 납니다. 그러나 이들이 듣는 이들을 즐겁게 해준 것은 물론 인간 본성과 주변 세계에 대한 이해를 풍부하게 해준 만큼 그 영향은 여전합니다.

 "데카메론"은 보카치오의 문학적 기량과 인간 경험의 본질을 포착하는 능력을 보여주는 작품으로 예술성, 유머, 그리고 삶과 사회에 대한 통찰력 있는 해설로 유명한 시대를 초월한 고전으로 남아 있습니다.

[Reading Comprehension]

1. Who is the author of "The Decameron"?
a) Dante Alighieri   b) Giovanni Boccaccio   c) Virgil   d) Petrarch

2. How many tales are there in "The Decameron"?
a) 50   b) 75   c) 100   d) 150

3. Why do the characters in "The Decameron" gather at a villa in the countryside?
a) To celebrate a wedding
b) To escape a war
c) To flee from the Black Death
d) To participate in a storytelling contest

4. What event serves as the backdrop for the frame story of "The Decameron"?
a) A royal banquet   b) A carnival
c) The Black Death epidemic   d) A religious pilgrimage

5. How many young people are part of the group telling stories in "The Decameron"?
a) 5   b) 7   c) 10   d) 12

6. What is the role of the elected king or queen each day in "The Decameron"?
a) To tell the first story
b) To choose the theme for the storytelling
c) To prepare meals for the group
d) To lead the group in song

7. What genres do the tales in "The Decameron" cover?
a) Only romance and comedy
b) Only tragedy and satire
c) Only romance and tragedy
d) Various genres including romance, comedy, tragedy, and satire

8. What is a recurring characteristic of the protagonists in the stories?
a) They are all royalty
b) They are all cunning and deceitful
c) They are all women
d) They use wit and intelligence to navigate challenges

9. What theme is often explored in the tales of "The Decameron"?
a) The power of magic
b) The mysteries of the universe
c) The complexities of human relationships
d) The struggles of animals in society

10. How does Boccaccio use storytelling to address societal issues in "The Decameron"?
a) He uses stories to promote religious dogma
b) He avoids societal issues in his tales
c) He critiques the church, nobility, and societal norms
d) He only focuses on entertainment without deeper meanings

11. What does the act of sharing tales provide for the characters in "The Decameron"?
a) Temporary relief from the rain
b) An opportunity to showcase their skills
c) Solace and escape from reality
d) A chance to compete for prizes

12. How many days do the characters tell stories in "The Decameron"?
a) 5 b) 7 c) 10 d) 14

13. What is the ultimate impact of the stories in "The Decameron"?
a) They lead to conflict among the characters
b) They provide a source of wealth for the characters
c) They enrich the listeners' understanding of human nature and the world
d) They lead to the downfall of the characters

14. What does "The Decameron" celebrate about the human spirit?
a) Its fragility in the face of adversity
b) Its tendency to give up easily
c) Its resilience and vitality even in challenging circumstances
d) Its lack of creativity

15. What is one aspect for which "The Decameron" is celebrated?
a) Its focus solely on romance
b) Its connection to ancient Greek mythology
c) Its artistry, humor, and insightful commentary
d) Its detailed description of the Italian countryside

[Grammar Check-up]

1. "The Decameron" is a collection of novellas _____ by the Italian author Giovanni Boccaccio in the 14th century.
a) written   b) writes   c) writing   d) wrote

2. It consists of 100 tales _____ by a group of young people who have fled Florence to escape the Black Death.
a) narrated   b) narrating   c) narrate   d) narrates

3. The work _____ a masterpiece of Italian literature and a precursor to the development of the short story genre.
a) has considered   b) is considering   c) considers   d) is considered

4. The frame story of "The Decameron" is set in 1348, _____ the height of the Black Death epidemic in Italy.
a) at   b) during   c) within   d) while

5. Ten young people, seven women, and three men, gather at a villa in the countryside near Florence, _____ from different social backgrounds and having diverse personalities.
a) coming   b) comes   c) came   d) come

6. To pass the time and distract themselves from the horrors of the plague, they decide to tell stories, _____ turns narrating a story that fits the chosen theme.
a) take   b) takes   c) taking   d) took

7. Each day, the group elects a new king or queen, who selects a theme for the day's storytelling. The members then take turns _____ a story that fits the chosen theme.
a) to narrate   b) narrating   c) narrates   d) narrated

8. The tales cover a wide range of genres, including romance, comedy, tragedy, and satire, _____ various aspects of human nature, society, and morality.
a) explore   b) explores   c) exploring   d) explored

9. The stories often feature clever protagonists who use wit, intelligence, and cunning to _____ difficult situations.
a) navigate   b) navigates   c) navigating   d) navigated

10. They showcase the complexities of human relationships, _____ of love, and the follies of human behavior.
a) the power   b) powerful   c) the powerful   d) powerfully

11. Some tales are humorous and lighthearted, while others are more serious _____ thought-provoking.
a) and   b) or   c) but   d) nor

12. Throughout "The Decameron," Boccaccio addresses social and moral issues of his time, critiquing the church, the nobility, and the _____ norms of the day.
a) societal   b) societies   c) society   d) socially

13. He also celebrates the vitality and resilience of the human spirit, even _____ the face of adversity.
a) on   b) in   c) at   d) with

14. One recurring theme in the stories is the transformative power of storytelling itself, _____ allows the characters to escape from their immediate reality.
a) who   b) that   c) which   d) whose

15. The act of sharing tales allows the characters to escape from their immediate reality and find solace in _____ world of fiction.
a) imagination   b) imaginative   c) imaginatively   d) imaginings

16. After ten days of storytelling, the group disperses, and the frame story ends with their return _____ Florence.
a) to   b) in   c) at   d) from

17. However, the impact of the stories lingers, _____ they have not only entertained but also enriched the listeners' understanding of human nature and the world around them.
a) for   b) as   c) so   d) but

18. "The Decameron" is a work that _____ Boccaccio's literary prowess and ability to capture the essence of the human experience.
a) showcase   b) showcasing   c) is showcased   d) showcases

19. It remains a timeless classic, celebrated _____ its artistry, humor, and insightful commentary on life and society.
a) to   b) for   c) with   d) at

20. "The Decameron" is a remarkable literary achievement, inspiring readers to reflect on _____ own lives and the power of storytelling.
a) his   b) their   c) its   d) our

[Writing Practice]

1. "The Decameron" _____ the Italian author Giovanni Boccaccio in the 14th century. ~에 의해 쓰여 진 단편소설(novella)들의 모음집이다

2. It _____ a group of young people who have fled Florence
~에 의해 전해지는(nar~) 100개의 이야기로 구성되어 있다   to escape the Black Death.

3. The work _____ Italian literature.
                    ~의 걸작으로 간주된다

4. They _____ and have diverse personalities.
                다른 사회적 배경으로부터 왔다

5. _____ the horrors of the plague, they
시간도 *보내고* 자신들을 ~로부터 *주의를 딴 데로 돌리기 위해서*   decide to tell stories.

6. The members then _____.
                    순서대로 선택한 주제에 맞는(fit) 이야기를 하다

7. They _____, society, and morality.
                인간본성의 다양한 측면들을 탐구한다

8. Some tales are humorous and lighthearted, _____
_____. 반면에 다른 이야기들은 더욱 진지하고 생각을 하게 만든다

9. He also celebrates the vitality and resilience of the human spirit, _____
_____ 심지어 역경(ad~)을 마주 하고도 (전치사구)

10. The act of sharing tales _____
                    등장인물들이 그들은 당면한 현실에서 벗어나게 해준다(all~)

- 54 -

[Word Quiz]

1. What does "precursor" mean?

a) A type of story   b) A person who tells a story

c) An introduction or forerunner   d) A protagonist's journey

2. Which word best describes a story's sequence of events?

a) Narrative   b) Distract   c) Resilience   d) Essence

3. What is the opposite of "homogeneous"?

a) Diverse   b) Navigate   c) Critique   d) Artistry

4. What does "distract" mean?

a) To focus intensely   b) To cause confusion or diversion

c) To enrich one's mind   d) To overcome adversity

5. Which term refers to a widespread and often deadly disease?

a) Plague   b) Satire   c) Solace   d) Imagination

6. Which word is associated with different styles or categories of artistic works?

a) Genres   b) Morality   c) Thought-provoking   d) Nobility

7. What is the purpose of "satire"?

a) To explore complexities   b) To provide solace

c) To critique and ridicule human flaws   d) To disperse ideas

8. Which term refers to principles of right and wrong conduct?

a) Morality   b) Navigate   c) Adversity   d) Enrich

9. Who are the main characters in a story?

a) Protagonists   b) Lighthearted   c) Societal norms   d) Insightful

10. What does it mean to "navigate" something?

a) To create complexities

b) To criticize thoroughly

c) To find a solution or explore through difficulties

d) To disperse and scatter

11. Which word means cheerful and carefree?

a) Lighthearted   b) Adversity   c) Literary prowess   d) Essence

12. What kind of art can be described as "thought-provoking"?
a) Solace   b) Diverse   c) Critique   d) Imagination

13. What does "critique" mean?
a) To provide solace and comfort   b) To navigate through complexities
c) To express insightful commentary   d) To celebrate and honor

14. Which word refers to a high social rank or class?
a) Nobility   b) Resilience   c) Precursor   d) Enrich

15. What are "societal norms"?
a) Complexities in society   b) Principles of morality
c) Celebrated values   d) Widely accepted customs and behaviors

16. What is the ability to recover and adapt in the face of challenges called?
a) Resilience   b) Satire   c) Imagination   d) Vitality

17. What does "adversity" mean?
a) A type of genre in literature   b) A state of tranquility and peace
c) A widespread disease   d) Difficulties and misfortune

18. What does "solace" mean?
a) To scatter and spread
b) To critique and analyze
c) To provide comfort and consolation
d) To navigate through complexities

19. What is the adjective form of "imagination"?
a) Artistry   b) Thought-provoking
c) Distracted   d) Imaginative

20. Which word means having profound insight and understanding?
a) Insightful   b) Commentary   c) Literary prowess   d) Essence

Unit 6: Canterbury Tales (1390)

"The Canterbury Tales" is a collection of stories written by Geoffrey Chaucer in the late 14th century. The frame narrative of the work is set as a storytelling competition among a group of pilgrims who are traveling together from London to the shrine of Saint Thomas Becket in Canterbury Cathedral.

At the Tabard Inn in Southwark, the narrator meets a diverse group of pilgrims, each representing a different social class and profession. There are 29 pilgrims in total, including nobles, clergy, merchants, craftsmen, and commoners. The host of the inn, Harry Bailey, suggests that to pass the time during their journey, each pilgrim should tell two tales on their way to Canterbury and two more on the way back. He proposes that upon their return, the pilgrim with the best story will be treated to a free dinner paid for by the rest of the group.

As the journey begins, the pilgrims take turns telling their tales. Each tale reflects the personality and interests of the storyteller and covers a wide range of genres and themes. The tales include stories of romance, adventure, morality, satire, and fables. Some are humorous and entertaining, while others offer moral lessons and social commentary.

The Knight is the first to tell a tale, narrating a chivalric romance about love and honor. The Miller follows with a comic and bawdy tale of trickery and deceit. The Reeve shares a story about a clever miller who is outwitted by two students, and the Wife of Bath narrates a tale of a knight who must discover what women truly desire.

Other memorable tales include the Pardoner's moral allegory about greed and deception, the Nun's Priest's lively fable of a cunning rooster, and the Physician's tragic tale of young love and treachery.

As the pilgrims share their stories, they engage in lively discussions and debates, revealing their differing viewpoints and worldviews. These interactions provide insights into the social, religious, and cultural issues of Chaucer's time.

However, the work remains unfinished, and Chaucer did not complete the planned 120 tales. The collection ends abruptly after only 24 tales, with the pilgrims still on their way to Canterbury.

Throughout the work, Chaucer uses the pilgrims and their stories to offer a vivid portrayal of medieval English society, with its various classes, customs, and values. "The Canterbury Tales" is a masterpiece of Middle English literature, renowned for its rich storytelling, skillful characterization, and keen observations of human nature and society. It remains a classic that continues to be studied, enjoyed, and appreciated by readers and scholars alike.

[Vocabulary]

Collection 모음 Competition 경쟁 Pilgrims 순례자들 Shrine 성지 Cathedral 성당 Diverse 다양한 Social class 사회 계급 Profession 직업 Nobles 귀족들 Clergy 성직자들 Merchants 상인들 Craftsmen 장인들 Commoners 일반 시민들 Host 주인장 Proposal 제안 Journey 여행 Personality 성격 Chivalric 기사도적인 Trickery 속임수 Deceit 속임수 Clever 영리한 Outwit 속이다 Knight 기사 Morality 도덕성 Allegory 우화 Cunning 교활한 Lively 생기 넘치는 Fable 우화 Treachery 배신 Characterization 성격묘사 Observations 관찰 Medieval 중세 시대의 Renowned 유명한 Appreciated 감사하는

[본문 해석] 캔터베리 이야기

"캔터베리 이야기"는 14세기 후반 제프리 초서가 쓴 이야기 모음집입니다. 작품의 프레임 서사는 런던에서 캔터베리 대성당의 성 토마스 베켓 성지까지 함께 여행하는 순례자 그룹의 이야기 대결로 설정되어 있습니다.

서더크의 타바드 여관에서 내레이터는 각각 다른 사회 계층과 직업을 대표하는 다양한 순례자 그룹을 만납니다. 귀족, 성직자, 상인, 장인, 평민을 포함하여 총 29명의 순례자가 있습니다. 여관 주인인 해리 베일리는 여행 중에 시간을 보내기 위해 각 순례자가 캔터베리로 가는 길에 두 가지 이야기를 하고 돌아오는 길에 두 가지 이야기를 더 해야 한다고 제안합니다. 돌아오는 길에, 가장 좋은 이야기를 가진 순례자가 저녁 식사를 무료로 대접받을 것을 그는 제안합니다.

여행이 시작되면서 순례자들은 돌아가면서 자신들의 이야기를 들려줍니다. 각각의 이야기는 이야기꾼의 성격과 흥미를 반영하고 다양한 장르와 주제를 다루고 있습니다. 이야기는 로맨스, 모험, 도덕, 풍자, 우화를 포함합니다. 어떤 것들은 유머러스하고 재미있는 반면, 다른 것들은 도덕적 교훈과 사회적 논평을 제공합니다.

기사는 사랑과 명예에 대한 기사도적 로맨스를 이야기한 첫 인물입니다. 방앗간 주인은 책략과 속임수에 대한 희극적이고 저속한 이야기를 이어갑니다. 장원청지기는 두 명의 대학생들에게 속아 넘어간 방앗간 주인에 대한 이야기를 하고, 바스의 아내는 여성이 진정으로 원하는 것이 무엇인지를 발견해야 하는 기사에 대한 이야기를 합니다.

다른 기억에 남는 이야기로는 탐욕과 속임수에 대한 면죄부 판매자의 도덕적 우화, 교활한 수탉에 대한 수녀원 사제의 생생한 우화, 그리고 젊은 사랑과 배신에 대한 의사의 비극적인 이야기가 있습니다.

순례자들이 자신들의 이야기를 나누면서 활발한 토론과 논쟁을 벌이며 서로 다른 관점과 세계관을 드러내는데, 이러한 상호작용은 초서 시대의 사회적, 종교적, 문화적 문제에 대한 통찰력을 제공합니다.

그러나, 이 작품은 미완성으로, 초서는 120편의 이야기를 모두 완성하지 못했습니다. 순례자들이 여전히 캔터베리로 가는 길에 불과 24편의 이야기 끝에 이 작품이 갑자기 끝납니다.

초서는 작품 내내 순례자들과 그들의 이야기를 통해 다양한 계급과 관습, 가치관을 지닌 중세 영국 사회를 생생하게 묘사하고 있으며, 풍부한 스토리텔링과 능숙한 성격 묘사, 인간의 본성과 사회에 대한 예리한 관찰로 유명한 중세 영국 문학의 걸작으로 독자와 학자 모두에게 연구되고, 즐기고, 감상되는 고전으로 남아 있습니다.

[Reading Comprehension]

1. What is the main theme of "The Canterbury Tales"?

a) Greed and deception   b) Love and honor

c) Tragedy and treachery   d) The diverse society and its stories

2. How many pilgrims are there in total?

a) 14 b) 24 c) 29 d) 120

3. Who suggests the storytelling competition among the pilgrims?

a) The Knight b) The Miller c) The Reeve d) Harry Bailey, the host of the inn

4. What is the first tale narrated in "The Canterbury Tales"?

a) A comic and bawdy tale

b) A chivalric romance about love and honor

c) A tragic tale of young love and treachery

d) A fable of a cunning rooster

5. What genre of tales does the work include?

a) Romance and adventure   b) Satire and fables

c) Morality and social commentary d) All of the above

6. Who tells the story of the clever miller outwitted by two students in one of the tales?

a) The Knight b) The Miller c) The Reeve d) The Wife of Bath

7. What does the Pardoner's tale allegorize?

a) Greed and deception   b) Love and honor

c) Trickery and deceit   d) The discovery of women's desires

8. What do the pilgrims do as they share their stories?

a) Write in their journals   b) Engage in lively discussions and debates

c) Remain silent and listen   d) Pray and fast

9. How many tales did Chaucer plan to complete in "The Canterbury Tales"?

a) 14 b) 24 c) 29 d) 120

10. What setting provides the backdrop for the storytelling competition?

a) Canterbury Cathedral   b) London

c) The Tabard Inn in Southwark   d) Saint Thomas Becket's shrine

11. Which pilgrim narrates a lively fable of a cunning rooster?

a) The Pardoner   b) The Nun's Priest   c) The Physician   d) The Reeve

12. What does Chaucer use to portray the pilgrims and their stories?

a) Modern English society

b) Medieval English society and its various classes, customs, and values

c) Social and cultural issues of the 19th century

d) Worldviews of different cultures

13. Which character follows the Knight's tale with a comic and bawdy story?

a) The Miller   b) The Reeve   c) The Wife of Bath   d) The Physician

14. How does the work "The Canterbury Tales" end?

a) Abruptly with the pilgrims still on their way to Canterbury

b) The pilgrims reach Canterbury and celebrate their journey

c) The host of the inn declares a winner of the storytelling competition

d) The pilgrims decide to tell more tales on their way back to London

15. What is "The Canterbury Tales" renowned for?

a) Its keen observations of human nature and society

b) Its portrayal of modern English society

c) Its depiction of the host of the inn, Harry Bailey

d) Its religious themes and sermons

[Grammar Check-up]

1. The pilgrims _____ their journey from London to Canterbury.
a) begins   b) began   c) beginning   d) has begun

2. Chaucer's portrayal of medieval English society is _____.
a) vividly   b) vivid   c) vividness   d) un-vivid

3. The tales in "The Canterbury Tales" cover a _____ range of genres and themes.
a) wide   b) wider   c) wideness   d) widen

4. The Pardoner's tale serves as a moral _____ about greed and deception.
a) allegory   b) allegories   c) allegorical   d) allegorize

5. The pilgrims engage in lively discussions and debates, revealing their differing _____.
a) viewpoints   b) viewpoint   c) view   d) viewable

6. The collection ends abruptly after only 24 tales, _____ the pilgrims still on their way to Canterbury.
a) yet   b) although   c) with   d) because

7. The narrator meets a diverse group of pilgrims, _____ represent different social classes and professions.
a) whom   b) which   c) who   d) whose

8. Chaucer uses the pilgrims and their stories to offer a _____ portrayal of medieval English society.
a) vivid   b) vividly   c) vividness   d) non-vivid

9. The Reeve shares a story about a clever miller who _____ outwitted by two students.
a) is   b) were   c) have been   d) are

10. The tales in "The Canterbury Tales" are _____ and entertaining.
a) humorous   b) humorously   c) humor   d) humorful

11. The pilgrims _____ turns telling their tales.
a) take   b) takes   c) taking   d) took

12. The Knight is the first to tell a tale, _____ a chivalric romance about love and honor.
a) narrates   b) narrating   c) narration   d) narrator

13. The work "The Canterbury Tales" remains a classic that continues to be studied, _____, and appreciated by readers and scholars alike.
a) enjoying   b) enjoyed   c) enjoyable   d) enjoy

14. Chaucer's keen _____ of human nature and society is evident in his storytelling.
a) observe   b) observation   c) observational   d) observer

15. The pilgrims _____ their tales as they travel to Canterbury.
a) tell   b) telling   c) tells   d) were told

16. Other memorable tales _____ the Pardoner's moral allegory about greed and deception
a) includes   b) include   c) are included   d) including

17. The narrator meets a diverse group of pilgrims, each _____ a different social class and profession.
a) representing   b) represents   c) represent   d) is represented

18. Chaucer's portrayal of medieval English society is vivid, offering _____ insights into its various classes, customs, and values.
a) deep   b) deeply   c) depth   d) deepness

19. The tales include stories of romance, adventure, morality, satire, and fables, each _____ a wide range of themes.
a) covering   b) covers   c) covered   d) cover

20. The collection ends abruptly after only 24 tales, leaving the readers _____ about the rest of the journey.
a) curious   b) curiosity   c) curiously   d) curios

[Writing Practice]

1. The frame narrative of the work is set as a storytelling competition among a group of pilgrims _____ to the shrine of Saint Thomas Becket in Canterbury Cathedral. 런던에서 ~까지 함께 여행하는 순례자들 (관계사)

2. At the Tabard Inn in Southwark, the narrator meets a diverse group of pilgrims, _____.
　　　각각은 다른 사회 계층과 직업을 나타낸다(re~) (분사구)

3. The host of the inn, Harry Bailey, suggests that to pass the time during their journey, _____ to Canterbury and two more on the way back.
　　　각각의 순례자는 ~로 가는 길에 2개의 이야기를 해야 한다

4. As the journey begins, the pilgrims _____.
　　　　　　　　　　　　　　순번대로 그들의 이야기를 한다

5. _____ and covers a wide range 각각의 이야기는 이야기를 하는 사람의 성격과 관심을 반영한다 　　of genres and themes.

6. _____ the Pardoner's moral allegory about greed and 다른 기억에 남을 만한 이야기들은 ~를 포함한다 　　　　　　　　　　　deception.

7. As the pilgrims share their stories, they engage in lively discussions and debates, _____.
그들의 다른 견해와 세계관을 드러낸다 (분사구)

8. _____
　　　이런 상호작용들은 사회적 그리고 종교적 문제(issue)들에 대한 통찰력을 제공한다

9. However, _____, and Chaucer did not complete the planned 120 tales. 그 작품은 미완성인 체로 남아있다

10. The collection ends abruptly after only 24 tales, _____
_____ 순례자들이 여전히 캔터베리(Canterbury)로 가는 중에 (with 분사구)

[Word Quiz]

1. What is a "collection"?
a) A type of competition   b) A group of people
c) A variety of items gathered together   d) A type of journey

2. What does "competition" refer to?
a) A group of diverse individuals   b) A religious place
c) A challenge to win or achieve something   d) A form of medieval literature

3. Who are "pilgrims"?
a) Skilled craftsmen   b) Members of the nobility
c) Travelers on a religious journey   d) Leaders of a community

4. What is a "shrine"?
a) A type of cathedral   b) A form of medieval artwork
c) A religious building   d) A place of worship

5. What is a "cathedral"?
a) A diverse gathering   b) A type of pilgrimage
c) A religious building of significance   d) A collection of stories

6. What does "diverse" mean?
a) Deceptive and misleading   b) Skilled and talented
c) Different and varied   d) Humorous and entertaining

7. What is a "social class"?
a) A group of craftsmen
b) A variety of professions
c) A hierarchy based on economic or social status
d) A gathering of nobles

8. What does "profession" refer to?
a) A form of medieval literature   b) A religious practice
c) A skilled trade or occupation   d) A journey of exploration

9. Who are "nobles"?
a) Common people   b) Skilled craftsmen
c) Members of the clergy   d) People of high social rank

10. What is the role of the "clergy"?
a) To engage in competition   b) To engage in deceit
c) To lead religious services   d) To lead social gatherings

11. Who are "merchants"?
a) People of high social rank   b) Religious leaders
c) Skilled craftsmen   d) Traders who buy and sell goods

12. What are "craftsmen" known for? craftsman
a) Leading social events   b) Telling allegorical stories
c) Creating skilled painting d) Practicing skilled handicraft or trades

13. What do "commoners" refer to?
a) People with diverse talents   b) Skilled craftsmen
c) People of lower social rank   d) Religious pilgrims

14. Who is a "host"?
a) A talented storyteller   b) A religious figure
c) A person who leads social gatherings   d) A person who provides hospitality

15. What is a "proposal"?
a) A form of medieval literature   b) A religious offering
c) An idea or plan suggested for consideration   d) A competition for a prize

16. What is a "journey"?
a) A diverse gathering   b) A form of pilgrimage
c) A challenge to win something   d) A religious building

17. What does "personality" refer to?
a) A collection of stories   b) The distinctive qualities that define an individual
c) A type of medieval art   d) A social class

18. What does "chivalric" mean?
a) Clever and deceitful   b) Humorous and entertaining
c) Related to knights and their code of conduct   d) Reflecting diverse viewpoints

19. What does "trickery" mean?
a) A form of medieval literature   b) Clever and skillful actions used to deceive
c) A type of religious practice   d) A diverse gathering

20. What is "morality"?
a) A religious building
b) Skilled craftsmanship
c) Principles concerning right and wrong conduct
d) A type of medieval artwork

Unit 7: Romeo and Juliet (1597)

"Romeo and Juliet" is a tragic play written by William Shakespeare around 1597. Set in the Italian city of Verona, the story revolves around two young lovers, Romeo Montague and Juliet Capulet, who belong to feuding families. Their love becomes the catalyst for a series of tragic events that ultimately leads to their untimely deaths.

The play begins with a longstanding conflict between the Montague and Capulet families, which permeates the entire city. Romeo, a Montague, attends a masked ball hosted by the Capulets, where he meets and falls in love with Juliet, the daughter of Lord Capulet. Unaware of each other's family backgrounds, Romeo and Juliet share a profound connection and secretly marry the following day with the help of Friar Laurence.

The situation worsens when Tybalt, Juliet's hot-tempered cousin, challenges Romeo to a duel. Romeo, who has married Juliet and now considers himself part of the Capulet family, refuses to fight Tybalt. However, Romeo's best friend Mercutio steps in and is killed by Tybalt. In a fit of rage, Romeo avenges Mercutio's death by slaying Tybalt. As a result, he is banished from Verona by the Prince.

Meanwhile, Juliet is pressured by her parents to marry Count Paris. In desperation, she seeks help from Friar Laurence, who devises a plan to reunite the lovers. He gives Juliet a potion that will make her appear dead temporarily, intending for Romeo to rescue her from the Capulet tomb. However, the message about the plan fails to reach Romeo, and he hears of Juliet's apparent death instead.

Heartbroken, Romeo rushes to the tomb and finds Juliet seemingly lifeless. Consumed by grief, he drinks a vial of poison and dies by her side. Upon waking from her drugged sleep, Juliet discovers Romeo's lifeless body and, unable to bear living without him, stabs herself with Romeo's dagger.

The tragic deaths of Romeo and Juliet serve as a catalyst for the reconciliation of their families, as they realize the senselessness of their feud and the devastating consequences it has brought upon their children. The play concludes with the Prince delivering a somber speech, highlighting the power of love to end hatred and the tragic consequences of unresolved conflict.

[Vocabulary]

Tragic 비극적인 Revolves 돌다, 회전하다 Catalyst 촉매 Untimely 때 이르지 않은 Conflict 갈등 Masked ball 가면무도회 Profound 깊은/심오한 Connection 연결 Secretly 비밀리에 Desperation 절망 Devise 고안하다 Reunite 재결합하다 Consume 태우다/소모하다 Grief 슬픔 Banished 추방된 Pressure 압박(하다) Rescue 구하다 Apparent 명백한 Heartbroken 비통한 Tomb 무덤 Poison 독 Reconciliation 화해 Senselessness 무모함 Devastating 파괴적인 Consequences 결과 Somber 침울한 Highlight 강조하다 Hatred 증오 Unaware 알지 못하는 Wed 결혼하다 Following 다음의 Challenge 도전하다 Refuse 거절하다

[본문 해석] 로미오와 줄리엣

　"로미오와 줄리엣"은 1597년경 윌리엄 셰익스피어에 의해 쓰여 진 비극적인 연극입니다. 이탈리아 도시 베로나를 배경으로, 그 이야기는 불화하는 가족에 속하는 두 명의 젊은 연인 로미오 몬테규와 줄리엣 캐퓰릿을 중심으로 전개됩니다. 그들의 사랑은 궁극적으로 그들의 때 아닌 죽음에 이르게 하는 일련의 비극적인 사건들의 촉매제가 됩니다.

　극은 도시 전체에 스며드는 몬테규 가문과 캐퓰릿 가문 사이의 오랜 갈등으로 시작합니다. 몬테규 가문인 로미오는 캐퓰릿 가문이 주최하는 가면무도회에 참석하는데, 그곳에서 캐퓰릿 경의 딸인 줄리엣을 만나 사랑에 빠지게 됩니다. 서로의 가정 배경을 모른 채 로미오와 줄리엣은 깊은 인연을 나누고 로렌스 수사의 도움을 받아 다음날 비밀리에 결혼합니다.

　줄리엣의 다혈질 사촌인 티볼트가 로미오에게 결투를 신청하면서 상황은 악화됩니다. 줄리엣과 결혼해 스스로를 캐퓰릿 가문의 일원으로 여기는 로미오는 티볼트와 싸우기를 거부합니다. 그러나 로미오의 가장 친한 친구 머큐쇼가 끼어들어 티볼트에게 죽임을 당합니다. 격분한 로미오는 티볼트를 살해함으로써 머큐쇼의 죽음에 복수합니다. 그 결과 왕자에 의해 베로나에서 추방당합니다.

　한편, 줄리엣은 부모님으로부터 파리스 백작과 결혼하라는 압력을 받습니다. 절망하여, 그녀는 연인들을 재회시킬 계획을 세운 로렌스 수사에게 도움을 구합니다. 그는 로미오가 캐퓰릿 무덤에서 그녀를 구출할 의도로 줄리엣에게 일시적으로 죽은 것처럼 보일 묘약을 줍니다. 그러나, 그 계획에 대한 메시지는 로미오에게 전달되지 못하고, 그는 대신 줄리엣의 분명한 죽음에 대해 듣습니다.

　슬픔에 잠긴 로미오는 무덤으로 달려갔고 줄리엣의 생명이 없는 것처럼 보이는 육체를 발견합니다. 슬픔에 사로잡힌 그는 독이 든 유리병을 마시고 그녀의 옆에서 죽습니다. 약에 취한 잠에서 깨어난 줄리엣은 로미오의 죽은 육체를 발견하고 그가 없이 사는 것을 견디지 못하고 로미오의 단검으로 자신을 찌릅니다.

　로미오와 줄리엣의 비극적 죽음은 그들의 불화의 무의미함과 그것이 그들의 아이들에게 가져다 준 파괴적인 결과들을 깨닫기 때문에 그들의 가족의 화해를 위한 촉매제 역할을 합니다. 극은 증오를 끝낼 사랑의 힘과 해결되지 않은 갈등의 비극적인 결과들을 강조하면서 왕자가 우울한 연설을 하는 것으로 끝을 맺습니다.

[Reading Comprehension]

1. When was "Romeo and Juliet" written?
a) Around 1497   b) Around 1597   c) Around 1697   d) Around 1797

2. Where is the story of "Romeo and Juliet" set?
a) Venice   b) Rome   c) Verona   d) Florence

3. What is the central conflict in "Romeo and Juliet"?
a) A war between two cities
b) A feud between two families
c) A dispute over land ownership
d) A struggle for political power

4. Who are the two main characters in "Romeo and Juliet"?
a) Romeo and Mercutio   b) Romeo and Tybalt
c) Romeo and Paris   d) Romeo and Juliet

5. How do Romeo and Juliet first meet?
a) At a marketplace   b) At a masked ball
c) At a church   d) At a funeral

6. Who assists Romeo and Juliet in getting married?
a) Friar Laurence   b) Mercutio   c) Lord Capulet   d) Tybalt

7. What causes Romeo to be banished from Verona?
a) His refusal to marry Juliet
b) His involvement in a brawl
c) His secret marriage to Juliet
d) His disrespect towards the Prince

8. How does Romeo avenge Mercutio's death?
a) By challenging Tybalt to a duel
b) By poisoning Tybalt
c) By getting Tybalt arrested
d) By seeking revenge from Lord Capulet

9. How does Friar Laurence help Juliet?
a) To escape from her parents' control   b) To find a suitable husband
c) To fake her own death   d) To rescue Romeo from banishment

10. What is Friar Laurence's plan to reunite Romeo and Juliet?
a) He arranges a secret marriage for them
b) He helps them run away to a different city
c) He gives Juliet a potion to make her appear dead
d) He convinces their families to reconcile

11. Why doesn't Romeo receive the message about Friar Laurence's plan?
a) Friar John, tasked with delivering the message to Romeo, is unable to do so
b) Friar Laurence changes his mind
c) Benvolio intercepts the message
d) The messenger is attacked by bandits

12. What is the outcome of Romeo's rush to Juliet's tomb?
a) He rescues Juliet from the tomb
b) He discovers that Juliet is alive
c) He dies by Juliet's side
d) He reunites with his family

13. How does Juliet react upon waking and finding Romeo dead?
a) She stabs herself with Romeo's dagger
b) She rushes to Friar Laurence for help
c) She calls for her parents to console her
d) She runs away to another city

14. What effect do the deaths of Romeo and Juliet have on their families?
a) Their families continue to feud
b) Their families become even more hostile
c) Their families reconcile and end their feud
d) Their families blame each other for the tragedy

15. How does the play "Romeo and Juliet" conclude?
a) With a grand wedding celebration
b) With Romeo's resurrection
c) With the Prince's speech about love and conflict
d) With a final duel between the Montagues and Capulets

[Grammar Check-up]

1. Romeo Montague and Juliet Capulet (are belonging, belong) to feuding families.

2. Their love becomes the catalyst for a series of tragic events that ultimately (leading, leads) to their untimely deaths.

3. The play begins with a longstanding conflict (between, both) the Montague and Capulet families, which permeates the entire city.

4. Romeo (attends to, attends) a masked ball (hosts, hosted) by the Capulets, (which, where) he meets and falls in love with Juliet, the daughter of Lord Capulet.

5. (Aware, Unaware) of each other's family backgrounds, Romeo and Juliet share a profound connection and (secretly, secret) marry the following day.

6. The situation (worsening, worsens) when Tybalt, Juliet's hot-tempered cousin, challenges Romeo to a duel.

7. Romeo, who (is married, has married) Juliet and now considers himself part of the Capulet family, refuses (to fight, fighting) Tybalt.

8. In a fit of rage, Romeo (is avenged, avenges) Mercutio's death by slaying Tybalt.

9. As a result, he (is banished, banishes) from Verona by the Prince.

10. Meanwhile, Juliet (is pressured, pressures) by her parents to marry Count Paris.

11. In desperation, she seeks help from Friar Laurence, who (devises, is devised) a plan to reunite the lovers.

12. He gives Juliet a potion (what, that) will make her appear dead temporarily, intending for Romeo to rescue her from the Capulet tomb.

13. However, the message about the plan fails to reach Romeo, and he hears of Juliet's (apparently, apparent) death instead.

14. (Heartbroken, Heartbreaking), Romeo rushes to the tomb and finds Juliet seemingly (lifelessness, lifeless).

15. (Consuming, Consumed) by grief, he drinks a vial of poison and dies by her side.

16. Upon waking from her drugged sleep, Juliet discovers Romeo's (lifeless, lifelessness) body and, (able, unable) to bear living without him, stabs herself with Romeo's dagger.

17. They realize the (senseless, senselessness) of their feud and the devastating consequences it (has, is) brought upon their children.

18. The play concludes with the Prince (delivers, delivering) a somber speech, (highlights, highlighting) the power of love to end hatred and the tragic consequences of unresolved conflict.

[Writing Practice]

1. The story revolves around two young lovers, Romeo Montague and Juliet Capulet, ------------------------------. 적대하는(feud~) 가문에 속하는 (관계사)

2. Their love becomes the catalyst for a series of tragic events --------------------. ------------------------ 궁극적으로 그들의 때 아닌 죽음을 불러일으키는 (관계사)

3. The play -------------------------------- the Montague and Capulet families, ~간의 오랜 갈등으로 시작한다 which permeates the entire city.

4. Romeo ----------------------------------- the Capulets, where he meets and 캐플릿 가문이 주최하는 가면무도회에 참석한다 falls in love with Juliet.

5. --------------------------------, Romeo and Juliet share a profound connection 서로의 가족 배경에 대해 알지 못하고 (분사구) and secretly marry the following day.

6. ----------------------------- Tybalt, Juliet's hot-tempered cousin, challenges ~하자 상황이 악화된다(wo~) Romeo to a duel.

7. ------------------------------------- Verona by the Prince. 그 결과, 그는 Verona로부터 추방당한다

8. ------------------------------------- her parents to marry Count Paris. 그동안, Juliet는 ~에 의해 압박을 받는다(pr~)

9. In desperation, she seeks help from Friar Laurence, --------------------------- the lovers. 그는 (연인들을) 재결합 시킬 계획을 생각해 낸다 (관계사)

10. He gives Juliet a potion ---------------------------------------, intending for 일시적으로 그녀가 죽은 것처럼 보이게 만들 독약 (관계사) Romeo to rescue her from the Capulet tomb.

11. Upon waking from her drugged sleep, Juliet discovers Romeo's lifeless body and, ------------------------------------, stabs herself with Romeo's dagger. 그 없이 살아가는 것을 견딜 수 없어서 (분사구) *able 응용

12. The play concludes with the Prince delivering a somber speech, -------------- ----------------------------- 증오를 끝내는 사랑의 힘을 강조하면서 (분사구)

[Word Quiz]

1. What does "tragic" mean?
a) Joyful and cheerful   b) Sad and sorrowful
c) Mysterious and enigmatic   d) Exciting and thrilling

2. If something "revolves," what does it do?
a) It stands still   b) It moves in a straight line
c) It rotates or orbits   d) It expands rapidly

3. What is a "catalyst"?
a) A barrier or obstacle   b) A triggering event or agent
c) A soothing remedy   d) A hidden treasure

4. What does "untimely" mean?
a) In the nick of time   b) At a suitable moment
c) Unexpectedly early   d) Right on schedule

5. What is a "conflict"?
a) Harmony and agreement   b) A struggle or disagreement
c) A mysterious occurrence   d) A celebration

6. What takes place at a "masked ball"?
a) A formal debate   b) A secret meeting
c) A funeral procession   d) A festive dance event

7. What is the meaning of "profound"?
a) Shallow and superficial   b) Deep and thoughtful
c) Loud and boisterous   d) Clear and concise

8. What is a "connection"?
a) A division or separation   b) A misunderstanding
c) A link or relationship   d) An isolation

9. What does "secretly" imply?
a) Openly and publicly   b) In a concealed or hidden manner
c) Loudly and audibly   d) Bravely and boldly

10. What is "desperation"?
a) Confidence and assurance b) A state of despair and urgency
c) Hope and optimism d) Calmness and tranquility

11. What is "devise"?
a) To abandon and neglect
b) To create or invent a plan
c) To confront and challenge
d) To follow a predetermined path

12. What happens when people "reunite"?
a) They separate and part ways
b) They meet again after being apart
c) They engage in a friendly competition
d) They argue and disagree

13. What does "consume" mean?
a) To save and preserve
b) To give away generously
c) To eat or use up
d) To neglect and disregard

14. What is "grief"?
a) Happiness and elation
b) Sorrow and sadness
c) Laughter and amusement
d) Excitement and thrill

15. What does it mean to be "banished"?
a) To be praised and honored
b) To be hidden and concealed
c) To be welcomed and embraced
d) To be forced to leave a place

Unit 8: Hamlet (1599)

"Hamlet" is a tragedy play written by William Shakespeare, believed to have been written between 1599 and 1601. It is one of Shakespeare's most well-known and frequently performed plays. The story is set in the kingdom of Denmark and follows the titular character, Prince Hamlet, as he grapples with grief, revenge, and the complexities of human nature. Here is a detailed storyline of the play:

The play opens at the royal castle in Elsinore, Denmark. The guards and Hamlet's friend, Horatio, encounter the ghost of the recently deceased King

Hamlet on the castle battlements. The ghost reveals that he was murdered by his own brother, Claudius, who is now the reigning king and has married Hamlet's mother, Queen Gertrude. The ghost implores Hamlet to avenge his murder.

Hamlet is disturbed by the revelation and pretends to be mad to hide his intentions. He becomes suspicious of his uncle Claudius and arranges for a troupe of actors to perform a play called "The Murder of Gonzago," which reenacts the murder of his father in front of Claudius and Gertrude. Claudius, who is watching the performance, avoids his seat with his complexion changed. Hamlet, who sees this, becomes convinced that Claudius killed his father. In this situation, a famous line that expresses the conflict within Hamlet comes: "To be or not to be, that is the question."

Hamlet's erratic behavior and the way he treats Ophelia, his love interest, leads Polonius, the father of Ophelia, to believe that Hamlet's madness is the result of his love for Ophelia. Hamlet, while interrogating her in his mother's room, mistakes Polonius, who is hiding behind the curtain, for Claudius and kills him. Shocked by his father's death, Ophelia falls into the water and dies. Claudius, fearing Hamlet's threat, tells Hamlet to flee to England because it is difficult to avoid a felony of murder, and later delivers an order to "kill Hamlet as soon as he arrives in England." But Hamlet comes back to Denmark alive after many twists and turns.

Meanwhile, Ophelia's brother, Laertes, hears this sad news and returns to Denmark to seek revenge. Recognizing this, Claudius recommends Laertes to to have a fencing match with Hamlet. To make sure of Hamlet being killed, Claudius puts poison on the tip of Laertes's sword, and Hamlet is stabbed with the sword. However, in the middle of the match, the swords change and Laertes is also stabbed with the poisoned sword. During the game, Gertrude drinks a poisoned drink prepared by the king to kill Hamlet, and Hamlet uses his last strength to stab Claudius with the poisoned sword. As Hamlet dies, the play ends by asking his friend Horatio to let others know what has happened so far.

"Hamlet" explores themes of revenge, madness, mortality, deception, corruption, and the complexities of human emotions. The character of Hamlet himself embodies the struggle with moral dilemmas and existential questions.

Shakespeare's "Hamlet" is a complex and richly layered play that has captivated audiences for centuries with its intricate characters and thought-provoking themes. This summary captures the main plot points, but the play is also full of memorable soliloquies, poetic language, and intricate psychological depth.

[Vocabulary]

tragedy 비극 confront 마주하다 revealing 드러내는 murdered 살해당한 embark 착수하다 indecision 우유부단 contemplation 숙고 philosophical 철학적인 soliloquy 혼잣말 mental state 정신 상태 unstable 불안정한 navigate 항해하다/빠져나가려고 애쓰다 deceit 거짓 betrayal 배신 moral dilemma 도덕적 딜레마 relationship 관계 manipulate 조종하다 courtier 궁궐인 calculating 계산적인/빈틈없는 confidant 친구 devise 꾸미다 reenacting 재연하는 internal conflicts 내부 갈등 sanity 제정신 take a toll on ~에 악영향을 미치다 tragic demise 비극적인 종말 fatal 치명적인 avenge 복수하다 responsibility 책임 restoration 복원 existentialism 실존주의 duel 대결/결투 poisoned 독이 든 restoration 회복 inevitability 불가피함 entrust A to B: A를 B에 맡기다

[본문 해석] 햄릿

"햄릿"은 1599년과 1601년 사이에 쓰여 진 것으로 추정되는 윌리엄 셰익스피어에 의해 쓰여진 비극입니다. 그것은 셰익스피어의 작품 중 가장 잘 알려져 있고 자주 공연되는 연극 중 하나입니다. 이야기는 덴마크 왕국을 배경으로 슬픔, 복수, 그리고 인간 본성의 복잡함과 투쟁하는 주인공인 햄릿 왕자를 중심으로 펼쳐집니다. 여기 연극의 자세한 줄거리가 있습니다:

덴마크의 엘시노어에 있는 왕궁에서 연극이 시작됩니다. 경비원들과 햄릿의 친구인 호레이쇼는 최근 성벽에서 죽은 햄릿 왕의 유령을 만나게 됩니다. 유령은 자신이 동생 클로디우스에 의해 살해당했다고 폭로합니다. 현재, 클로디우스는 햄릿의 어머니 거트루드 여왕과 결혼한 상태입니다.

햄릿은 이 폭로에 의해 혼란스러워 하며, 자신의 의도를 숨기기 위해 미친 척합니다. 그는 삼촌 클로디우스를 의심하게 되고, 클로디우스와 거트루드 앞에서 아버지를 살해한 장면을 재연하는 연극 '곤자고의 살인'을 배우들이 공연하도록 주선합니다. 공연을 보던 중 클로디우스는 안색이 변한 채 자리를 피하고, 이를 본 햄릿은 클로디우스가 아버지를 살해한 것이라고 확신하게 됩니다. 이러한 상황에서 '사느냐 죽느냐 그것이 문제로다'란 유명한 말이 나오게 됩니다.

햄릿의 변덕스러운 행동과 그의 연인인 오필리어를 대하는 태도는 햄릿의 광기가 오필리어에 대한 사랑의 결과라고 믿게 만듭니다. 햄릿은 어머니의 방에서 그녀를 추궁하던 중 커튼 뒤에 숨어있던 폴로니어스를 클로디우스로 오인하여 죽이게 됩니다. 오필리어는 아버지의 죽음에 충격을 받아 물에 빠져 죽게 됩니다. 햄릿의 위협을 두려워한 클로디우스는 햄릿에게 살인죄를 피하기 어려우니 영국으로 도망치라고 말하고, 나중에 "햄릿이 영국에 도착하자마자 죽여 버리라"는 명령을 전하지만 햄릿은 우여곡절 끝에 살아서 덴마크로 돌아옵니다.

한편 오필리어의 오빠 레어티즈는 이 슬픈 소식을 듣고 덴마크로 돌아와 복수를 추구합니다. 이를 알고 클로디우스는 레어티즈에게 햄릿과 검술 시합을 하라고 권합니다. 햄릿을 확실히 죽이기 위해, 클로디우스는 레어티즈의 검 끝에 독을 바르고, 햄릿은 그 칼에 찔리게 됩니다. 그러나 경기 중간에 검이 바뀌면서 레어티즈 또한 독 묻은 칼에 찔리게 됩니다. 게임 도중 거트루드는 햄릿을 죽이기 위해 왕이 준비해둔 독이 든 음료를 마시게 되고, 햄릿은 마지막 힘을 다해 독이 든 검으로 클로디우스를 찌릅니다. 햄릿은 죽어가며 그의 친구 호레이쇼에게 지금까지 일어난 일을 다른 사람들에게 알려달라고 부탁하는 것으로 이 비극은 끝이 납니다.

"햄릿"은 복수, 광기, 죽음, 기만, 부패, 인간 감정의 복잡성을 탐구하며, 햄릿의 캐릭터는 도덕적 딜레마와 실존적 질문과의 투쟁을 구체화합니다. 셰익스피어의 "햄릿"은 복잡한 인물들과 사고를 유발하는 주제들로 수세기 동안 관객들을 사로잡았던 복잡하고 풍부한 층위의 연극입니다. 이 요약은 주요 줄거리를 포착하지만, 또한 기억에 남는 독백과 시적인 언어, 그리고 복잡한 심리적 깊이로 가득 차 있습니다.

[Reading Comprehension]

1. When was "Hamlet" written?
a) 1605   b) 1599-1601   c) 1623   d) 1587

2. In which kingdom is the play "Hamlet" set?
a) England   b) France   c) Denmark   d) Italy

3. Who encounters the ghost of King Hamlet on the castle battlements?
a) Queen Gertrude   b) Claudius   c) Polonius   d) Horatio

4. Why does the ghost of King Hamlet appear to Prince Hamlet?
a) To warn him of an impending invasion
b) To ask for forgiveness
c) To reveal his murderer and seek revenge
d) To offer him the throne

5. How does Hamlet react to the news of his father's murder?
a) He immediately confronts Claudius
b) He pretends to be mad
c) He goes into exile
d) He seeks counsel from Ophelia

6. What event does Hamlet arrange to confirm Claudius's guilt?
a) A royal feast
b) A hunting party
c) A fencing match
d) A play reenacting the murder

7. Which famous line reflects Hamlet's inner turmoil and contemplation?
a) "All the world's a stage."
b) "To be or not to be, that is the question."
c) "Et tu, Brute?"
d) "Wherefore art thou, Romeo?"

8. Who does Hamlet mistakenly kill in his mother's room?
a) Ophelia
b) Polonius
c) Laertes
d) Horatio

9. What prompts Claudius to send Hamlet to England?

a) To arrange a diplomatic marriage

b) To study abroad

c) To avoid Hamlet's threats

d) To make Hamlet study abroad

10. How does Ophelia die?

a) She is poisoned by Claudius

b) She drowns in water

c) She is stabbed by Hamlet

d) She dies in a fencing match

11. What does Laertes seek when he returns to Denmark?

a) Revenge for his father's murder

b) A reconciliation with Hamlet

c) The crown of Denmark

d) Ophelia's hand in marriage

12. How does the fencing match between Hamlet and Laertes turn fatal?

a) Hamlet accidentally falls off the castle walls

b) Laertes stabs Hamlet with a poisoned sword

c) Hamlet poisons Laertes's drink

d) Gertrude intervenes and is killed

13. Who survives the fencing match and stab Claudius?

a) Horatio b) Hamlet c) Laertes d) Gertrude

14. How does Hamlet ultimately kill Claudius?

a) He stabs him with a dagger

b) He poisons his drink

c) He shoots him with a crossbow

d) He stabs him with a poisoned sword

15. What does Hamlet ask Horatio to do before he dies?

a) Avenge his death

b) Kill Claudius

c) Tell his story to others

d) Marry Ophelia

[Grammar Check-up]

1. "Hamlet" is a tragedy written by William Shakespeare, (believing, believed) to have been written between 1599 and 1601.

2. The play follows the story of Prince Hamlet of Denmark, who (confronts, is confronted) by the ghost of his father, King Hamlet.

3. King Hamlet (reveals, revealing) that he (murdered, was murdered) by his own brother, Claudius, (whom, who) has since become the new king and married Hamlet's mother, Queen Gertrude.

4. (Driving, Driven) by grief and a sense of duty, Hamlet (embarking, embarks) on a mission to avenge his father's death.

5. However, he (plagues, is plagued) by indecision and contemplation, often engaging in philosophical soliloquies that (explore, explores) the nature of life, death, and the human condition.

6. Hamlet's mental state becomes (increasingly, increasing) unstable as he struggles to navigate the complex web of deceit, betrayal, and moral dilemmas (surrounding, surrounded) him.

7. Throughout the play, Hamlet's relationships with (another, other) characters unfold, including his love interest Ophelia, who (manipulates, is manipulated) by her father and brother to test Hamlet's sanity.

8. The play also (is featured, features) the witty and manipulative courtier Polonius, the ambitious and calculating Claudius, and the loyal and morally upright Horatio, who (is served, serves) as Hamlet's confidant.

9. (Since, As) the plot progresses, Hamlet devises a plan to confirm Claudius's guilt by staging a play reenacting his father's murder.

10. Claudius's reaction confirms his guilt, and Hamlet contemplates killing him but decides (delaying, to delay) his revenge.

11. Meanwhile, the weight of his internal conflicts takes a toll on Hamlet's sanity, (leads, leading) to the tragic demise of several characters, (including, includes) Polonius and Ophelia.

12. In the (finally, final) act, Hamlet (is confronted, confronts) Claudius in a duel and successfully kills him, but not before being fatally wounded by a poisoned sword.

13. As he (lays, lies) dying, Hamlet entrusts the responsibility of avenging his death to his friend, Fortinbras, the prince of Norway.

14. The play concludes with the entrance of Fortinbras, (symbolizes, symbolizing) the restoration of order and the inevitability of fate.

15. It (remains, is remained) one of Shakespeare's most celebrated works, known for its psychological depth, and the introspective journey of its tragic hero, Hamlet.

[Writing Practice]

1. "Hamlet" _____ 1599 and 1601.
   ~사이에 쓰여 진 것으로 생각 된다(believe) (완료부정사)

2. The play follows the story of Prince Hamlet of Denmark, who is confronted by the ghost of his father, King Hamlet, _____ his own brother, Claudius.
   그가 ~에 의해서 살해되었다는 것을 폭로하다(reveal) (분사구, 접속사)

3. Driven by grief and a sense of duty, Hamlet _____ his father's death.
   ~를 복수하려는 임무에 착수하다(em~)

4. However, he is plagued by indecision and contemplation, often engaging in philosophical soliloquies _____.
   삶, 죽음, 그리고 인간의 조건/상황의 본질을 탐구하는 (관계사)

5. Hamlet's mental state _____ navigate the complex web of deceit.   그가 ~하려고 투쟁함에 따라 점점(increase~) 불안정해 진다.

6. Hamlet's relationships with other characters unfold, including his love interest Ophelia, _____ her father and brother to test Hamlet's sanity.
   ~에 의해서 조종당하는 Ophelia (관계사)

7. As the plot progresses, Hamlet devises a plan to confirm Claudius's guilt
_____
그의 아버지의 살해를 재연하는(reenact) 연극을 무대에 올림으로써

8. Hamlet contemplates killing him but _____.
   그의 복수를 연기하기로 결심한다.

9. Meanwhile, the weight of his internal conflicts takes a toll on Hamlet's sanity, _____ several characters, including Polonius and Ophelia.
~의 비극적인 죽음(d~)을 초래한다. (분사구)

10. It _____, known for its psychological
   그의 가장 유명한 작품 중의 하나로 남아 있다

[Word Quiz]

1. What is the meaning of "avenge"?
a) To betray someone
b) To calculate accurately
c) To seek revenge for a wrongdoing
d) To confront a challenge

2. What does "betrayal" involve?
a) Seeking revenge
b) Accurate calculations
c) Deceiving or being disloyal to someone's trust
d) Navigating through difficulties

3. What does "calculating" mean?
a) Being honest and sincere
b) Carefully considering options
c) Seeking revenge
d) Engaging in conflicts

4. Who is a "confidant"?
a) Someone who calculates accurately
b) A close and trusted friend
c) A manipulative person
d) An unstable individual

5. What are "conflicts"?
a) Honest conversations
b) Harmonious relationships
c) Disagreements or disputes
d) Peaceful resolutions

6. What happens when you "confront" something?
a) You engage in betrayal
b) You calculate accurately
c) You carefully consider options
d) You face a challenge directly

7. What does "contemplation" involve?
a) Engaging in conflicts
b) Navigating through challenges
c) Careful thought and consideration
d) Betraying someone's trust

8. Who is a "courtier"?
a) Someone who calculates accurately
b) A manipulative person
c) A person in the royal court or social circle
d) An unstable individual

9. What is "deceit"?
a) Honest and sincere behavior
b) Accurate calculations
c) Manipulative and dishonest actions
d) Confronting challenges

10. What is the meaning of "demise"?
a) A final resolution
b) Accurate calculations
c) A tragic death or downfall
d) Navigating through challenges

11. What does "devise" mean?
a) To engage in conflicts
b) To manipulate others
c) To navigate through difficulties
d) To create or invent a plan

12. What is a "dilemma"?
a) A harmonious relationship
b) A peaceful resolution
c) A difficult choice between two options
d) An inevitable situation

13. What is a "duel"?
a) A friendly competition
b) A manipulative tactic
c) A serious fight or conflict between two individuals
d) A philosophical debate

14. What happens when you "embark" on something?
a) You engage in betrayal
b) You calculate accurately
c) You navigate through challenges
d) You start a new journey or undertaking

15. What does "entrust" mean?
a) To manipulate others
b) To reveal secrets
c) To place trust or responsibility in someone's care
d) To engage in conflicts

16. What does "existentialism" refer to?
a) A philosophical belief that emphasizes individual existence, freedom, and choice
b) A state of happiness and contentment
c) A strong moral code
d) A calculating approach to life

17. What is "fatal"?
a) Unpredictable and uncertain
b) Manipulative and deceptive
c) Resulting in death or disaster
d) Philosophical and introspective

18. What is "indecision"?
a) A clear and definite choice
b) A calculating approach
c) A state of confusion and inability to choose
d) A harmonious relationship

19. What does "inevitability" mean?
a) A calculated outcome
b) A philosophical debate
c) The quality of being unavoidable
d) A mental state of manipulation

20. What does "internal" refer to?
a) An unstable individual
b) A harmonious relationship
c) Occurring within oneself
d) A calculating approach

Unit 9: Othello (1603)

"Othello" is a tragic play written by William Shakespeare around 1603. Set primarily in the city-state of Venice, the story revolves around the Moorish general Othello, his wife Desdemona, and the manipulative ensign Iago. The play explores themes of jealousy, manipulation, and the destructive power of suspicion.

Othello, a highly respected military leader, secretly marries Desdemona, a young Venetian woman. Iago, a low-ranking officer, harbors deep-seated resentment towards Othello, who excluded Iago from the promotion by promoting Cassio instead. Iago begins scheming and manipulating those around him, seeking to destroy Othello's life and reputation.

Iago cunningly convinces Othello that his wife Desdemona has been unfaithful to him, using planted evidence and insidious suggestions. Othello becomes consumed by jealousy and suspicion, descending into a state of emotional turmoil. Despite Desdemona's protestations of innocence, Othello believes Iago's lies and becomes determined to seek revenge.

As the play progresses, Iago manipulates other characters, including Desdemona's father, Brabantio, and the gullible Roderigo, to further his scheme. He orchestrates situations that appear to confirm Desdemona's infidelity, leading Othello to the brink of madness.

In a tragic turn of events, Othello suffocates Desdemona, believing he is justified in his actions. Emilia, Iago's wife and Desdemona's attendant, discovers the truth behind Iago's manipulations and exposes him. Realizing the extent of Iago's deceit, Othello is filled with remorse and kills himself.

The play ends with the exposure of Iago's villainy and his subsequent punishment. The characters remaining alive are left to grapple with the consequences of their actions and the devastating effects of jealousy and betrayal.

"Othello" explores themes of racism, trust, and the destructive power of unchecked jealousy. It delves into the human psyche and the tragic consequences that arise from succumbing to base emotions and manipulative influences.

[Vocabulary]

Revolve 회전하다 Moorish 모로코의 General 장군 Manipulative 조종하는 Jealousy 질투 Manipulation 조작 Destructive 파괴적인 Suspicion 의심 Secretly 비밀리에 Anger 화나게 하다 Frustrate 좌절시키다 Harbor 품다 Resentment 원한 Scheming 음모를 꾸미는 Destroy 파괴하다 Reputation 평판 Cunningly 교활하게 Convince 납득시키다 Unfaithful 불신의 Planted evidence 조작 증거 Insidious 음흉한 Be consumed 사로잡히다 Protestations 항변 Innocence 결백 Revenge 복수 Progress 진행되다 Brink 가장자리 Madness 광기 Suffocate 질식시키다 Justified 정당화된 Actions 행동 Attendant 시종 Discover 발견하다 Deceit 기만 Remorse 후회 Racism 인종주의

[본문 해석] 오셀로

"오셀로(Othello)"는 윌리엄 셰익스피어가 1603년경에 쓴 비극적인 연극입니다. 주로 베네치아 (Venice)의 도시국가를 배경으로 하며, 이 이야기는 모어인 장군 오셀로, 그의 아내 데스데모나, 그리고 음모를 꾸미는 부관 이아고를 중심으로 펼쳐집니다. 이 연극은 질투, 조작 그리고 의심의 파괴적인 힘과 같은 주제들을 탐구합니다.

존경 받는 군사 지도자 오셀로는 베네치아의 젊은 여성 데스데모나와 비밀리에 결혼합니다. 하급 장교인 이아고는 카시오를 승진시킴으로써 자신을 승진에서 제외시킨 오셀로에게 깊은 분노를 품고 있습니다. 이아고는 오셀로의 삶과 명성을 파괴하기 위해 그의 주변 사람들을 계획하고 조종하기 시작합니다.

이아고는 계획된 증거와 음흉한 암시들을 이용하여, 교활하게도 오셀로 하여금 그의 아내 데스데모나가 부정을 저질렀다고 확신하게 만듭니다. 오셀로는 질투와 의심에 사로잡혀 감정적 혼란에 빠져들게 됩니다. 데스데모나가 자신의 결백을 주장해도, 오셀로는 이아고의 거짓말을 믿고 복수하기로 결심합니다.

연극이 진행됨에 따라, 이아고는 데스데모나의 아버지 브라반티오와 속이기 쉬운 로드리고를 포함하여 다른 등장인물들도 조종합니다. 그는 데스데모나의 부정을 확신시킬 상황을 계획하여 오셀로가 광기에 빠지게 합니다.

비극적인 사건이 벌어지면서, 오셀로는 자신의 행동이 옳다고 믿고 데스데모나를 목 졸라 죽입니다. 이아고의 아내이자 데스데모나의 시종인 에밀리아가 이아고의 조작에 대한 진실을 발견하고 그를 폭로합니다. 이아고의 속임수의 정도를 깨닫게 된 오셀로는 후회로 가득 차 스스로 목숨을 끊습니다.

연극은 이아고의 악행이 드러나고 뒤따르는 그에 대한 처벌로 끝나게 됩니다. 살아남은 등장인물들은 자신들의 행동의 결과와 질투와 배신의 파괴적인 영향에 대해 고심하게 됩니다.

"오셀로"는 인종주의, 신뢰 그리고 억눌리지 않은 질투의 파괴적인 힘과 같은 주제들을 탐구합니다. 이 작품은 인간의 심리로 파고들며 기절적인 감정과 조작적인 영향에 굴복하는 것으로 인해 생기는 비극적인 결과를 다룹니다.

[Reading Comprehension]

1. Who is the main character of the play "Othello"?
a) Desdemona   b) Iago   c) Othello   d) Emilia

2. What are the primary themes explored in the play?
a) Love and friendship   b) Trust and betrayal
c) Revenge and forgiveness   d) Greed and ambition

3. Where is the setting of the play "Othello" primarily located?
a) Paris   b) London   c) Venice   d) Rome

4. Why does Iago want to destroy Othello's life and reputation?
a) He is jealous of Othello's military success
b) He feels deep-seated resentment towards Othello involving promotion
c) He is seeking revenge because Othello loves his wife
d) He wants to take over Othello's position

5. How does Iago convince Othello of Desdemona's unfaithfulness?
a) By providing solid evidence of her infidelity
b) By using insidious suggestions and planted evidence
c) By forcing Desdemona to confess her affair
d) By manipulating other characters to lie about her

6. What is the tragic consequence of Othello's jealousy and suspicion?
a) He kills Iago   b) He commits suicide
c) He runs away from Venice   d) He seeks forgiveness from Desdemona

7. Who exposes Iago's deceit in the end?
a) Roderigo   b) Emilia   c) Brabantio   d) Desdemona

8. What do the characters remaining alive do to grapple with at the end of the play?
a) The consequences of their actions   b) The joys of their newfound freedom
c) Their plans for revenge   d) The celebration of their victory

9. What are some of the themes explored in "Othello"?
a) Happiness and contentment   b) Racism, trust, and unchecked jealousy
c) Hope and optimism   d) Political intrigue and power struggles

10. How does the play "Othello" delve into the human psyche?
a) By focusing on supernatural elements
b) By exploring the subconscious mind
c) By revealing the inner thoughts and emotions of characters
d) By depicting characters with extraordinary abilities

[Grammar Check-up]

1. "Othello" is a (tragedy, tragic) play written by William Shakespeare around 1603.

2. (Set, Setting) primarily in the city-state of Venice, the story revolves around the Moorish general Othello, his wife Desdemona, and the manipulative ensign Iago.

3. The play (explore, explores) themes of jealousy, manipulation, and the destructive power of (suspicion, suspicious).

4. Othello, a highly (respected, respecting) military leader, secretly marries Desdemona, a young Venetian woman.

5. This marriage (angry, angers) and frustrates Iago, (who, whose) harbors deep-seated resentment towards Othello.

6. Iago begins scheming and (manipulating, manipulate) those around him, seeking to destroy Othello's life and reputation.

7. Iago (cunningly, cunning) convinces Othello that his wife Desdemona has been unfaithful to him, (using, used) planted evidence and insidious suggestions.

8. Othello becomes (consuming, consumed) by jealousy and suspicion, descending into a state of emotional turmoil.

9. (Although, Despite) Desdemona's protestations of innocence, Othello believes Iago's lies and becomes determined (seeking, to seek) revenge.

10. As the play progresses, Iago manipulates other (characters, character), (included, including) Desdemona's father, Brabantio, and the gullible Roderigo, to further his scheme.

11. He orchestrates situations that appear to confirm Desdemona's infidelity, (leads, leading) Othello to the brink of madness.

12. In a tragic turn of events, Othello (is suffocated, suffocates) Desdemona, believing he is justified in his actions.

13. Emilia, Iago's wife and Desdemona's attendant, (discovers, discovering) the truth behind Iago's manipulations and exposes him.

14. (Realized, Realizing) the extent of Iago's deceit, Othello is filled with remorse and (is killed, kills) himself.

15. The play ends with the exposure of Iago's villainy and his (subsequent, subsequently) punishment.

16. The characters (remaining, remained) alive are left to grapple with the consequences of their actions and the devastating effects of jealousy and betrayal.

17. "Othello" explores themes of racism, trust, and the (destruction, destructive) power of unchecked jealousy.

18. It delves into the human psyche and the tragic consequences that (raise, arise) from succumbing to base emotions and manipulative influences.

[Writing Practice]

1. _____ Venice, the story revolves around the Moorish
주로 Venice라는 도시국가를 배경으로(set) 한 (분사구)
general Othello, his wife Desdemona, and the manipulative ensign Iago.

2. Othello, _____, secretly marries Desdemona, a young
Venetian woman. 매우 존경받는 군 지도자인 (동격)

3. This marriage angers and frustrates Iago, _____ Othello.
Othello를 향해 깊이 자리 잡은 원한을 가진 (관계사)

4. Iago begins scheming and manipulating those around him, _____.
_____ Othello의 삶과 명성을 파괴하기를 추구하면서 (분사구)

5. Iago cunningly convinces Othello that his wife Desdemona has been unfaithful to
him, _____.
계획된 증거와 교활한 (insidious) 암시들을 사용하여 (분사구)

6. Othello _____, descending into a state of emotional
turmoil. 질투와 의심으로 초췌해(consume~) 진다

7. Despite Desdemona's protestations of innocence, Othello believes Iago's lies and
_____. 복수하기로 결심한다

8. He orchestrates situations that appear to confirm Desdemona's infidelity,
_____. Othello를 광기의 벼랑까지 이끈다 (분사구)

9. In a tragic turn of events, Othello suffocates Desdemona, _____
_____.   그는 그의 행동들이 정당하다고 믿으며 (분사구, 접속사)

10. _____ grapple with the consequences of their
살아남은 등장인물들은 ~하도록 남겨진다(leave)
actions and the devastating effects of jealousy and betrayal.

[Word Quiz]

1. She _____ her keys on the kitchen counter and headed out the door.
a) Planted   b) Revolve   c) Anger   d) Progress

2. The detective carefully examined the _____ left at the crime scene.
a) Attendant   b) evidence   c) Cunningly   d) Unfaithful

3. The scientist's ground-breaking research _____ a new understanding of the human brain.
a) Destroy   b) Resentment   c) Discover   d) Scheming

4. The movie's _____ special effects captivated the audience.
a) Destructive   b) Manipulative   c) Deceit   d) Manipulation

5. He always _____ his actions with logical reasoning.
a) Racism   b) Justified   c) Frustrate   d) Remorse

6. What word refers to the state of being free from guilt, sin, or moral wrongdoing?
a) Revenge   b) Innocence   c) Anger   d) Cunningly

7. What word refers to information that is kept hidden, not shared?
a) Jealousy   b) Secret   c) Protestations   d) Be Brink

8. The company's unethical practices _____ the trust of their customers.
a) Be Brink   b) Insidious   c) Harbor   d) consumed

9. The suspect's _____ behavior raised suspicions among the investigators.
a) Revolve   b) Anger   c) Manipulative   d) Innocence

10. The athlete's dedication and hard work led to an impressive _____ in her performance.
a) Revolve   b) Anger   c) Progress   d) Madness

11. Despite his _____ attempts to cover his tracks, the truth eventually came out.
a) Cunning b) Destroy c) Resentment d) Attendant

12. The novel's plot was filled with _____ twists and turns that kept readers engaged.
a) Scheming b) Frustrate c) Manipulation d) Actions

13. The scientist's theory was met with skepticism and _____ from some of his colleagues.
a) Revenge b) Racism c) Suspicion d) Harbor

14. What word refers to a deep and painful regret for a past action or wrongdoing?
a) Remorse b) Anger c) Happiness d) Frustration

15. The company's unethical business practices led to a tarnished _____ in the industry.
a) Reputation b) Insidious c) Secretly d) Manipulative

16. She tried to _____ her innocence through heartfelt protestations.
a) Convince b) Insidious c) Jealousy d) Suffocate

17. What words refers to the forward movement or advancement towards a goal?
a) Destructive b) Moorish c) Progress d) Cunningly

18. The villain's _____ plans were revealed in the final act of the story.
a) Manipulative b) Destroy c) Actions d) Be Brink

19. What word refers to a formal statement made to express strong disapproval?
a) Madness b) Revolve c) Remorse d) Protestation

20. What word refers to a state of severe mental illness?
a) Unfaithful b) Attendant c) Anger d) Madness

Unit 10: King Lear (1605)

"King Lear" is a tragic play written by William Shakespeare around 1605. Set in ancient Britain, the story revolves around the aging King Lear, who decides to divide his kingdom among his three daughters based on their flattery of him. The play explores themes of power, betrayal, madness, and the consequences of flawed judgment.

King Lear, wanting to retire from the responsibilities of ruling, asks his daughters Goneril, Regan, and Cordelia to express their love for him. Goneril and Regan, driven by ambition, flatter their father with exaggerated declarations of love, while Cordelia, the youngest and most sincere daughter, refuses to engage in such empty praise. Outraged, Lear disowns Cordelia and divides his kingdom between Goneril and Regan.

As Lear gradually realizes the depth of his mistake, he finds himself at the mercy of his ruthless daughters, who quickly abuse their newfound power. Goneril and Regan strip Lear of his authority, mistreat him, and reduce his retinue of loyal servants. Feeling betrayed and abandoned, Lear descends into madness, wandering the stormy heath accompanied by his Fool and the loyal

Earl of Kent.

Parallel to Lear's story, the subplot involves the Earl of Gloucester and his two sons, Edgar and Edmund. Edmund, fueled by ambition, manipulates his father into believing that Edgar is plotting against him. Edgar, unjustly accused, is forced to go into hiding and takes on a disguise. Eventually, Edgar and Gloucester are reconciled, and they join forces to aid the dethroned Lear.

The play reaches its tragic climax when Lear and Cordelia are captured by Edmund, who has now aligned himself with Goneril and Regan. Despite their father's deteriorating mental state, Cordelia remains fiercely loyal to him. In a climactic battle, Cordelia is hanged, and Lear, overcome by grief, dies holding her lifeless body.

The play ends with a sense of despair and moral reckoning. Lear's mistakes and the treachery of those around him lead to catastrophic consequences. The surviving characters are left to reflect on the destructive nature of power, the fleeting nature of human existence, and the consequences of unchecked ambition and betrayal.

"King Lear" is a profound exploration of human folly, the complexities of family dynamics, and the vulnerability of those in positions of authority. It delves into themes of madness, redemption, and the inevitability of mortality.

[Vocabulary]

Ancient Britain 고대 브리튼 Aging 노화 Kingdom 왕국 Flattery 아부 Ambition 야망 Exaggerated 과장된 Declarations 선언 Refuse 거부하다 Engage 참여하다 Outraged 분노한 Disown 버리다 Gradually 점차적으로 Ruthless 무자비한 Mistreat 학대하다 Abandoned 버려진 Madness 광기 Subplot 부가적인 줄거리 Reconcile 화해시키다 Dethrone 왕위를 빼앗다 Deteriorating 악화되는 Grief 슬픔 Despair 절망 Moral reckoning 도덕적 징계 Exploration 탐구 Folly 어리석음 Dynamics 역학 Vulnerability 취약성 Authority 권위 Inevitability 불가피성 Redemption 구원 Consequences 결과 Human existence 인간의 존재 Unchecked 통제되지 않은 Betrayal 배신

[본문 해석] 리어왕

"리어왕(King Lear)"은 윌리엄 셰익스피어가 약 1605년경에 쓴 비극적 연극입니다. 옛 대영국을 배경으로 이야기는 늙은 리어왕을 중심으로 전개됩니다. 리어왕은 딸들의 아부에 따라 왕국을 세 딸들에게 나누기로 결정합니다. 이 연극은 권력, 배신, 광기 그리고 결함이 있는 판단의 결과와 같은 주제들을 탐구합니다.

리어왕은 통치의 책임으로부터 물러나고자 하며, 딸들 고너릴, 리건, 코델리아에게 자신에 대한 사랑을 표현하도록 요구합니다. 고너릴과 리건은 야망에 사로잡힌 채로 과장된 사랑의 선언으로 아버지에게 아부합니다. 반면에 막내이자 가장 진실한 딸인 코델리아는 그러한 허튼 칭찬에 참여하지 않습니다. 분노한 리어는 코델리아를 제외하고 고너릴과 리건 사이에 왕국을 나눕니다.

리어왕은 점차 자신의 실수 깊이를 깨닫게 되며, 그들이 새로 얻은 권력을 재빨리 남용하려고 하는 그의 무자비한 딸들의 손에 운명이 맡겨졌음을 알게 됩니다. 고너릴과 리건은 리어왕으로부터 권위를 박탈하고, 그를 학대하며, 그에게 충성하는 하인들을 줄입니다. 배신당하고 버림받았다고 느낀 리어왕은 광기에 빠져 그의 광대와 충성스런 켄트 백작과 함께 폭풍우 속을 떠돌게 됩니다.

"리어왕"의 이야기와 병행하여, 글로스터 백작과 그의 두 아들, 에드거와 에드먼드의 이야기도 나옵니다. 야망에 불타는 에드먼드는 아버지를 속여 에드거가 자신을 음모하고 있다고 믿게 합니다. 무고하게 책망을 당한 에드거는 은신처로 들어가 위장을 하게 됩니다. 결국, 에드거와 글로스터는 화해하고 퇴위당한 리어를 돕기 위해 힘을 합칩니다.

연극은 리어왕과 코델리아가 고너릴과 리건과 한 편이 된 에드먼드에게 잡히는 비극적 절정에 이르게 됩니다. 아버지의 점점 악화되는 정신 상태에도 불구하고 코델리아는 그에게 강한 충성심을 유지합니다. 절정적인 전투에서 코델리아는 교수형에 처해지고, 슬픔에 휩싸인 리어왕은 그녀의 시체를 안고 죽습니다.

연극은 절망감과 도덕적 징계로 끝납니다. 리어왕의 실수와 주변인들의 배신은 비극적인 결과를 초래합니다. 생존한 인물들은 권력의 파괴적 본성, 인간 존재의 덧없음 그리고 억제되지 않은 야망과 배신의 결과에 대해 되돌아봅니다.

"리어왕"은 인간의 어리석음, 가족 역학의 복잡성, 그리고 권위 있는 자들의 취약성에 대해 깊이 탐구하는 책 입니다. 이 책은 광기, 구원, 그리고 죽음의 불가피성과 같은 주제들에 대해 파헤칩니다.

[Reading Comprehension]

1. Who is the main character in "King Lear"?

a) Goneril   b) Cordelia   c) Regan   d) King Lear

2. What are the three themes explored in the play?

a) Love, Happiness, Wealth

b) Power, Betrayal, Madness

c) Friendship, Forgiveness, Adventure

d) Knowledge, Wisdom, Truth

3. How does King Lear divide his kingdom among his daughters?

a) Based on their intelligence

b) Based on their loyalty to him

c) Based on their flattery of him

d) Based on their wealth

4. What happens to Cordelia when she refuses to flatter her father?

a) She is disowned by Lear

b) She is given the largest portion of the kingdom

c) She becomes the Queen

d) She is praised for her honesty

5. Who manipulates his father into believing that Edgar is plotting against him?

a) Goneril

b) Regan

c) Cordelia

d) Edmund

6. How do Goneril and Regan treat King Lear after gaining power?

a) They mistreat him and reduce his retinue of servants

b) They show him great love and respect

c) They give him more authority

d) They apologize for their previous behavior

7. Who accompanies Lear while he wanders the stormy heath in madness?

a) Fool and Edgar

b) Edgar and Kent

c) Fool and Goneril

d) Cordelia and Regan

8. What is the ultimate fate of Cordelia?

a) She becomes the new Queen

b) She is hanged

c) She becomes a powerful ruler

d) She escapes with Edgar

9. How does the play end?

a) Lear reconciles with Goneril and Regan

b) Lear dies holding Cordelia's lifeless body

c) Cordelia becomes the ruler of the kingdom

d) Cordelia forgives Lear for his mistakes

10. How does the subplot involving the Earl of Gloucester and his sons parallel the main storyline of King Lear?

a) Gloucester's illegitimate son, Edmund, seeks to overthrow Lear.

b) Edgar disguises himself to escape Lear's wrath.

c) Gloucester's manipulation by Edmund mirrors Lear's betrayal by his daughters.

d) Gloucester and Edgar reconcile to help Lear reclaim his throne.

[Grammar Check-up]

1. Set in ancient Britain, the story revolves around the aging King Lear, who (decide, decides) to divide his kingdom among his three daughters (base, based) on their flattery of him.
2. The play (exploring, explores) themes of power, betrayal, madness, and the consequences of flawed judgment.
3. King Lear, wanting to retire from the responsibilities of ruling, asks his daughters Goneril, Regan, and Cordelia (to express, expressing) their love for him.
4. Goneril and Regan, (driving, driven) by ambition, flatter their father with (exaggerating, exaggerated) declarations of love, while Cordelia, the youngest and most sincere daughter, refuses (engaging, to engage) in such empty praise.
5. Outraged, Lear disowns Cordelia and (divides, is divided) his kingdom between Goneril and Regan.
6. As Lear (gradually, gradual) realizes the depth of his mistake, he finds himself at the mercy of his ruthless daughters, who quickly (abuses, abuse) their newfound power.
7. Goneril and Regan strip Lear of his authority, mistreat him, and (reducing, reduce) his retinue of loyal servants.
8. Feeling betrayed and abandoned, Lear descends into madness, (wandering, wanders) the stormy heath accompanied by his Fool and the loyal Earl of Kent.
9. Parallel to Lear's story, the subplot (involves, is involved) the Earl of Gloucester and his two sons, Edgar and Edmund.
10. Edmund, (fueling, fueled) by ambition, manipulates his father into believing that Edgar is plotting against him.
11. Edgar, unjustly accused, (forces, is forced) to go into hiding and takes on a disguise.
12. Eventually, Edgar and Gloucester are reconciled, and they join forces to aid the (dethroned, dethroning) Lear.
13. The play reaches its tragic climax (which, when) Lear and Cordelia are captured by Edmund, who has now aligned himself with Goneril and Regan.
14. (Although, Despite) their father's deteriorating mental state, Cordelia (remains, is remained) fiercely loyal to him.
15. In a climactic battle, Cordelia (hangs, is hanged), and Lear, overcome by grief, dies holding her lifeless body.
16. Lear's mistakes and the treachery of those around him (leading, lead) to catastrophic consequences.
17. The surviving characters (leave, are left) to reflect on the destructive nature of power, the fleeting nature of human existence, and the consequences of unchecked ambition and betrayal.

[Writing Practice]

1. Set in ancient Britain, the story revolves around the aging King Lear, _____ his three daughters based on their flattery of him. 그의 왕국을 ~간에 나누어 주려고 결심한 리어왕 (관계사)

2. The play _____ and the consequences of flawed judgment.   권력, 배반, 광기란 주제들을 탐구한다

3. King Lear, _____, asks his daughters Goneril, Regan, and Cordelia to express their love for him. 통치의 책임으로부터 물러나기를 바라며

4. Goneril and Regan, driven by ambition, flatter their father with exaggerated declarations of love, while Cordelia, the youngest and most sincere daughter, _____ 그런 어리석은 칭찬에 관여하기를 거부하다

5. As Lear gradually realizes the depth of his mistake, he finds himself at the mercy of his ruthless daughters, _____.
그들의 새로 찾은 권력을 재빨리 남용 한다 (관계사)

6. _____, Lear descends into madness, wandering
배신당하고 버림받았다고 느끼고 (분사구)
the stormy heath accompanied by his Fool and the loyal Earl of Kent.

7. _____, the subplot involves the Earl of Gloucester and his two sons, Edgar and Edmund. 리어 왕의 이야기와 유사한(pa~) (분사구)

8. Edmund, fueled by ambition, _____ that Edgar is plotting against him.   그의 아버지가 ~를 믿도록 조종 한다 (ma~)

9. Edgar, _____, is forced to go into hiding and takes on a disguise.
부당하게 고발당해 (분사구)

10. _____, and they join forces to aid the dethroned Lear.   마침내, 그들은 화해한다

[Word Quiz]

1. What term refers to a former time period characterized by historical significance?
a) Ancient   b) Kingdom   c) Ambition   d) Refuse

2. Which word denotes a state or realm ruled by a monarch or queen?
a) Flattery   b) Declaration   c) Refuse   d) Kingdom

3. Which term describes excessive praise or admiration, often used to gain favor or advantage?
a) Exaggerate   b) Outraged   c) Ambition   d) Flattery

4. What action involves making an official statement or announcement?
a) Engage   b) Mistreat   c) Declaration   d) Disown

5. Which word means to reject or decline an offer, request, or invitation?
a) Refuse   b) Gradually   c) Redemption   d) Consequences

6. Which term refers to becoming involved or participating in an activity or discussion?
a) Engage   b) Abandon   c) Subplot   d) Reconcile

7. What emotion is felt in response to an offensive or unjust action?
a) Grief   b) Dynamics   c) Vulnerability   d) Authority

8. Which action involves severing ties or relationships with someone, often familial?
a) Dethrone   b) Disown   c) Mistreat   d) Exploration

9. What term describes a gradual decline or worsening of a situation or condition?
a) Deteriorate   b) Refuse   c) Betrayal   d) Unchecked

10. Which word signifies extreme sorrow or sadness, often due to loss or disappointment?
a) Despair   b) Moral reckoning   c) Folly   d) Redemption

11. What concept refers to the exploration or examination of unknown territories or ideas?
a) Exploration   b) Ambition   c) Vulnerability   d) Inevitability

12. Which word denotes a lack of control or restraint, often resulting in negative consequences?
a) Authority   b) Unchecked   c) Consequences   d) Human existence

13. What term signifies an act of treachery against someone's trust?
a) Betrayal   b) Refuse   c) Reconcile   d) Redemption

14. Which action involves overstating the truth for effect or emphasis?
a) Exaggerate   b) Gradually   c) Disown   d) Mistreat

15. What word denotes a secondary or subordinate storyline within a larger narrative?
a) Subplot   b) Dethrone   c) Folly   d) Dynamics

16. What concept refers to the restoration of harmony or resolution of conflict between parties?
a) Reconcile   b) Kingdom   c) Redemption   d) Vulnerability

17. Which term describes the stripping of power or authority from a ruler or leader?
a) Dethrone   b) Engage   c) Consequences   d) Moral reckoning

18. What word signifies the process of becoming morally or ethically corrupt?
a) Betrayal   b) Outraged   c) Deteriorate   d) Exploration

19. What emotion is experienced in response to an irreversible loss or tragic event?
a) Grief   b) Ambition   c) Refuse   d) Gradually

20. Which term refers to the unavoidable nature of certain events or outcomes?
a) Inevitability   b) Reconciliation   c) Mistreat   d) Abandon

Unit 11: Macbeth (1623)

"Macbeth" is a tragedy written by William Shakespeare and first performed in the early 17th century. The play revolves around the ambitious Scottish general, Macbeth, and his wife, Lady Macbeth, as they seek power and glory. Here is a brief plot summary of "Macbeth":

The play opens with three witches, also known as the Weird Sisters, who prophesy that Macbeth will become the Thane of Cawdor and eventually the King of Scotland. Macbeth and his friend, Banquo, encounter the witches and are intrigued by their prophecies. Macbeth receives news that he has been named the Thane of Cawdor, fulfilling the first part of the witches' prophecy. Upon hearing the witches' prediction, Macbeth becomes consumed with ambition and contemplates murdering King Duncan to claim the throne.

With the encouragement of his wife, Lady Macbeth, Macbeth decides to carry out the murder of King Duncan while he is a guest at their castle.

Macbeth kills King Duncan in his sleep and becomes the new king of Scotland. Suspicion falls on Duncan's sons, Malcolm and Donalbain, and they flee the country.

Macbeth becomes increasingly paranoid and starts to eliminate anyone he sees as a threat to his throne. Banquo becomes suspicious of Macbeth's actions but is murdered by hired assassins under Macbeth's orders. At a royal banquet, Macbeth is haunted by the ghost of Banquo, revealing his growing guilt.

Macbeth seeks out the witches again for further prophecies and is told to beware of Macduff. Macbeth orders the killing of Macduff's family in an attempt to eliminate any opposition.

Lady Macbeth's guilt and madness begin to consume her, and she sleepwalks, revealing the horrors of their actions. Macduff joins forces with Malcolm and other Scottish nobles to overthrow Macbeth's tyrannical rule. In the final battle, Macbeth faces Macduff and is told that he cannot be killed by any man "of woman born." Macduff reveals that he was "untimely ripped" from his mother's womb, and thus, he fulfills the witches' prophecy. Macduff kills Macbeth, and Malcolm is proclaimed the new king of Scotland.

The play delves into themes of ambition, power, guilt, and the corrupting influence of unchecked ambition. "Macbeth" remains one of Shakespeare's most famous and frequently performed tragedies, exploring the consequences of one's actions and the destructive nature of ruthless ambition.

[Vocabulary]

tragedy 비극 ambitious 야심적인 Scottish 스코틀랜드의 general 장군 prophecy 예언 Thane 대작/귀족 intrigue 흥미를 끌다 fulfilling 이행하는 prediction 예측 ambition 야망 contemplate 숙고하다 throne 왕위 encouragement 격려 murder 살해 suspicion 의심 paranoid 편집증적인 eliminate 제거하다 assassins 암살자들 haunted 시달리는 prophecies 예언들 beware 경계하다 opposition 반대 guilt 죄책감 madness 광기 sleepwalk 잠꼬대를 하다 revealing 드러내는 horrors 공포 overthrow 전복시키다 tyrannical 폭정적인 battle 전투 proclaimed 선포된 themes 주제 consequences 결과 destructive 파괴적인 corrupting 부패시키는 frequently 자주 performed 공연되는 explore 탐구하다 unchecked 억눌리지 않은

[본문 해석] 맥베스

"맥베스"는 윌리엄 셰익스피어가 쓴 비극으로, 17세기 초에 처음 공연되었습니다. 이 연극은 야심찬 스코틀랜드 장군 맥베스와 그의 아내 레이디 맥베스를 중심으로 권력과 영광을 추구해 나가는 이야기입니다. "맥베스"의 간단한 줄거리 요약은 다음과 같습니다:

연극은 마녀 자매로 알려진 세 명의 마녀가 맥베스가 코더의 영주가 되고, 마침내 스코틀랜드의 왕이 될 것이라 예언을 하는데서 시작됩니다. 맥베스와 그의 친구 뱅쿠오는 이 마녀들을 우연히 만나게 되고, 그들의 예언에 흥미를 느낍니다. 맥베스는 코더의 영주로 지명을 받았다는 소식을 듣게 되는데, 이것은 마녀들의 첫 번째 예언이 실행되었음을 의미합니다. 마녀들의 예언을 듣자마자 맥베스는 야망에 사로잡혀 왕위를 차지하기 위해 던컨 왕을 살해할 것을 고려합니다.

그의 아내 레이디 맥베스로부터 자극을 받은 맥베스는 던컨 왕이 그들의 성에 손님으로 머물 때 그를 살해하기로 결심합니다. 맥베스는 던컨 왕을 잠자는 동안 죽이고 스코틀랜드의 새로운 왕이 됩니다. 던컨 왕의 아들들인 말콤과 도널베인에게 의심이 쏠리고, 그들은 나라를 떠납니다.

맥베스는 점점 편집증적으로 변하며, 왕위를 위협하는 사람들을 제거하기 시작합니다. 뱅쿠오는 맥베스의 행동에 의심을 품게 되고 결국 맥베스의 명령에 따라 고용한 암살자들에게 죽임당합니다. 왕실 연회에서 맥베스는 증가하는 죄책감을 드러내며, 뱅쿠오의 유령에 시달립니다.

맥베스는 다시 마녀들을 찾아가 더 많은 예언을 듣게 되는데, 이때 맥더프를 조심하라는 경고를 받습니다. 맥베스는 반대하는 자들을 모두 제거하기 위해 맥더프의 가족을 죽이라고 명령합니다.

레이디 맥베스의 죄책감과 광기는 그녀를 사로잡고, 그녀는 잠꼬대를 하며 그들의 행동의 무서움을 드러냅니다. 맥더프는 말콤과 다른 스코틀랜드 귀족들과 연합하여 맥베스의 폭정을 끝내기 위해 힘을 합칩니다. 최종 전투에서 맥베스는 맥더프와 맞서게 되고, 그는 "여자가 낳은 자"에 의해 죽지 않는다는 예언이 있다고 말합니다. 이에 맥더프는 자신이 제왕절개로 태어났음을 밝힙니다. 그리하여 그는 마녀들의 예언을 이행하게 됩니다. 맥더프가 맥베스를 죽이고 말콤이 스코틀랜드의 새로운 왕으로 선포됩니다.

이 연극은 야망, 권력, 죄책감, 그리고 억눌리지 않은 야망의 타락적인 영향에 대한 주제를 탐구합니다. "맥베스"는 셰익스피어의 가장 유명하고 자주 공연되는 비극 중 하나로, 행동의 결과와 무자비한 야망의 파괴적인 본성을 탐구합니다.

[Reading Comprehension]

1. What is the main focus of the play "Macbeth"?
a) Love and romance
b) Ambition and power
c) Friendship and loyalty
d) Betrayal and revenge

2. Who are the Weird Sisters in "Macbeth"?
a) The king's advisors
b) Macbeth's cousins
c) Three witches
d) Banquo's allies

3. What do the Weird Sisters prophesy to Macbeth?
a) He will become a wealthy merchant.
b) He will become the Thane of Cawdor and the King of Scotland.
c) He will marry Lady Macbeth.
d) He will travel to foreign lands.

4. How does Macbeth become the Thane of Cawdor?
a) He wins a battle against the current Thane of Cawdor.
b) He is appointed by King Duncan.
c) He marries Lady Macbeth, who is the Thane of Cawdor's daughter.
d) He inherits the title from his father.

5. What role does Lady Macbeth play in Macbeth's decision to kill King Duncan?
a) She encourages and persuades him to carry out the murder.
b) She reports his plans to the king.
c) She tries to convince him to wait for a better opportunity.
d) She has no knowledge of his plans.

6. What happens to Malcolm and Donalbain after the murder of King Duncan?
a) They become advisors to Macbeth.
b) They are accused of the murder and go into hiding.
c) They leave Scotland to seek refuge in a neighboring country.
d) They are imprisoned by Macbeth.

7. How does Macbeth react to seeing the ghost of Banquo?

a) He laughs and dismisses it as a trick.

b) He becomes terrified and confesses his crimes.

c) He becomes angry and blames his wife for the ghost's appearance.

d) He invites the ghost to join the banquet.

8. What warning does Macbeth receive from the witches in his second encounter with them?

a) He should beware of Macduff.

b) He should beware of Banquo.

c) He should beware of Malcolm.

d) He should beware of Lady Macbeth.

9. How does Macbeth plan to eliminate Macduff as a threat?

a) He sends him into exile.

b) He frames him for a crime he didn't commit.

c) He hires assassins to murder Macduff's family.

d) He challenges him to a duel.

10. What happens to Lady Macbeth as the play progresses?

a) She becomes increasingly power-hungry.

b) She is revealed to be a spy for Macduff.

c) She is haunted by guilt and descends into madness.

d) She escapes from Scotland to avoid prosecution.

11. Who leads the forces against Macbeth in the final battle?

a) Macduff and Malcolm

b) Lady Macbeth and Donalbain

c) Banquo and Duncan

d) The witches and Macbeth's ghost

12. How does Macbeth meet his end?

a) He is killed by his own henchmen.

b) He is executed by order of Malcolm.

c) He is defeated in battle by Macduff.

d) He dies of natural causes.

13. What theme does "Macbeth" primarily explore?

a) Love conquering all obstacles

b) The danger of excessive ambition and unchecked power

c) The triumph of good over evil

d) The inevitability of fate

14. What is the ultimate fate of Macbeth?

a) He escapes to a foreign land and lives in exile.

b) He becomes a humble servant in another kingdom.

c) He is forgiven by the people of Scotland and regains his throne.

d) He is defeated and killed in battle.

15. How does the play "Macbeth" address the consequences of ambition?

a) By portraying ambition as a positive trait that leads to success.

b) By showing that ambitious individuals always achieve their goals.

c) By illustrating how uncontrolled ambition can lead to ruin and destruction.

d) By suggesting that ambition is irrelevant to the events of the play.

[Grammar Check-up]

1. "Macbeth" is a tragedy written by William Shakespeare and first (performs, performed) in the early 17th century.

2. The play (revolves, is revolved) around the ambitious Scottish general, Macbeth, and his wife, Lady Macbeth, as they seek power and glory.

3. The play opens with three witches, also (to know, known) as the Weird Sisters, who (prophet, prophesy) that Macbeth will become the Thane of Cawdor and eventually the King of Scotland.

4. Macbeth and his friend, Banquo, encounter the witches and are (intriguing, intrigued) by their prophecies.

5. Macbeth (receives, is received) news that he has been (naming, named) the Thane of Cawdor, fulfilling the first part of the witches' prophecy.

6. (For, Upon) hearing the witches' prediction, Macbeth becomes consumed with ambition and contemplates murdering King Duncan (claiming, to claim) the throne.

7. With the (encourage, encouragement) of his wife, Lady Macbeth, Macbeth decides to carry out the murder of King Duncan (while, whereas) he is a guest at their castle.

8. Macbeth becomes increasingly paranoid and starts to eliminate anyone he (see, sees) as a threat to his throne.

9. Banquo becomes (suspicion, suspicious) of Macbeth's actions but is murdered by (hiring, hired) assassins under Macbeth's orders.

10. At a royal banquet, Macbeth is haunted by the ghost of Banquo, (reveals, revealing) his growing guilt.

11. Macbeth seeks out the witches again for (further, farther) prophecies and is told to beware of Macduff.

12. Macbeth orders the killing of Macduff's family in an attempt (to eliminate, eliminating) any opposition.

13. Lady Macbeth's guilt and madness begin to consume her, and she sleepwalks, (reveals, revealing) the horrors of their actions.

14. Macduff joins forces with Malcolm and other Scottish (nobles, noble) to overthrow Macbeth's tyrannical rule.

15. In the final battle, Macbeth (is faced, faces) Macduff and (tells, is told) that he cannot be killed by any man "of woman born."

16. Macduff reveals that he was "untimely ripped" from his mother's womb, and thus, he (fulfills, fulfilling) the witches' prophecy.

17. Macduff kills Macbeth, and Malcolm (proclaims, is proclaimed) the new king of Scotland.

[Writing Practice]

1. The play opens with three witches, also known as the Weird Sisters, _____
_____ the Thane of Cawdor and eventually the King of Scotland.
Macbeth가 ~가 될 것이라고 예언한 (관계사, 접속사)

2. Macbeth and his friend, Banquo, encounter the witches and _____
_____.   그들의 예언들에 호기심을 가진다 (in~)

3. Macbeth receives news _____ the Thane of Cawdor, fulfilling
the first part of the witches' prophecy. 그가 ~로 임명되었다는 소식 (접속사, 현재완료)

4. _____, Macbeth becomes consumed with ambition and
        마녀들의 예언을 듣자마자
contemplates murdering King Duncan to claim the throne.

5. With the encouragement of his wife, Lady Macbeth, Macbeth _____
King Duncan while he is a guest at their castle.   ~의 살해를 실행하기로 결심한다

6. Macbeth becomes increasingly paranoid and starts _____
_____ 그가 그의 왕좌에 위협으로 여기는(see) 자는 누구든지 제거하기 시작한다

7. Banquo _____ Macbeth's actions but is murdered by
hired assassins under Macbeth's orders. ~에 대해 의심을 받게 된다

8. Macbeth orders the killing of Macduff's family _____.
                        어떤 반발(opp~)이든 제거하려는 시도로

9. Lady Macbeth's guilt and madness begin to consume her, and she sleepwalks,
_____. 그들의 행동에 대한 잔혹함(ho~)를 폭로한다

10. In the final battle, Macbeth faces Macduff and _____
any man "of woman born."   ~에 의해서 죽임을 당할 수는 없다고 듣는다

[Word Quiz]

1. What is the synonym for "aspiring"?
a) General   b) Prophecy   c) Ambitious   d) Fulfilling

2. Which word refers to a foretelling of a future event?
a) Murder   b) Suspicion   c) Prediction   d) Contemplate

3. What word refers to a strong desire to achieve success, power, or wealth?
a) Ambition   b) Completion   c) Contemplation   d) Encouragement

4. Which word means to think deeply or ponder?
a) Paranoid   b) Contemplate   c) Murder   d) Opposition

5. What is a seat of power for a ruler called?
a) Haunted   b) Throne   c) Ambition   d) Predict

6. Which term means providing support or motivation?
a) Prophecy   b) Encouragement   c) Prediction   d) Madness

7. What is the act of murdering a public figure by surprise attack?
a) Paranoid   b) Eliminate   c) Assassination   d) Murder

8. Which word means to get rid of or remove completely?
a) Beware   b) Paranoid   c) Eliminate   d) Revealing

9. What is the adjective for someone who is excessively fearful or suspicious?
a) Paranoid   b) Murder   c) Guilt   d) Opposition

10. Which word means a prediction believed to be divinely inspired or foretelling future events?
a) Prophecy   b) Paranoid   c) Explore   d) Contemplate

11. What word refers to the act of resisting or confronting something?
a) Opposition   b) Revealing   c) Prophecy   d) Proclaimed

12. Which word means to publicly announce or declare?
a) Paranoid b) Proclaim c) Themes d) Assassins

13. Which term refers to the result of one's actions?
a) Destructive b) Corrupting c) Consequence d) Opposition

14. What is an adverb that describes something occurring often or at regular intervals?
a) Completely b) Frequently c) Formally d) Casually

15. Which word means to investigate or examine thoroughly?
a) Contemplate b) Haunt c) Explore d) Uncheck

16. What is the opposite of a benevolent and just ruler?
a) Revealing b) Tyrant c) Opposition d) Encouragement

17. What is the term for a prolonged and intense struggle, often involving armies?
a) Madness b) Battle c) Prediction d) Fulfilling

18. Which word means to disclose information?
a) Haunted b) Murder c) Revealing d) Themes

19. What is the adjective for something that is causing harm or damage?
a) Destructive b) Explore c) Encouragement d) Ambition

20. Which term means to take down from power, often forcefully?
a) Proclaimed b) Overthrow c) Murder d) Intrigue

Unit 12: Don Quixote (1605)

"Don Quixote," written by Miguel de Cervantes, is a two-part novel published in 1605 and 1615. The story follows the adventures of a man named Alonso Quixano, who becomes so obsessed with tales of chivalry and knights-errant that he loses touch with reality and transforms himself into "Don Quixote," a self-proclaimed knight on a quest to revive chivalry and defend the helpless.

Don Quixote persuades an innkeeper to dub him a knight, even though the inn is just a regular tavern. This is the starting point of his delusional adventures. Don Quixote declares a skinny horse as his noble steed,

Rocinante, and falls in love with a peasant woman named Aldonza Lorenzo, whom he imagines to be a noble lady named Dulcinea del Toboso. One of the most famous episodes in the novel is when Don Quixote mistakes windmills for giants and charges at them. He is thrown from his horse and injured, and Sancho Panza, a simple farmer, becomes his loyal squire after the incident. Don Quixote comes across a group of prisoners being transported, and he decides to free them. In the process, he antagonizes the guards and releases the prisoners. This leads to chaos and confusion.

Don Quixote decides to undertake a period of penance as a knight-errant and sets himself up as a penitent at an inn. He endures various comical situations, much to the amusement of the inn's guests. Don Quixote encounters a group of merchants he believes are oppressing innocent travelers. He valiantly attacks them, but in reality, the merchants are just carrying on with their normal business. Don Quixote meets a young man named Cardenio, who tells him a tragic tale of lost love. The story involves a beautiful woman named Lucinda, Cardenio's love interest, and his friend Fernando. Don Quixote encounters a group of actors, and one of them, pretending to be a princess from a far-off land, seeks his help. He agrees to accompany her, believing her fictional story.

Don Quixote returns home briefly and his friends and family are concerned about his delusions. They try to persuade him to give up his knightly pursuits. Despite the pleas of his friends, Don Quixote decides to set out on a second expedition, accompanied by Sancho Panza, who now has dreams of wealth and power. Don Quixote and Sancho Panza encounter the Duke and Duchess, who have read about Don Quixote's adventures and decide to play tricks on him for their amusement. Don Quixote faces a challenging opponent, the Knight of the Mirrors (Sanson Carrasco in disguise), who tricks Don Quixote into looking into a mirror to confront his own delusions. The Duke and Duchess promise Sancho an island to govern, and he becomes the governor of Barataria. His rule, however, is marked by comical misunderstandings and naive decisions. Altisidora, a lady at the Duke and Duchess's court, falls in love with Don Quixote and pretends to be sick for his attention. Don Quixote's reaction adds to the humor of the situation.

Cardenio reappears, and his story of lost love continues. He seeks revenge on Fernando for betraying him and stealing Lucinda.

Don Quixote comes across a statue of Dulcinea, which he believes has been enchanted. He is convinced that the enchantment is the reason she appears different than he remembers.

In the climax of the novel, Don Quixote faces a series of misadventures and confrontations with various characters, ultimately leading to his defeat and return to sanity. Don Quixote returns home once more, where he renounces his knighthood and returns to his true identity as Alonso Quixano. He falls seriously ill and, surrounded by friends and family, passes away. The novel concludes with Cervantes reflecting on the legacy of Don Quixote and expressing his hope that the story will serve as both entertainment and a lesson for readers.

"Don Quixote" is a rich and multifaceted work that explores themes of reality and illusion, the power of imagination, the nature of heroism, and the complexities of human folly and nobility. It remains a timeless and influential piece of literature, often regarded as the first modern novel.

[Vocabulary]

Adventures 모험 Obsessed 집착하는 Chivalry 기사도 Knights-errant 유랑 기사들 Reality 현실 Transform 변모시키다 Self-proclaimed 자칭의 Quest 탐험 Revive 부활시키다 Defend 지키다 Obscene 음란한 Heroic 영웅적인 Excessive 지나친 Sanity 제정신 Adopt 채택하다 Delusional 환각적인 Declarations 선언 Peasant 농민 Imagination 상상력 Antagonize 적대시하다 Chaos 혼돈 Undertake 착수하다 Penance 회개 Oppressing 억압하는 Valiantly 용감하게 Disguise 위장 Misunderstandings 오해 Naive 순진한 Pretend 가장하다 Enchantment 마법 Climax 절정 Defeat 패배 Renounce 포기하다 Legacy 유산 Region 지역 Innkeeper 여관주인 Confusion 혼란 Penitent 뉘우치는 Expedition 원정 Accompany 동반하다 Challenging 도전적인 Confront 직면하다 Revenge 복수 Enchanted 마법에 걸린 Confrontation 대립 Renounce 포기하다 Reflect 반성/반사하다

[본문 해석] 돈키호테

  "돈키호테"는 미겔 세르반테스(Miguel de Cervantes)에 쓰여 진, 1605년과 1615년에 출판된 2부작 소설입니다. 이 소설은 스페인의 라만차 지역에 사는 알론소 키하노(Alonso Quixano)라는 남자의 모험을 따릅니다. 알론소 키하노는 기사도와 편력하는 기사 이야기에 심취한 나머지 현실과의 접촉을 잃고 스스로가 "돈키호테"로 변신합니다. 그는 기사도를 부활시키고 무력한 자들을 지키는 자칭 기사단으로서의 임무를 수행하기 위해 떠납니다.

  돈키호테는 사실 평범한 주점의 여관주인을 설득하여 자신을 기사로 임명하게 합니다. 이것이 그의 망상적 모험의 시작점이 됩니다. 돈키호테는 삐쩍 바른 말인 로시난테를 그의 고귀한 종마로 선언하며, 농사를 짓는 여성인 알돈사 로렌조에게 사랑에 빠져 그녀를 둘시네아라고 이름 짓고 그녀가 귀족이라고 상상합니다. 이 소설에서 가장 유명한 에피소드 중 하나는 돈키호테가 풍차를 거인으로 오해하고 공격하는 장면입니다. 그는 말에서 떨어져 상처를 입게 되고, 이 사건 이후 단순한 농부인 산초 판자가 그의 충성스러운 하인이 됩니다. 돈키호테는 우연히 수송 중인 수감자들을 목격하고 그들을 해방시키기로 결심합니다. 이 과정에서 그는 호송원들과 대적하고 죄수들을 풀어주게 되는 데, 이로 인해 혼돈과 혼란이 발생합니다.

  돈키호테는 편력하는 기사로서 참회의 기간을 갖기로 결정하고, 한 여관에서 자신을 참회자로 설정합니다. 그는 여관 손님들을 즐겁게 할 정도로 다양한 희극적인 상황들을 견뎌냅니다. 돈키호테는, 그가 생각하기에, 무고한 여행객들을 억압하고 있는 상인들과 마주칩니다. 그는 용감하게 그들을 공격하지만, 현실에서 그 상인들은 그들의 평범한 사업을 계속하고 있을 뿐입니다. 돈키호테는 카르데니오라는 이름의 젊은 남자를 만나는데, 그는 돈키호테에게 실연에 대한 비극적인 이야기를 들려줍니다. 그 이야기는 카르데니오의 연인인 루신다라는 아름다운 여성과 그의 친구 페르난도가 관련되어 있습니다. 돈키호테는 한 무리의 배우들을 만나게 되는데, 그들 중 한 명이 먼 나라의 공주인 척하며 그의 도움을 구합니다. 그는 그녀가 지어낸 이야기를 믿고 그녀와 동행하는데 동의합니다.

  돈키호테는 잠시 동안 집으로 돌아오고 그의 친구와 가족들은 그의 망상에 대해 걱정을 합니다. 그들은 그가 기사 생활을 포기하도록 설득하려고 노력합니다. 그러나 친구들의 탄원에도 불구하고, 돈키호테는 부하가 되는 산초 판자를 동반하여 떠나기로 결정합니다. 산초 판자는 이제 부와 권력에 대한 꿈을 갖게 되었습니다. 돈키호테와 산초 판자는 기사와 공작부인을 만납니다. 그들은 돈키호테의 모험에 관해 읽은 후, 그들을 놀리기로 결정합니다. 돈키호테는 도전적인 상대인 '거울의 기사'(Sanson Carrasco가 위장한 것)와 대면하게 됩니다. 그는 돈키호테를 속여 자신의 망상과 대적하도록 거울을 들여다보게 합니다. 공작부인과 공작은 산초 판자에게 지배할 섬을 주기로 약속하고, 그는 바라타리아의 통치자가 됩니다. 그러나 그의 통치는 유쾌한 오해와 순진한 결정으로 가득 차 있습니다. 공작부인의 궁정에 있는 여인 알티시도라(Altisidora)는 돈키호테에게 사랑에 빠지고 그의 관심을 끌기 위해 아픈 척합니다. 돈키호테의 반응은 상황에 대해 유머를 더합니다. 카르데니오가 다시 나타나고, 그의 실연에 관한 이야기가 계속됩니다. 그는 페르난도가 자신을 배신하고 루신다를 빼앗은 것에 대한 복수를 추구합니다.

돈키호테는 우연히 둘시네아의 조각상을 만나고, 그것이 마법에 걸렸다고 믿습니다. 그는 그녀가 그가 기억하는 것과 다르게 보이는 이유가 마법 때문이라고 확신합니다.

이 소설의 절정에서 돈키호테는 다양한 인물들과의 일련의 우발적 사건과 대결에 직면하며, 결국 패배하고 제정신으로 돌아옵니다. 돈키호테는 다시 집으로 돌아가, 기사도를 포기하고 알론소 키하노의 진정한 정체성으로 되돌아옵니다. 그는 심각하게 병에 걸려 가족과 친구들에게 둘러싸여 세상을 떠납니다. 소설은 세르반테스가 돈키호테의 이야기가 우리에게 남긴 것에 대해 되돌아보고, 이 이야기가 독자들에게 즐거움과 교훈을 제공할 것을 희망하는 것으로 끝납니다.

"돈키호테"는 현실과 환상, 상상력의 힘, 영웅성의 본질, 인간의 어리석음과 고귀함 등 다양한 주제를 탐구하는 풍부하고 다면적인 작품입니다. 이것은 언제나 세계적으로 영향력이 크며, 최초의 현대 소설로서 높이 평가되는 문학 작품입니다.

[Reading Comprehension]

1. What is the name of the main character in "Don Quixote"?
a) Alonso Lorenzo b) Miguel Cervantes c) Sancho Panza d) Alonso Quixano

2. What is the reason for Alonso Quixano's transformation into Don Quixote?
a) His desire for power
b) His obsession with books about knights
c) A traumatic event from his childhood
d) His love for Aldonza Lorenzo

3. What does Don Quixote mistakenly believe Aldonza Lorenzo's true name to be?
a) Lucinda b) Dulcinea c) Rocinante d) Altisidora

4. What does Don Quixote mistake for giants and charge at, resulting in injury?
a) Windmills b) Lions c) Knights d) Prisoners

5. Who becomes Don Quixote's loyal squire after his charge at the windmills?
a) Fernando b) Cardenio c) Sancho Panza d) Sanson Carrasco

6. What is the primary reason for Don Quixote's return to sanity in the climax of the novel?
a) Defeat in confrontations with various characters
b) Encountering a statue of Dulcinea
c) Falling seriously ill
d) Renouncing his knighthood

7. What is the Duke and Duchess's motivation for playing tricks on Don Quixote?
a) They admire his bravery
b) They want to help him regain his sanity
c) They find amusement in his delusions
d) They are trying to steal his wealth

8. What is the name of the character who tricks Don Quixote into confronting his own delusions?
a) Cardenio b) Sancho Panza c) Altisidora d) Sanson Carrasco

9. What role does Sancho Panza assume during his time with the Duke and Duchess?
a) Knight-Errant   b) Governor   c) Jester   d) Squire

10. Who falls in love with Don Quixote and pretends to be sick for his attention?
a) Aldonza Lorenzo   b) Lucinda   c) Altisidora   d) The Duchess

11. What event marks the climax of the novel, where Don Quixote faces various misadventures and confrontations?
a) Don Quixote's return to sanity
b) The Lion Incident
c) The encounter with Cardenio
d) The battle with the Knight of the Mirrors

12. How does "Don Quixote" conclude?
a) Don Quixote becomes king
b) Don Quixote defeats all his enemies
c) Don Quixote renounces his knighthood and passes away
d) Don Quixote marries Dulcinea

13. What themes are explored in "Don Quixote"?
a) Romantic love and betrayal
b) Exploration of space and time
c) The power of imagination and the complexities of human folly
d) Political intrigue and power struggles

14. How does the novel conclude, according to the passage?
a) Don Quixote defeats all his adversaries and becomes a renowned knight.
b) Don Quixote remains delusional until the end of the story.
c) Don Quixote renounces his knighthood and returns to his true identity.
d) Don Quixote's friends and family betray him, leading to his demise.

15. What is the significance of "Don Quixote" in literary history?
a) It is the first science fiction novel
b) It is the first modern novel and explores various themes
c) It is a collection of short stories about knights
d) It is a tragedy about the downfall of a nobleman

[Grammar Check-up]

1. The story follows the adventures of a man named Alonso Quixano, who becomes so (obsessed, obsessing) with tales of chivalry and knights-errant that he (is lost, loses) touch with reality and transforms himself into "Don Quixote."

2. He is well-read, (particular, particularly) in books about knights, chivalry, and heroic deeds.

3. (because, Due to) his excessive reading, Alonso Quixano loses his sanity and becomes (obsessed, obsessing) with the idea of becoming a knight-errant himself.

4. He decides (adopting, to adopt) the name "Don Quixote" and sets out on a quest to become a hero.

5. Don Quixote persuades an innkeeper to (be dubbed, dub) him a knight, even though the inn is just a regular tavern.

6. This is the starting point of his (delusion, delusional) adventures.

7. Don Quixote declares a skinny horse as his noble steed, Rocinante, and falls in love with a peasant woman (named, who names) Aldonza Lorenzo.

8. One of the most famous episodes in the novel (are, is) when Don Quixote mistakes windmills (of, for) giants and charges at them.

9. He (is thrown, throws) from his horse and injured, and Sancho Panza, a simple farmer, becomes his loyal squire after the incident.

10. Don Quixote comes across a group of prisoners being (transported, transporting), and he decides to free them.

11. Don Quixote decides to (be undertaken, undertake) a period of penance as a knight-errant and sets himself up as a penitent at an inn.

12. He endures various comical (situations, situation), much to the amusement of the inn's guests.

13. Don Quixote encounters a group of merchants he believes (is, are) oppressing innocent travelers.

14. He (valiantly, valiant) attacks them, but in reality, the merchants are just carrying on with their normal business.

15. Don Quixote meets a young man named Cardenio, who (tells, is told) him a tragic tale of lost love.

16. The story (is involved, **involves**) a beautiful woman named Lucinda, Cardenio's love interest, and his friend Fernando.

17. Don Quixote encounters a group of actors, and one of them, (pretending, **pretends**) to be a princess from a far-off land, seeks his help.

18. He agrees to accompany her, (**believing**, believes) her fictional story.

19. Don Quixote returns home briefly and (recognizes, **is recognized**) by his friends and family who (is, **are**) concerned about his delusions.

20. They try to persuade him (**to give up**, giving up) his knightly pursuits.

21. (**Despite**, Even thought) the pleas of his friends, Don Quixote (deciding, **decides**) to set out on a second expedition, (accompanying, **accompanied**) by Sancho Panza, who now has dreams of wealth and power.

22. Don Quixote and Sancho Panza encounter the Duke and Duchess, who (**have**, has) read about Don Quixote's adventures.

23. Don Quixote (**faces**, is faced) a challenging opponent, the Knight of the Mirrors (Sanson Carrasco in disguise), (which, **who**) tricks Don Quixote into looking into a mirror to confront his own delusions.

24. The Duke and Duchess promise Sancho an island (**to govern**, governing), and he becomes the governor of Barataria.

25. Don Quixote comes across a statue of Dulcinea, (**who**, which) he believes has been enchanted.

26. He (**is convinced**, convinces) that the enchantment is the reason she appears (different, **differently**) than he remembers.

27. In the climax of the novel, Don Quixote (is faced, **faces**) a series of misadventures and confrontations with various characters, (**ultimately**, ultimate) leading to his defeat and return to sanity.

28. Don Quixote returns home once more, (**where**, which) he renounces his knighthood and returns to his true identity as Alonso Quixano.

29. He falls (**seriously**, serious) ill and, surrounded by friends and family, passes away.

30. "Don Quixote" remains a timeless and influential piece of literature, often (is regarded, **regarded**) as the first modern novel.

[Writing Practice]

1. "Don Quixote," written by Miguel de Cervantes, is _____
1605 and 1615   ~년에 발표된 2부로 된 소설이다

2. Alonso Quixano, _____ *tales of chivalry* _____
reality.   너무 *기사도 이야기*에 사로잡혀 있어서 현실과의 접촉을 잃었다 (접속사, 과거)

3. _____, Alonso Quixano loses his sanity.
     그의 과도한 독서로 인해

4. Don Quixote _____, even though the inn is just
a regular tavern. 그를 기사로 부르도록 여관주인을 설득하다

5. _____ Aldonza Lorenzo, whom he imagines to
그는 ~라고 불리는 시골뜨기(pea~) 여성과 사랑에 빠진다
be a noble lady named Dulcinea del Toboso.

6. _____ is when Don Quixote mistakes
그 소설에서 가장 유명한 에피소드 중 하나는   windmills for giants and charges at them.

7. Don Quixote comes across *a group of* _____, and he
decides to free them.   이송중인(transport) *한 무리의* 죄수들 (관계사)

8. He encounters a group of merchants _____ *innocent travelers*.
                    ~를 억압하고 있다고 <u>그가 믿는</u> 상인들 (관계사, 삽입구)

9. The story _____ Lucinda, Cardenio's love interest, and his
friend Fernando. ~라고 불리는 아름다운 여인과 관련 있다

10. They _____ *his knightly pursuits*.
          그가 ~를 포기하도록 설득하려고 시도한다

11. _____, Don Quixote decides to set out on a second
expedition.   그의 친구들의 간청에도 불구하고

[Word Quiz]

1. What term refers to exciting or daring experiences, typically involving risk and excitement?
a) Adventures   b) Obsessed   c) Chivalry   d) Knights-errant

2. Which word describes being excessively preoccupied or fixated on something?
a) Reality   b) Transform   c) Obsessed   d) Quest

3. Which term denotes the medieval code of conduct for knights, emphasizing qualities like honor, bravery, and courtesy?
a) Chivalry   b) Defend   c) Heroic   d) Excessive

4. What are wandering knights, often in pursuit of noble quests or adventures, called?
a) Knights-errant   b) Revive   c) Delusion   d) Declaration

5. What is the term for the state or quality of being real or existent?
a) Reality   b) Adopt   c) Misunderstandings   d) Antagonize

6. Which word means to change or alter drastically in form, appearance, or nature?
a) Transform   b) Enchantment   c) Disguise   d) Legacy

7. What adjective describes someone who proclaims or declares something about themselves without external validation or authority?
a) Self-proclaimed   b) Penance   c) Oppressing   d) Valiantly

8. What term refers to a long or arduous journey, often undertaken in pursuit of a goal or objective?
a) Quest   b) Undertake   c) Peasant   d) Confusion

9. What does it mean to bring back to life or restore to consciousness?
a) Revive   b) Region   c) Climax   d) Defeat

10. Which word means to protect or guard against attack, danger, or harm?
a) Defend   b) Renounce   c) Legacy   d) Oppressing

11. What adjective describes something offensive to decency or morality, typically in a sexual context?

a) Obscene b) Imagination c) Misunderstandings d) Naive

12. Which term refers to showing extreme courage or bravery, especially in the face of danger or difficulty?

a) Valiantly b) Disguise c) Pretend d) Enchantment

13. What does it mean to be beyond what is reasonable, usual, or necessary?

a) Excessive b) Sanity c) Penitent d) Expedition

14. What term describes the state of having a healthy and rational mind?

a) Sanity b) Undertake c) Confusion d) Legacy

15. Which word means to take on or accept something, such as a belief, practice, or identity?

a) Adopt b) Reflection c) Accompany d) Revenge

16. What is the noun form of the belief in something that is not true or based on reality?

a) Delusion b) Declaration c) Oppressing d) Challenging

17. Which term refers to a formal or explicit statement or announcement?

a) Declaration b) Peasant c) Expedition d) Confront

18. What term describes a person of low social status who works on the land, typically in agriculture?

a) Peasant b) Legacy c) Confrontation d) Reflect

19. Which word describes the faculty or action of forming new ideas, images, or concepts not present to the senses?

a) Imagination b) Challenging c) Revenge d) Enchanted

20. What does it mean to cause someone to become hostile or to provoke someone into taking action?

a) Antagonize b) Chaos c) Enchantment d) Climax

Unit 13: The Pilgrim's Progress (1678)

"The Pilgrim's Progress" is a Christian allegorical novel written by John Bunyan, first published in 1678. The book is considered one of the most significant works of religious literature in English. It tells the story of a man named Christian and his journey from the City of Destruction to the Celestial

City, representing his spiritual pilgrimage from a life of sin to eternal salvation.

The story begins with a man named Christian living in the City of Destruction. He becomes burdened with a sense of sin and realizes that his city will be destroyed due to its sinful nature. He reads a book (the Bible) that tells him to flee from the city's impending doom.

Christian meets Evangelist, who directs him to a narrow gate and a difficult path that leads to the Celestial City. Evangelist encourages Christian to begin his journey immediately. Christian tries to find the Wicket Gate (representing salvation) but faces distractions and temptations along the way. Eventually, he finds the gate and enters the straight and narrow path. Christian stops at the Interpreter's House, where he sees various allegorical visions illustrating different aspects of the Christian life and its challenges.

Christian faces challenges and trials as he climbs the Hill Difficulty. He meets a fellow traveler named Help, and together they overcome obstacles and continue their journey. Christian reaches the Palace Beautiful, where he is welcomed and refreshed by the inhabitants. He learns more about the journey and the wonders of the Celestial City. Christian travels through a dangerous valley, facing fear and despair. He relies on his faith and the Word of God to guide him through the darkness.

Christian arrives at Vanity Fair, a bustling marketplace symbolizing worldly temptations and distractions. He resists the allure of material possessions and pleasures, leading to conflict with the townspeople. Christian falls into a deep, muddy bog called the Slough of Despond, representing the weight of his sins and the challenges of the spiritual life. He is rescued by a man named Help.

Christian and his companion Hopeful are captured by the giant Despair and imprisoned in Doubting Castle. Despite their hardships, they eventually find the key of Promise, which unlocks their prison and sets them free. Christian and Hopeful find themselves on the Delectable Mountains, where they meet shepherds who offer them guidance and comfort.

The travelers reach a place called the Enchanted Ground, where the air induces a sleepy forgetfulness of their purpose. They are warned of the danger and press on. Christian and Hopeful enter the Land of Beulah, a place of peace and rest, where they can see the Celestial City in the distance. As they approach the end of their journey, Christian and Hopeful must cross the River of Death. Angels carry them safely to the Celestial City, where they are joyously received.

The second part of the book follows Christian's wife, Christiana, and her children as they also embark on a pilgrimage to the Celestial City, guided by Greatheart, a valiant and faithful companion. Christiana and her children encounter similar challenges and trials but ultimately reach the Celestial City, where they are reunited with Christian and live in eternal bliss.

"The Pilgrim's Progress" is a powerful and enduring allegory of the Christian journey, using vivid characters and situations to depict the challenges, triumphs, and ultimate rewards of a life devoted to faith and righteousness.

[Vocabulary]

Allegorical 은유적인 Significant 중요한 Religious 종교적인 Literature 문학 Spiritual 영적인 Pilgrimage 순례 Impending 다가오는 Distractions 주의산만 Temptations 유혹 Interpreter 해석가 Challenges 도전 Obstacles 장애물 Inhabitants 거주자들 Despair 절망 Imprisoned 갇힌 Enchanted 마법에 걸린 Forgetfulness 망각 Reunite 재회하다 Devoted 헌신적인 Allegory 은유 Celestial 천국적인 Destruction 파멸 Rescued 구조된 Valiant 용감한 Embark 착수하다 Vanity 허영 Muddy 진흙투성이의 Induce 유도하다 Bliss 행복 Shepherds 목자들 Journey 여정 Conflicts 갈등 Salvation 구원 Strait 협소한/해협 Companion 동료 Weight 무게 Destructive 파괴적인 Refreshed 상쾌해진 Trials 시험들 Ultimate 궁극적인 Triumphs 승리 Eternal 영원한 Allure 유혹(하다) Hazard 위험 Glimpse 흘끗 봄 Rejoice 기뻐하다

[본문 해석] 천로역정

"천로역정"은 1678년에 존 번연에 의해 쓰여 진 기독교적 우화 소설로, 영어로 된 종교 문학 중에서 가장 중요한 작품 중 하나로 여겨집니다. 이 책은 크리스천(청교도인)이라는 남자와 그의 여정을 다룹니다. 그는 파멸의 도시로부터 천상의 도시까지 여정을 떠나며, 이는 그의 죄에서 영원한 구원으로의 영적 순례를 상징합니다.

이야기는 파멸의 도시에서 살고 있는 크리스천이라는 남자로 시작합니다. 그는 죄의식으로 무거운 짐을 짊어지게 되고, 그의 도시가 죄악의 본성으로 인해 파괴될 것임을 깨닫습니다. 그는 자신에게 도시의 임박한 파멸로부터 도망가라고 말해주는 책(성경)을 읽게 됩니다.

크리스천은 복음전도사를 만나게 되는데, 그는 그에게 좁은 문과 천상의 도시로 이끄는 힘든 길로 안내합니다. 복음전도사는 크리스천에게 즉시 그의 여정을 시작하도록 격려합니다. 크리스천은 구원을 상징하는 좁은 문을 찾으려고 시도하지만, 그 길은 유혹과 시험으로 가득합니다. 결국 그는 그 문을 찾아 좁고 곧은길로 들어갑니다. 크리스천은 '해설자'의 집을 방문하게 되고, 그곳에서 그는 기독교적 삶의 다른 양상들과 도전들을 보여주는 다양한 우화적 비전을 보게 됩니다.

크리스천 '어려움'이라는 언덕을 어려움을 오르는 동안 도전과 시험에 직면합니다. 그는 동료 여행자인 '도움'이라는 사람을 만나서 함께 장애물을 극복하고 여정을 계속합니다. 크리스천은 아름다운 궁전에 도착하여 그곳에 거주하는 사람들에게 환영받고 기운을 차립니다. 그는 여정과 천상의 도시의 신기한 것들에 대해 더 많이 배우게 됩니다. 크리스천은 위험한 계곡을 여행하면서 두려움과 절망과 마주하게 됩니다. 그는 자신의 믿음과 하나님의 말씀에 의지하여 어둠을 헤쳐 나갑니다.

크리스천은 세속의 유혹과 방해를 상징하는 화려한 장터인 '허영 시장'에 도착합니다. 그는 물질적인 소유와 즐거움의 유혹에 저항하여 도시 주민들과 갈등을 겪습니다. 크리스천은 그의 죄와 영적인 삶의 어려움을 상징하는 '먹물의 구렁'이라고 불리는 깊고 진흙 수렁에 빠지게 되지만, '도움'이라는 사람에 의해 구출됩니다.

크리스천과 그의 친구 '희망'은 거인인 '절망'에게 잡혀 '의심의 성'에 가둬지게 됩니다. 그들의 고난에도 불구하고, 그들은 결국 감옥의 문을 열고 그들을 자유롭게 해주는 '약속의 열쇠'를 찾습니다. 크리스천과 '희망'은 유쾌한 산에 있는 자신들을 발견합니다. 그리고 그곳에서 그들은 길잡이와 위로를 제공해주는 양치기들을 만나게 됩니다.

여행자들은 '마법의 땅'이라고 불리는 곳에 도달하는데, 그곳에의 공기는 그들의 목적을 잊게 하는 졸음을 유도합니다. 그들은 위험에 대해 경고를 받지만 계속 밀어붙입니다. 크리스천과 '희망'은 평화와 휴식의 땅, 멀리 천상의 도시를 볼 수 있는 '뿔라'(빛나는 미래를 상징)의 땅으로 들어갑니다. 그들의 여행의 마지막이 가까워지면서, 크리스천과 '희망'은 죽음의 강을 건너야 합니다. 천사들은 그들을 천상의 도시로 안전하게 데려다 주고, 그곳에서 그들은 기꺼이 받아 들여

집니다.

2부에서 크리스천의 아내인 크리스티안과 그녀의 아이들이 용감하고 충실한 동반자인 '위대한 마음'의 안내로 천상의 도시로 순례를 떠나는 과정을 그립니다. 크리스티안과 아이들은 비슷한 도전과 시련을 겪지만 궁극적으로 천상의 도시에 도달하여 크리스천과 재회하고 영원한 행복 속에서 살게 됩니다. "천로역정"은 신앙과 정의에 바친 삶의 도전, 승리, 그리고 궁극적인 보상을 묘사하기 위해 생생한 인물과 상황을 사용하는 기독교 여행의 강력하고 지속되는 우화입니다.

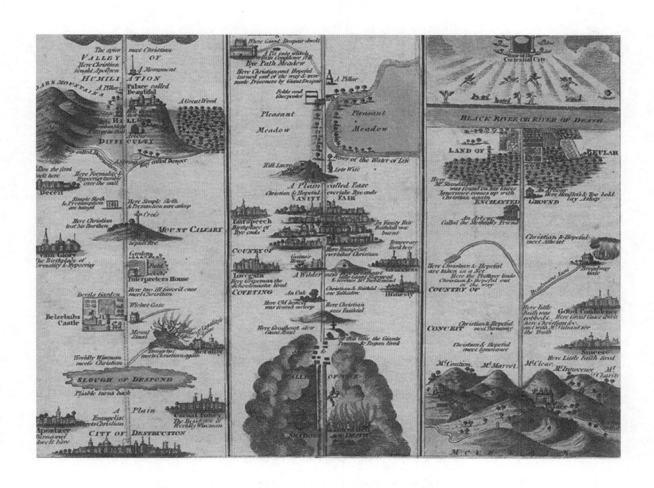

[Reading Comprehension]

1. What is "The Pilgrim's Progress" about?
a) A journey from the City of Destruction to the Celestial City
b) A love story between two characters
c) A political allegory of the 17th century
d) A science fiction novel

2. What is the significance of the City of Destruction?
a) It represents a place of peace and rest.
b) It symbolizes the weight of sins and challenges of the spiritual life.
c) It is the starting point of Christian's journey.
d) It is the destination of the pilgrimage.

3. What book does Christian read to know about his city's impending doom?
a) The Pilgrim's Progress
b) The Bible
c) Vanity Fair
d) The City of Destruction

4. Who guides Christian to the Celestial City?
a) Evangelist   b) Help   c) Greatheart   d) Hopeful

5. What does the Wicket Gate represent?
a) Salvation   b) Worldly temptations   c) Fear and despair   d) Sinful nature

6. Where does Christian stop to see allegorical visions about the Christian life?
a) Vanity Fair   b) The Interpreter's House
c) The Enchanted Ground   d) The Delectable Mountains

7. What challenges does Christian face while climbing the Hill Difficulty?
a) Temptations   b) Imprisonment   c) Fear and despair   d) Obstacles

8. Who is Christian's companion when he faces the challenges on the Hill Difficulty?
a) Evangelist   b) Vanity Fair   c) Help   d) Hopeful

9. Where does Christian find refuge and refreshment during his journey?
a) The City of Destruction   b) Vanity Fair
c) The Palace Beautiful   d) The Slough of Despond

10. What does the Slough of Despond represent?

a) A dangerous valley

b) The weight of sins and spiritual challenges

c) Worldly temptations and distractions

d) A narrow gate

11. How does Christian get rescued from the Slough of Despond?

a) He finds the key of Promise.

b) He meets the shepherds of Delectable Mountains.

c) He meets Help, who rescues him.

d) He is carried by angels to the Celestial City.

12. What do Christian and Hopeful find on the Delectable Mountains?

a) The Land of Beulah

b) Shepherds offering guidance and comfort

c) The Interpreter's House

d) The Celestial City

13. What happens on the Enchanted Ground?

a) Christian finds the Wicket Gate.

b) The air induces forgetfulness of their purpose.

c) They are warned of the danger ahead.

d) Christian meets Evangelist.

14. What does the Land of Beulah symbolize?

a) Worldly temptations and distractions

b) Peace and rest

c) Fear and despair

d) Vanity Fair

15. How do Christian and Hopeful reach the Celestial City in the end?

a) They cross the River of Death with the help of angels.

b) They face challenges and trials.

c) They meet Evangelist.

d) They are rescued by Greatheart.

[Grammar Check-up]

1. "The Pilgrim's Progress" was written by John Bunyan in 1678, _____ it a Christian allegorical novel.
a) making b) makes c) made d) make

2. Christian, _____ in the City of Destruction, embarks on a spiritual journey.
a) living b) lived c) lives d) live

3. He reads the Bible, _____ advises him to flee from the city's impending doom.
a) who b) which c) whom d) whose

4. Evangelist, _____ Christian to take a difficult path leading to the Celestial City.
a) directs b) to direct c) directing d) have directed

5. Christian faces distractions and temptations _____ finding the Wicket Gate.
a) when b) while c) as d) during

6. At the Interpreter's House, Christian sees allegorical visions _____ different aspects of the Christian life.
a) illustrating b) illustrated c) illustrates d) illustrate

7. Christian relies on his faith and the Word of God _____ him through the darkness.
a) to guiding b) guided c) guides d) guiding

8. Vanity Fair represents a bustling marketplace _____ worldly temptations and distractions.
a) within b) of c) for d) in

9. Christian resists the allure of material possessions, _____ leading to conflict with the townspeople.
a) consequently b) subsequently c) consequence d) thereby

10. The Slough of Despond symbolizes the weight of Christian's sins _____ the challenges of the spiritual life.
a) as long as b) coupled with c) as well as d) despite

11. Christian and Hopeful, _____ by the giant Despair, are imprisoned in Doubting Castle.
a) capturing   b) captured   c) captures   d) have captured

12. Despite their hardships, they eventually find the key of Promise, _____ their prison.
a) unlocking   b) unlocked   c) unlocks   d) to unlock

13. On the Delectable Mountains, Christian and Hopeful meet shepherds _____ them guidance and comfort.
a) offering   b) offered   c) offers   d) offer

14. The Enchanted Ground induces a _____ forgetfulness of the travelers' purpose.
a) joyful   b) somber   c) sleepy   d) determined

15. Christian and Hopeful enter the Land of Beulah, _____ peace and rest.
a) find   b) finding   c) finds   d) to find

16. Angels _____ Christian and Hopeful safely across the River of Death.
a) guides   b) hinder   c) trap   d) carry

17. The second part of the book follows Christian's wife, Christiana, _____ her children on a pilgrimage.
a) and   b) also   c) within   d) or

18. Guided by Greatheart, Christiana and her children encounter challenges _____ to Christian's journey.
a) similar   b) similarity   c) similarities   d) similarly

19. Greatheart is described as a valiant and faithful companion, _____ helps Christiana's family.
a) which   b) whose   c) who   d) whom

20. The allegory of "The Pilgrim's Progress" depicts the _____ of a life devoted to faith and righteousness.
a) challenged   b) challengeful   c) challenging   d) challenges

[Writing Practice]

1. The book _____ in English.
   이 책은 종교 문학의 가장 중요한 작품 중 하나로 여겨진다

2. The story begins with _____.
   파괴의 도시에 사는 Christian이라는 남자

3. He becomes burdened with a sense of sin and realizes that _____
   _____. 그의 도시가 죄악의 본성으로 인해 파괴될 것이다

4. He reads a book _____ the city's impending doom.
   ~으로부터 도망치라고 그에게 말하는 (관계사)

5. Christian meets Evangelist, _____ and a difficult path
   that leads to the Celestial City. 그리고 그는 그를 좁은 문으로 안내한다 (관계사)

6. 에반젤리스트는 그를 좁은 문으로 안내하고, 그는 천상의 도시로 향하는 어려운 길로 안내한
   다.
   _____

7. Eventually, _____.
   그는 문을 발견하고 곧고 좁은 길로 들어간다

8. Christian stops at the Interpreter's House, _____
   _____ the Christian life and its challenges.
   그리고 그곳에서 그는 ~의 다른 측면들을 보여주는(il~) 다양한 우화적 비전을 본다 (관계사)

9. Christian _____ as he climbs the Hill Difficulty.
   도전과 시련(tr~)에 직면한다

10. Christian reaches the Palace Beautiful, _____
    그리고 그곳에서 주민들에게 환영을 받는다 (관계사)

- 134 -

[Word Quiz]

1. Which term refers to a symbolic story or representation, often used to convey deeper meaning?
a) Allegorical   b) Religious   c) Literature   d) Spiritual

2. What word describes something of great importance or significance?
a) Significant   b) Pilgrimage   c) Impending   d) Distractions

3. What term relates to beliefs, rituals, and practices associated with the divine or supernatural?
a) Religious   b) Challenges   c) Obstacles   d) Inhabitants

4. Which word pertains to written works, especially those of lasting artistic merit?
a) Literature   b) Spiritual   c) Temptations   d) Interpreter

5. What adjective describes something relating to the soul or inner essence?
a) Spiritual   b) Forgetfulness   c) Reunite   d) Devoted

6. A journey to a sacred place or for a higher purpose is known as a _____.
a) Pilgrimage   b) Vanity   c) Muddy   d) Induce

7. Which word means imminent or about to happen?
a) Impending   b) Enchanted   c) Destruction   d) Rescued

8. What are things that divert attention or disturb concentration?
a) Distractions   b) Shepherds   c) Conflicts   d) Salvation

9. Which term refers to desires or inclinations to do something wrong or unwise?
a) Temptations   b) Embark   c) Companion   d) Weight

10. Someone who translates languages is known as an _____.
a) Interpreter   b) Challenges   c) Vanity   d) Glimpse

11. What do you call difficult situations or tasks that test someone's abilities?
a) Challenges   b) Forgetfulness   c) Refreshed   d) Trials

12. What are things that hinder progress or success?
a) Obstacles   b) Ultimate   c) Triumphs   d) Eternal

13. Who are the people who live in a particular place?
a) Inhabitants   b) Despair   c) Imprisoned   d) Shepherds

14. What word describes a feeling of hopelessness or loss of hope?
a) Despair   b) Destruction   c) Valiant   d) Celestial

15. What term means confined or restricted, especially against one's will?
a) Imprisoned   b) Reunite   c) Devoted   d) Enchanted

16. When something is under a spell or has a magical quality, it is said to be _____.
a) Enchanted   b) Spiritual   c) Bliss   d) Vanity

17. What word refers to the state of being unable to remember?
a) Forgetfulness   b) Vanity   c) Muddy   d) Induce

18. To come together again after being apart is to _____.
a) Reunite   b) Allegory   c) Strait   d) Allure

19. What adjective describes someone deeply committed or loyal?
a) Devoted   b) Refreshed   c) Hazard   d) Glimpse

20. A symbolic representation, especially in literature, is known as an _____.
a) Allegory   b) Vanity   c) Shepherds   d) Rejoice

Unit 14: Robinson Crusoe (1719)

"Robinson Crusoe" is a novel written by Daniel Defoe, first published in 1719. The story follows the life and adventures of a young man named Robinson Crusoe.

Robinson Crusoe, a young Englishman from York, dreams of a life of adventure and exploration at sea, much to the dismay of his family. Ignoring his father's wishes to pursue a more stable profession, Crusoe sets sail against all odds in 1651. Initially, his voyages prove successful, but as he embarks on his third sea journey, disaster strikes. A violent storm wrecks his ship off the coast of a deserted island in the Caribbean.

Stranded and alone on the island, Crusoe must learn to survive in this harsh and unforgiving environment. Using his wits and ingenuity, he manages to salvage supplies from the wreckage and sets up a makeshift shelter. Over time, he becomes proficient in hunting, fishing, and farming, which enables him to sustain himself.

Isolation becomes both a blessing and a curse for Crusoe. While he enjoys the solitude, he also grapples with loneliness and despair. He befriends a parrot and a dog that survived the shipwreck, but human companionship remains absent. Nevertheless, he finds solace in his faith and begins to reflect on his past life and the decisions that led him to this predicament.

After several years of isolation, Crusoe encounters a footprint on the beach, indicating that he is not alone on the island. Fearing that it may belong to cannibals, he fortifies his dwelling and prepares for a potential threat. However, to his relief, he discovers that the footprint belongs to natives who do not pose any immediate danger to him.

With newfound companionship, Crusoe rescues one of the natives from his enemies and names him Friday. Crusoe teaches Friday English and introduces him to Christianity, fostering a deep bond between them. Friday becomes loyal to Crusoe and assists him in various tasks.

Years pass, and Crusoe and Friday witness a group of Europeans arriving on the island, who are taken captive by a group of mutineers. Crusoe devises a plan to rescue the prisoners, successfully overpowering the mutineers and freeing the captives. Among the prisoners is a kind Portuguese captain who offers Crusoe and Friday safe passage back to England.

Crusoe, Friday, and the captain set sail for England, and after a long and eventful journey, they finally return home. Despite the hardships he endured, Crusoe emerges from his adventure and becomes a changed man. He learns the value of companionship, the importance of faith, and gains a new appreciation for the comforts of civilization.

"Robinson Crusoe" is a timeless tale of survival, self-discovery, and the resilience of the human spirit in the face of adversity. It has become a classic in world literature and continues to captivate readers with its themes of isolation, redemption, and the triumph of the human spirit.

[Vocabulary]

adventures 모험들 exploration 탐험 dismay 실망 pursue 추구하다 profession 직업 odds 낙제조건 voyages 항해들 successful 성공적인 embark 시작하다 disaster 재앙 violent storm 폭풍우 wreckage 파괴 stranded 갇힌 survive 살아남다 unforgiving 용서하지 않는 environment 환경 salvage 구해내다 makeshift 임시로 만든 shelter 보호소 proficient 능숙한 enable 가능하게 하다 isolation 고립 blessing 축복 curse 저주 grapple 씨름하다 despair 절망 companionship 교제 fortify 강화하다 potential 잠재적인 resilience 회복력

[본문 해석] 로빈슨 크루소

"로빈슨 크루소"는 다니엘 디포(Daniel Defoe)가 1719년에 처음 출판한 소설입니다. 이 소설은 젊은 남성 로빈슨 크루소의 삶과 모험을 따릅니다.

로빈슨 크루소는 영국의 요크 출신으로, 가족들이 실망스럽게도 모험과 항해에 대한 꿈을 꾸고 있습니다. 안정적인 직업을 추구하길 원했던 아버지의 바람을 무시하고 크루소는 1651년에 모든 역경에 맞서 항해를 떠납니다. 처음 몇 차례의 항해는 성공적이었으나, 세 번째 항해를 시작하자 재앙이 찾아왔습니다. 폭풍우가 그의 배를 파괴하고 그는 카리브해의 한 무인도에 그의 배를 난파시킵니다.

그 섬에 좌초되고 혼자인 크루소는 이 혹독하고 힘든 환경에서 살아남는 법을 배워야만 합니다. 그의 재치와 독창성을 사용하여, 그는 난파된 배의 잔해에서 보급품을 인양하고 임시 거처를 설치합니다. 시간이 지나면서, 그는 사냥, 낚시, 그리고 농사에 능숙해지는데, 이것은 그가 스스로를 지탱할 수 있게 해줍니다.

고독은 크루소에게 축복이자 저주가 됩니다. 그는 그 고독을 즐기는 동안 외로움과 절망을 겪기도 합니다. 그는 난파선에서 살아남은 앵무새와 개와 친구가 되지만 인간의 우정은 여전히 부재합니다. 그럼에도 불구하고, 그는 자신의 믿음에서 위안을 찾고 자신의 지난 삶과 이 곤경에 이르게 한 결정들에 대해 반성하기 시작합니다.

몇 년 동안 고립된 후, 크루소는 그가 그 섬에 혼자가 아니라는 것을 나타내는 발자국을 해변에서 발견하게 됩니다. 그것이 식인종의 것일지도 모른다는 두려움에 그는 그의 주거를 강화하고 잠재적인 위협에 대비합니다. 그러나 다행스럽게도, 그는 그 발자국이 그에게 어떤 즉각적인 위험을 가하지 않는 원주민들의 것이라는 것을 알게 됩니다.

새로운 우정으로, 크루소는 그의 적들로부터 원주민 중 한 명을 구하고 그에게 프라이데이라고 이름을 붙입니다. 크루소는 프라이데이에게 영어를 가르치고 그에게 기독교를 소개하여 그들 사이에 깊은 유대감을 조성합니다. 프라이데이는 크루소에게 충성하게 되고 다양한 일에서 그를 돕습니다.

세월이 흐르고, 크루소와 프라이데이는 섬에 도착한 한 무리의 유럽인을 목격하게 되고, 그들이 반란군에 의해 포로로 잡혀 있음을 알게 됩니다. 크루소는 포로들을 구출하기 위한 계획을 생각해 내어 반란군들을 성공적으로 제압하고 포로들을 석방합니다. 포로들 중에는 크루소와 프라이데이를 영국으로 안전하게 돌아갈 수 있게 도움을 줄 친절한 포르투갈인 선장이 있습니다.

크루소, 프라이데이, 그리고 선장은 영국으로 출항했고, 길고 다사다난한 여행 후에, 그들은 마침내 집으로 돌아옵니다. 그가 견뎌낸 고난에도 불구하고, 크루소는 그의 모험에서 벗어나 변화된 사람이 됩니다. 그는 우정의 가치, 믿음의 중요성을 배우고, 문명의 안락함에 대한 새로운 감사를 얻습니다.

"로빈슨 크루소"는 역경에 직면한 인간 정신의 생존, 자기 발견, 회복력에 대한 시대를 초월하는 이야기입니다. 그것은 세계 문학의 고전이 되었고 고립, 구원, 그리고 인간 정신의 승리라는 주제로 독자들의 마음을 계속 사로잡고 있습니다.

[Reading Comprehension]

1. Who is the author of the novel "Robinson Crusoe"?
a) Charles Dickens   b) Mark Twain   c) Daniel Defoe   d) Jules Verne

2. What is the occupation Robinson Crusoe's family wants him to pursue?
a) Sailor   b) Explorer   c) Farmer   d) Stable profession

3. In what year did Robinson Crusoe set sail on his ill-fated journey?
a) 1601   b) 1651   c) 1701   d) 1751

4. Where does the shipwreck occur in the story?
a) Mediterranean Sea   b) Atlantic Ocean   c) Indian Ocean   d) Caribbean Island

5. How does Crusoe manage to survive on the deserted island?
a) He builds a mansion
b) He befriends the natives
c) He uses his wits and skills to hunt and farm
d) He communicates with passing ships

6. What does Crusoe use to fortify his dwelling after seeing a footprint on the beach?
a) Cannons   b) Wooden walls   c) Moat   d) Drawbridge

7. Who is the first person Crusoe encounters on the island after years of isolation?
a) A cannibal   b) Another shipwreck survivor
c) A pirate   d) A native named Friday

8. How does Crusoe meet Friday?
a) Friday saves him from a wild animal
b) Friday rescues him from captivity
c) Friday is his loyal dog
d) Friday is a parrot that speaks English

9. What does Crusoe teach Friday during their time together?
a) Sword fighting   b) Farming techniques
c) English language and Christianity   d) Navigation skills

10. Who arrives on the island after many years, leading to the rescue of Crusoe and Friday?

a) Cannibals   b) Pirates   c) Mutineers   d) Explorers

11. How does Crusoe eventually return to England?

a) He builds a raft

b) He constructs a small boat

c) He hitches a ride with passing sailors

d) He returns thanks to the help of a Portuguese captain

12. What are the themes explored in "Robinson Crusoe"?

a) Romance and mystery

b) Comedy and adventure

c) Survival, isolation, and the human spirit

d) Science fiction and technology

13. What does Robinson Crusoe learn during his time on the island?

a) He learns to hate humanity

b) He learns to be self-sufficient

c) He learns to avoid challenges

d) He learns to fear the unknown

14. How is the relationship between Crusoe and Friday characterized?

a) Hostile

b) Competitive

c) Distrustful

d) Bond of friendship and loyalty

15. What is the significance of the novel "Robinson Crusoe" in literature?

a) It is a romantic love story

b) It emphasizes the dangers of exploration

c) It explores themes of survival, self-discovery, and resilience

d) It predicts the future of technology

[Grammar Check-up]

1. Robinson Crusoe, a young Englishman from York, (dreaming, dreams) of a life of adventure and exploration at sea, much to the dismay of his family.
2. (Ignoring, Ignore) his father's wishes to pursue a more stable profession, Crusoe sets sail against all odds in 1651.
3. (Initially, Initial), his voyages prove successful, but as he embarks on his third sea journey, disaster (striking, strikes).
4. (Stranding, Stranded) and alone on the island, Crusoe must learn to survive in this harsh and (unforgiving, unforgiven) environment.
5. Using his wits and ingenuity, he manages (salvaging, to salvage) supplies from the wreckage and sets up a makeshift shelter.
6. Over time, he becomes (proficient, proficiently) in hunting, fishing, and farming, which (able, enables) him to sustain himself.
7. Isolation becomes (between, both) a blessing and a curse for Crusoe. While he enjoys the solitude, he also (grappling, grapples) with loneliness and despair.
8. He befriends a parrot and a dog that survived the shipwreck, but human companionship remains (absently, absent).
9. Nevertheless, he (is found, finds) solace in his faith and begins to reflect on his past life and the decisions that led him to this predicament.
10. After several (years, year) of isolation, Crusoe encounters a footprint on the beach, (indicating, indicates) that he is not alone on the island.
11. Fearing that it may belong to cannibals, he fortifies his dwelling and prepares for a (potentially, potential) threat.
12. However, to (his, him) relief, he discovers that the footprint belongs to natives who (does, do) not pose any immediate danger to him.
13. With newfound companionship, Crusoe rescues one of the (natives, native) from his enemies and names him Friday.
14. Crusoe teaches Friday English and introduces him to Christianity, (fosters, fostering) a deep bond between them.
15. Friday becomes loyal to Crusoe and assists him in various (task, tasks).
16. Years pass, and Crusoe and Friday witness a group of Europeans (arrive, -arriving) on the island, only to be taken captive by a group of mutineers.
17. Crusoe devises a plan (rescuing, to rescue) the prisoners, successfully overpowering the mutineers and freeing the captives.
18. Among the prisoners (is, are) a kind Portuguese captain who (offer, offers) Crusoe and Friday safe passage back to England.
19. (Although, Despite) the hardships he endured, Crusoe emerges from his adventure a changed man.

[Writing Practice]

1. Robinson Crusoe, a young Englishman from York, dreams of a life of adventure and exploration at sea, _____. 그의 가족들이 너무나 당황스럽게도

2. _____, Crusoe sets sail against all odds in 1651. 더욱 안정적인 직업을 찾으라는 그의 아버지의 소망을 무시하고 (분사구)

3. Initially, his voyages prove successful, but _____, disaster strikes.   그가 그의 세 번째 바다 여행을 시작할 때

4. _____, Crusoe must learn to survive in this harsh and unforgiving environment. 섬에 고립되어(st~) 홀로 남아 (분사구)

5. Using his wits and ingenuity, _____ *from* the wreckage and sets up a makeshift shelter. 그는 가까스로 공급품들을 ~로부터 구하다(sa~)

6. Over time, he becomes proficient in hunting, fishing, and farming, _____. 이것은 그가 자신을 부양할 수 있게 해준다 (관계사)

7. _____, he also grapples with loneliness and despair.
        그가 고독(so~)을 즐기는 동안

8. Nevertheless, he finds solace in his faith and begins to reflect on his past life and _____. 그를 이러한 곤경으로 이끈 결정들 (관계사)

9. _____, Crusoe encounters a footprint on the beach,
        몇 년간의 고립 후에   indicating that he is not alone on the island.

10. _____ cannibals, he fortifies his dwelling and prepares 그것이 식인종들의 것일지도 모른다고 두려워하면서 (분사구, belong)   for a potential threat.

11. However, to his relief, he discovers that the footprint belongs to natives _____ _____. 그에게 어떤 즉각적인 위험도 취하지(pose) 않는 (관계사)

12. With newfound companionship, Crusoe _____ and names him Friday.   그의 적들로부터 원주민중의 한 사람을 구한다

[Word Quiz]

1. What is the meaning of "adventures"?
a) Difficulties   b) Exciting experiences
c) Misfortunes   d) Predictable situations

2. Which word is a synonym for "exploration"?
a) Disaster b) Pursue c) Dismay d) Investigation

3. How would you define "dismay"?
a) A strong desire   b) To begin a journey
c) A feeling of shock or distress   d) A successful outcome

4. Which word can be a synonym for "pursue"?
a) Escape b) Abandon c) Follow d) Hide

5. What does "profession" refer to?
a) A type of exploration   b) A successful endeavor
c) An occupation or career   d) A temporary shelter

6. In the phrase "against all odds," what does "odds" mean?
a) Unfavorable circumstances   b) Endless opportunities
c) Easy challenges   d) Predictable outcomes

7. What is the meaning of "voyages"?
a) Failed attempts   b) Difficulties
c) Long journeys, often by sea or air   d) Temporary stays

8. What is the opposite of "disaster"?
a) Violent storm b) Success c) Wreckage d) Stranded

9. Which word means to start a journey or venture?
a) Pursue b) Embark c) Explore d) Survive

10. What does "violent storm" describe?

a) A calm weather condition

b) A gentle breeze

c) A strong, destructive weather event

d) A bright and sunny day

11. What does "wreckage" refer to?

a) A successful outcome

b) A shelter made of natural materials

c) The remains of something that has been destroyed

d) A type of adventure

12. What does "stranded" mean?

a) Stuck or left in a difficult situation

b) Skilled and proficient

c) Abandoned by choice

d) Unaffected by challenges

13. What does it mean to "survive"?

a) To give up

b) To find companionship

c) To overcome difficulties and stay alive

d) To embark on a journey

14. How would you describe an "unforgiving" environment?

a) A friendly and welcoming atmosphere

b) A harsh and relentless setting

c) A temporary dwelling

d) A successful endeavor

15. What does "salvage" mean?

a) To abandon

b) To destroy

c) To save or recover something from wreckage

d) To explore

16. What is a "makeshift shelter"?

a) A permanent residence

b) A luxurious mansion

c) A temporary and improvised place of refuge

d) A successful journey

17. What does it mean to be "proficient" in a skill?

a) To struggle with a task

b) To be a beginner

c) To be skilled or competent

d) To give up easily

18. What does "enable" mean?

a) To disable or hinder

b) To make possible or provide the means for something

c) To explore

d) To be stranded

19. What is the meaning of "isolation"?

a) A state of companionship

b) A feeling of success

c) Being alone or separated from others

d) A type of adventure

20. How would you define a "curse"?

a) A fortunate event

b) A state of isolation

c) A negative consequence or bad luck

d) A successful outcome

Unit 15: Gulliver's Travels (1726)

"Gulliver's Travels" is a satirical novel written by Jonathan Swift and first published in 1726. The story follows the travels and adventures of Lemuel Gulliver, a ship's surgeon who embarks on four remarkable voyages to different fantastical lands, each with its own unique inhabitants and customs.

In the first voyage, Gulliver finds himself shipwrecked on the island of Lilliput. There, he encounters a race of tiny people no more than six inches tall. Despite their small size, they possess a complex society and engage in petty conflicts and political intrigue. Gulliver becomes embroiled in their internal struggles and eventually helps the Lilliputians in their war against their neighboring island, Blefuscu.

In his second voyage, Gulliver discovers the opposite extreme as he arrives in Brobdingnag. In this land, everything is gigantic, including the inhabitants. Gulliver, now the miniature one, faces numerous challenges and dangers but eventually gains favor with the kindly and wise Brobdingnagian king. Through his observations and conversations, Gulliver criticizes the flaws of humanity, including its vanity, greed, and corruption.

The third voyage takes Gulliver to the flying island of Laputa, a realm inhabited by eccentric intellectuals who are detached from practical matters. Laputans are preoccupied with abstract theories, music, and mathematics while neglecting the everyday needs of their society. Swift satirizes the absurdity of intellectual pursuits without practical application.

In the final voyage, Gulliver reaches the land of the Houyhnhnms, a race of highly rational and intelligent horses. The Houyhnhnms possess a utopian society where reason and virtue prevail. However, Gulliver also encounters the Yahoos, primitive and savage humanoid creatures. Swift uses this encounter to criticize humanity's base instincts, contrasting them with the noble qualities of the Houyhnhnms.

Throughout his travels, Gulliver's experiences challenge his perceptions of humanity, society, and his own identity. He becomes disillusioned with human nature and questions the values and institutions of his own world.

"Gulliver's Travels" is a complex work that combines adventure, satire, and social commentary. It uses the lens of different imaginary lands to criticize and satirize various aspects of society, including politics, human nature, science, and intellectualism. Swift's novel remains a classic and influential piece of literature, known for its wit, imagination, and enduring social criticism.

[Vocabulary]

Satirical 풍자적인 Remarkable 놀라운 Fantastical 환상적인 Inhabitants 주민들 Customs 관습 Shipwrecked 난파한 Encounters 만남 Petty 사소한 Embroiled 엇갈린 Struggles 투쟁 Engage 종사하다 Intrigue 음모 Internal 내부의 Neighboring 인접한 Gigantic 거대한 Miniature 소형의 Numerous 많은 Challenges 도전 Flaws 결점 Humanity 인류 Vanity 허영심 Corruption 부패 Inhabited 사람이 살고 있는 Eccentric 별난 Detached 분리된 Preoccupied 사로잡혀있는 Abstract 추상적인 Swift 신속한 Satirize 풍자적으로 비판하다 Absurdity 터무니없음 Pursuits 추구 Practical 실용적인 Encounter 마주하다 Base 천박한 Instincts 본능 Contrasting 대조적인 Noble 고귀한 Perception 인식 Disillusioned 환멸을 느낀 Institutions 기관들 Commentary 주석 Imaginary 상상의 Politics 정치 Intellectualism 지성주의

[본문 해석] 걸리버 여행기

"걸리버 여행기"는 조나단 스위프트에 의해 쓰여 져 1726년에 처음 출판된 풍자적인 소설입니다. 그 이야기는 각각 독특한 거주민과 관습을 지닌 환상적인 땅으로 네 번의 놀라운 항해를 떠나는 외과 의사 레무엘 걸리버의 여행과 모험을 따릅니다.

첫 번째 항해에서 걸리버는 릴리퍼트 섬에서 난파된 자신을 발견합니다. 그곳에서 그는 키가 6인치가 채 되지 않는 작은 사람들의 종족과 마주칩니다. 그들의 왜소한 크기에도 불구하고, 그들은 복잡한 사회를 소유하고 있으며 사소한 갈등과 정치적 음모에도 관여하고 있습니다. 걸리버는 그들의 내부 투쟁에 휘말리게 되고 결국 그들의 이웃 섬 블레푸스쿠와의 전쟁에서 릴리푸트 사람들을 도웁니다.

그의 두 번째 항해에서 걸리버는 브로브딩내그에 도착하면서 정반대의 극을 발견합니다. 이 땅에서, 주민들을 포함하여 모든 것이 거대합니다. 걸리버는 이제 소인으로 수많은 도전과 위험에 직면하게 되지만 결국 친절하고 현명한 브로브딩내그 왕의 총애를 받습니다. 걸리버는 그의 관찰과 대화를 통해 허영심, 탐욕, 그리고 부패를 포함하여 인간의 결점을 비판합니다.

세 번째 항해는 걸리버를 현실적인 문제에 초연한 괴짜 지식인들이 거주하는 영역인 하늘을 나는 섬 라퓨타로 데려갑니다. 라퓨타 사람들은 추상적인 이론, 음악, 수학에 몰두하면서 그들 사회의 일상적인 필요는 도외시합니다. 스위프트는 현실적인 적용이 없는 지적 추구의 부조리를 풍자합니다.

마지막 항해에서 걸리버는 매우 이성적이고 지적인 말의 종족인 후이넘의 땅에 도착합니다. 후이넘 족은 이성과 미덕이 우세한 유토피아 사회를 소유하고 있습니다. 그러나 걸리버는 또한 원시적이고 야만적인 인간형 생명체인 야후족과 마주칩니다. 스위프트는 이 만남을 인류의 기본 본능을 비판하기 위해 후이넘 족의 고귀한 특성과 대조하여 이용합니다.

그의 여행 내내, 걸리버의 경험은 인류, 사회, 그리고 정체성에 대한 그의 인식에 도전합니다. 그는 인간 본성에 환멸을 느끼게 되고 그 자신의 세계의 가치와 제도에 의문을 제기합니다.

"걸리버 여행기"는 모험, 풍자, 그리고 사회 비평이 결합된 복잡한 작품입니다. 그것은 정치, 인간 본성, 과학, 그리고 지성주의를 포함하여, 사회의 다양한 측면을 비판하고 풍자하기 위해 다른 상상의 땅의 렌즈를 사용합니다. 스위프트의 소설은 재치, 상상력, 그리고 지속되는 사회 비평으로 유명한 고전적이고 영향력 있는 문학 작품으로 남아 있습니다.

[Reading Comprehension]

1. "Gulliver's Travels" is a novel written by:
a) Charles Dickens b) Mark Twain c) Jonathan Swift d) J.K. Rowling

2. How many voyages does Lemuel Gulliver embark on?
a) Three b) Five c) Four d) Six

3. In which land does Gulliver find himself shipwrecked with tiny people?
a) Laputa b) Brobdingnag c) Lilliput d) Houyhnhnms

4. What is the size of the tiny people in Lilliput?
a) Six inches tall b) One foot tall c) One inch tall d) Two feet tall

5. What does Gulliver criticize in humanity during his adventures?
a) Their kindness
b) Their courage
c) Their flaws, including vanity, greed, and corruption
d) Their intelligence

6. Which voyage introduces Gulliver to highly rational and intelligent horses?
a) First voyage b) Second voyage c) Third voyage d) Final voyage

7. The Laputans are primarily interested in:
a) Politics
b) Music and mathematics
c) Literature
d) Sports

8. The race of highly rational and intelligent horses is called:
a) Lilliputians
b) Yahoos
c) Laputans
d) Houyhnhnms

9. Gulliver becomes disillusioned with:
a) The tiny people of Lilliput
b) Human nature
c) The Brobdingnagian king
d) The Houyhnhnms

10. Which aspect does "Gulliver's Travels" criticize and satirize through imaginary lands?

a) Human nature

b) Mathematics

c) The wonders of Brobdingnag

d) The kindness of Houyhnhnms

11. What is the primary genre of "Gulliver's Travels"?

a) Mystery

b) Science fiction

c) Satire

d) Romance

12. Gulliver's occupation is that of a _____.

a) Scientist

b) Ship's surgeon

c) Adventurer

d) King

13. The flying island of Laputa is inhabited by:

a) Giants

b) Intellectuals

c) Animals

d) Robots

14. In which voyage does Gulliver face numerous challenges and dangers due to his miniature size?

a) First voyage

b) Second voyage

c) Third voyage

d) Final voyage

15. What does Swift criticize through Gulliver's encounter with the Yahoos?

a) Humanity's base instincts

b) The intelligence of the Houyhnhnms

c) The beauty of the land of Brobdingnag

d) The vanity of the Lilliputians

[Grammar Check-up]

1. The story follows the travels and adventures of Lemuel Gulliver, a ship's surgeon who embarks (at, on) four remarkable voyages to different fantastical lands, each with its own (unique, uniquely) inhabitants and customs.

2. In the first voyage, Gulliver finds himself (shipwrecked, shipwrecking) on the island of Lilliput.

3. There, he (is encountered, encounters) a race of tiny people no more than six inches tall.

4. (Even though, Despite) their small size, they possess a complex society and engage in petty conflicts and political intrigue.

5. Gulliver becomes (embroiling, embroiled) in their internal struggles and eventually helps the Lilliputians in their war against their neighboring island, Blefuscu.

6. In his second voyage, Gulliver discovers the opposite (extreme, extremely) as he arrives in Brobdingnag.

7. In this land, everything (is, are) gigantic, including the inhabitants.

8. Gulliver, now the miniature one, (faces, facing) numerous challenges and dangers but eventually gains favor with the kindly and wise Brobdingnagian king.

9. (Despite, Through) his observations and conversations, Gulliver criticizes the flaws of humanity, (included, including) its vanity, greed, and corruption.

10. The third voyage takes Gulliver to the flying island of Laputa, a realm (inhabited, inhabiting) by eccentric intellectuals who (detach, are detached) from practical matters.

11. Laputans are (preoccupying, preoccupied) with abstract theories, music, and mathematics while (neglecting, neglect) the everyday needs of their society.

12. Swift satirizes the (absurd, absurdity) of intellectual pursuits without practical application.

13. In the final voyage, Gulliver (reaches, reaches to) the land of the Houyhnhnms, a race of highly rational and intelligent horses.

14. The Houyhnhnms possess (a, an) utopian society (which, where) reason and virtue prevail.

15. However, Gulliver also (is encountered, encounters) the Yahoos, primitive and savage humanoid creatures.

16. Swift uses this encounter to criticize humanity's base instincts, (contrast, contrasting) them with the noble qualities of the Houyhnhnms.

17. (Thought, Throughout) his travels, Gulliver's experiences challenge his perceptions of humanity, society, and his own identity.

18. He (becomes disillusioned, disillusions) with human nature and questions the values and institutions of his own world.

19. "Gulliver's Travels" is a complex work (what, that) combines adventure, satire, and social commentary.

20. It (uses, is used) the lens of different imaginary lands to criticize and satirize various (aspect, aspects) of society, including politics, human nature, science, and intellectualism.

[Writing Practice]

1. The story follows the travels and adventures of Lemuel Gulliver, *a ship's surgeon*
_____ different fantastical lands.
~로 4번의 놀라운 항해를 시작하는 *배의 외과의사* (관계사)

2. In the first voyage, Gulliver _____ on the island of Lilliput.
자신이 난파당했다는 것을 알게 되다 (5형식)

3. There, he encounters a race of tiny people _____.
키가 단지 6인치에 지나지 않는

4. Despite their small size, they _____ petty
conflicts and political intrigue.   복잡한 사회를 갖추고(po~) ~에 종사하고 있다

5. In his second voyage, Gulliver _____ as he arrives
in Brobdingnag.   정반대의 극단을 발견한다

6. Laputans _____, music, and mathematics
추상적인 이론들에 사로잡혀(pre~) 있다
while neglecting the everyday needs of their society.

7. In the final voyage, Gulliver _____ the Houyhnhnms, a race
of highly rational and intelligent horses. ~의 땅에 도착한다(re~)

8. He _____ human nature and questions the values
~에 환멸을 느끼다   and institutions of his own world.

9. "Gulliver's Travels" is *a complex work* _____ *and*
social commentary.   모험, 풍자, 그리고 *사회적 논평을 결합한 복합적인 작품* (관계사)

10. It uses the lens of different imaginary lands _____
_____, including politics, human nature, science, and intellectualism.
사회의 다양한 양상들을 비판하고 풍자화하기 위하여

[Word Quiz]

1. Which word describes something that is characterized by wit, irony, or sarcasm?
a) Intrigue   b) Satirical   c) Encounters   d) Fantastical

2. What term refers to the people living in a particular place or area?
a) Inhabitants   b) Struggles   c) Vanity   d) Corruption

3. What adjective is used to describe something extraordinary or unusual?
a) Petty   b) Intrigue   c) Remarkable   d) Base

4. Which word refers to the traditional practices and behaviors of a particular group or society?
a) Customs   b) Embroiled   c) Swift   d) Contrasting

5. If a ship has been destroyed or damaged in a sea-related accident, it is said to be:
a) Detached   b) Satirical   c) Shipwrecked   d) Shipment

6. What term refers to something of little importance or trivial significance
a) Challenges   b) Petty   c) Intrigue   d) Pursuits

7. Which word refers to something that is situated or occurring within something else?
a) Noble   b) Internal   c) Eccentric   d) Numerous

8. What word involves participation, commitment, or interaction in various contexts?
a) Engage   b) Institutions   c) Commentary   d) Disillusioned

9. Which term refers to both the act of scheming or plotting as well as the effect of something being mysterious or captivating?
a) Vanity   b) Imaginary   c) Encounters   d) Intrigue

10. If something is very large and immense in size, it is described as:
a) Gigantic   b) Miniature   c) Swift   d) Absurdity

11. What word describes a situation where someone is lost in thought or occupied with something else?
a) Detached   b) Abstract   c) Preoccupied   d) Instincts

12. Which term refers to the state of being involved in secret or underhanded plots or schemes?
a) Noble   b) Embroiled   c) Pursuits   d) Intellectualism

13. What adjective describes something that is separated or disconnected from something else?
a) Contrasting   b) Disillusioned   c) Detached   d) Satirical

14. Which word means to criticize or mock someone or something using irony or humor?
a) Encounter   b) Satirize   c) Corruption   d) Vanity

15. Which term is concerned with the actual doing of things rather than with theories and ideas?
a) Swift   b) Imaginary   c) Noble   d) Practical

16. What term refers to the act of meeting or confronting someone or something?
a) Absurdity   b) Encounter   c) Intrigue   d) Perception

17. Which word describes the basic, fundamental, or lowest part of something?
a) Base   b) Humanity   c) Commentary   d) Institutions

18. What adjective means showing marked difference between two things?
a) Noble   b) Contrasting   c) Internal   d) Vanity

19. When someone is _____, they have become disenchanted or disappointed because reality does not match their previous beliefs or hopes.
a) Noble   b) Absurdity   c) Intrigue   d) Disillusioned

20. Which term refers to the governing bodies or organizations within a society?
a) Commentary   b) Imaginary   c) Institutions   d) Intellectualism

1800년대 문학 작품

Unit 16: Faust 파우스트 (1808)

Unit 17: Pride and Prejudice 오만과 편견 (1813)

Unit 18: Frankenstein 프랑켄슈타인 (1818)

Unit 19: Oliver Twist 올리버 트위스트 (1838)

Unit 20: The Count of Monte Cristo 몬테 크리스토 백작 (1844)

Unit 21: Jane Eyre 제인 에어 (1847)

Unit 22: Wuthering Heights 폭풍의 언덕 (1847)

Unit 23: Moby-Dick 모비딕 (1851)

Unit 24: Walden 월든 (1854)

Unit 25: Great Expectations 위대한 유산 (1861)

Unit 26: Crime and Punishment 죄와 벌 (1866)

Unit 27: War and Peace 전쟁과 평화 (1869)

Unit 28: 20,000 Leagues Under the Sea 해저 2만리 (1870)

Unit 29: Anna Karenina 안나 카레니나 (1877)

Unit 30: Treasure Island 보물섬 (1883)

Unit 31: What Men Live By 인간은 무엇으로 사는가? (1885)

Unit 32: The Brothers Karamazov 카라마조프가의 형제들 (1880)

Unit 33: Thus Spoke Zarathustra 차라투스트라는 이렇게 말했다 (1883)

Unit 34: Dr. Jekyll and Mr. Hyde 지킬박사와 하이드 (1886)

Unit 35: Resurrection 부활 (1899)

Unit 16: Faust (1808)

The writing of Johann Wolfgang von Goethe's "Faust" spanned many decades, as Goethe continually revised and expanded upon the work. "Faust" first written in 1772, and the first part was published in 1808 and the second part in 1832. Therefore, the entire process of writing "Faust" took around 60 years.

The play begins with a wager between God and Mephistopheles, a devil. God believes that Faust can be saved from his despair by saying, "My servant, he!"

and "A good man has still an instinct of the one true way through obscurest aspiration" while Mephistopheles is confident he can lead Faust astray saying "Gently upon my road to train him!"

Faust, a disillusioned scholar, contemplates suicide due to his dissatisfaction with life's limitations. He desires to experience true fulfillment and understanding of the world. He makes a pact with Mephistopheles, agreeing to sell his soul to the devil in exchange for unlimited knowledge and boundless pleasure. Faust says that Mephistopheles can take his soul when he says "thou art so fair" towards the moment. With the pact, Mephistopheles becomes Faust's guide and companion.

Mephistopheles takes Faust on a journey that rejuvenates him. Faust becomes infatuated with Gretchen, a young and innocent woman. Mephistopheles helps Faust seduce Gretchen, leading to a passionate but ultimately tragic love affair. Faust's influence indirectly leads to Gretchen's mother's death. He also impregnates Gretchen, and she gives birth to a child out of wedlock. The child dies, and Gretchen is socially rejected, spiraling into a state of despair and isolation. At last, she is imprisoned due to these incidents, waiting for being executed.

As Gretchen's situation worsens, Faust is wracked with guilt and remorse. He attempts to save her by helping her escape from prison, but she rejects Faust's proposal and tries to find salvation through her faith in God.

Part Two opens with Faust's yearning for new experiences and ambitions. He strives to shape the world around him through wealth, power, and the mastery of nature. Faust becomes involved in political and economic affairs, collaborating with rulers and leaders to advance his vision. He aims to achieve a utopian society, blending science, technology, and culture.

Faust embarks on a journey to a classical realm, where he seeks to enhance his understanding of beauty, culture, and art. He encounters figures like Helen of Troy and experiences unfulfilled desires.

Faust's insatiable ambition leads him to strive for god-like power. He attempts to harness the forces of nature to create a utopia. However, his plans lead to destruction and chaos.

Gretchen, who has found salvation through her faith, reunites with Faust in a vision. She embodies divine forgiveness and redemption, symbolizing spiritual renewal. As Faust's life draws to a close, he reflects on his actions and desires for deeper understanding. His striving spirit yearns for the infinite, and in his final moments, he achieves salvation through God's grace.

"Faust" is a profound exploration of human aspirations, the pursuit of knowledge, the consequences of unchecked ambition, and the interplay between good and evil. It blends elements of tragedy, philosophy, spirituality, and social commentary, offering a multi-layered narrative that has inspired countless interpretations and discussions over the centuries.

[본문 해석] 파우스트

요한 볼프강 폰 괴테의 "파우스트"의 집필은 괴테가 작품을 계속해서 수정하고 확장하면서 수십 년에 걸쳐 이루어졌습니다. "파우스트"는 1772년에 처음 쓰여 졌고, 1부는 1808년에, 2부는 1832년에 출판되었습니다. 따라서, "파우스트"를 쓰는 전체 과정은 약 60년이 걸렸습니다.

"파우스트"는 신과 악마 메피스토펠레스 사이의 내기로 시작됩니다. 신은 "파우스트가 자신의 종"이고 "선한 인간은 어두운 충동 속에서도 올바를 길을 잘 알고 있다"고 말합니다, 반면 메피스토펠레스는 "그 자를 나의 길로 슬쩍 이끌고 가리다"라고 말하며 그가 파우스트를 올바른 길에서 벗어나게 할 수 있다고 확신합니다.

망상에서 깨어난 학자 파우스트는 삶의 한계에 대해 불만을 느끼며 자살을 생각합니다. 그는 진정한 성취감과 세상에 대한 이해를 경험하기를 갈망합니다. 그는 메피스토펠레스와 계약을 하여, 무한한 지식과 즐거움을 대가로 자신의 영혼을 악마에게 팔기로 합의합니다. 파우스트는 자신이 순간을 향해 "너 참 아름답구나!"라고 말할 때 그의 영혼을 가져가도 좋다고 말합니다. 이 계약으로 메피스토펠레스는 파우스트의 안내자이자 동반자가 됩니다.

메피스토펠레스는 파우스트가 다시 활력을 되찾게 하는 여행으로 데려갑니다. 파우스트는 젊고 순진한 여자 그레첸에게 푹 빠지게 됩니다. 메피스토펠레스는 파우스트가 그레첸을 유혹하는 것을 도와 그가 열정적이지만 궁극적으로는 비극적인 연애를 하게 만듭니다. 파우스트의 영향은 간접적으로 그레첸의 어머니의 죽음을 초래합니다. 그는 또한 그레첸이 임신을 하게 만들고, 그녀는 결혼을 하지 않은 상태에서 아이를 낳게 됩니다. 아이가 죽고 자신이 사회적으로 거부당하자 그녀는 절망과 고립의 상태로 빠져듭니다. 결국 그녀는 이러한 사건들로 인해 감옥에 갇히게 됩니다.

그레첸의 상황이 악화되면서 파우스트는 죄책감과 양심의 가책에 휩싸이게 되고, 그는 그녀를 감옥에서 탈출시켜 구하려 하지만 그녀는 파우스트의 제안을 거절하고 하느님에 대한 믿음을 통해 구원을 찾고자 합니다.

2부는 파우스트의 새로운 경험과 야망으로 시작됩니다. 그는 부와 권력, 자연의 지배를 통해 그를 둘러싼 세계를 형성하려고 노력합니다. 파우스트는 정치와 경제 문제에 관여하게 되고, 통치자와 지도자들과 협력하여 그의 비전을 발전시킵니다. 그는 과학, 기술, 문화를 융합한 유토피아 사회를 이루는 것을 목표로 합니다.

파우스트는 아름다움, 문화, 예술에 대한 그의 이해를 증진시키기 위해 고전적인 세계로의 여행을 시작합니다. 그는 트로이의 헬렌과 같은 인물들을 만나고 이루지 못한 욕망을 경험합니다. 그의 끝없는 야망은 그로 하여금 신과 같은 힘을 얻기 위해 노력하게 하고, 그는 자연의 힘을 이용하여 유토피아를 창조하려 하지만, 그의 계획은 파멸과 혼란을 초래합니다.

그녀의 믿음을 통해 구원을 찾은 그레첸은 파우스트와 환영 속에서 재회합니다. 그녀는 신적인 용서와 구원을 구현하며 영적인 부활을 상징합니다. 파우스트의 삶이 끝나갈 무렵, 그는 자신의 행동과 더욱 깊은 이해를 위한 욕망에 대해 되새겨 봅니다. 그의 분투하는 정신은 무한을 갈망하고, 마지막 순간에 하나님의 은혜를 통해 구원을 얻습니다.

"파우스트"는 인간의 열망, 지식의 추구, 억제되지 않은 야망의 결과, 선과 악의 상호작용에 대한 심오한 탐구입니다. 그것은 비극, 철학, 영성, 그리고 사회 비평의 요소들을 융합하여, 수세기에 걸쳐 수많은 해석과 토론에 영감을 준 다층적인 이야기를 제공합니다.

[Vocabulary]

Span (시간이) ~에 걸치다 Revised 개정된 Expanded 확장된 Posthumously 사후에 Despair 절망 Instinct 본능 Obscure 불명확한 Aspiration 열망 Astray 길을 잃어 Disillusioned 망상에서 벗어난 Dissatisfaction 불만 Fulfillment 충족감 Boundless 무한한 Pact 계약 Infatuated 반한/열중한 Seduce 유혹하다 Passionate 열정적인 Influence 영향 Indirectly 간접적으로 Impregnate 임신시키다 Out of wedlock 혼외의 Socially rejected 사회적 배척을 받은 Isolation 고립 Execute 처형하다 Remorse 양심의 가책 Proposal 제안 Utopian 이상적인 Embark on 착수하다 Unfulfilled 미흡한 Insatiable 만족할 줄 모르는 Consequence 결과 Unchecked 억제되지 않은 Pursuit 추구 Ambition 야망 Interplay 상호 작용 Philosophy 철학 Multi-layered 다층의

[Reading Comprehension]

1. How long did it take Johann Wolfgang von Goethe to write "Faust"?
A) 10 years   B) 20 years   C) 30 years   D) 60 years

2. What is the subject of the wager at the beginning of the play?
A) A race between God and Mephistopheles
B) A bet on the outcome of a war
C) Faust's ability to seduce Gretchen
D) Faust's potential salvation or damnation

3. What is Faust's main motivation for making a pact with Mephistopheles?
A) Unlimited wealth
B) Boundless pleasure
C) True fulfillment and understanding
D) Revenge against his enemies

4. What phrase does Faust utter that allows Mephistopheles to take his soul?
A) "I am yours"
B) "Thou art so fair"
C) "I surrender"
D) "Guide me, devil"

5. What is the consequence of Faust's influence on Gretchen's life?
A) She becomes a queen
B) Her child is born healthy
C) Her mother dies
D) She gains unlimited knowledge

6. What leads to Gretchen's imprisonment?
A) Her involvement in politics
B) Her rejection of Faust's proposal
C) Her social rejection and incidents in her life
D) Her attempts to seduce Faust

7. How does Gretchen seek salvation in Part Two?
A) Through her relationship with Faust
B) Through her wealth and power
C) Through her faith in God
D) Through her pursuit of knowledge

8. What is Faust's goal in Part Two of the play?
A) To become a famous artist   B) To achieve a utopian society
C) To become a powerful ruler   D) To find true love

9. What happens as a result of Faust's attempts to harness the forces of nature?
A) He achieves god-like power   B) He creates a utopian society
C) Destruction and chaos ensue   D) He gains unlimited knowledge

10. How does Gretchen symbolize spiritual renewal in the play?
A) Through her pursuit of wealth
B) Through her tragic love affair
C) Through her interactions with Mephistopheles
D) Through her faith and forgiveness

11. What themes does "Faust" explore according to the passages?
A) The history of classical literature
B) The consequences of unchecked ambition
C) The pursuit of unlimited pleasure
D) The rivalry between God and the devil

12. What elements does "Faust" blend according to the passages?
A) Tragedy, science, and politics
B) Philosophy, spirituality, and comedy
C) Art, culture, and adventure
D) Tragedy, philosophy, spirituality, and social commentary

13. What is the central character's profession?
A) Scientist B) Scholar C) Warrior D) Artist

14. What does Faust ultimately achieve in his final moments?
A) Wealth and power
B) Salvation through God's grace
C) Victory over Mephistopheles
D) Knowledge of the universe's secrets

15. What is the primary focus of Faust's ambition in Part Two?
A) Pursuit of knowledge
B) Pursuit of love
C) Creation of a utopian society
D) Defeating Mephistopheles

[Grammar Check-up]

1. "Faust" is a tragic play written by Johann Wolfgang von Goethe, (was published, published) in two parts in 1808 and 1832.

2. It tells the story of a scholar named Heinrich Faust who, (is dissatisfied, dissatisfied) with his life and thirsting for knowledge, makes a pact with the devil

3. In the beginning, Faust (disillusions, is disillusioned) with his studies and yearns for a deeper understanding of life's meaning and pleasures.

4. He strikes a deal with Mephistopheles, (offering, offered) his soul in exchange for unlimited knowledge and worldly experiences.

5. Mephistopheles becomes Faust's companion and guide, (tempts, tempting) him with various indulgences and adventures.

6. Faust's journey (divides, is divided) into several significant episodes.

7. In the first part, Faust (engaging, engages) in a romantic relationship with Gretchen (Margarete), a young woman of innocence and virtue.

8. However, their relationship becomes tragic as Faust's desires and Mephistopheles' influence (lead, leading) to Gretchen's downfall.

9. She gives birth to Faust's child out of wedlock, (where, which) results in the death of the child and her (subsequent, subsequently) spiral into despair and madness.

10. In the second part, Faust embarks (for, on) a series of ambitious ventures.

11. He becomes (involving, involved) in politics, (seeks, seeking) to reshape the world and achieve power and wealth.

12. With Mephistopheles' (assist, assistance), Faust engages in grand projects such as land reclamation, building cities, and (amassing, amass) vast wealth.

13. However, these (endeavor, endeavors) ultimately (leads, lead) to ecological destruction and societal decay.

14. Throughout the play, Faust is (constantly, constant) torn between his longing for spiritual fulfillment and his pursuit of earthly desires.

15. He experiences moments of (deep, deeply) introspection and wrestles with the consequences of his actions.

16. In the (finally, final) scenes, Faust seeks redemption and spiritual salvation through (selflessness, selfless) acts and a yearning for transcendence.

17. His striving and search for meaning (rewarded, are rewarded), and he finds eternal rest and fulfillment.

18. It delves into the complexities of human desires, the consequences of (unchecking, unchecked) ambition, and the possibility of spiritual transformation.

19. Goethe's epic work (is remained, remains) a seminal piece of German literature, showcasing the timeless struggle of the human condition.

[Writing Practice]

1. It tells the story of a scholar named Heinrich *Faust* _____,
_____ makes a pact with the devil.
그의 삶에 실망하고 지식을 갈망하는 *파우스트* (관계사)

2. In the beginning, *Faust* _____ his studies and yearns for a
deeper understanding of life.   *파우스트는 ~에 환멸을 느낀다*

3. He strikes a deal with Mephistopheles, _____ unlimited
knowledge and worldly experiences.   ~를 얻는 대가로 그의 영혼을 제공한다 (분사구)

4. Mephistopheles becomes Faust's companion and guide, _____
various indulgences and adventures.   그가 ~하도록 유혹한다 (분사구)

5. Faust's journey _____ episodes.
           몇몇 중요한 사건들로 나눠진다.

6. In the first part, Faust _____ Gretchen.
            ~와 낭만적인 관계를 시작한다(en~)

7. However, their relationship _____ *Faust's desires and
Mephistopheles' influence lead to Gretchen's downfall.* ~함에 따라 비극적이 된다.

8. She _____ out of wedlock, _____ the death of
           파우스트의 아이를 낳는다   그리고 그것은 ~를 초래한다 (관계사)
the child and her subsequent spiral into despair and madness.

9. In the second part, Faust _____.
             일련의 야심찬 모험을 시작한다(em~)

10. He _____ politics, seeking to reshape the world and
        ~에 관여하게 된다   achieve power and wealth.

11. With Mephistopheles' assistance, Faust _____ *land reclamation,
building cities, and amassing vast wealth.* ~와 같은 큰 프로젝트를 착수한다(en~)

12. However, _____ ecological destruction and
societal decay.   이러한 노력들은 궁극적으로 ~를 초래한다

[Word Quiz]

1. What does the word "Span" mean?
A) To measure length   B) A type of footwear
C) To cross a river   D) To extend across a period of time

2. Which word means "to review and make changes"?
A) Revise B) Expand C) Obscure D) Instinct

3. Which term describes something "occurring after the death of the author"?
A) Posthumous B) Aspiration C) Execute D) Influence

4. What is the synonym of "Hopelessness"?
A) Obscure B) Despair C) Boundless D) Fulfillment

5. What is an "innate tendency or impulse" known as?
A) Obscure B) Pact C) Instinct D) Execute

6. What does "Astray" mean?
A) Boundless B) Execute C) Lost or off the right path D) Fulfillment

7. Which term means "not clearly understood or expressed"?
A) Execute B) Obscure C) Posthumously D) Passionate

8. What is a strong desire for achievement known as?
A) Pact B) Influence C) Aspiration D) Embark on

9. What term describes the ability of someone or something to impact?
A) Execute B) Influence C) Expanded D) Passionate

10. What does "Impregnate" mean?
A) To inspire B) To make pregnant C) To execute D) To fulfill

11. What does "Out of wedlock" mean?
A) A type of lock   B) During a wedding
C) Without being married D) Outside of a castle

12. What does "Socially rejected" mean?
A) Embraced by society   B) Isolated from society
C) Accepted by society   D) Cast out by society

13. What does "Isolation" mean?

A) The act of joining a group   B) Being alone and separated

C) The pursuit of knowledge   D) The result of a pact

14. What is the synonym of "Carry out"?

A) Execute B) Remorse C) Dissatisfaction D) Interplay

15. What is a feeling of regret or guilt known as?

A) Proposal B) Execute C) Remorse D) Aspiration

16. What is a formal suggestion or plan known as?

A) Ambition B) Execute C) Proposal D) Influence

17. What does "Utopian" mean?

A) Imaginative or visionary, usually describing an ideal society

B) Cynical or pessimistic

C) Pragmatic and realistic

D) Full of despair

18. Which term means "to start or engage in"?

A) Execute B) Embark on C) Influence D) Pursuit

19. What is the antonym of "Fulfilled"?

A) Unchecked B) Aspiration C) Unfulfilled D) Expanded

20. What does "Consequence" mean?

A) A decision

B) A pact

C) The outcome or result of an action

D) An aspiration

Unit 17: Pride and Prejudice (1813)

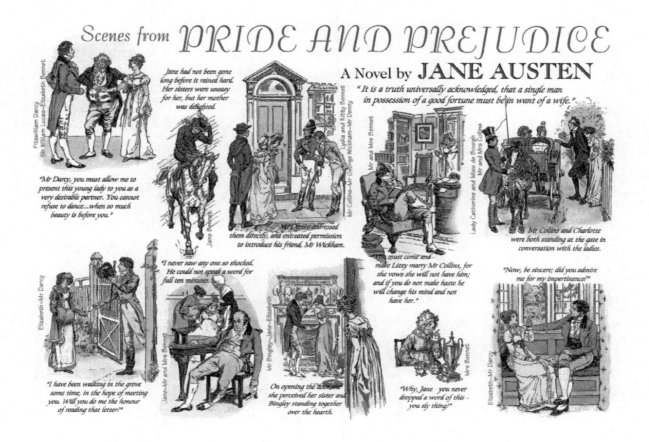

"Pride and Prejudice" is a novel written by Jane Austen and published in 1813. It is a classic work of English literature that explores themes of love, marriage, social class, and the impact of first impressions.

The story is set in rural England during the early 19th century and follows the lives of the Bennet family. The protagonist is Elizabeth Bennet, a witty and independent-minded young woman, who is one of five sisters. The Bennets are of modest means and their mother is determined to marry them off to wealthy suitors.

The narrative begins with the arrival of a wealthy and eligible bachelor named Charles Bingley in the neighboring estate of Netherfield. Bingley is well-received by the Bennet family and sparks the interest of Mrs. Bennet, who hopes that one of her daughters will win his affections. Bingley's friend, Fitzwilliam Darcy, a wealthy and proud man, accompanies him and quickly earns a bad reputation for his haughty demeanor.

The central focus of the novel revolves around the complicated relationship between Elizabeth Bennet and Fitzwilliam Darcy. Initially, their pride and prejudice lead them to form negative opinions of each other. However, as the story progresses, their feelings undergo a transformation as they come to know and understand each other better.

Alongside the central romance, Austen weaves a tapestry of social commentary, depicting the lives and aspirations of the various characters in the novel. She satirizes the conventions and social expectations of the time, exposing the hypocrisy and superficiality of certain characters.

"Pride and Prejudice" is renowned for its sharp wit, engaging dialogue, and memorable characters. It explores the complexities of love and the importance of seeing beyond first impressions and societal expectations. Austen skillfully crafts a world that examines the limitations imposed on women, the role of class in society, and the pursuit of personal happiness.

The novel is a timeless exploration of human relationships, social dynamics, and the power of self-reflection and growth. It has remained popular for centuries and continues to be celebrated as one of the greatest works of English literature.

[Vocabulary]

pride 오만, 자부심 prejudice 선입견 impact 영향 impressions 첫인상 rural 시골의 protagonist 주인공 independent-minded 독립적인 마음을 가진 determined 결심한 eligible 유능한 bachelor 독신 남성 neighboring 이웃하는 well-received 호의적으로 받아들여진 spark 자극하다 affections 애정 haughty 거만한 central 중심적인 transformation 변화 undergo 겪다 narrative 서술 tapestry 벽걸이 융단 commentary 주석 depict 묘사하다 aspirations 염원 satirize 풍자하다 conventions 관습 renowned 유명한 engaging 매력적인 explore 탐구하다 complexities 복잡성 limitations 제약 social dynamics 사회적 역동성 pursuit 추구 celebrated 기념되고 있는

[본문 해석] 오만과 편견

"오만과 편견"은 제인 오스틴이 쓴 소설로, 1813년에 출판되었습니다. 이 책은 사랑, 결혼, 사회 계급, 그리고 첫인상의 영향력과 같은 주제를 탐구하는 영어 문학의 고전작품입니다.

이 이야기는 19세기 초 영국 시골에서 베넷 가족의 삶을 따라가고 있습니다. 주인공은 엘리자베스 베넷으로, 똑똑하고 독립적인 성격의 젊은 여성이며, 총 5명의 자매 중 한 명입니다. 베넷 가족은 소득이 낮아서, 그녀의 어머니는 딸들을 부유한 남자들과 결혼시키기로 결심합니다.

이야기는 네더필드의 이웃 사유지에 부유하고 결혼상대로 바람직한 찰스 빙글리라는 총각이 도착하면서 시작됩니다. 빙글리는 베넷 가족에게 좋은 평가를 받으며 딸 중 한 명이 그의 사랑을 얻기를 바라는 베넷 부인의 흥미를 유발합니다. 빙글리의 친구인 부유하고 자랑스러운 남자 피츠윌리엄 다아시가 그와 동행하고 그는 거만한 태도로 인해 재빠르게 나쁜 평판을 얻습니다.

소설의 중심은 엘리자베스 베넷과 피츠윌리엄 다아시의 복잡한 관계를 중심으로 전개됩니다. 처음에 그들의 자부심과 편견은 그들이 서로에 대한 부정적인 의견을 형성하게 합니다. 그러나 이야기가 진행됨에 따라 그들의 감정은 서로를 더 잘 알고 이해하게 되면서 변화를 겪게 됩니다.

중심 로맨스와 함께 오스틴은 소설에 등장하는 다양한 인물들의 삶과 열망을 묘사하는 사회적 논평이라는 태피스트리를 짜 넣습니다. 그녀는 특정 인물들의 위선과 천박성을 노출시키며 당시의 관습과 사회적 기대를 풍자합니다.

"오만과 편견"은 날카로운 재치, 매력적인 대화 및 기억에 남는 등장인물들로 유명합니다. 그것은 사랑의 복잡성과 첫 인상과 사회적 기대를 넘어서는 사람을 보는 것에 대한 중요성을 탐구합니다. 오스틴은 여성에게 부과된 한계, 사회에서 계급의 역할 및 개인적 행복 추구에 대해 고찰하는 세계를 능숙하게 만듭니다.

그 소설은 인간관계, 사회적 역학, 그리고 자기 성찰과 성장의 힘에 대한 시대를 초월한 탐구입니다. 그것은 수세기 동안 인기를 유지해왔고 영문학의 가장 위대한 작품 중 하나로 계속해서 기념되고 있습니다.

[Reading Comprehension]

1. What is the title of the novel written by Jane Austen and published in 1813?
a) Sense and Sensibility
b) Emma
c) Pride and Prejudice
d) Mansfield Park

2. In "Pride and Prejudice," the story is set in which location?
a) Urban London
b) Rural England
c) Paris, France
d) New York City, USA

3. Who is the protagonist of the novel?
a) Charles Bingley
b) Fitzwilliam Darcy
c) Mrs. Bennet
d) Elizabeth Bennet

4. What reputation does Fitzwilliam Darcy earn upon his arrival?
a) Friendly and welcoming
b) Modest and humble
c) Haughty and proud
d) Reserved and shy

5. Initially, what leads Elizabeth Bennet and Fitzwilliam Darcy to form negative opinions of each other?
a) Love and attraction
b) Pride and prejudice
c) Social status
d) Family expectations

6. Besides the central romance, what else does Jane Austen depict in the novel?
a) Political intrigue
b) Social commentary
c) Science fiction elements
d) Mystery and suspense

7. What is "Pride and Prejudice" renowned for?

a) Its tragic ending

b) Its witty humor

c) Its action-packed plot

d) Its fantasy elements

8. According to the passage, what does Austen skillfully craft in the novel?

a) A world of magic and sorcery

b) A tapestry of social commentary

c) A science fiction universe

d) A dystopian society

9. What themes does "Pride and Prejudice" explore?

a) Love and social class

b) Marriage and personal happiness

c) Impact of first impressions and societal expectations

d) All of the above

10. How has "Pride and Prejudice" been received over the years?

a) It has been criticized for its lack of depth.

b) It has remained popular and celebrated as a great work of English literature.

c) It has been largely forgotten and ignored.

d) It has been adapted into a successful movie franchise.

[Grammar Check-up]

1. "Pride and Prejudice" is a classic work of English literature (what, that) explores themes of love, marriage, social class, and the impact of first impressions.
2. The story is set in rural England during the early 19th century and (follows, following) the lives of the Bennet family.
3. The protagonist is Elizabeth Bennet, a witty and independent-minded young woman, who (are, is) one of five sisters.
4. The Bennets are of modest means and their mother (determines, is determined) to marry them off to wealthy suitors.
5. The narrative begins with the (arriving, arrival) of a wealthy and eligible bachelor named Charles Bingley in the neighboring estate of Netherfield.
6. Bingley is (well-received, well-receiving) by the Bennet family and sparks the interest of Mrs. Bennet, who hopes that one of her daughters will win his affections.
7. Bingley's friend, Fitzwilliam Darcy, a wealthy and proud man, (is accompanied, accompanies) him and quickly earns a reputation for his haughty demeanor.
8. The central focus of the novel revolves around the (complicated, complicating) relationship between Elizabeth Bennet and Fitzwilliam Darcy.
9. (Initial, Initially), their pride and prejudice lead them (form, to form) negative opinions of each other.
10. However, as the story progresses, their feelings (is undergone, undergo) a transformation as they come to know and understand each other better.
11. Alongside the central romance, Austen weaves a tapestry of social commentary, (depicting, depicts) the lives and aspirations of the various characters in the novel.
12. She (is satirized, satirizes) the conventions and social expectations of the time, exposing the hypocrisy and superficiality of certain characters.
13. "Pride and Prejudice" is renowned for (their, its) sharp wit, engaging dialogue, and memorable characters.
14. It explores the complexities of love and the importance of (being seen, seeing) beyond first impressions and societal expectations.
15. Austen (skillfully, skillful) crafts a world that examines the limitations (imposed, imposing) on women, the role of class in society, and the pursuit of personal happiness.
16. The novel is a (timeless, timelessly) exploration of human relationships, social dynamics, and the power of self-reflection and growth.
17. It (is remained, has remained) popular for centuries and continues to be celebrated as one of the greatest (work, works) of English literature.

[Writing Practice]

1. The protagonist is Elizabeth Bennet, a witty and independent-minded young woman, _____. 그리고 그녀는 다섯 자매 중 한명이다 (관계사)

2. The Bennets are of modest means and their mother _____
wealthy suitors.   그들을 ~와 결혼시키기로 결심한다(det~)

3. The narrative _____a wealthy and eligible bachelor
named Charles Bingley. ~의 도착과 함께 시작한다

4. Bingley is well-received by the Bennet family and sparks the interest of Mrs.
Bennet, who *hopes that* _____.
              그녀의 딸 중 한명이 그의 애정을 얻기를 *바란다*

5. The central focus of the novel _____ *Elizabeth
Bennet and Fitzwilliam Darcy.*   *~간의* 복잡한 관계를 중심으로 일어난다 (rev~)

6. Initially, their pride and prejudice _____
              서로에 대한 부정적인 견해를 형성하도록 그들을 이끈다

7. Their feelings undergo a transformation _____.
              그들이 서로를 더 잘 알게 되고 이해하게 됨에 따라

8. Alongside the central romance, Austen weaves a tapestry of social commentary,
_____ in the novel.
다양한 인물들의 삶과 열망(as~)을 묘사하는 (분사구)

9. "Pride and Prejudice" _____, engaging dialogue,
and memorable characters.   그것의 날카로운 위트로 유명하다

10. Austen skillfully crafts a world that examines _____, the
role of class in society, and the pursuit of personal happiness. 여성에게 부과된 제한들

[Word Quiz]

1. What word refers to a feeling of deep pleasure and satisfaction in one's achievements or qualities?
a) Prejudice b) Determined c) Pride d) Impact

2. What term is used to describe preconceived opinions that are not based on reason or actual experience?
a) Rural b) Impression c) Prejudice d) Spark

3. Which word indicates a powerful or major influence or effect on something or someone?
a) Eligible b) Impact c) Affections d) Central

4. What term refer to an idea, belief, or opinion formed about someone or something?
a) Impression b) Transformation c) Determination d) Protagonist

5. Which term refers to something related to the countryside or areas located away from cities and towns?
a) Pursuit b) Rural c) Haughty d) Narrative

6. Who is the main character or leading figure in a literary work like a novel or play?
a) Aspirations b) Protagonist c) Commentary d) Engaging

7. What adjective describes someone who thinks and acts in a self-reliant manner?
a) Engaging b) Independent-minded c) Celebrated d) Renowned

8. What adjective means showing firmness and a strong sense of purpose or resolve?
a) Determined b) Central c) Prejudice d) Limitations

9. Which word describes someone who is considered suitable for marriage or partnership?
a) Transformations b) Bachelor c) Rural d) Well-received

10. What term refers to the person living next door to or near another person?
a) Neighbor b) Pursuit c) Tapestry d) Impact

11. What word refer to going through a process, situation, or change?
a) Impact b) Narrate c) Undergo d) Haughty

12. What is a spoken or written account of connected events, experiences, or stories?
a) Tapestry b) Narrative c) Engaging d) Explore

13. What word refers to a complex or intricate pattern or structure, often used metaphorically?
a) Commentary b) Depict c) Tapestry d) Aspirations

14. Which word means to describe or represent someone or something through artistic expression?
a) Transformations b) Depict c) Conventions d) Satirize

15. What does "renowned" mean?
a) Social dynamics b) Pursuit c) Celebrated d) Determined

16. What adjective describes something that is attractive, interesting, and capable of holding attention?
a) Engaging b) Impacted c) Underwent d) Eligible

17. What word means to examine or investigate something thoroughly and in detail?
a) Engaging b) Explore c) Limitations d) Spark

18. What does "complexities" refer to?
a) The impact of first impressions
b) The rural setting of the story
c) Complicated and intricate aspects or factors
d) The protagonist's aspirations

19. What term signifies the restrictions on someone or something?
a) Pursuit b) Prejudice c) Limitations d) Central

20. What term describes the interactions and behaviors of individuals within a social group or society?
a) Social dynamics b) Haughty c) Transformations d) Commentary

Unit 18: Frankenstein (1818)

"Frankenstein" is a novel written by Mary Shelley and first published in 1818. The story follows the journey of Victor Frankenstein, a young Swiss scientist who becomes obsessed with the idea of creating life. Here's a detailed plot summary:

The novel opens with a series of letters from Robert Walton, an explorer, to his sister, Margaret. Walton is on a voyage to the North Pole and comes across Victor Frankenstein, who is stranded and in poor health. Victor agrees to share his story with Walton as a warning.

Victor Frankenstein is born to a loving family in Geneva, Switzerland. He grows up with a strong interest in science and alchemy. After witnessing a lightning strike that destroys a tree, Victor becomes fascinated with the idea of harnessing the power of electricity to create life.

As a university student, Victor becomes obsessed with his experiment of creating life. He spends years studying and experimenting in secret. Finally, he succeeds in bringing a creature to life, but he is horrified by its appearance and abandons it.

The creature, abandoned and alone, wanders the countryside, seeking companionship and acceptance. However, he is rejected and shunned by society due to his monstrous appearance. This rejection fills the creature with anger and bitterness toward his creator, whom he refers to as his "Frankenstein."

The creature eventually confronts Victor and demands that he create a companion for him, so he won't be alone. Victor initially agrees but later changes his mind, fearing that the two creatures could cause untold harm to humanity.

The creature, feeling rejected once again, seeks revenge against Victor. He murders several of Victor's loved ones, including his younger brother, best friend, and eventually his newlywed wife, Elizabeth. Victor vows to hunt down the creature and destroy him.

Victor follows the creature to the Arctic, where he encounters Walton. The two men form a bond over their mutual isolation and pursuit of knowledge. Despite Victor's pleas to destroy the creature, Walton is determined to continue his exploration. Weakened by his pursuit and loss, Victor succumbs to illness and dies on Walton's ship. Before his death, he warns Walton of the dangers of unrestrained ambition and obsession. After Victor's death, the creature appears on the ship and laments the death of his creator. He expresses regret for his actions and vows to end his own life by immolating himself on a funeral pyre.

The novel concludes with Walton returning to England. He reflects on Victor's tragic tale and the consequences of unchecked ambition. He decides to abandon his quest for the North Pole and return home, understanding the importance of family and human connection.

"Frankenstein" is a cautionary tale that explores themes of ambition, responsibility, the consequences of playing God, and the importance of compassion and empathy.

[Vocabulary]

explorer 탐험가 voyage 항해 stranded 고립된 cautionary 경고적인 consequence 결과 responsibility 책임 obsession 집착 fascination 매혹 harness 이용하다 electricity 전기 companionship 교제 abandonment 버림 rejection 거부 monstrous 괴물 같은 vengeance 복수 regret 후회 pursuit 추구 destruction 파괴 tragedy 비극 immortal 불멸의 exploration 탐사 caution 주의 electrical 전기의 experiment 실험 ambition 야망 phenomenon 현상 transformation 변화 essence 본질 philosophy 철학 creature 생물 humanity 인류 isolation 고립 melancholy 우울함 determination 결단 vulnerability 취약성 mortality 죽어야 할 운명 empathy 감정이입/공감 iconic 상징적인 immolate 희생으로 바치다

[본문 해석] 프랑켄슈타인

"프랑켄슈타인"은 메리 셸리가 쓴 소설로, 1818년에 첫 출판되었습니다. 이 이야기는 젊은 스위스 과학자인 빅토르 프랑켄슈타인의 여정을 따라갑니다. 빅토르는 생명을 창조하려는 생각에 사로잡히게 됩니다. 다음은 자세한 줄거리 요약입니다:

소설은 탐험가 로버트 월튼이 자신의 여동생 마가렛에게 보내는 일련의 편지로 시작합니다. 월튼은 북극 지역으로 항해 중에 몸이 꽁꽁 얼고 건강이 악화된 빅토르 프랑켄슈타인을 만나게 됩니다. 빅토르는 월튼에게 자신의 이야기를 경고 차원에서 공유하기로 합니다.

빅토르 프랑켄슈타인은 스위스 제네바에서 사랑스러운 가정에서 태어났습니다. 그는 과학과 연금술에 강한 흥미를 느끼며 성장합니다. 나무를 파괴하는 번개를 목격한 후 빅토르는 전기의 힘을 이용하여 생명을 창조하려는 아이디어에 매혹되게 됩니다.

대학생으로서, 빅토르는 생명을 창조하는 실험에 사로잡힙니다. 그는 여러 해 동안 비밀리에 공부하고 실험하는 시간을 보냅니다. 마침내 살아있는 생명체를 만들어내지만, 그 외모에 경악하고 이를 버리게 됩니다.

버림받고 홀로 남은 그 생명체는 교우 관계와 받아 줄 곳을 찾아 시골을 떠돌게 됩니다. 하지만, 그는 괴물 같은 외모 때문에 사회로부터 거부당하고 외면당합니다. 이러한 거부는 그가 "프랑켄슈타인"이라고 부르는 그의 창조자에 대한 분노와 씁쓸함으로 그 생명체의 마음을 가득 채웁니다.

그 생명체는 결국 빅토르에게 맞서 그가 혼자가 되지 않도록 그를 위해 동반자를 만들 것을 요구합니다. 빅토르는 처음에 동의했지만 나중에 그 두 생명체가 인류에게 말할 수 없는 해를 끼칠 수 있다고 두려워 마음을 바꿉니다.

그 생명체는 다시 한 번 거부당한 기분으로 빅토르에게 복수하려고 합니다. 그는 그의 남동생, 가장 친한 친구, 그리고 결국 그의 신혼 아내 엘리자베스를 포함하여 빅토르의 사랑하는 사람들 중 몇 명을 살해합니다. 빅토르는 그 생명체를 잡아 파괴할 것을 맹세합니다.

빅토르는 그 생물체를 따라 북극으로 가서 월튼과 마주칩니다. 그 두 남자는 그들의 상호 고립과 지식의 추구에 대해 유대감을 형성합니다. 이 생명체를 파괴해 달라는 빅토르의 간청에도 불구하고, 월튼은 그의 탐험을 계속하기로 결심합니다. 추구와 상실로 약해진 빅토르는 월튼의 배에서 병에 굴복하여 사망합니다. 죽기 전에 그는 월튼에게 억제되지 않은 야망과 집착의 위험성을 경고합니다. 빅토르가 죽은 후, 그 생명체는 배에 나타나 자신을 만든 이의 죽음을 애도합니다. 그는 자신의 행동에 대해 유감을 표하고 장작더미에 자신을 불태움으로써 자신의 삶을 끝내겠다고 맹세합니다.

소설은 월튼이 영국으로 돌아오는 것으로 마무리됩니다. 그는 빅토르의 비극적인 이야기와 억제되지 않은 야망의 결과에 대해 숙고합니다. 그는 가족과 인간관계의 중요성을 이해하면서 북극에 대한 탐구를 포기하고 집으로 돌아가기로 결정합니다.

"프랑켄슈타인"은 야망, 책임, 신의 역할을 한 결과, 그리고 연민과 공감의 중요성에 대한 주제를 탐구하는 경고적인 이야기입니다.

[Reading Comprehension]

1. What is the title of the novel written by Mary Shelley?
a) The North Pole Voyage   b) Victor Frankenstein
c) Frankenstein   d) The Swiss Scientist

2. Who does Robert Walton write letters to at the beginning of the novel?
a) Victor Frankenstein   b) Margaret
c) The North Pole   d) The Creature

3. Why does Victor Frankenstein become fascinated with electricity?
a) He witnesses a lightning strike that destroys a tree.
b) He sees a documentary about electricity.
c) He experiments with electrical devices in his lab.
d) He learns about electricity in school.

4. What does Victor Frankenstein do after successfully bringing the creature to life?
a) He embraces and loves the creature.
b) He is horrified by its appearance and abandons it.
c) He immediately destroys the creature.
d) He shares the creature's existence with the world.

5. What does the creature demand from Victor Frankenstein?
a) To be left alone in the Arctic
b) To create a companion for him
c) To bring back his loved ones
d) To teach him alchemy

6. What fills the creature with anger and bitterness toward Victor?
a) Victor's success as a scientist
b) The rejection and shunning by society
c) Victor's love and compassion
d) The creature's own actions

7. What is the creature's nickname for Victor Frankenstein?
a) His "Brother" b) His "God" c) His "Monster" d) His "Creator"

8. What does the creature do to seek revenge against Victor?

a) He destroys Victor's lab.

b) He takes over Victor's family estate.

c) He murders several of Victor's loved ones.

d) He challenges Victor to a duel.

9. Where does Victor Frankenstein follow the creature to?

a) England   b) The North Pole   c) Switzerland   d) The Arctic

10. What does Victor warn Robert Walton about before he dies?

a) The dangers of unrestrained ambition and obsession.

b) The beauty of the North Pole.

c) The creature's desire for companionship.

d) The importance of family and human connection.

11. What does the creature express regret for?

a) His own existence

b) His actions and the death of his creator

c) Seeking revenge against Victor

d) Failing to create a companion

12. How does the novel conclude?

a) Victor destroys the creature and returns home.

b) Walton returns to the Arctic to continue his exploration.

c) The creature immolates himself on a funeral pyre.

d) Walton decides to abandon his quest for the North Pole.

13. What themes does "Frankenstein" explore?

a) Ambition, responsibility, and compassion

b) Exploration, science, and technology

c) Love, betrayal, and forgiveness

d) Revenge, vengeance, and friendship

14. Who is often mistakenly called "Frankenstein" in the novel?

a) Victor Frankenstein   b) Robert Walton

c) The creature   d) Margaret, Walton's sister

15. What is the creature's nickname for himself?

a) Monster   b) Victor   c) The Swiss Scientist   d) Frankenstein's Creation

[Grammar Check-up]

1. The story follows the journey of Victor Frankenstein, a young Swiss scientist who becomes (obsessed, obsession) with the idea of creating life.

2. Here's a (detail, detailed) plot summary.

3. Walton is on a voyage to the North Pole and comes across Victor Frankenstein, who is (stranding, stranded) and in poor health.

4. Victor agrees to share his story (within, with) Walton as a warning.

5. He grows up with a strong (interest, interested) in science and alchemy.

6. After witnessing a lightning strike (that, what) destroys a tree, Victor becomes fascinated with the idea of (harness, harnessing) the power of electricity to create life.

7. As (an, a) university student, Victor becomes obsessed (for, with) his experiment of creating life.

8. He spends years (to study, studying) and experimenting in secret.

9. Finally, he succeeds in bringing a creature to life, but he is horrified by its appearance and (abandons, is abandoned) it.

10. The creature, (abandoned, abandoning) and alone, wanders the countryside, seeking companionship and acceptance.

11. However, he (rejects, is rejected) and shunned by society due to his monstrous appearance.

12. This rejection (is filled, fills) the creature with anger and bitterness toward his creator, whom he (refers, is referred) to as his "Frankenstein."

13. The creature eventually confronts Victor and demands that he (creates, create) a companion for him, so he won't be alone.

14. Victor initially agrees but later changes his mind, fearing that the two creatures could cause (untelling, untold) harm to humanity.

15. The creature, (feels, feeling) rejected once again, seeks revenge against Victor.

16. He murders several of Victor's loved ones, including his younger brother, best friend, and eventually his (newlywed, newly wedding) wife, Elizabeth.

17. Victor follows the creature to the Arctic, (which, where) he encounters Walton.

18. The two men form a bond over their (mutual, mutually) isolation and pursuit of knowledge.

19. Despite Victor's pleas to destroy the creature, Walton (determines, is determined) to continue his exploration.

20. (Weakened, Weaken) by his pursuit and loss, Victor succumbs to illness and dies on Walton's ship.

21. Before his death, he warns Walton of the dangers of (restrained, unrestrained) ambition and obsession.

22. After Victor's death, the creature (appears, is appeared) on the ship and laments the death of his creator.

23. He expresses regret for his actions and vows to end his own life (to immolate, by immolating) himself on a funeral pyre.

24. He reflects on Victor's tragic tale and the consequences of (checked, unchecked) ambition.

25. He decides to abandon his quest for the North Pole and return home, (understanding, understands) the importance of family and human connection.

[Writing Practice]

1. The story follows the journey of Victor Frankenstein, a young Swiss *scientist*

생명을 창조하려는 생각에 사로잡힌 *과학자* (관계사)

2. Victor _____ *Walton* as a warning.
　　　　　　그의 이야기를 ~*와* 공유하는데 동의한다

3. He _____ science and alchemy.
　　　　~에 대한 강한 관심을 가지고 성장한다

4. He _____ in secret.
　　　　공부하고 실험하는 데 여러 해를 보낸다

5. This rejection _____ *his creator*.
　　　　　~를 향한 분노와 쓰라림으로 그 생명체(cr~)를 충만하게 하다(fi~)

6. The creature eventually confronts Victor and _____.
　　　　　Victor가 그를 위해 친구를 만들어주어야 한다고 요구한다(de~) *접속사

7. _____, Walton is determined to continue
his exploration. 그 생명체를 파괴하려는 Victor의 간청에도 불구하고

8. Before his death, he _____ unrestrained ambition
and obsession. 　　　　Walton에게 ~의 위험에 대해서 경고한다

9. He reflects on Victor's tragic tale and _____.
　　　　　　　　　　　　　　　　　억제되지 않은 야망의 결과

10. He _____ the North Pole and return
home. 　　~을 향한 그의 탐색을 포기하기로 결심한다

[Word Quiz]

1. What is the synonym of "voyage"?
a) Stranded   b) Exploration   c) Responsibility   d) Regret

2. What does "cautionary" mean?
a) Fascination   b) Destruction   c) Warning   d) Empathy

3. What is the consequence of a reckless action?
a) Immortality   b) Responsibility   c) Melancholy   d) Iconic

4. What is the opposite of "abandonment"?
a) Companionship   b) Pursuit   c) Vulnerability   d) Transformation

5. What does "monstrous" describe?
a) Empathy   b) Regret   c) Fascination   d) Resembling a monster

6. What is a synonym for "determination"?
a) Consequence   b) Exploration   c) Responsibility   d) Resolve

7. What is the meaning of "obsession"?
a) Isolation   b) Immolation   c) Intense preoccupation   d) Transformation

8. What is the synonym of "fascination"?
a) Melancholy   b) Ambition   c) Empathy   d) Enchantment

9. What do you "harness" when you use a tool?
a) Humanity   b) Electricity   c) Mortality   d) Abandonment

10. What word describes something that happens or exists and is notable or unusual in some way?
a) Exploration   b) Ambition   c) Phenomenon   d) Essence

11. What is the opposite of "rejection"?
a) Stranded   b) Companionship   c) Tragedy   d) Caution

12. What is the meaning of "pursuit"?
a) Exploration   b) Responsibility   c) Immolation   d) Chasing or seeking

13. What word refers to a significant change in form, appearance, nature, or character?
a) Empathy b) Ambition c) Transformation d) Regret

14. Which term refers to any event or situation characterized by sorrow, loss?
a) Comedy b) Tragedy c) Play d) Drama

15. What does "immortal" mean?
a) Lacking empathy
b) Eternal or undying
c) Monstrous in nature
d) Melancholic

16. What is the act of "exploration"?
a) Empathy b) Immolation c) Investigation d) Rejection

17. What term refers to the obligation, duty, or accountability for one's actions, decisions, or obligations?
a) Responsibility b) Vulnerability c) Stranded d) Abandonment

18. What is the synonym of "ambition"?
a) Transformation b) Essence c) Aspiration d) Humanity

19. Which term refers to a feeling or state of deep sadness, often accompanied by sorrowful reflection?
a) Empathy
b) Vulnerability
c) Melancholy
d) Caution

20. What is the act of "immolate"?
a) To abandon
b) To reject
c) To sacrifice by fire
d) To harness electricity

Unit 19: Oliver Twist (1838)

"Oliver Twist" is a classic novel written by Charles Dickens, first published in 1838. The story follows the life of a young orphan named Oliver Twist and the challenges he faces as he navigates the harsh and often cruel world of 19th-century London.

The story begins with the birth of Oliver Twist in a workhouse in a small town. After his mother dies during childbirth, he grows up in an orphanage under the care of the cruel Mr. Bumble and the heartless Mrs. Mann.

At the age of nine, Oliver is sent to work as an apprentice to an undertaker, Mr. Sowerberry. Due to the mistreatment and cruelty he faces there, Oliver runs away to London, hoping for a better life.

In London, Oliver meets the charismatic and mischievous Artful Dodger, who introduces him to Fagin, a cunning and elderly criminal. Fagin runs a gang of pickpockets and thieves, and Oliver is unwittingly drawn into their world.

Oliver's innocence is contrasted with the dangerous and brutal characters he encounters, such as the ruthless criminal Bill Sikes. The kind-hearted prostitute Nancy takes pity on Oliver and tries to protect him from the darker aspects of Fagin's gang.

Oliver's first pickpocketing attempt during a visit to the countryside goes awry, and he is wrongly accused of stealing by the victim, Mr. Brownlow. Despite the misunderstanding, Mr. Brownlow takes Oliver into his care and provides him with a loving home.

Fagin, worried that Oliver might reveal the secrets of his gang, sends Bill Sikes and Nancy to recapture Oliver. They forcefully return him to Fagin's hideout. Nancy, feeling guilty for her role in Oliver's abduction, decides to help him escape from Fagin and Sikes. She meets secretly with Rose Maylie, a kind-hearted young lady, and Mr. Brownlow to devise a plan.

Nancy's plan to save Oliver is discovered by Bill Sikes, who, in a fit of rage and jealousy, murders her. A massive manhunt ensues to capture Bill Sikes, who flees London with Oliver as his hostage. Eventually, Sikes meets a tragic end during a botched robbery attempt.

After a series of the dramatic events, Oliver finds a loving home with Mr. Brownlow and Rose Maylie. The novel concludes with Oliver's newfound happiness and the fates of the other characters, including Fagin's capture and subsequent sentencing to death.

"Oliver Twist" is a compelling tale of social injustice, poverty, and redemption, with Dickens' characteristic critique of the societal issues of his time. It remains one of his most beloved and enduring works, highlighting the resilience of the human spirit against all odds.

[Vocabulary]

navigate 항해하며 orphan 고아 cruel 잔혹한 workhouse 노동원/소년원 childbirth 분만 orphanage 고아원 apprentice 견습생 undertaker 장의사 mistreatment 학대 charismatic 매력적인 mischievous 장난기 많은 cunning 교활한 the elderly 노인 pickpocket 소매치기(하 다) unwittingly 의도치 않게 innocence 순수함 dangerous 위험한 brutal 잔혹한 encounter 마주하게 되다 ruthless 무자비한 prostitute 기생 accused 비난받은/기소당한 victim 피해자 misunderstanding 오해 recapture 재탈환 hideout 은신처 parentage 혈통 respectable 존경 할 만한 consequences 결과 abduction 납치 jealousy 질투 manhunt 인간 사냥 hostage 인 질 dramatic 극적인 sentencing 징계 compelling 설득력 있는 injustice 부당함 poverty 빈곤 redemption 구원 enduring 오래 지속되는 resilience 회복력 subsequent 그 후의 highlight 강조하다

- 191 -

[본문 해석] 올리버 트위스트

"올리버 트위스트"는 찰스 디킨스가 쓴 고전 소설로, 1838년에 처음으로 출판되었습니다. 이 이야기는 어린 고아인 올리버 트위스트의 삶과 그가 19세기 런던의 가혹하고 종종 잔혹한 세계를 항해하면서 직면하는 도전들을 따라갑니다.

이 이야기는 작은 마을의 구빈원(poorhouse)에서 올리버 트위스트가 태어나면서 시작됩니다. 어머니가 출산 중에 사망한 후, 그는 잔혹한 범블 씨와 무자비한 맨 부인의 보호 하에 고아원에서 자라납니다.

아홉 살 때 올리버는 장의사인 소어베리의 견습생으로 보내집니다. 그곳에서 마주한 학대와 잔인함으로 인해 올리버는 더 나은 삶을 바라며 런던으로 도망칩니다. 런던에서 올리버는 카리스마 있고 짓궂은 장난꾸러기 아트풀 도저를 만나고, 그는 올리버를 교활하고 나이 든 범죄자 페이긴에게 소개합니다. 페이긴은 소매치기와 도둑들의 무리를 운영하고 있는데, 올리버는 자신도 모르게 그들의 세계에 빠지게 됩니다.

올리버의 순수함은 무자비한 범죄자 빌 시이크스 같은 인물과 대조됩니다. 하지만 따뜻한 마음을 지닌 창녀 낸시는 올리버를 불쌍히 여겨 페이긴의 갱단의 어두운 면들로부터 그를 보호하려고 노력합니다.

올리버가 시골을 방문한 동안 시도한 첫 소매치기는 성공하지 못하지만, 그는 피해자인 브라운로 씨로부터 도둑질을 한 것으로 부당하게 고발을 당합니다. 오해에도 불구하고, 브라운로 씨는 올리버를 돌보며 사랑이 깃든 집을 제공합니다.

올리버가 자신의 패거리의 비밀을 폭로할까봐 걱정된 페이긴은 빌 시크스와 낸시를 보내 올리버를 다시 잡아 옵니다. 그들은 그를 페이긴의 은신처로 강제로 돌려보냅니다. 낸시는 올리버의 납치에서 그녀가 한 역할에 대해 죄책감을 느끼고, 올리버가 페이긴과 시크스로부터 탈출하는 것을 돕기로 결심합니다. 계획을 세우기 위해 그녀는 마음씨 좋은 젊은 여성인 로즈 메이리와 브라운로우씨를 비밀리에 만납니다.

올리버를 구하기 위한 낸시의 계획은 빌 시크스에 의해 발견되고, 그는 분노와 질투로 그녀를 죽입니다. 올리버를 인질로 잡고 런던을 탈출하는 빌 시크스를 붙잡기 위해 대대적인 범인 수색이 이어집니다. 결국 시크스는 강도 시도를 하던 중 실패하고 비극적인 최후를 맞이합니다.

일련의 극적인 사건들 후에, 올리버는 브라운로우와 로즈 메이리와 함께 사랑이 가득한 가정을 찾게 됩니다. 소설은 올리버의 새로운 행복과 페이긴의 체포, 그 이후의 사형 선고를 포함한 다른 등장인물들의 운명으로 마무리됩니다.

"올리버 트위스트"는 디킨슨 시대의 사회적 문제에 대한 그의 특징적인 비평과 함께 사회적 불평등, 가난, 그리고 구원에 대한 설득력 있는 이야기입니다. 그것은 모든 역경에 맞서는 인간 정신의 회복력을 강조하면서 그의 가장 사랑 받고 지속되는 작품 중 하나로 남아 있습니다.

[Reading Comprehension]

1. When was "Oliver Twist" first published?
a) 1830   b) 1838   c) 1845   d) 1852

2. Where was Oliver Twist born?
a) America   b) Paris   c) Workhouse   d) Orphanage

3. Who takes care of Oliver in the orphanage?
a) Mr. Sowerberry   b) Mr. Bumble   c) Nancy   d) Mr. Brownlow

4. At what age was Oliver sent to work as an apprentice?
a) 6   b) 8   c) 9   d) 12

5. Who introduces Oliver to Fagin?
a) Bill Sikes   b) Mr. Sowerberry   c) Artful Dodger   d) Mrs. Mann

6. What does Fagin run?
a) Orphanage
b) Gang of pickpockets and thieves
c) Workhouse
d) Undertaker shop

7. Whom does Oliver meet in London?
a) Mr. Brownlow   b) Artful Dodger   c) Mrs. Mann   d) Mr. Bumble

8. What aspect of Fagin's gang does Nancy try to protect Oliver from?
a) Kindness   b) Innocence   c) Darker aspects   d) Cunning

9. What goes awry during Oliver's pickpocketing attempt?
a) He gets caught by the police.
b) The victim dies.
c) He is wrongly accused.
d) He succeeds in stealing.

10. Who takes Oliver into his care after the misunderstanding?
a) Artful Dodger
b) Mr. Brownlow
c) Bill Sikes
d) Fagin

11. Why does Fagin send Bill Sikes and Nancy to recapture Oliver?

a) To protect Oliver from danger

b) To give Oliver a reward

c) To prevent Oliver from revealing their secrets

d) To help Oliver escape

12. Who takes pity on Oliver and tries to protect him from the darker aspects of Fagin's gang?

a) Mr. Brownlow

b) Nancy

c) Bill Sikes

d) The victim, Mr. Brownlow

13. Who discovers Nancy's plan to save Oliver?

a) Oliver Twist

b) Mr. Brownlow

c) Bill Sikes

d) Fagin

14. What does Bill Sikes do in a fit of rage and jealousy?

a) Kidnap Oliver

b) Murder Nancy

c) Steal from Fagin's gang

d) Surrender to the police

15. How does "Oliver Twist" conclude?

a) Oliver becomes a pickpocket.

b) Oliver is sentenced to death.

c) Fagin's gang takes over London.

d) Oliver finds happiness with Mr. Brownlow and Rose Maylie.

[Grammar Check-up]

1. The classic novel "Oliver Twist" was _____ by Charles Dickens.
a) writing b) written c) writes d) write

2. Oliver Twist, the protagonist of the story, _____ in a workhouse after his mother's death.
a) was born b) bears c) bear d) bore

3. The orphanage, under the care of Mr. Bumble and Mrs. Mann, was _____ for its harsh treatment of the children.
a) known b) knowing c) knows d) know

4. Oliver's mistreatment at the undertaker's made him _____ run away to London.
a) decided b) decidedly c) deciding d) decide

5. Artful Dodger, _____ introduces Oliver to the criminal world, is a charismatic and mischievous character.
a) who b) whom c) which d) whose

6. Fagin, _____ a cunning and elderly criminal, runs a gang of pickpockets and thieves.
a) which b) whose c) who is d) whom

7. Oliver is unwittingly drawn _____ the dangerous world of Fagin's gang.
a) at b) into c) on d) onto

8. Nancy, _____ takes pity on Oliver, is a kind-hearted prostitute.
a) which b) who c) whom d) whose

9. Oliver is wrongly accused of stealing by Mr. Brownlow, _____ provides him with a loving home.
a) who b) which c) whose d) whom

10. Fagin sends Bill Sikes and Nancy to recapture Oliver, _____ forcefully return him to Fagin's hideout.
a) who b) whom c) whose d) which

11. Nancy, _____ for her role in Oliver's abduction, decides to help him escape.
a) feel b) feels c) feeling d) felt

12. The novel concludes with Oliver's newfound happiness and the fates of the other characters, _____ Fagin's capture and subsequent sentencing to death.
a) inclusion b) include c) includes d) including

13. She meets secretly with Rose Maylie, _____ young lady, and Mr. Brownlow to devise a plan.
a) a kind-hearted b) who kind-hearted c) kind-hearted d) kind-heartedly

14. Nancy's plan to save Oliver is discovered by Bill Sikes, who _____ her in a fit of rage and jealousy.
a) murdering b) murders c) was murdered d) murder

15. A massive manhunt _____ to capture Bill Sikes, who flees London with Oliver as his hostage.
a) ensure b) ensues c) ensuing d) is ensued

16. Oliver finds a loving home with Mr. Brownlow and Rose Maylie, where he _____ his newfound happiness.
a) is discovered b) discovering c) discovers d) discover

17. The novel "Oliver Twist" concludes with _____ of the other characters and Fagin's sentencing to death.
a) fatal b) fates c) fating d) fated

18. Charles Dickens' characteristic critique of societal issues _____ throughout the novel.
a) are shined b) shining c) shines d) shine

19. "Oliver Twist" remains one of his most beloved and enduring works, highlighting the _____ of the human spirit.
a) resilience b) resiliency c) resilient d) resolute

20. The novel explores themes of social injustice, poverty, and redemption, _____ captivate readers to this day.
a) in which b) whose c) which d) who

[Writing Practice]

1. The orphanage, under the care of Mr. Bumble and Mrs. Mann, _____
_____ 어린이들에 대한 가혹한 대우로 알려져 있었습니다.

2. _____ there, Oliver runs away to London,
　　　그가 직면한 학대와 잔혹함으로 인해　　　　　　　　hoping for a better life.

3.
Artful Dodger, _____, is a charismatic and
mischievous character. 범죄 세계에 Oliver를 소개한 *Dodger*는 (관계사)

4. Oliver _____ *Mr. Brownlow*, who provides him with
　　Oliver는 ~에 의해 도둑질 혐의로 잘못 기소된다　　　　　　　　　a loving home.

5. _____, and his connection to respectable
　　Oliver의 태생(par~)에 대한 진실이 밝혀지고　　　　individuals becomes known.

6. Nancy, _____, decides to help him
　　　　　liver의 유괴에 대한 자신의 역할을 느끼고 (분사구)　　　　　　escape.

7. _____, who murders her in a fit of rage
Oliver를 구하기 위한 Nancy의 계획이 Bill Sikes에 의해 발각되다

8. Oliver finds a loving home with Mr. Brownlow and Rose Maylie,
_____
　　거기서 그는 그가 새로 발견한 행복을 경험 한다 (관계사)

9. Charles Dickens' characteristic critique of societal issues shines
_____ 소설 전체에

10. A massive manhunt ensues to capture *Bill Sikes*, _____
_____ 그의 인질로 올리버와 함께 런던에서 도망치려던 *Bill Sikes* (관계사)

[Word Quiz]

1. Which term refers to the act of guiding a vessel or vehicle through a course, often involving navigation tools?
a) Orphan   b) Navigate   c) Cruel   d) Workhouse

2. What term describes a child who has lost both parents or has been abandoned?
a) Mistreatment   b) Orphan   c) Charismatic   d) Apprentice

3. What word characterizes behavior or actions that cause pain or suffering to others?
a) Innocence   b) Mischievous   c) Cruel   d) Undertaker

4. Which term refers to a place where impoverished people, especially the homeless or destitute, are housed and required to work?
a) Workhouse   b) Orphanage   c) Pickpocket   d) Mistreatment

5. What is the term for the process of giving birth to a child?
a) Childbirth   b) Innocence   c) Encounter   d) Abduction

6. Which word describes a facility where the children without parents are cared for and housed?
a) Apprenticeship   b) Orphanage   c) Ruthless   d) Prostitute

7. What term refers to someone who is learning a trade or skill under a skilled worker?
a) Undertaker   b) Apprentice   c) Misunderstanding   d) Hideout

8. Which word describes the person responsible for arranging and conducting funerals?
a) Resilience   b) Charismatic   c) Undertaker   d) Jealousy

9. What term denotes the act of treating someone badly or unfairly?
a) Mistreatment   b) Hideout   c) Respectable   d) Parentage

10. Which word describes having a compelling charm or appeal that inspires devotion in others?
a) Mischievous   b) Charismatic   c) Cruel   d) Innocence

11. What term describes behavior, especially of a child, that is playful and mildly naughty?
a) Cunning b) Ruthless c) Mischievous d) Accused

12. Which word describes having or showing skill in achieving one's ends by deceit or evasion?
a) Cunning b) Pickpocket c) Misunderstanding d) Hostage

13. What term refers to people who are older, typically used to describe a group within a community?
a) The elderly b) The victim c) The accused d) The orphan

14. Which word describes someone who steals from the pockets or purses of others, especially in crowded areas?
a) Unwittingly b) Jealousy c) Pickpocket d) Subsequent

15. What term describes something done without being aware of the consequences or implications?
a) Innocence b) Highlight c) Unwittingly d) Misunderstanding

16. Which word denotes the state of being free from guilt or moral wrongdoing?
a) Innocence b) Dangerous c) Hostage d) Redemption

17. What term describes likely to cause harm or injury?
a) Dramatic b) Dangerous c) Cunning d) Resilience

18. Which word describes exceptionally cruel or savage behavior?
a) Brutal b) Subsequent c) Innocence d) Mischievous

19. What term refers to a meeting, especially one that is unexpected or violent?
a) Encounter b) Sentencing c) Compelling d) Abduction

20. Which word describes having no compassion or mercy; showing no remorse?
a) Innocence b) Ruthless c) Redemption d) Respectable

Unit 20: The Count of Monte Cristo (1844)

"The Count of Monte Cristo" is a novel written by Alexandre Dumas and published in 1844. It tells the story of Edmond Dantès, a young sailor who is unjustly accused of treason and imprisoned on the island of Château d'If. The novel follows his journey of revenge and redemption.

The story begins when Edmond Dantès, a kind-hearted and ambitious sailor, is about to marry his beloved fiancée, Mercédès. However, his life takes a drastic turn when he is betrayed by his friends and falsely accused of being a Bonapartist conspirator. He is arrested and imprisoned without trial.

During his imprisonment, Dantès befriends another inmate named Abbé Faria, an old priest who becomes his mentor and imparts a vast amount of knowledge to him. Faria also reveals the existence of a hidden treasure on the island of Monte Cristo.

After Faria's death, Dantès manages to escape from prison, using the priest's corpse to fake his own death. He then acquires the hidden treasure on Monte Cristo and transforms himself into the enigmatic and wealthy Count of Monte Cristo. With his newfound wealth, Dantès sets out on a mission of vengeance against those who wronged him.

As the Count, Dantès systematically orchestrates the downfall of his enemies. He exposes their secrets, manipulates their lives, and uses their own actions against them. Throughout his quest for revenge, he encounters a diverse cast of characters, including the greedy banker Danglars, the cowardly Fernand Mondego, the corrupt magistrate Villefort, and the remorseful Caderousse.

However, as Dantès carries out his vengeance, he also begins to question the morality of his actions and the toll it takes on his own soul. Along the way, he reunites with Mercédès, who has married Fernand Mondego, and discovers the impact his actions have had on the innocent.

In the end, Dantès realizes that true justice cannot be achieved through revenge alone. He learns to forgive and finds redemption through acts of kindness and mercy. The novel concludes with Dantès abandoning his pursuit of vengeance and seeking a new life of love and happiness.

"The Count of Monte Cristo" is a tale of betrayal, revenge, forgiveness, and the ultimate triumph of good over evil. It explores themes of justice, morality, and the consequences of one's actions. The novel has captivated readers for generations and has been adapted into numerous films, plays, and television series.

[Vocabulary]

Unjustly 불공평하게 Treason 배신 Imprisoned 감옥에 갇힌 Drastic 급격한 Conspirator 음모자 Betrayed 배신당한 Falsely 거짓으로 Mentor 멘토/조언자 Impart 전수하다 Enigmatic 수수께끼로 가득한 Orchestrate 조직하다 Diverse 다양한 Cowardly 겁쟁이 Corrupt 부패한 Pursuit 추구 Redemption 구원 Vengeance 복수 Reunite 재회하다 Impact 영향 Justice 정의 Morality 도덕성 Conclude 끝나다/결론을 내리다 Triumph 승리 Captivated 매료된 Adapted 적응된 Betrayal 배신 Forgiveness 용서 Ultimate 궁극적인 Consequences 결과 Ambitious 야심 있는 Kind-hearted 착한 마음을 지닌 Imprisonment 투옥/수감 Existence 존재 Newfound 새롭게 얻은 Morality 도덕성

[본문 해석] 몬테크리스토 백작

"몬테크리스토 백작"은 알렉상드르 뒤마에 의해 쓰여 져 1844년에 출판된 소설입니다. 이것은 반역죄로 억울하게 기소되어 샤토 디프 섬에 수감된 젊은 선원 에드몽 돈테스에 대한 이야기합니다. 소설은 그의 복수와 구원의 여정을 따릅니다.

이야기는 마음씨 좋고 야망 있는 선원인 에드몽 돈테스가 사랑하는 약혼자 메르세데스와 결혼을 앞두고 있을 때 시작됩니다. 그러나 친구들에게 배신당하고 나폴레옹 지지자와 공모한 자로 잘못 기소되면서 그의 인생은 급격하게 바뀌게 됩니다. 그는 재판 없이 체포되고 투옥됩니다.

감옥에 있는 동안, 돈테스는 그의 스승이 되어 그에게 방대한 양의 지식을 주는 늙은 사제인 아베 파리아라는 또 다른 수감자와 친구가 됩니다. 파리아는 몬테 크리스토 섬에 숨겨진 보물의 존재를 밝힙니다.

파리아가 죽은 후, 돈테스는 자신의 죽음을 가장하기 위해 그 사제의 시체를 사용하여 가까스로 감옥에서 탈출합니다. 그리고 나서 그는 몬테 크리스토 섬에 숨겨진 보물을 얻고 부유하고 미스테리한 몬테크리스토 백작으로 변신합니다. 그의 새로운 재산으로, 돈테스는 그에게 죄를 지은 사람들에게 복수하는 임무를 시작합니다.

백작으로서, 돈테스는 그의 적들의 몰락을 체계적으로 계획합니다. 그는 그들의 비밀을 폭로하고, 그들의 삶을 조종하고, 그들이 한 행동을 이용하여 그들에게 대항합니다. 복수를 위한 그의 탐색을 통해, 그는 탐욕스러운 은행가 태그라르, 비겁한 페르난도 몬데고, 부패한 치안판사 빌포르, 그리고 양심의 가책을 느끼는 카데루스를 포함한 다양한 인물들을 만나게 됩니다.

그러나 돈테스가 복수를 하면서 그는 또한 자신이 한 행동의 도덕성, 그리고 그 행동이 자신의 영혼에 끼치는 피해에 대해 의문을 품기 시작합니다. 그 과정에서 그는 페르난도 몬데고와 결혼한 메르세데스와 재회하고 자신의 행동이 무고한 사람들에게 미치는 영향을 발견하게 됩니다.

결국 돈테스는 복수만으로는 진정한 정의를 이룰 수 없음을 깨닫게 되고, 용서를 배우고 친절과 자비의 행위를 통해 구원을 찾게 됩니다. 소설은 돈테스가 복수를 추구하는 것을 버리고 사랑과 행복의 새로운 삶을 찾는 것으로 끝이 납니다.

"몬테 크리스토 백작"은 배신, 복수, 용서, 그리고 악에 대한 선의 궁극적인 승리에 대한 이야기입니다. 그것은 정의, 도덕, 그리고 한 사람의 행동의 결과에 대한 주제들을 탐구합니다. 그 소설은 수 세대 동안 독자들을 사로잡았고 수많은 영화, 연극, 그리고 텔레비전 시리즈로 각색되었습니다.

[Reading Comprehension]

1. What is the primary theme of "The Count of Monte Cristo"?
a) Love and happiness
b) Betrayal, revenge, and forgiveness
c) Greed and corruption
d) Political intrigue and conspiracy

2. Why is Edmond Dantès imprisoned on the island of Château d'If?
a) He committed murder.
b) He was falsely accused of treason.
c) He stole a valuable treasure.
d) He was involved in a political conspiracy.

3. Who becomes Edmond Dantès' mentor during his imprisonment?
a) Mercédès
b) Abbé Faria
c) Fernand Mondego
d) Villefort

4. What does Abbé Faria reveal to Edmond Dantès during their time in prison?
a) The existence of a hidden treasure on Monte Cristo
b) The identity of the real traitor
c) How to escape from Château d'If
d) The location of Mercédès

5. How does Edmond Dantès escape from prison?
a) He. bribes the guards.
b) He tunnels his way out.
c) He uses Abbé Faria's corpse to fake his own death.
d) He is released on parole.

6. What does Edmond Dantès become after acquiring the hidden treasure on Monte Cristo?
a) A wealthy banker   b) A priest   c) The Count of Monte Cristo   d) A pirate

7. What is the Count of Monte Cristo's main goal after gaining wealth?
a) To find true love
b) To seek revenge against his enemies
c) To travel the world
d) To become a recluse

8. Who is one of the Count's enemies that he seeks revenge against?
a) Abbé Faria   b) Mercédès   c) Danglars   d) Fernand Mondego

9. What is the Count's method for seeking revenge against his enemies?
a) Direct confrontation and violence
b) Blackmail and extortion
c) Forgiveness and reconciliation
d) None of the above

10. What makes the Count of Monte Cristo question the morality of his actions?
a) The discovery of a hidden treasure
b) The impact of his actions on the innocent
c) His inability to achieve revenge
d) His desire for more wealth

11. Who does Edmond Dantès reunite with during his quest for revenge?
a) Mercédès   b) Villefort   c) Danglars   d) Abbé Faria

12. What does Edmond Dantès ultimately learn about justice and redemption?
a) That revenge is the only path to justice
b) That justice cannot be achieved through revenge alone
c) That forgiveness is a sign of weakness
d) That wealth is the key to redemption

13. What are some of the themes explored in "The Count of Monte Cristo"?
a) Justice, morality, and consequences of one's actions
b) Love, betrayal, and revenge
c) Greed, corruption, and political intrigue
d) All of the above

14. How has "The Count of Monte Cristo" been adapted over the years?
a) It has been turned into numerous films, plays, and television series.
b) It has only been adapted into novels.
c) It has remained unchanged since its publication.
d) It is a relatively unknown work.

15. In the end, what does Edmond Dantès choose to pursue instead of revenge?
a) Wealth and power
b) Love and happiness
c) Isolation and solitude
d) Further acts of revenge

[Grammar Check-up]

1. It tells the story of Edmond Dantès, a young sailor who is unjustly (accused, accusing) of treason and imprisoned on the island of Château d'If.
2. The story begins when Edmond Dantès, a kind-hearted and ambitious sailor, (who is, is) about to marry his beloved fiancée, Mercédès.
3. However, his life takes a drastic turn when he is betrayed by his friends and (falsely accused, false accuse) of being a Bonapartist conspirator.
4. He is arrested and (imprison, imprisoned) without trial.
5. (While, During) his imprisonment, Dantès befriends (another, other) inmate named Abbé Faria, an old priest (becomes, who becomes) his mentor and imparts a vast amount of knowledge to him.
6. Faria also (is revealed, reveals) the existence of a hidden treasure on the island of Monte Cristo.
7. After Faria's death, Dantès manages to escape from prison, (is used, using) the priest's corpse to fake his own death.
8. He then (is acquired, acquires) the hidden treasure on Monte Cristo and transforms himself into the enigmatic and wealthy Count of Monte Cristo.
9. With his (newfind, newfound) wealth, Dantès sets out on a mission of vengeance against those (who, which) wronged him.
10. As the Count, Dantès (systematically, systenatical) orchestrates the downfall of his enemies.
11. He (is exposed, exposes) their secrets, manipulates their lives, and uses their own actions against them.
12. (Throughout, Thought) his quest for revenge, he encounters a diverse cast of characters, including the greedy banker Danglars and others.
13. However, as Dantès carries out his vengeance, he also begins to question the (moral, morality) of his actions and the toll it takes on his own soul.
14. Along the way, he reunites with Mercédès, who has married Fernand Mondego, and discovers the impact his actions have (had on, had) the innocent.
15. In the end, Dantès realizes that true justice cannot (be achieved, achieve) through revenge alone.
16. He learns (forgiving, to forgive) and finds redemption through acts of kindness and mercy.
17. The novel concludes with Dantès (abandoning, abandon) his pursuit of vengeance and seeking a new life of love and happiness.
18. "The Count of Monte Cristo" is a tale of (betrayal, betray), revenge, forgiveness, and the ultimate triumph of good over evil.

[Writing Practice]

1. It tells the story of Edmond Dantès, *a young sailor* _____
_____ on the island of Château d'If.
부당하게 반역죄(tr~)로 기소되어 투옥된 *젊은 항해사* (관계사)

2. The story begins when Edmond Dantès, a kind-hearted and ambitious sailor,
_____ his beloved fiancée, Mercédès.
막 ~와 결혼하려고 할 때

3. However, his life takes a drastic turn _____
_____ *being* a Bonapartist conspirator.
그가 그의 친구들에 의해 배반당하고 거짓으로 ~로 고발당하자 (접속사)

4. During his imprisonment, Dantès _____ *Abbé*
Faria, an old priest.   *Abbé Faria*라고 불리는 또 다른 수감자(in~)와 친구가 된다

5, Faria also _____ on the island of Monte Cristo.
            숨겨진 보물의 존재를 밝힌다(re~)

6. After Faria's death, Dantès _____, using the priest's
corpse to fake his own death.   가까스로 감옥에서 탈출한다

7. He then acquires the hidden treasure on Monte Cristo and _____
_____ of Monte Cristo.
그 자신을 정체모를(enig~) 부유한 백작으로 바꾼다(tr~)

8. He _____, and uses their own actions against them.
   그들의 비밀들을 폭로하고 그들의 삶을 조종한다

9. Along the way, he reunites with Mercédès, who has married Fernand Mondego, and
discovers _____.
            그의 행동들이 결백한 사람들에게 끼쳤던 영향을 *발견하다* (관계사)

10. He _____ *acts of kindness and mercy*.
            용서하는 것을 배우고 ~를 통해 구원을 찾는다

[Word Quiz]

1. What does "unjustly" mean?
a) Rightfully   b) Fairly   c) Unfairly   d) Justifiably

2. What is the act of betraying one's country known as?
a) Justice   b) Morality   c) Treason   d) Redemption

3. Which word means being confined in a prison or jail?
a) Imprisoned   b) Ambitious   c) Ultimate   d) Captivated

4. What term describes a sudden and severe change?
a) Drastic   b) Adapted   c) Impart   d) Impact

5. Who is a person involved in a conspiracy or plot?
a) Cowardly   b) Mentor   c) Conspirator   d) Kind-hearted

6. What happens when someone is deceived or let down by someone they trusted?
a) Betrayed   b) Orchestrate   c) Conclude   d) Triumph

7. What does "falsely" mean?
a) Honestly   b) Truthfully   c) Untruthfully   d) Sincerely

8. Who is a person who provides guidance and advice to someone less experienced?
a) Mentor   b) Reunite   c) Diverse   d) Vengeance

9. What word describes something that is mysterious and puzzling?
a) Impart   b) Unjustly   c) Enigmatic   d) Corrupt

10. Which term means to organize or plan something carefully and in detail?
a) Pursuit   b) Drastic   c) Orchestrate   d) Existence

11. What word means having various different forms or aspects?
a) Cowardly   b) Diverse   c) Betrayal   d) Impact

12. What does "corrupt" mean?

a) Honest b) Pure c) Dishonest d) Forgiving

13. What is the act of seeking or following something, especially a goal or objective?

a) Justice b) Pursuit c) Adapted d) Unjustly

14. What is the act of being saved or set free from sin or evil?

a) Redemption b) Triumph c) Ambitious d) Conclude

15. What is the act of seeking revenge for a perceived wrongdoing?

a) Betrayal b) Imprisoned c) Vengeance d) Mentor

16. What happens when people come together again after being apart?

a) Pursuit b) Impact c) Reunite d) Impart

17. What is the effect or influence that an event, action, or decision has on something or someone?

a) Morality b) Impact c) Ultimate d) Consequences

18. What is the concept of fairness, righteousness, and moral rightness?

a) Justice b) Captivated c) Existence d) Kind-hearted

19. How do you call the act of reaching a decision or drawing a conclusion?

a) Conclude b) Triumph c) Adapted d) Corrupt

20. What word describes the state of being victorious or successful?

a) Captivated b) Ultimate c) Triumph d) Unjustly

Unit 21: Jane Eyre (1847)

"Jane Eyre" is a novel written by Charlotte Brontë, first published in 1847. The story revolves around the life of the eponymous protagonist, Jane Eyre. Here is a summary of the plot:

Jane Eyre is an orphan who is raised by her cruel and unkind aunt, Mrs. Reed, after her parents' death. She suffers mistreatment and abuse from her cousins and is sent away to a strict boarding school called Lowood Institution. The conditions at Lowood are harsh, but Jane befriends Helen Burns, who teaches her the value of endurance and piety. Unfortunately, Helen passes away due to an illness, leaving Jane feeling even more alone.

As she grows older, Jane becomes a teacher at Lowood, but she desires more from life. She advertises for a governess position and receives an offer from Thornfield Hall, to be the governess for a young French girl named Adele. The master of Thornfield Hall is Mr. Edward Rochester, a mysterious and brooding man.

Jane develops a strong bond with Adele and slowly falls in love with Mr. Rochester. Their relationship deepens, and they become close despite their differences in social status. However, strange occurrences in the house, including eerie laughter and a fire, add to the mystery surrounding Mr. Rochester.

Jane soon learns that Mr. Rochester has a dark secret. He is already married to a mentally ill woman named Bertha, whom he keeps locked away in Thornfield's attic. Distraught and heartbroken, Jane leaves Thornfield Hall and embarks on a journey to find a new life. She encounters a kind family, the Rivers, who take her in and help her find work as a teacher at a small village school.

St. John Rivers, one of the members of the Rivers family, becomes Jane's friend and proposes marriage to her, asking her to accompany him to India as a missionary's wife. Jane contemplates the offer but realizes that she cannot marry St. John without love.

Despite her strong feelings for Mr. Rochester, Jane believes she must never return to Thornfield Hall. However, fate has other plans, and one night, she hears Mr. Rochester's voice calling her from afar. She rushes back to find Thornfield Hall burned to the ground by Bertha's actions. Mr. Rochester was injured while trying to save Bertha, leaving him blind and physically impaired.

Jane and Mr. Rochester are reunited, and she cares for him during his recovery. They confess their love for each other and decide to marry, their social and economic differences no longer a barrier. The novel ends with Jane narrating her contented life as Mrs. Rochester and the mother of a son.

"Jane Eyre" is a timeless classic that explores themes of love, independence, morality, and social class. It is celebrated for its strong, independent female protagonist and its portrayal of a passionate and unconventional love story.

[Vocabulary]

protagonist 주인공 eponymous 자기 이름으로 된 orphan 고아 mistreatment 학대 abuse 학대하다 boarding school 기숙학교 harsh 가혹한 endurance 인내 piety 독실함 governess 가정교사 mysterious 신비로운 brooding 생각에 잠긴 relationship 관계 social status 사회적 지위 occurrences 사건들 eerie 기묘한 attic 다락방 distraught 괴로워하는 heartbroken 비탄에 잠긴 embark 떠나다 contemplate 숙고하다 realization 깨달음 recovery 회복 confess 고백하다 barrier 장벽 contented 만족스러운 narrating 서술 timeless 영원한 explore 탐구하다 independence 독립성 morality 도덕성 celebrated 칭송받는 portrayal 묘사

[본문 해석] 제인 에어

"제인 에어"는 샬롯 브론테가 쓴 소설로, 1847년에 처음 출판되었습니다. 이 이야기는 주인공 제인 에어의 삶을 중심으로 전개됩니다. 다음은 줄거리의 요약입니다:

제인 에어는 부모님이 돌아가신 후 잔인하고 불친절한 이모인 리드 부인에게 길러진 고아입니다. 그녀는 사촌들로부터 학대와 학대를 당하고 로우드 기관이라고 불리는 엄격한 기숙학교로 보내집니다. 로우드의 환경은 가혹하지만 제인은 그녀에게 인내심과 경건함의 가치를 가르쳐주는 헬렌 번스와 친구가 됩니다. 불행하게도 헬렌은 병으로 세상을 떠나고, 제인은 더욱 더 외로워집니다.

나이가 들면서 제인은 로우드의 선생님이 되지만 삶에서 더 많은 것을 원합니다. 그녀는 가정교사 자리를 광고하고 손필드 저택으로부터 아델이라는 젊은 프랑스 소녀의 가정교사가 되어 달라는 제안을 받습니다. 손필드 저택의 주인은 신비롭고 음울한 남자인 에드워드 로체스터입니다.

제인은 아델과 강한 유대감을 형성하고 로체스터와 서서히 사랑에 빠집니다. 그들의 관계는 깊어지고, 사회적 지위의 차이에도 불구하고 가까워집니다. 하지만 섬뜩한 웃음과 화재를 포함한 집안의 이상한 사건들은 로체스터를 둘러싼 미스터리를 더합니다.

제인은 곧 로체스터가 어두운 비밀을 가지고 있다는 것을 알게 됩니다. 그는 이미 베르타라는 정신 질환이 있는 여성과 결혼했고, 그 여성은 손필드 저택의 다락방에 가두어 둡니다. 정신이 혼미하고 비통한 제인은 손필드 저택을 떠나 새로운 삶을 찾기 위한 여행을 떠납니다. 그녀는 그녀를 받아 들여 작은 마을 학교에서 선생님으로 일하는 것을 도와주는 친절한 가족 '리버스'를 만나게 됩니다.

리버스 가족 중 한 명인 세인트 존 리버스는 제인의 친구가 되어 그녀에게 청혼하고, 그녀에게 선교사의 아내로 인도에 그와 동행해 달라고 부탁합니다. 제인은 그 제안을 고려하지만 사랑이 없으면 세인트 존과 결혼할 수 없다는 것을 깨닫습니다.

로체스터에 대한 강한 감정에도 불구하고, 제인은 절대 손필드 저택으로 돌아가서는 안 된다고 생각합니다. 하지만 운명에는 다른 계획이 있고, 어느 날 밤, 멀리서 자신을 부르는 로체스터의 목소리를 듣습니다. 그녀는 급히 돌아왔지만 손필드 저택이 베르타의 행동에 의해 불에 타버린 것을 발견하게 됩니다. 로체스터 씨는 베르타를 구하려다 부상을 입었고, 장님이 되고 신체적으로 손상을 입었습니다.

제인과 로체스터는 재회했고, 그가 회복되는 동안 그녀는 그를 돌봅니다. 그들은 서로에 대한 사랑을 고백하고 결혼하기로 결정하는데, 그들의 사회적, 경제적 차이는 더 이상 장벽이 되지 않습니다. 소설은 제인이 로체스터 부인이자 아들의 어머니로서 만족스러운 삶을 이야기하는 것으로 끝이 납니다.

"제인 에어"는 사랑, 독립, 도덕, 그리고 사회 계급의 주제를 탐구하는 시대를 초월한 고전입니다. 그것은 강하고, 독립적인 여성 주인공과 열정적이고 파격적인 사랑 이야기의 묘사로 유명합니다.

[Reading Comprehension]

1. Who is the author of the novel "Jane Eyre"?
A) Charlotte Brontë
B) Jane Eyre
C) Mr. Edward Rochester
D) Mrs. Reed

2. What is the name of the boarding school where Jane Eyre is sent?
A) Lowood Institution
B) Thornfield Hall
C) Rivers' School
D) St. John's School

3. What does Jane befriend at Lowood Institution?
A) Adele   B) Bertha   C) Mr. Rochester   D) Helen Burns

4. What is the dark secret of Mr. Rochester?
A) He is already married to Bertha.
B) He is secretly wealthy.
C) He is not the real owner of Thornfield Hall.
D) He is planning to leave the country.

5. Where is Bertha kept hidden in Thornfield Hall?
A) In the garden
B) In the attic
C) In the basement
D) In a secret room

6. Who proposes marriage to Jane, asking her to accompany him to India?
A) Mr. Edward Rochester
B) Mr. Rivers
C) Adele
D) Mrs. Reed

7. Why does Jane leave Thornfield Hall?
A) To find a new job
B) To visit her family
C) Because she is mistreated by Mr. Rochester
D) Because Mr. Rochester is already married

8. What happens to Thornfield Hall in the end?

A) It is burned down by Bertha's actions.

B) It is sold to another owner.

C) It is renovated and becomes a school.

D) It is inherited by Jane.

9. How does Mr. Rochester get injured?

A) In a horse-riding accident

B) Trying to save Bertha from a fire

C) In a fight with Mr. Rivers

D) Trying to escape from the attic

10. What are the themes explored in "Jane Eyre"?

A) Mystery and suspense

B) Love, independence, morality, and social class

C) Wealth and poverty

D) War and politics

11. What is Jane's profession at Lowood Institution?

A) Governess   B) Teacher   C) Maid   D) Cook

12. What is the relationship between Jane and Adele?

A) Cousins

B) Mother and daughter

C) Teacher and student

D) Friends

13. What does Jane desire more from life as she grows older?

A) Fame and fortune

B) A loving family

C) Adventure and travel

D) A higher social status

14. Who becomes Jane's close friend and proposes marriage to her?

A) Mr. Rochester   B) Mr. Rivers   C) Helen Burns   D) St. John Rivers

15. How does the novel "Jane Eyre" end?

A) With Jane becoming a governess

B) With Jane narrating her contented life as Mrs. Rochester

C) With Jane and Mr. Rochester parting ways

D) With Jane discovering her true identity and inheritance

[Grammar Check-up]

1. Jane Eyre is an orphan who is (rosen, raised) by her cruel and unkind aunt, Mrs. Reed, after her parents' death.

2. She suffers mistreatment and abuse from her cousins and (sends, is sent) away to a strict boarding school called Lowood Institution.

3. The conditions at Lowood (are, is) harsh, but Jane (is friends, befriends) Helen Burns, who (teach, teaches) her the value of endurance and piety.

4. Unfortunately, Helen passes away due to an illness, (leaves, leaving) Jane feeling even more alone.

5. (As long as, As) she grows older, Jane becomes a teacher at Lowood, but she desires more from life.

6. She advertises for a governess position and (receives, is received) an offer from Thornfield Hall, to be the governess for a young French girl named Adele.

7. Jane (develops, is developed) a strong bond with Adele and slowly (fallen, falls) in love with Mr. Rochester.

8. Their relationship (deeps, deepens), and they become close (despite of, despite) their differences in social status.

9. However, strange occurrences in the house, including eerie laughter and a fire, (add, adds) to the mystery surrounding Mr. Rochester.

10. He is already married to a (mentally, mental) ill woman named Bertha, whom he keeps (locked, locking) away in Thornfield's attic.

11. Distraught and (heartbreaking, heartbroken), Jane leaves Thornfield Hall and embarks on a journey to find a new life.

12. She encounters a kind family, the Rivers, who (takes, take) her in and help her find work as a teacher at a small village school.

13. St. John Rivers, one of the members of the Rivers family, (becomes, become) Jane's friend and proposes marriage to her, (asks, asking) her to accompany him to India as a missionary's wife.

14. Jane contemplates the offer but (is realized, realizes) that she cannot marry St. John without love.

15. (Due to, Despite) her strong feelings for Mr. Rochester, Jane believes she must never return to Thornfield Hall.

16. However, fate has (other, another) plans, and one night, she hears Mr. Rochester's voice (to call, calling) her from afar.

17. She rushes back to find Thornfield Hall (burning, burned) to the ground by Bertha's actions.

18. Mr. Rochester was injured while trying to save Bertha, leaving him blind and physically (impairing, impaired).

[Writing Practice]

1. Jane Eyre is *an orphan* _____ her cruel and unkind aunt, Mrs. Reed, after her parents' death. ~에 의해 길러진 *고아* (관계사)

2. She suffers mistreatment and abuse from her cousins and _____ a strict boarding school called Lowood Institution. ~로 멀리 보내어 진다

3. The conditions at Lowood is harsh, but Jane befriends *Helen Burns*, _____ _____ and piety.
   그녀에게 인내의 가치를 가르쳐준 *Helen Burns* (관계사)

4. She advertises for a governess position and _____
   ~로부터 제안을 받는다
   Thornfield Hall, _____ a young French girl named Adele.
   ~를 위한 가정교사가 되어 달라는

5. Jane _____ Adele and slowly falls in love with Mr. Rochester.
   ~와 강한 유대를 발전시킨다

6. They _____ *social status*.
   사회적 지위에서의 그들의 차이에도 불구하고 가까워진다

7. _____, Jane leaves Thornfield Hall and embarks on a
   혼란스럽고 비통한 심정으로 (분사구)   journey to find a new life.

8. She encounters *a kind family*, the Rivers, _____
   _____ as a teacher at a small village school. 그녀를 받아들이고 그녀가
   일자리를 찾도록 도와준 *친절한 가족* (관계사)

9. St. John Rivers becomes Jane's friend and proposes marriage to her, _____
   _____ to India as a missionary's wife.
   그녀에게 그와 동반해 줄 것을 요청하면서 (분사구)

10. _____ *Mr. Rochester*, Jane believes she must never return to
    *Mr. Rochester*를 향한 강한 감정에도 불구하고   Thornfield Hall.

[Word Quiz]

1. What is the term for the main character in a story?
a) Eponymous   b) Orphan   c) Protagonist   d) Abuse

2. Which word describes a person who has lost both parents?
a) Endurance   b) Orphan   c) Governess   d) Mistreatment

3. Which word means the act of treating someone with cruelty or violence?
a) Boarding school   b) Abuse   c) Harsh   d) Piety

4. Where might a character in a novel experience mistreatment and harsh conditions?
a) Orphanage   b) Mysterious place   c) Social status   d) Relationship

5. What word describes the act of being left alone to face difficult situations?
a) Endurance   b) Eerie   c) Embark   d) Contented

6. What term refers to a character's devotion to religious principles?
a) Governess   b) Piety   c) Realization   d) Recovery

7. Who is typically responsible for the education and care of children in a private household?
a) Abuse   b) Endurance   c) Governess   d) Mistreatment

8. Which word describes something that is difficult to understand and mysterious?
a) Boarding school   b) Brooding   c) Mysterious   d) Relationship

9. What term can be used to describe someone who is deep in thought and appears gloomy?
a) Celebrated   b) Distraught   c) Harsh   d) Brooding

10. What word represents the connection between two or more people?
a) Relationship   b) Social status   c) Occurrences   d) Barrier

11. What is the word for one's position in society or the community?
a) Independence b) Morality c) Social status d) Eponymous

12. Which term refers to events or happenings?
a) Eerie b) Occurrences c) Narrating d) Independence

13. What word describes something that is strange and unsettling in a supernatural way?
a) Eerie b) Attic c) Celebrated d) Contented

14. Where might a character hide away in a story, often in secrecy?
a) Eerie b) Attic c) Endurance d) Embark

15. What word best describes someone who is deeply saddened and upset?
a) Heartbroken b) Realization c) Confess d) Mistreatment

16. Which word means to begin a journey or adventure?
a) Recover b) Embark c) Contemplate d) Governess

17. What term refers to the act of thinking deeply or considering something?
a) Recovery b) Endurance c) Contemplate d) Heartbroken

18. Which word signifies the moment when one becomes aware of something previously unknown?
a) Recovery b) Realization c) Confess d) Boarding school

19. What is the word for the process of getting better or healing?
a) Confess b) Recovery c) Barrier d) Independence

20. What word means to admit or acknowledge something, often a wrongdoing?
a) Celebrated b) Narrating c) Confess d) Morality

Unit 22: Wuthering Heights (1847)

"Wuthering Heights" is a classic novel written by Emily Brontë, first published in 1847. It is a complex and haunting tale that spans several generations and explores themes of love, revenge, social class, and the destructive power of passion. The story is set in the desolate moorlands of Yorkshire, England, and revolves around two neighboring estates: Wuthering Heights and Thrushcross Grange.

The novel begins with Mr. Lockwood, a city-dwelling man, renting Thrushcross Grange from Heathcliff. Intrigued by his landlord's mysterious personality, Lockwood visits Wuthering Heights, where Heathcliff resides. Lockwood's narrative shifts to the past, as he hears the story of Wuthering Heights and its inhabitants from Nelly Dean, the housekeeper at Thrushcross Grange.

In the late 18th century, Mr. Earnshaw, the owner of Wuthering Heights, brings home an orphan boy from Liverpool, whom he names Heathcliff.

Earnshaw's daughter, Catherine, forms a deep bond with Heathcliff, while his son, Hindley, resents the boy's presence. As Catherine and Heathcliff grow up together, their friendship turns into a passionate and intense love. However, Catherine's desire for social advancement leads her to become close to Edgar Linton, a wealthy neighbor, eventually causing friction between Heathcliff and Edgar. Catherine is torn between her love for Heathcliff and her ambition for a higher social status by marrying Edgar. In a famous quote, she declares, "I am Heathcliff." Despite her love for Heathcliff, she chooses to marry Edgar, leading Heathcliff to leave Wuthering Heights heartbroken.

After a three-year absence, Heathcliff returns as a wealthy and sophisticated man. He is determined to exact revenge on those who wronged him, particularly Hindley and Edgar. He also seeks to win back Catherine, who is now married to Edgar and living at Thrushcross Grange. Heathcliff marries Edgar's sister, Isabella, in a vengeful act against the Linton family. However, the marriage is tumultuous and ends in misery for Isabella. Meanwhile, Catherine gives birth to a daughter, Cathy, but her health deteriorates rapidly. Catherine dies after giving birth to her daughter, and her death devastates Heathcliff. His grief and obsession with Catherine's memory drive him further into darkness and cruelty.

The focus of the story shifts to the next generation. Cathy, Catherine's daughter, grows up under the influence of her father, Edgar, and her cousin, Hareton Earnshaw, the son of Hindley. Hareton, though uneducated, possesses good qualities and develops feelings for Cathy. Heathcliff's relentless pursuit of revenge consumes him, and he descends into madness. Tormented by visions of Catherine, he becomes a tormented and haunted soul. Eventually, his desire for vengeance wanes, and he longs for death to reunite with Catherine.

As Cathy and Hareton spend time together, their mutual affection grows, and they fall in love. Through their relationship, the cycle of hatred and vengeance is broken, bringing hope for the future.

After a night of strange occurrences and visions, Heathcliff is found dead. His passing brings an end to his suffering and the dark cloud that had hung over Wuthering Heights. With Heathcliff's death, Cathy and Hareton are free to love each other and work towards rebuilding Wuthering Heights and Thrushcross Grange. The novel concludes on a note of hope and redemption as the younger generation rises above the mistakes of their predecessors.

"Wuthering Heights" is a tale of passion, revenge, and the enduring power of love that explores the complexities of human relationships and the destructive consequences of unchecked emotions.

[Vocabulary]

complex 복잡한 haunting 자주 떠오르는 generations 세대 revenge 복수 destructive 파괴적인 passion 열정 desolate 황량한 moorlands 황야 neighboring 이웃하는 estates 부지 mysterious 신비로운 personality 성격 narrative 서술 shift 변화하다 resentment 원한 intense 강렬한 friction 갈등 torn 갈라진 quote 인용구 declare 선언하다 heartbroken 비통함을 느끼는 absence 부재 sophisticated 세련된 vengeful 복수심에 찬 tumultuous 격동의 misery 비통 devastating 파괴적인 deteriorate 악화되다 obsession 집착 cruelty 잔혹함 relentless pursuit 끈질긴 추구 tormented 괴로워하는 redemption 구원

[본문 해석] 폭풍의 언덕

"폭풍의 언덕(Wuthering Heights)"는 에밀리 브론테(Emily Brontë)가 쓴 고전 소설로, 처음으로 1847년에 출판되었습니다. 이는 몇 세대를 걸쳐 사랑, 복수, 계급 사회, 그리고 열정의 파괴적인 힘과 같은 주제를 탐구하는 복잡하고 괴로운 이야기입니다. 이 소설은 잉글랜드 요크셔의 황량한 지대를 배경으로 하고 있으며 워더링 하이츠와 스러시크로스 그레인지라는 두 이웃하는 저택을 중심으로 이야기가 전개됩니다.

이 소설은 도시 거주자인 록우드가 히스클리프로부터 스러시크로스 그레인지에 세입자가 되는 것으로 시작합니다. 호기심 많은 록우드는 그의 집주인인 히스클리프의 신비로운 성격에 끌려 워더링 하이츠를 방문합니다. 록우드의 서술은 과거로 변하며, 스러시크로스 그레인지의 하녀인 넬리 딘으로부터 워더링 하이츠와 그 주민들의 이야기를 듣게 됩니다.

18세기 후반에 워더링 하이츠의 소유주인인 언쇼는 리버풀에서 만난 고아 소년을 집으로 데려와 히스클리프라고 이름 짓습니다. 언쇼의 딸 캐서린은 히스클리프와 깊은 유대를 형성하며, 그의 아들 힌들리는 그 소년의 존재를 못마땅해 합니다. 캐서린과 히스클리프는 함께 성장함에 따라 그들의 우정은 열정적이고 격렬한 사랑으로 바뀝니다. 그러나 캐서린의 사회적 지위에 대한 욕망으로 인해 그녀는 부유한 이웃인 에드거 린턴과 가까워지게 되고, 결국 히스클리프와 에드거 사이에 마찰이 일어나게 됩니다. 캐서린은 히스클리프를 사랑하면서도 에드거와 결혼하여 더 높은 사회적 지위를 얻기 위한 야망 사이에서 갈등합니다. "나는 히스클리프다"라는 유명한 구절을 남길 정도로 히스클리프를 사랑하면서도, 그녀는 에드거와 결혼을 선택하게 되고, 히스클리프는 상실의 아픔으로 워더링 하이츠를 떠나게 됩니다.

떠난 지 3년 후, 히스클리프는 부유하고 세련된 사람으로서 돌아옵니다. 그는 자신을 해치려던 사람들, 특히 힌들리와 에드거에게 복수하려고 합니다. 또한 지금은 에드거와 결혼하고 스러시크로스 그레인지에서 살고 있는 캐서린을 되찾으려 합니다. 히스클리프는 에드거의 여동생 이자벨라와 결혼하게 되는데, 이는 린턴 가족에 대한 복수심에 의한 행동입니다. 하지만 이 결혼은 격동적이며 이사벨라의 불행한 결말로 끝이 납니다. 한편, 캐서린은 딸 캐시를 낳으나 건강이 빠르게 악화됩니다. 캐서린은 딸을 낳은 직후 사망하며, 그녀의 죽음은 히스클리프에게 큰 충격을 줍니다. 히스클리프는 캐서린의 기억에 사로잡힌 채 어둠과 잔혹함에 빠져들게 됩니다.

이야기의 초점은 다음 세대로 옮겨갑니다. 캐서린의 딸인 캐시는 아버지인 에드거와 사촌인 힌들리의 영향을 받으며 자라갑니다. 힌들리의 아들인 헤어튼은 교육은 받지 못했지만 좋은 품성을 지니고 캐시에게 애정을 품게 됩니다. 히스클리프는 복수에 대한 끊임없는 추구로 인해 광기에 빠지게 되며, 캐서린의 환영에 시달리는 고통 받는 영혼이 되어갑니다. 결국 그의 복수심를 향한 욕망은 사그라들고, 캐서린과의 재회를 바라며 죽음을 갈망하게 됩니다.

캐시와 헤어튼이 함께 시간을 보내며 그들의 서로에 대한 애정이 깊어지고 사랑에 빠지게 됩니다. 그들의 관계를 통해 증오와 복수의 연속이 깨어지며 미래에 대한 희망이 실현됩니다.

이상한 사건과 환영이 뒤따르는 어느 밤이 지나고 히스클리프는 죽음을 맞습니다. 그의 사망은 그의 고통과 워더링 하이츠에 머물던 어둠의 그림자를 종식시킵니다. 히스클리프의 죽음으로 캐시와 헤어튼은 서로를 사랑하고 워더링 하이츠와 스러시크로스 그레인지를 재건하기 위한 노력을 할 수 있게 됩니다. 소설은 어린 세대가 그들보다 앞서 살았던 자들의 실수를 뛰어넘으며 희망과 구원의 노트로 끝납니다. "폭풍의 언덕"는 사랑, 복수, 그리고 무제한한 감정의 파괴적인 결과를 탐구하며, 인간관계의 복잡성을 탐험하는 열정적인 이야기입니다.

[Reading Comprehension]

1. Who is the author of "Wuthering Heights"?
a) Jane Austen   b) Emily Brontë   c) Charlotte Brontë   d) William Shakespeare

2. What year was "Wuthering Heights" first published?
a) 1847   b) 1799   c) 1920   d) 1865

3. The novel is set in which location?
a) London, England   b) Yorkshire, England   c) New York, USA   d) Paris, France

4. What are the two main estates around which the story revolves?
a) Thornfield Hall and Pemberley
b) Wuthering Heights and Mansfield Park
c) Wuthering Heights and Thrushcross Grange
d) Baskerville Hall and Highbury

5. Who rents Thrushcross Grange from Heathcliff at the beginning of the novel?
a) Catherine Earnshaw   b) Edgar Linton   c) Nelly Dean   d) Mr. Lockwood

6. What does Catherine's desire for social advancement lead her to do?
a) Marry Edgar Linton
b) Run away from Wuthering Heights
c) Become a housekeeper at Thrushcross Grange
d) Form a bond with Heathcliff

7. What famous quote does Catherine say about Heathcliff?
a) "Heathcliff is my enemy."   b) "I am Catherine Earnshaw."
c) "I am Heathcliff."   d) "Heathcliff is my love."

8. Why does Heathcliff return to Wuthering Heights after a three-year absence?
a) To exact revenge on Hindley and Edgar
b) To take over ownership of the estate
c) To find Catherine's hidden treasure
d) To reconcile with his past mistakes

9. Whom does Heathcliff marry as an act of revenge against the Linton family?

a) Catherine Earnshaw

b) Isabella Linton

c) Nelly Dean

d) Cathy Earnshaw

10. What happens to Catherine shortly after giving birth to her daughter?

a) She leaves Wuthering Heights to live with Edgar at Thrushcross Grange.

b) Her health deteriorates rapidly, and she dies.

c) She runs away with Heathcliff to start a new life.

d) She becomes a recluse in Wuthering Heights.

11. Who raises Cathy, Catherine's daughter, after her mother's death?

a) Hindley Earnshaw b) Edgar Linton c) Hareton Earnshaw d) Heathcliff

12. How does Heathcliff's relentless pursuit of revenge affect him?

a) He becomes wealthy and sophisticated.

b) He descends into madness and darkness.

c) He finds peace and forgiveness.

d) He forgets about his past grievances.

13. What brings an end to Heathcliff's suffering and obsession?

a) His marriage to Isabella Linton

b) The birth of his daughter, Cathy

c) His reunion with Catherine in death

d) His reconciliation with Hindley

14. Who eventually breaks the cycle of hatred and vengeance in the story?

a) Catherine   b) Edgar   c) Heathcliff   d) Cathy and Hareton

15. How does the novel "Wuthering Heights" conclude?

a) With Catherine's marriage to Heathcliff

b) With Heathcliff's death and hope for the future

c) With a tragic ending for all the characters

d) With the younger generation repeating the mistakes of their predecessors

[Grammar Check-up]

1. "Wuthering Heights" is a complex and haunting tale that (is span, spans) several generations and explores themes of love and revenge.
2. The novel begins with Mr. Lockwood, a (city-dwelled, city-dwelling) man, renting Thrushcross Grange from Heathcliff.
3. Intrigued by his landlord's mysterious personality, Lockwood visits Wuthering Heights, (where, which) Heathcliff resides.
4. Lockwood's narrative shifts to the past, as he hears the story of Wuthering Heights and its (inhabits, inhabitants) from Nelly Dean.
5. In the (late, lately) 18th century, Mr. Earnshaw, the owner of Wuthering Heights, brings home an orphan boy from Liverpool, whom he (is named, names) Heathcliff.
6. Earnshaw's daughter, Catherine, forms a deep bond with Heathcliff, while his son, Hindley, (presents, resents) the boy's presence.
7. As Catherine and Heathcliff grow up together, their friendship (turns, is turned) into a passionate and intense love.
8. However, Catherine's desire for social advancement leads her (to become, becoming) close to Edgar Linton, a wealthy neighbor.
9. Catherine (tears, is torn) between her love for Heathcliff and her ambition for a higher social status by marrying Edgar.
10. Despite her love for Heathcliff, she chooses to marry Edgar, (leads, leading) Heathcliff to leave Wuthering Heights heartbroken.
11. After a three-year absence, Heathcliff returns as a wealthy and (sophisticated, sophisticating) man.
12. He is (determining, determined) to exact revenge on those who wronged him, particularly Hindley and Edgar.
13. He also seeks to win back Catherine, who (now marries, is now married) to Edgar and living at Thrushcross Grange.
14. Heathcliff (marries, is married) Edgar's sister, Isabella, in a vengeful act against the Linton family.
15. Meanwhile, Catherine gives birth to a daughter, Cathy, but her health deteriorates (rapid, rapidly). Catherine dies after giving birth to her daughter, and her death (devastates, is devastated) Heathcliff.
16. His grief and (obsess, obsession) with Catherine's memory drive him further into darkness and cruelty.
17. (Tormenting, Tormented by) visions of Catherine, he becomes a tormented and haunted soul.
18. Eventually, his desire for vengeance (wane, wanes), and he longs for death to reunite with Catherine.

[Writing Practice]

1. "Wuthering Heights" is a complex and haunting tale _____ and explores themes of love and revenge.　　　　　몇 세대에 걸친(span) 이야기 (관계사)

2. _____, Lockwood visits Wuthering Heights, where Heathcliff resides. 그의 집주인의 신비스러운 성격에 호기심을 느껴 (intrigue, 분사구)

3. _____ Mr. Earnshaw, brings home an orphan boy from
　　　　　　18세기 말에　　　　　　　　Liverpool, whom he (is named, names) Heathcliff.

4. Earnshaw's daughter, Catherine, forms a deep bond with Heathcliff, while his son, Hindley, _____. 그의 존재에 대해 분개한다(resent)

5. As Catherine and Heathcliff grow up together, their friendship _____
_____. 열정적이고 강렬한 사랑으로 변한다

6. However, Catherine's desire for social advancement _____
Edgar Linton, a wealthy neighbor.　　　　　　　　그녀가 ~에게 가까워지도록 이끈다

7. _____ Heathcliff, she chooses to marry Edgar, leading
~에 대한 그녀의 사랑에도 불구하고 Heathcliff to leave Wuthering Heights heartbroken.

8. _____ Heathcliff returns as a wealthy and sophisticated man. 3년간의 부재 후에

9. Meanwhile, Catherine _____, Cathy, but her health _____.
　　　　　　　　　　　　　　딸을 낳고　　　　　　　　　　　　　　　　급속히 악화된다

10. _____ Catherine's memory drive him further into
　　　　그의 슬픔과 ~에 대한 집착은　　　　　　　　　　　　　　darkness and cruelty.

- 228 -

[Word Quiz]

1. What is the meaning of "complex"?
a) Simple b) Difficult c) Complicated d) Easy

2. Which word best describes a "haunting" experience?
a) Joyful b) Scary c) Memorable d) Boring

3. "Generations" refer to:
a) An individual's lifespan   b) A group of people born at the same time
c) A single family tree   d) Ancient history

4. What is another word for "revenge"?
a) Forgiveness b) Justice c) Retaliation d) Peace

5. What is the opposite of "destructive"?
a) Creative b) Harmful c) Damaging d) Instructive

6. "Passion" is most closely related to:
a) Apathy b) Love c) Indifference d) Boredom

7. How would you describe a "desolate" place?
a) Lively b) Populated c) Deserted d) Colorful

8. "Moorlands" are characterized by:
a) Dense forests   b) Rocky mountains
c) Vast grasslands   d) Marshy and boggy areas

9. What does "neighboring" mean in a geographical context?
a) Distant   b) Far away   c) Nearby   d) Isolated

10. In real estate, "estates" typically refer to:
a) Large properties or landholdings
b) Small apartments in urban areas
c) Houses with swimming pools
d) Vacation resorts

11. What is an appropriate synonym for "mysterious"?
a) Transparent b) Puzzling c) Obvious d) Clear

12. "Personality" refers to a person's:

a) Physical appearance   b) Inner thoughts and feelings

c) Social status   d) Educational background

13. What is a "narrative"?

a) A plot twist   b) A summary

c) A story or account of events   d) A prediction

14. What does "shift" imply in a work environment?

a) Stability b) Change c) Predictability d) Uniformity

15. "Resentment" often arises from:

a) Forgiveness   b) Gratitude

c) Positive experiences   d) Negative experiences

16. Which word best describes an "intense" emotional experience?

a) Mild b) Overwhelming c) Neutral d) Calm

17. What is likely to cause "friction" between colleagues?

a) Effective communication   b) Shared goals

c) Conflicting opinions   d) Teamwork

18. When you feel "torn," it means you are:

a) Confident b) Indecisive c) Excited d) Pleased

19. What is a "quote"?

a) A picture   b) A passage from a book

c) A famous saying or expression   d) A short story

20. When do people usually "declare" their feelings for someone?

a) When they're feeling indifferent

b) When they're afraid of rejection

c) When they're not interested in a relationship

d) When they want to express their emotions openly

Unit 23: Moby-Dick (1851)

"Moby-Dick" is a novel written by American author Herman Melville and published in 1851. It tells the story of Captain Ahab's obsessive quest for revenge against a giant white whale known as Moby Dick. The novel explores themes of obsession, fate, human nature, and the struggle between man and nature.

The story is narrated by Ishmael, a young sailor who joins the whaling ship Pequod, commanded by the enigmatic and vengeful Captain Ahab. Ahab has lost his leg to Moby Dick and is determined to find and kill the whale as an act of personal vendetta. The crew, consisting of a diverse group of sailors from different backgrounds, is drawn into Ahab's dangerous and single-minded pursuit.

As the Pequod embarks on its voyage, Ishmael provides vivid descriptions of whaling techniques, the camaraderie among the sailors, and philosophical musings on life, nature, and the human condition. The narrative is interspersed with chapters exploring various aspects of whales and whaling, serving as both informative interludes and metaphorical reflections.

During their journey, the Pequod encounters other whaling ships, each with its own unique captain and crew. These encounters offer glimpses into different perspectives on whaling and the human relationship with nature. The crew members of the Pequod include Queequeg, a harpooner of Polynesian descent and Ishmael's close friend, as well as Starbuck, the first mate who questions Ahab's dangerous obsession.

As the Pequod sails deeper into the ocean, Ahab's obsession with Moby Dick consumes him, and he becomes increasingly detached from his crew and consumed by madness. The pursuit of the elusive whale leads the ship into treacherous waters and dangerous encounters, culminating in a climactic battle between Ahab and Moby Dick.

In the final confrontation, the white whale proves to be a formidable force of nature, leading to the destruction of the Pequod and the death of most of its crew. Ishmael, the sole survivor, clings to a coffin and is rescued by a passing ship, reflecting on the tragic events and pondering the mysteries of life and death.

"Moby-Dick" is renowned for its rich symbolism, complex characters, and intricate exploration of human nature. It delves into themes of hubris, the destructive power of obsession, the limits of human knowledge, and the sublime vastness of the natural world. It is considered a masterpiece of American literature and a profound examination of the human condition.

[Vocabulary]

author 작가 revenge 복수 whale 고래 themes 주제들 obsession 집착 fate 운명 human nature 인간의 본성 struggle 투쟁 narrate 이야기하다 whaling ship 고래 사냥선 enigmatic 수수께끼의 vengeful 복수심이 강한 vendetta 원한 camaraderie 동료애 philosophical musings 철학적 고찰 interspersed 흩뿌려진/산재한 informative interludes 정보를 담은 간주절 metaphorical reflections 은유적인 반영 encounters 만남들 perspectives 관점들 harpooner 고래작살을 던지는 자 Polynesian descent 폴리네시아 계통 first mate 일등항해사 obsession 집착 elusive 교묘히 빠져나가는 treacherous 배반하는 formidable 어마어마한 climactic 절정의 destruction 파괴 profound 심오한 hubris 오만함/과도한 자만 destructive power 파괴적인 sublime vastness 숭고한 광활함 masterpiece 걸작

[본문 해석] 모비딕

"모비 딕"은 미국 작가 허먼 멜빌이 쓴 소설로, 1851년에 출판되었습니다. 이 소설은 선장 아합의 거대한 백색고래인 모비 딕에 대한 집착적인 복수를 추구하는 이야기를 다룹니다. 이 소설은 집착, 운명, 인간의 본성 및 인간과 자연 사이의 투쟁과 같은 주제를 탐구합니다.

이 이야기는 미스테리하고 복수심에 불타는 선장 아합의 지휘를 받는 포경선 피쿼드에 합류하는 젊은 선원 이스마엘에 의해 서술됩니다. 아합은 모비 딕에게 다리를 잃었고 개인적인 복수심으로 고래를 찾아서 죽이기로 결심했습니다. 다른 배경을 가진 다양한 선원 집단으로 구성된 선원들은 아합의 위험하고 외골수적인 추적에 말려들게 됩니다.

피쿼드호가 항해를 시작하면서, 이스마엘은 고래잡이 기술에 대한 생생한 설명, 선원들 사이의 동지애, 그리고 삶, 자연, 그리고 인간의 상태에 대한 철학적인 사색을 제공합니다. 그 이야기는 고래와 고래잡이의 다양한 측면을 탐구하는 장들로 가득 차 있고, 유용한 정보를 제공하는 에피소드들과 비유적인 생각들을 제공합니다.

그들의 여행 동안, 피쿼드호는 각각 독특한 선장과 선원이 있는 다른 포경선들을 마주칩니다. 이러한 만남은 포경과 자연과의 인간관계에 대한 다양한 관점을 살짝 보여줍니다. 피쿼드호의 선원들은 아합의 위험한 집착에 의문을 제기하는 일등 항해사인 스타 벅뿐만 아니라, 폴리네시아 혈통의 작살잡이이자 이스마엘의 가까운 친구인 퀴퀘그를 포함합니다.

피쿼드호가 바다 속으로 더 깊이 항해하면서 모비딕에 대한 아합의 집착은 그를 소모시키고, 그는 점점 더 선원들로부터 분리되고 광기에 사로잡히게 됩니다. 잡기 힘든 고래를 쫓는 것은 배를 위험한 바다와 위험한 만남으로 이끌고, 결국 아합과 모비딕 사이의 절정에 이른 싸움으로 끝납니다.

마지막 대결에서 흰 고래는 피쿼드호를 파괴하고 선원 대부분을 죽음에 이르게 하는 강력한 자연의 힘임이 증명됩니다. 유일한 생존자인 이스마엘은 나무판에 매달려 있다가 지나가는 배에 의해 구조되어, 비극적인 사건들을 반성하고 삶과 죽음의 신비를 곰곰이 생각하게 됩니다.

"모비딕"은 풍부한 상징성, 복잡한 캐릭터, 그리고 인간 본성에 대한 복잡한 탐구로 유명합니다. 그것은 자만심, 집착의 파괴적인 힘, 인간 지식의 한계, 그리고 자연 세계의 숭고한 광대함의 주제들을 탐구합니다. 그것은 미국 문학의 걸작으로 여겨지며 인간 상태에 대한 심오한 검토의 대상으로 여겨집니다.

[Reading Comprehension]

1. Who is the author of the novel "Moby-Dick"?
a) Mark Twain   b) Edgar Allan Poe   c) Herman Melville   d) Nathaniel Hawthorne

2. What is the main target of Captain Ahab's revenge in the novel?
a) A giant squid   b) A white shark
c) A giant white whale named Moby Dick   d) A rogue pirate captain

3. How is the story of "Moby-Dick" narrated?
a) By Captain Ahab himself
b) Through the eyes of the white whale
c) Through the perspective of Ishmael, a young sailor
d) Through the eyes of a Polynesian harpooner

4. What is the name of the whaling ship commanded by Captain Ahab?
a) Pequod   b) Leviathan   c) Nautilus   d) Sea Serpent

5. What drives Captain Ahab's obsession with the white whale?
a) The whale stole his treasure
b) Ahab's lost leg due to an encounter with the whale
c) Ahab's desire for adventure
d) Ahab's fascination with marine life

6. Who is Queequeg in the novel "Moby-Dick"?
a) The ship's cook
b) The ship's doctor
c) A Polynesian harpooner and Ishmael's close friend
d) The ship's navigator

7. What is Starbuck's role on the Pequod?
a) Captain Ahab's personal assistant
b) The ship's first mate
c) The ship's cook
d) The ship's lookout

8. How does Captain Ahab's obsession affect his interactions with the crew?
a) He becomes more compassionate and understanding
b) He becomes more engaged in building friendships
c) He becomes increasingly detached and consumed by madness
d) He becomes a mentor to Ishmael

9. What happens to the Pequod during its pursuit of Moby Dick?
a) It returns to port
b) It encounters peaceful waters
c) It faces dangerous encounters and destruction
d) It reaches a new land

10. What does Ishmael cling to for survival after the Pequod's destruction?
a) A lifeboat   b) A harpoon   c) A barrel of oil   d) A coffin

11. Who is the sole survivor of the Pequod's destruction?
a) Captain Ahab   b) Queequeg   c) Starbuck   d) Ishmael

12. What themes does "Moby-Dick" explore?
a) Only the theme of revenge
b) Themes of obsession, fate, human nature, and the struggle between man and nature
c) Themes of romance and fantasy
d) Themes of politics and social inequality

13. How is the relationship between man and nature portrayed in the novel?
a) Nature is completely submissive to human will
b) Man and nature are in harmonious balance
c) There is a constant struggle and tension between man and nature
d) Nature has no impact on the characters' lives

14. What is the outcome of the final confrontation between Captain Ahab and Moby Dick?
a) Ahab successfully kills Moby Dick and survives
b) Moby Dick kills Ahab and spares the rest of the crew
c) The crew manages to capture Moby Dick alive
d) The Pequod is destroyed and most of the crew dies

15. How does the novel "Moby-Dick" end?
a) Captain Ahab becomes the new captain of the Pequod
b) Ishmael reflects on the tragic events and is rescued
c) Moby Dick and Captain Ahab join forces
d) The Pequod sails away to an unknown destination

[Grammar Check-up]

1. "Moby-Dick" tells the story of Captain Ahab's (obsessively, obsessive) quest for revenge against a giant white whale (is known, known) as Moby Dick.
2. The novel explores themes of (obsessive, obsession), fate, human nature, and the struggle between man and nature.
3. The story is narrated by Ishmael, a young sailor (who. which) joins the whaling ship Pequod, (commanding, commanded) by the vengeful Captain Ahab.
4. Ahab has lost his leg to Moby Dick and is (determining, determined) to find and kill the whale as an act of personal vendetta.
5. The crew, (consisting, consisted) of a diverse group of sailors from different backgrounds, is drawn into Ahab's dangerous and single-minded pursuit.
6. As the Pequod embarks on its voyage, Ishmael (provides, providing) vivid descriptions of whaling techniques and the camaraderie among the sailors.
7. The narrative (intersperses, is interspersed) with chapters exploring various aspects of whales and whaling, (serving, serves) as both informative interludes and metaphorical reflections.
8. (For, During) their journey, the Pequod encounters (other, another) whaling ships, each with its own unique captain and crew.
9. (These, this) encounters offer glimpses into different perspectives on whaling and the human relationship with nature.
10. The crew members of the Pequod (are included, include) Queequeg, a harpooner of Polynesian descent and Ishmael's close friend, as well as Starbuck.
11. As the Pequod sails deeper into the ocean, Ahab's obsession with Moby Dick consumes him, and he becomes (increasingly, increasing) detached from his crew and consumed by madness.
12. The (pursuit, pursue) of the elusive whale leads the ship into treacherous waters and dangerous encounters, (culminates, culminating) in a climactic battle between Ahab and Moby Dick.
13. In the final confrontation, the white whale proves to be a (formidable, formidably) force of nature, (leads, leading) to the destruction of the Pequod.
14. And the death of most of its crew. Ishmael, the sole survivor, (clinging, clings) to a coffin and is rescued by a passing ship, reflecting on the tragic events and (ponders, pondering) the mysteries of life and death.
15. "Moby-Dick" is renowned for (its, their) rich symbolism, complex characters, and intricate exploration of human nature.
16. It delves into themes of hubris, the (destructive, destruction) power of obsession, the limits of human knowledge, and the sublime vastness of the natural world.
17. It (is considered, considers) a masterpiece of American literature and a profound examination of the human condition.

[Writing Practice]

1. "Moby-Dick" tells the story of Captain *Ahab's* _____ a giant white whale known as Moby Dick. ~에 대한 *Ahap의* 복수를 위한 집착적인 탐색

2. The novel explores themes of obsession, fate, human nature, and _____.
인간과 자연 사이의 투쟁

3. The story is narrated by Ishmael, a young sailor who joins the whaling ship Pequod, _____ *Captain Ahab.*
수수께끼 같고 복수심에 불타는 *선장 Ahab*에 의해서 지휘되는 (분사구)

4. Ahab has lost his leg to Moby Dick and _____ as an act of personal vendetta. 그 고래를 찾아 죽이기로 결의한다

5. The crew, _____ from different backgrounds, is drawn
다양한 선원들로 구성된 (분사구) into Ahab's dangerous pursuit.

6. As the Pequod embarks on its voyage, Ishmael _____
whaling techniques and camaraderie among the sailors. ~에 대한 생생한 묘사를 제공한다

7. As the Pequod sails deeper into the ocean, Ahab's obsession with Moby Dick consumes him, and he _____ his crew and consumed by madness.
점차 ~로부터 이탈하게(detach) 된다

8. _____ leads the ship into treacherous waters
교묘히 빠져나가는 고래의 추격은 and dangerous encounters.

9. In the final confrontation, the white whale _____.
자연의 가공할 힘이라는 것이 증명된다

10. Ishmael, the sole survivor, _____ a passing ship.
관에 매달려(cling) 지나가는 배에 의해 구조된다

11. "Moby-Dick" _____, complex characters, and intricate
그것의 풍부한 상징성으로 유명하다 exploration of human nature.

12. It _____ and a profound examination of
미국 문학의 걸작으로 간주된다 the human condition.

[Word Quiz]

1. What is the term for the act of seeking retaliation for a perceived wrongdoing?
a) Revenge b) Whale c) Themes d) Obsession

2. What is a large marine mammal that is often depicted in literature and folklore?
a) Whale b) Fate c) Human nature d) Struggle

3. What are recurring subjects or ideas explored in a literary work?
a) Themes b) Narrate c) Whaling ship d) Enigmatic

4. What is an intense preoccupation with someone or something?
a) Obsession b) Vengeful c) Vendetta d) Camaraderie

5. Which term refers to the predetermined course of events in a person's life?
a) Fate b) Philosophical musings c) Interspersed d) Informative interludes

6. What is the inherent quality or characteristics of human beings?
a) Human nature b) Struggle c) Encounters d) Perspectives

7. What is the term for a prolonged effort or conflict?
a) Struggle b) Harpooner c) Polynesian descent d) First mate

8. Which word means to tell a story or give an account of events?
a) Narrate b) Elusive c) Treacherous d) Formidable

9. What is a vessel specifically designed for hunting and capturing whales?
a) Whaling ship b) Enigmatic c) Vengeful d) Vendetta

10. What describes something mysterious or puzzling?
a) Enigmatic b) Camaraderie c) Philosophical musings d) Interspersed

11. Which term describes a deep desire for revenge?
a) Vengeful b) Obsession c) Climactic d) Destruction

12. What is a prolonged bitter feud or conflict?

a) Vendetta   b) Hubris   c) Destructive power   d) Sublime vastness

13. What term refers to the mutual trust and friendship among people?

a) Camaraderie   b) Elusive   c) Treacherous   d) Formidable

14. What are thoughtful reflections on philosophical ideas?

a) Philosophical musings   b) Informative interludes

c) Metaphorical reflections   d) Encounters

15. Which term means scattered or dispersed at intervals?

a) Interspersed   b) Perspectives   c) Harpooner   d) Polynesian descent

16. What are brief sections of a literary work providing additional information?

a) Informative interludes   b) Harpooner   c) Treacherous   d) Climactic

17. Which term describes symbolic representations or comparisons?

a) Metaphorical reflections   b) Destructive power

c) Vengeful   d) Profound

18. What are chance meetings or confrontations between characters?

a) Encounters   b) Perspectives   c) Themes   d) Masterpiece

19. What term refers to the viewpoints or attitudes presented in a literary work?

a) Perspectives   b) Whale   c) Fate   d) Obsession

20. What is a person skilled in the use of a harpoon, especially on a whaling ship?

a) Harpooner   b) Polynesian descent   c) First mate   d) Elusive

Unit 24: Walden (1854)

"Walden" is a book written by Henry David Thoreau, first published in 1854. It is a reflection on his two-year experience of living in a cabin near Walden Pond, a small body of water in Concord, Massachusetts. Thoreau embarked on this experiment in simple living from 1845 to 1847, seeking to find a deeper connection to nature and to live deliberately with only the essentials.

The book begins with Thoreau describing his reasons for moving to Walden Pond. He wanted to escape the distractions of modern society and live a life of simplicity and self-sufficiency. Thoreau built a small cabin on the shores of the pond and settled there to observe nature and learn from it.

Throughout the book, Thoreau reflects on his daily life at Walden Pond and the lessons he learned. He observes the changing seasons and the beauty of nature, which he finds to be a source of deep spiritual and intellectual insight. Thoreau spends his time exploring the woods, fishing, and cultivating a small plot of land for crops. He lives off the land and carefully considers his relationship with nature, recognizing the interdependence of humans and the natural world.

Thoreau also explores the idea of self-reliance and individuality. He advocates for people to live authentically and not be governed by societal norms and material possessions. He believes in the importance of living deliberately, with purpose and intention, and not being consumed by the pursuit of wealth and status.

The book also delves into Thoreau's philosophical and social commentary on various topics. He discusses the role of government and questions its legitimacy, advocating for civil disobedience when faced with unjust laws. He critiques the materialistic society of his time and the loss of individuality and connection with nature.

Thoreau's time at Walden Pond comes to an end after two years. He decides to leave the cabin and return to society, but he carries with him the lessons and insights he gained from his experience. Thoreau's "Walden" is a testament to the importance of simplicity, self-reliance, and the deep connection between humans and nature. It remains a classic work of American literature and a source of inspiration for those seeking to live a more meaningful and deliberate life.

[Vocabulary]

reflection 반추/성찰 experience 경험 cabin 오두막 embark on 착수하다 simplicity 간소함 deliberately 의도적으로/신중하게 essentials 필수품 distractions 주의 산만 settle 정착하다 observe 관찰하다 spiritual 영적인 intellectual 지적인 insight 통찰 explore 탐험하다 cultivate 경작하다 interdependence 상호의존성 self-reliance 자기 의존 individuality 개성 authenticity 진정성 be governed 통제되다 philosophical 철학적인 commentary 논평 legitimacy 합법성 advocate 옹호하다 civil disobedience 시민 불복종 materialistic 물질주의 material possessions 물질적 소유물 pursuit 추구 delve into 탐구하다 critique 비평하다 loss 상실 inspiration 영감 testament 증거/고백 deliberate 의도적인 meaningful 의미 있는

[본문 해석] 월든

"월든(Walden)"은 헨리 데이비드 소로우(Thoreau)가 1854년에 처음 출간한 책입니다. 이 책은 소로우가 매사추세츠 주 콩코드의 월든 연못 근처 작은 오두막에서 2년간의 경험을 회상한 것입니다. 소로는 1845년부터 1847년까지 이 간단한 생활 실험을 시작하며 자연과 깊은 연결을 찾고 필요한 것들만으로 의식적으로 살아보려는 노력을 합니다.

이 책은 소로우가 월든 연못으로 이사하는 이유를 설명하는 부분으로 시작합니다. 그는 현대 사회의 방해와 도성 같은 삶을 떠나 간단하고 자기 충족적인 삶을 살고자 했습니다. 소로우는 연못의 해변에 작은 오두막을 짓고 거기서 자연을 관찰하고 배우기 위해 살게 됩니다.

이 책 전반에 걸쳐 소로우는 월든 연못에서의 일상생활과 그로부터 얻은 교훈에 대해 성찰합니다. 그는 계절의 변화와 자연의 아름다움을 관찰하며 이들이 깊은 영적이고 지적 통찰의 원천이라고 느끼게 됩니다. 소로는 숲을 탐험하고 낚시하며 작은 땅에서 농사를 짓습니다. 그는 대지에서 생활하며 인간과 자연의 상호 의존성을 깊이 생각합니다.

소로우는 또한 자립과 개성에 대해 탐구합니다. 그는 사람들에게 진정한 삶을 살도록 권장하고 사회적 규범과 물질적 소유에 의해 통제되지 말라고 합니다. 그는 목적과 의도를 가지고 의식적으로 살고, 부와 지위를 추구하는 데에 빠져들지 않아야 한다고 믿습니다.

이 책은 또한 소로우의 철학적이고 사회적 주제에 대한 논평을 다룹니다. 그는 정부의 역할에 대해 논하고, 정부의 정당성을 의심하며 불의한 법에 직면했을 때 시민 불복종을 옹호합니다. 그는 그 시대의 물질주의 사회를 비판하며 개인성과 자연과의 연결의 상실을 지적합니다.

소로우의 월든 연못에서의 시간은 2년 후에 끝나게 됩니다. 그는 오두막을 떠나 사회로 돌아가지만 그 경험으로부터 얻은 교훈과 통찰을 함께 가지고 갑니다. 소로우의 "월든"은 간소함, 자립, 그리고 인간과 자연 사이의 깊은 연관성의 중요성에 대한 증거입니다. 이 책은 미국 문학의 고전적인 작품이며 더욱 의미 있는 의식적인 삶을 추구하는 이들에게 영감을 주는 원천으로 남아 있습니다.

[Reading Comprehension]

1. When was "Walden" first published?
a) 1854 b) 1845 c) 1847 d) 1852

2. What is the main focus of "Walden"?
a) Thoreau's reflections on living in a cabin
b) Thoreau's exploration of the woods
c) Thoreau's observations of changing seasons
d) Thoreau's experiences at Walden Pond

3. Why did Thoreau move to Walden Pond?
a) To live a life of simplicity and self-sufficiency
b) To escape the distractions of modern society
c) To observe nature and learn from it
d) All of the above

4. What is Thoreau's purpose in living at Walden Pond?
a) To find a deeper connection to nature
b) To seek wealth and status
c) To cultivate crops and fish
d) To build a cabin near the water

5. What does Thoreau believe in regarding self-reliance and individuality?
a) People should follow societal norms
b) People should be governed by material possessions
c) People should live authentically
d) People should avoid living deliberately

6. What does Thoreau advocate for in the face of unjust laws?
a) Civil disobedience
b) Obedience and compliance
c) Avoiding any confrontation
d) Seeking government intervention

7. What is Thoreau's critique of society during his time?

a) Society is too simple and lacks complexity

b) Society values material possessions too much

c) Society is too focused on nature

d) Society lacks connection with the government

8. How long did Thoreau stay at Walden Pond?

a) One year

b) Five years

c) Two years

d) Three years

9. What is the lasting impact of "Walden"?

a) A testament to the importance of simplicity and self-reliance

b) A reflection on Thoreau's daily life at Walden Pond

c) A book about government roles

d) A source of inspiration for fishing enthusiasts

10. "Walden" is considered a classic work of _____.

a) British literature

b) French literature

c) American literature

d) German literature

[Grammar Check-up]

1. Thoreau's book "Walden" was _____ in 1854.
a) written   b) writing   c) writes   d) wrote

2. "Walden" is a reflection on Thoreau's _____ life at Walden Pond.
a) day   b) daily   c) today   d) days

3. Thoreau wanted to find a deeper _____ to nature during his time at Walden Pond.
a) connection   b) connected   c) connects   d) connecting

4. Thoreau embarked on an experiment in _____ living from 1845 to 1847.
a) simple   b) simply   c) simplicity   d) simpleness

5. He built a small cabin on the shores of Walden Pond and _____ there to observe nature.
a) settles   b) settled   c) settling   d) settle

6. Thoreau finds nature to be a source of deep _____ insight.
a) spiritual   b) spiritually   c) spirits   d) spirituality

7. He spends his time _____ the woods and cultivating crops.
a) explores   b) exploring   c) explored   d) explore

8. Thoreau advocates for people to live _____ and not be governed by societal norms.
a) authentically   b) authentic   c) authenticate   d) authenticity

9. He believes in the _____ of living deliberately and with purpose.
a) import   b) importance   c) important   d) importantly

10. Thoreau's book delves into philosophical and social _____ on various topics.
a) commandment   b) commentary   c) commented   d) commenting

11. Thoreau discusses the _____ of government and questions its legitimacy.
a) role b) rule c) rules d) rolling

12. He advocates for civil disobedience when faced with _____ laws.
a) unjust b) justly c) justice d) justness

13. Thoreau critiques the materialistic _____ of his time.
a) socially b) societal c) society d) social

14. He recognizes the _____ of humans and the natural world.
a) interdependence   b) interdepend
c) interdepending   d) interdependently

15. Thoreau's time at Walden Pond comes to _____ after two years.
a) end b) an end c) the end d) endless

16. He decides to leave the cabin and _____ to society.
a) take turns b) returning c) returned d) return

17. Thoreau's "Walden" is a testament to the _____ of simplicity and self-reliance.
a) importing b) importantly c) importance d) import

18. It remains a classic _____ of American literature.
a) worked b) work c) workings d) workable

19. "Walden" is a source of inspiration for those seeking to live a _____ life.
a) meaningfully b) meaningful c) meaning d) meaningless

20. Thoreau's experiences at Walden Pond are a _____ of his reflections.
a) test b) testifies c) testified d) testament

[Writing Practice]

1. Thoreau embarked on this experiment in simple living from 1845 to 1847, _____
_____ and to live deliberately with only the essentials.
자연과의 더 깊은 연관성을 찾아서 (분사구)

2. He _____ and live a life of simplicity
　　　　　현대 사회의 산만함에서 벗어나기를 원했다　　　　　and self-sufficiency.

3. Thoreau built a small cabin on the shores of the pond and _____
_____. 자연을 관찰하고 그것으로부터 배우기 위해 그곳에 정착했다

4. He observes the changing seasons and the beauty of nature, _____
_____
그는 그것이 깊은 영적이고 지적인 통찰력의 원천이라고 생각한다(find) (관계사)

5. Thoreau _____ a small plot
　　　　　숲을 탐험하고, 낚시하고, 경작하는 데 그의 시간을 보낸다　of land for crops.

6. He lives off the land and carefully considers his relationship with nature,
_____.
인간과 자연 세계의 상호 의존성을 인식하면서 (분사구)

7. He advocates for _____ and
material possessions.　사회적 규범에 의해 지배당하지 않고 진정하게 살아가는 사람들

8. He believes in *the importance* of living deliberately, with purpose and intention,
and *of* _____.
　　　　　부와 지위를 추구에 의해 낭비되지(consume) 않는 *것의 중요성*

9. He decides to leave the cabin and return to society, but he _____
_____
그는 그의 경험에서 얻은 교훈과 통찰력을 가지고 간다 (carry A with B)

10. It remains a classic work of American literature and a source of inspiration
_____
더 의미 있고 신중한 삶을 살고자 하는 사람들을 위해

[Word Quiz]

1. What term refers to thoughtful consideration or contemplation?
a) Reflection   b) Experience   c) Embark on   d) Simplicity

2. Which word means to begin or start something, especially a journey or project?
a) Embark on   b) Settle   c) Explore   d) Cultivate

3. What is the quality of being plain, uncomplicated, or straightforward?
a) Deliberately   b) Essentials   c) Distractions   d) Simplicity

4. Which term describes acting with intention or purpose?
a) Deliberately   b) Observing   c) Intellectual   d) Spiritual

5. What are fundamental or necessary items or principles?
a) Distractions   b) Essentials   c) Settle   d) Explore

6. Which word refers to factors that divert one's attention or focus?
a) Distractions   b) Observing   c) Spiritual   d) Authenticity

7. What does it mean to establish oneself in a new environment or situation?
a) Settle   b) Observe   c) Cultivate   d) Advocate

8. Which term involves watching or paying attention to something carefully?
a) Settle   b) Observe   c) Interdependence   d) Pursuit

9. What relates to matters of the spirit or soul rather than the physical body?
a) Intellectual   b) Spiritual   c) Insight   d) Authenticity

10. What word describes the ability to reason and think critically?
a) Interdependence   b) Self-reliance   c) Individuality   d) Intellectual

11. What is the understanding or perception of a deeper truth or meaning?
a) Interdependence   b) Insight   c) Explore   d) Cultivate

12. What term means to investigate or traverse new territory?

a) Individuality   b) Authenticity   c) Explore   d) Advocate

13. What is the concept of mutual reliance or dependence between entities?

a) Cultivate   b) Interdependence   c) Pursuit   d) Delve into

14. Which word describes the ability to rely on oneself rather than others?

a) Self-reliance   b) Authenticity   c) Deliberate   d) Meaningful

15. What refers to the unique characteristics or qualities of a person?

a) Exploration   b) Individuality   c) Insight   d) Legitimacy

16. What is the quality of being genuine or true to oneself?

a) Exploration   b) Individuality   c) Authenticity   d) Commentary

17. What does it mean to be controlled or influenced by something?

a) Be governed   b) Philosophical   c) Materialistic   d) Pursuit

18. Which term relates to the examination and discussion of ideas?

a) Be governed   b) Commentary   c) Legitimacy   d) Advocate

19. What is the state of being lawful, valid, or justifiable?

a) Legitimacy   b) Advocate   c) Civil disobedience   d) Material possessions

20. What refers to the active support or promotion of a cause or idea?

a) Legitimacy   b) Advocate   c) Civil disobedience   d) Material possessions

Unit 25: Great Expectations (1861)

"Great Expectations" is a novel written by Charles Dickens and was first published in 1861. The story is narrated by the protagonist, Philip Pirrip, who is known as Pip. The novel follows Pip's life from his childhood to adulthood, and it is set in the early 19th century.

The novel opens with young Pip living with his abusive sister, Mrs. Joe Gargery, and her kind-hearted husband, Joe, a blacksmith. Pip's parents are deceased, and he lives in a humble cottage on the marshes of Kent, England. One evening, while visiting the graves of his parents, Pip encounters an escaped convict named Abel Magwitch, who threatens him into bringing food and a file to remove his shackles. Pip does what he is told, but he's afraid he feels guilty of helping the prisoner.

Pip is invited to the grand and decaying Satis House by Miss Havisham, an eccentric and wealthy woman who wears her wedding dress, still waiting for her long-lost love. Miss Havisham asks Pip to play with her adopted daughter,

Estella, who is cold and disdainful toward him. Despite the harsh treatment, Pip falls in love with Estella, and his desire to become a gentleman is ignited.

One day, Pip receives news that he has "great expectations" - an anonymous benefactor has provided him with the means to become a gentleman and move to London. Pip assumes that Miss Havisham is his benefactor, and he leaves for London, leaving Joe and his simple country life behind. In London, he is tutored by Mr. Pocket and becomes friends with Herbert Pocket, who is also Miss Havisham's relative.

Pip becomes ashamed of his humble background and tries to become a refined gentleman. He spends money recklessly and incurs debts. He also distances himself from Joe and Biddy, his childhood friend who has always cared for him. Pip's infatuation with Estella continues, but she remains emotionally distant.

Pip discovers that his true benefactor is not Miss Havisham but the convict he once helped, Abel Magwitch, who has become a successful criminal. Magwitch, once a fatherly figure to Pip, returns to England to see his "gentleman" prosper. Pip is devastated by this revelation, but he still wants to help Magwitch escape the law.

Miss Havisham realizes the damage she has caused, particularly to Estella, and she suffers great remorse. She is accidentally killed in a fire at Satis House, and before she dies, she asks Pip for his forgiveness. Pip forgives her, and her death marks a turning point in Pip's life, leading him to reevaluate his values and priorities.

After Magwitch's capture and death, Pip falls into severe illness. He is nursed back to health by Joe, who comes to London to take care of him. During his recovery, Pip realizes the true worth of Joe and Biddy and understands the importance of love and loyalty.

Pip returns to the marshes and reconciles with Joe and Biddy. Pip realizes that he was blind to the genuine love and care they offered him throughout his life. Pip decides to start anew and becomes a humble blacksmith with Joe.

Estella, who was raised to be heartless by Miss Havisham, suffers from an abusive marriage. After her husband dies, she becomes more compassionate and acknowledges the mistakes she made. Pip and Estella meet again, and though their futures remain uncertain, they part as friends.

"Great Expectations" is a bildungsroman, or a coming-of-age novel, that explores themes of identity, social class, love, forgiveness, and the corrupting influence of ambition. Pip's journey from a poor, humble boy to a gentleman and back again is a tale of self-discovery and moral growth, making it one of Dickens' most enduring and celebrated works.

[본문 해석] 위대한 유산

  "위대한 유산"은 찰스 디킨스가 쓴 소설로 1861년에 처음 출판되었습니다. 그 이야기는 핍으로 알려진 주인공 필립에 의해 시작됩니다. 그 소설은 핍의 어린 시절부터 성인기까지의 삶을 따라가고, 그것은 19세기 초를 배경으로 합니다.

  이 소설은 핍을 학대하는 누나 조 가저리 부인과 마음씨 고운 남편 대장장이 조와 함께 사는 어린 핍으로 시작합니다. 핍의 부모님은 돌아가셨고, 그는 영국 켄트의 습지에 있는 초라한 오두막에서 살고 있습니다. 어느 날 저녁, 핍은 부모님의 무덤을 방문하던 중 아벨 매그위치라는 탈출한 죄수를 만나게 되고, 그는 그에게 음식과 족쇄를 제거하기 위한 줄(쇠붙이를 가는 도구)을 가져오라고 위협합니다. 핍은 시키는 대로 하지만 그가 죄수를 도운 것에 대해 죄의식을 느낍니다.

  핍은 아직도 오랫동안 잃어버렸던 사랑을 기다리며 웨딩드레스를 입고 사는 엉뚱하고 부유한 여성인 미스 헤비셤에 의해 웅장하고 쇠퇴한 사티스 저택으로 초대됩니다. 미스 헤비셤은 핍에게 자신의 차갑고 경멸하는 성질을 지닌 입양한 딸 에스텔러의 놀이 친구가 되어 것을 부탁합니다. 가혹한 대우에도 불구하고, 핍은 에스텔러와 사랑에 빠지게 되고, 신사가 되고 싶다는 그의 욕망이 점화됩니다.

  어느 날, 핍은 그가 엄청난 유산을 상속받게 될 것이라는 소식을 듣습니다. - 어느 익명의 후원자가 그에게 런던으로 이사 가 신사가 될 수 있는 재산을 제공했습니다. 핍은 헤비셤이 그의 후원자라고 생각하고, 조와 그의 소박한 시골 생활을 뒤로하고 런던으로 떠납니다. 런던에서, 그는 허버트 포킷 씨의 지도를 받으며 헤비셤의 친척이기도 한 그와 친구가 됩니다.

  핍은 자신의 초라한 배경을 부끄러워하고 세련된 신사가 되려고 노력합니다. 그는 돈을 무모하게 쓰고 빚을 집니다. 또한 그는 매형 조와 자신을 항상 아껴주던 소꿉친구인 비디와 거리를 둡니다. 핍은 에스텔러에 대한 미련이 계속되지만, 그녀는 감정적으로 거리를 두고 있습니다.

  핍은 자신의 진정한 은인이 미스 헤비셤이 아니라 성공한 범죄자, 한때 자신을 도왔던 죄수인 아벨 매그위치라는 것을 알게 됩니다. 한때 핍에게 아버지 같은 존재였던 매그위치는 그가 만든 "신사" 핍이 성공하는 것을 보기 위해 영국으로 돌아옵니다. 핍은 이러한 폭로에 충격을 받았지만, 여전히 매그위치가 법망에서 벗어날 수 있도록 돕고 싶어 합니다.

  헤비셤은 자신이 특히 에스텔러에게 입힌 피해를 깨닫고 큰 후회를 합니다. 그녀는 사티스 저택에서 발생한 화재로 우연히 사망하고, 그녀가 죽기 전에 핍에게 용서를 구합니다. 핍은 그녀를 용서하고, 그녀의 죽음은 핍의 삶에 전환점을 맞이하게 하며, 그가 그의 가치와 우선순위를 재평가하도록 이끌었습니다.

  매그위치가 붙잡혀 죽은 후, 핍은 심각한 병에 걸립니다. 그는 그를 돌보기 위해 런던으로 온 조에 의해 건강을 되찾게 됩니다. 그가 회복되는 동안, 핍은 조와 누나, 친구 비디의 진정한 가치를 깨닫고 사랑과 충절의 중요성을 이해하게 됩니다.

  핍은 고향의 평원으로 되돌아오고, 조 그리고 비디와 화해합니다. 핍은 그가 평생 동안 그들이 제공한 진정한 사랑과 보살핌에 눈이 멀었다는 것을 깨닫습니다. 핍은 새로운 시작을 하기로 결정하고 조와 함께 소박한 대장장이가 됩니다.

  미스 헤비셤에 의해 비정하게 자란 에스텔러는 학대적인 결혼 생활로 고통을 받습니다. 남편이 죽은 후, 그녀는 더 동정심이 많아지고 자신이 저지른 실수를 인정합니다. 핍과 에스텔러는 다시 만나게 되고, 그들의 미래는 불확실하지만, 그들은 친구로서 헤어집니다.

  "위대한 유산"은 정체성, 사회 계급, 사랑, 용서 그리고 야망의 부패한 영향에 대한 주제를 탐구하는 교양소설 또는 성장소설입니다. 가난하고 소박한 소년에서 신사로 그리고 다시 예전으로 돌아온 핍의 여행은 자아 발견과 도덕적인 성장에 대한 이야기이며, 그것을 디킨스의 가장 오래 지속되고 유명한 작품 중 하나로 만듭니다.

[Vocabulary]

abusive 학대적인 deceased 사망한 encounter 마주치다 convict 유죄자/죄인 threaten 협박하다 shackles 족쇄 grand 웅장한 decaying 부패한 eccentric 기이한 disdainful 경멸적인 benefactor 후원자 refined 세련된 infatuation 짝사랑 revelation 폭로 devastation 황폐화 remorse 후회 accidentally 우연히 turning point 전환점 reconcile 화해하다 blind 무감각한 genuine 진정한 heartless 무정한 compassionate 동정적인 acknowledge 인정하다 corrupting influence 타락적인 영향력 bildungsroman 성장소설 identity 정체성 forgiveness 용서 self-discovery 자기발견 moral growth 도덕적 성장 enduring 지속되는 celebrate 기념하다 protagonist 주인공 humble 겸손한 cottage 오두막집 marshes 습지대

[Reading Comprehension]

1. Who is the protagonist and narrator of "Great Expectations"?
a) Abel Magwitch   b) Miss Havisham   c) Philip Pirrip (Pip)   d) Joe Gargery

2. Where does Pip live with his abusive sister and kind-hearted husband?
a) London   b) Satis House
c) The marshes of Kent, England   d) Blacksmith shop

3. What does Pip encounter while visiting the graves of his parents?
a) A convict named Abel Magwitch
b) Soldiers looking for him
c) A wealthy benefactor
d) A mysterious treasure map

4. Who invites Pip to the grand and decaying Satis House?
a) Joe Gargery   b) Estella   c) Miss Havisham   d) Mr. Pocket

5. What is Pip's infatuation with Estella despite her harsh treatment?
a) He wants to become a gentleman like her
b) He believes she is a long-lost relative
c) He is seeking revenge on her
d) He wants to marry her and inherit her wealth

6. What news does Pip receive that changes his life?
a) His parents are alive
b) He has inherited a fortune from a wealthy relative
c) He is invited to join a secret society
d) He is going to be married to Estella

7. Who is Pip's true benefactor providing him with "great expectations"?
a) Miss Havisham   b) Mr. Pocket
c) Abel Magwitch   d) Joe Gargery

8. What does Miss Havisham realize about her actions?
a) She wants to adopt Pip as her son
b) She regrets adopting Estella
c) She caused damage to Estella
d) She wants to become a blacksmith

9. How does Pip react when he discovers Abel Magwitch is his benefactor?
a) He is devastated
b) He is excited to meet him
c) He is angry and seeks revenge
d) He doesn't care

10. What happens to Miss Havisham in the end?
a) She gets married to Joe Gargery
b) She dies in a fire at Satis House
c) She runs away with Abel Magwitch
d) She forgives Estella

11. Who takes care of Pip during his severe illness?
a) Herbert Pocket
b) Miss Havisham
c) Joe Gargery
d) Abel Magwitch

12. How does Pip's attitude towards Joe and Biddy change?
a) He becomes more distant from them
b) He becomes more appreciative of their love and care
c) He becomes jealous of them
d) He forgets about them completely

13. What does Estella suffer from after her husband's death?
a) Poverty
b) An abusive marriage
c) Loneliness
d) Illness

14. What are the themes explored in "Great Expectations"?
a) Mystery and adventure
b) Identity, social class, love, and forgiveness
c) Science and technology
d) War and peace

15. What genre does "Great Expectations" belong to?
a) Mystery
b) Romance
c) Bildungsroman (coming-of-age novel)
d) Fantasy

[Grammar Check-up]

1. The novel follows Pip's life from his childhood (and, to) adulthood, and it is set in the early 19th century.

2. The novel opens with young Pip (who live, living) with his abusive sister, Mrs. Joe Gargery, and her kind-hearted husband, Joe, a blacksmith.

3. Pip's parents are (deceasing, deceased), and he lives in a (humbly, humble) cottage on the marshes of Kent, England.

4. One evening, while (visit, visiting) the graves of his parents, Pip encounters an escaped convict (who names, named) Abel Magwitch, who (threatening, threatens) him into bringing food and a file to remove his shackles.

5. Pip (invites, is invited) to the grand and decaying Satis House by Miss Havisham, an eccentric and wealthy woman who (wearing, wears) her wedding dress, still waiting for her long-lost love.

6. Miss Havisham asks Pip to play with her (adopted, adopting) daughter, Estella, who is cold and disdainful toward him.

7. Despite the harsh treatment, Pip falls in love with Estella, and his desire to become a gentleman is (ignited, igniting).

8. One day, Pip (is received, receives) news that he has "great expectations" - an anonymous benefactor has provided him with the (mean, means) to become a gentleman and move to London.

9. Pip (assumes, is assumed) that Miss Havisham is his benefactor, and he leaves for London, leaving Joe and his simple country life behind.

10. In London, he is (tutoring, tutored by) Mr. Pocket and becomes friends with Herbert Pocket, who is also Miss Havisham's relative.

11. Pip becomes (ashame, ashamed) of his humble background and tries to become a refined gentleman.

12. He (is spent, spends) money recklessly and incurs debts.

13. He also distances himself from Joe and Biddy, his childhood friend who (have, has) always cared for him.

14. Pip's infatuation with Estella continues, but she remains emotionally (distant, distantly).

15. Pip discovers that his true benefactor is not Miss Havisham (and, but) the convict he once helped, Abel Magwitch, who has become a successful criminal.

16. Magwitch, once a fatherly figure to Pip, (returns, returning) to England to see his "gentleman" prosper.

17. Pip is (devastated by, devastating) this revelation, but he still wants to help Magwitch escape the law.

18. Miss Havisham realizes the damage she has caused, (particular, particularly) to Estella, and she suffers great remorse.

19. She is (accidentally, accidental) killed in a fire at Satis House, and before she dies, she asks Pip for his forgiveness.

20. Pip forgives her, and her death marks a turning point in Pip's life, leading him (to reevaluate, reevaluate) his values and priorities.

21. He is (nursing, nursed) back to health by Joe, who comes to London to take care of him.

22. (While, During) his recovery, Pip realizes the true worth of Joe and Biddy and understands the importance of love and loyalty.

23. Pip realizes that he was blind to the (genuinely, genuine) love and care they offered him throughout his life.

24. Pip decides to start (anew, new) and becomes a humble blacksmith with Joe.

25. Estella, who was (risen, raised) to be heartless by Miss Havisham, suffers from an abusive marriage.

26. After her husband dies, she becomes more compassionate and acknowledges the mistakes she (was made, made).

27. Pip and Estella meet again, and though their futures remain (uncertain, uncertainly), they part as friends.

28. "Great Expectations" is a bildungsroman, or a coming-of-age novel, that (exploring, explores) themes of identity, social class, love, forgiveness, and the corrupting influence of ambition.

29. Pip's journey from a poor, humble boy to a gentleman and back again is a tale of (self-discover, self-discovery) and moral growth, making it one of Dickens' most enduring and celebrated (work, works).

[Writing Practice]

1. One evening, _____, Pip encounters an
escaped convict named Abel Magwitch. 그의 부모님의 무덤을 방문하는 동안

2. Pip _____ by Miss Havisham, an eccentric
　　　　　웅장하고 쇠퇴해가는 Satis House에 초대받는다　　　　　and wealthy woman.

3. Miss Havisham _____, Estella, who is cold and
disdainful toward him. Pip에게 그녀의 입양한 딸과 놀아주도록 부탁한다

4. Despite the harsh treatment, Pip falls in love with Estella, and _____
_____. 신사가 되려는 그의 욕망이 불붙는다(ignite)

5. One day, Pip receives news that he has "great expectations" – an anonymous
benefactor _____ a gentleman and move to London.
　　　　　그에게 ~가 되기 위한 수단을 제공했다 (현재완료)

6. Pip _____ and tries to become a refined
　　　　　그의 비천한 배경에 대해 수치심을 느낀다　　　　　　　　　　gentleman.

7. He also distances himself from Joe and Biddy, his childhood friend _____
_____ 늘 그를 돌봐 주었던 (관계사, 현재완료)

8. _____at Satis House, and before
　　　　그녀는 우연히 화재로 죽는다　　　　she dies, she asks Pip for his forgiveness.

9. Pip realizes that he was blind to the genuine *love and care* _____
_____ 그들이 그에게 그의 일생 내내 제공했던 *사랑과 돌봄* (관계사)

10. Estella, _____ by Miss Havisham,
suffers from an abusive marriage. 비정하도록 길러진 (관계사, 과거)

[Word Quiz]

1. What is the meaning of "abusive"?

a) Humble   b) Kind-hearted   c) Cruel and harmful   d) Gentle and caring

2. What word means "dead"?

a) Deceased   b) Remorse   c) Genuine   d) Turning point

3. What does "encounter" mean?

a) To threaten   b) To reconcile

c) To meet or come across unexpectedly   d) To celebrate

4. Which word refers to a person found guilty of a crime?

a) Threaten   b) Benefactor   c) Convict   d) Infatuation

5. What is the meaning of "threaten"?

a) To acknowledge   b) To celebrate

c) To offer help   d) To express intent to harm or cause fear

6. What are "shackles"?

a) A grand event

b) A humble dwelling

c) Chains or restraints on someone's wrists or ankles

d) A turning point in a story

7. What does "grand" mean?

a) Genuine   b) Decaying   c) Humble   d) Impressive and magnificent

8. What is the meaning of "decaying"?

a) Cruel and harmful   b) Genuine

c) Humble   d) In a state of rot or deterioration

9. Which word describes someone who is unconventional or peculiar?

a) Remorse   b) Eccentric   c) Reconcile   d) Compassionate

10. What does "disdainful" mean?

a) Kind-hearted

b) Cruel and harmful

c) Expressing scorn or contempt

d) A genuine revelation

11. What is a "benefactor"?

a) A grand event

b) A person who causes devastation

c) A person who offers help or financial aid

d) A person who is remorseful

12. What does "refined" mean?

a) To acknowledge

b) To reconcile

c) To become humble

d) Cultured and polished

13. What is an "infatuation"?

a) Genuine love and care

b) A turning point in a story

c) An intense but short-lived passion or admiration

d) A remorseful feeling

14. What does "revelation" mean?

a) A grand event

b) A turning point in a story

c) An accidental discovery

d) Genuine and sincere

15. What does "devastation" refer to?

a) A genuine revelation

b) A state of rot or deterioration

c) A state of extreme destruction and ruin

d) An accidental encounter

16. What is "remorse"?

a) Kind-heartedness

b) Cruelty

c) Genuine and sincere   ·

d) A feeling of regret and guilt for past actions

17. What does "accidentally" mean?

a) Cruelly

b) Genuinely

c) By chance or without intention

d) Magnificently

18. What is a "turning point"?

a) A grand event

b) A state of rot or deterioration

c) A moment of significant change or decision in a story

d) A genuine revelation

19. What does "reconcile" mean?

a) To express scorn or contempt

b) To offer help or financial aid

c) To restore friendly relations after a disagreement

d) To become eccentric

20. What is the meaning of "blind" in the context of a person?

a) Unable to see

b) Unable to hear

c) Unable to feel

d) Unaware or insensitive to certain things

Unit 26: Crime and Punishment (1866)

"Crime and Punishment" is a novel written by Fyodor Dostoevsky and first published in 1866. The story is set in St. Petersburg, Russia, during the mid-19th century and follows the life of Rodion Raskolnikov, an impoverished former student.

Rodion Raskolnikov is a deeply troubled and impoverished young man. He has dropped out of university and lives in a small, rundown apartment. Overwhelmed by poverty and his nihilistic beliefs, Raskolnikov develops a theory that extraordinary individuals are above traditional moral laws and can commit crimes for the greater good. He decides to test this theory by murdering Alyona Ivanovna, an elderly pawnbroker, and her innocent sister, Lizaveta, for their money. Raskolnikov believes that he will use the stolen money to help others and prove his superiority.

After committing the double murder, Raskolnikov becomes overwhelmed with guilt and fear of being caught. He becomes mentally unstable and struggles to cope with the consequences of his actions. Meanwhile, the investigating magistrate, Porfiry Petrovich, becomes suspicious of Raskolnikov and begins to closely monitor his movements.

Raskolnikov befriends Marmeladov, a drunkard and the father of Sonya, a young woman who turns to prostitution to support her family. Sonya's unwavering faith and self-sacrifice deeply affect Raskolnikov, and he starts to see the possibility of redemption for his crimes.

As Raskolnikov's mental state continues to deteriorate, he is haunted by hallucinations and visions, particularly of a malevolent figure named Mephistopheles. He confesses his crime to Sonya, who becomes his confidante and moral compass. Raskolnikov becomes increasingly torn between the idea of confessing to the police and maintaining his theory of superiority.

During the investigation, Porfiry Petrovich cleverly manipulates Raskolnikov, trying to lead him into a confession. Meanwhile, Raskolnikov's mother, Pulcheria Alexandrovna, and sister, Avdotya Romanovna (Dounia), arrive in St. Petersburg. They have been receiving financial support from a wealthy suitor, Luzhin, but Dounia rejects him after learning about his vile intentions.

Raskolnikov's friend, Razumikhin, discovers that Raskolnikov is the murderer and confronts him. Raskolnikov, in a state of extreme emotional distress, falls seriously ill. Sonya, driven by her love for him, stays by his side and takes care of him.

As Raskolnikov recovers, he finally decides to confess his crime to the authorities. He is brought to the police station, where he admits to the murders and is subsequently sentenced to exile in Siberia. Throughout the process, Raskolnikov experiences a profound spiritual transformation and accepts his guilt.

In the epilogue, Raskolnikov is shown in Siberia, where he begins his sentence. He is filled with remorse and repentance, and his interactions with other prisoners and Sonya provide a glimpse of hope for his redemption.

"Crime and Punishment" is a profound exploration of human nature, morality, guilt, and the consequences of one's actions. It delves into the psychological and philosophical struggles of its characters, making it a timeless and powerful work of literature.

[Vocabulary]

Impoverished 빈곤한 Nihilistic 허무주의의 Extraordinary 비범한 Consequences 결과 Commit 범하다 Investigation 수사 Magistrate 사법관 Prostitution 매춘 Unwavering 동요하지 않는 Redemption 구원 Deteriorate 악화되다 Hallucinations 환각 Malevolent 악의적인 Confess 고백하다 Manipulate 조작하다 Financial 재정적인 Confront 맞서다 Emotional 감정적인 Authorities 당국 Exile 망명 Subsequently 이후에 Profound 심오한 Transformation 변형 Epilogue 맺음말 Remorse 후회 Repentance 회개 Redemption 구원 Exploration 탐구 Morality 도덕성 Guilt 죄책감 Psychological 심리적인 Philosophical 철학적인 Timeless 영구한 Confession 고백

[본문 해석] 죄와 벌

"죄와 벌"은 러시아 소설가 표도르 도스토옙스키에 의해 쓰여 진 소설로 1866년에 처음 출판되었습니다. 이야기는 19세기 중반 러시아 상트페테르부르크를 배경으로 가난한 전직 학생인 라스콜니코프의 삶을 따라갑니다.

라스콜니코프는 매우 근심이 많은 가난한 젊은이입니다. 그는 대학을 중퇴하고 쇠퇴한 작은 아파트에서 살고 있습니다. 가난과 허무주의적인 신념에 압도된 라스콜니코프는 비범한 개인은 전통적인 도덕 법칙 위에 있고 더 큰 선을 위해 범죄를 저지를 수 있다는 이론을 발전시킵니다. 그는 나이 든 전당포 주인인 알료나 이바노브나와 그녀의 무고한 여동생 리자베타를 그들의 돈을 위해 살해함으로써 이 이론을 시험하기로 결정합니다. 라스콜니코프는 그가 훔친 돈을 다른 사람들을 돕고 자신의 우월함을 증명하는 데 사용할 것이라고 믿습니다.

이중 살인을 저지른 후 라스콜니코프는 죄책감과 붙잡힐 것에 대한 두려움에 휩싸이게 됩니다. 그는 정신적으로 불안정해지고 자신의 행동이 초래할 결과에 대처하기 위해 고군분투합니다. 한편 수사 치안판사 포르피리 페트로비치는 라스콜니코프를 의심하게 되고 그의 움직임을 면밀히 감시하기 시작합니다.

라스콜니코프는 술주정뱅이이자 가족을 부양하기 위해 성매매로 전향한 젊은 여성 소냐의 아버지인 마르멜라도프와 친구가 됩니다. 소냐의 변함없는 믿음과 자기희생은 라스콜니코프에게 깊은 영향을 미치고, 그는 자신의 범죄에 대한 구원의 가능성을 보기 시작합니다.

라스콜니코프의 정신 상태가 계속 악화되면서 그는 환각과 환영, 특히 메피스토펠레스라는 사악한 인물의 환영에 시달립니다. 그는 소냐에게 자신의 범행을 고백하고, 소냐는 자신의 친구이자 도덕적 나침반이 됩니다. 라스콜니코프는 경찰에게 고백해야 한다는 생각과 자신의 우월론을

유지해야 한다는 생각 사이에서 점점 갈팡질팡하게 됩니다.

수사가 진행되는 동안, 포르피리 페트로비치는 라스콜니코프를 교묘하게 조종하여 그를 자백으로 인도합니다. 한편, 라스콜니코프의 어머니 풀체리아 알렉산드로브나와 여동생 아브도티야 로마노프나(두니아)가 상트페테르부르크에 도착합니다. 그들은 부유한 구혼자 루진으로부터 재정적인 지원을 받고 있지만, 두니아는 그의 사악한 의도를 알고 그를 거부합니다.

라스콜니코프의 친구 라주미킨은 라스콜니코프가 살인자라는 것을 발견하고 그와 대면합니다. 극심한 감정적 고통에 빠진 라스콜니코프는 심각한 병에 걸립니다. 그에 대한 사랑에 이끌려 소냐는 그의 곁을 지키며 그를 돌봅니다.

라스콜니코프가 회복하면서 마침내 당국에 자신의 범죄를 고백하기로 결정합니다. 그는 경찰서로 이송되어 살인을 인정하고 이후 시베리아로 추방 판결을 받습니다. 과정 전반에 걸쳐 라스콜니코프는 심대한 정신적 변화를 경험하고 죄책감을 받아들입니다.

에필로그에서 라스콜니코프는 시베리아에서 그의 형기를 시작하는 모습을 보여줍니다. 그는 회환과 회개로 가득 차 있고, 그의 다른 죄수들과 소냐와의 상호작용은 그의 구원에 대한 희미한 희망을 제공합니다. "죄와 벌"은 인간의 본성, 도덕성, 죄의식, 그리고 자신의 행동의 결과에 대한 심오한 탐구입니다. 그것은 그것을 시대를 초월하고 강력한 문학 작품으로 만들면서, 그것의 등장인물들의 심리적인 그리고 철학적인 투쟁을 파고듭니다.

[Reading Comprehension]

1. What is the title of the novel written by Fyodor Dostoevsky?
a) War and Peace
b) Crime and Punishment
c) Anna Karenina
d) The Brothers Karamazov

2. In which city is the story set?
a) Moscow   b) St. Petersburg   c) London   d) Paris

3. Who is the protagonist of the novel?
a) Alyona Ivanovna
b) Lizaveta
c) Rodion Raskolnikov
d) Porfiry Petrovich

4. Why does Raskolnikov murder Alyona Ivanovna and Lizaveta?
a) For revenge
b) To test his theory of superiority
c) For money
d) To protect Sonya

5. What is Raskolnikov's theory about extraordinary individuals?
a) They are above the law
b) They are destined for greatness
c) They are inherently evil
d) They are guided by a higher power

6. Who becomes Raskolnikov's confidante and moral compass?
a) Marmeladov
b) Porfiry Petrovich
c) Sonya
d) Pulcheria Alexandrovna

7. What is Raskolnikov's reaction after committing the double murder?
a) He feels triumphant
b) He becomes mentally unstable and overwhelmed with guilt
c) He plans his next crime
d) He feels no remorse

8. What role does Porfiry Petrovich play in the story?
a) He is Raskolnikov's friend
b) He is Raskolnikov's mother
c) He is the investigating magistrate
d) He is the murder victim

9. Who takes care of Raskolnikov when he falls seriously ill?
a) Marmeladov   b) Razumikhin   c) Sonya   d) Pulcheria Alexandrovna

10. What does Raskolnikov finally decide to do at the end of the novel?
a) Escape to another country
b) Commit suicide
c) Confess his crime to the authorities
d) Continue his life of crime

11. Where is Raskolnikov sentenced to exile?
a) Moscow   b) Paris   c) London   d) Siberia

12. What does the epilogue of the novel show?
a) Raskolnikov's trial
b) Raskolnikov's confession to Sonya
c) Raskolnikov's life in Siberia
d) Raskolnikov's escape from the police

13. What themes does "Crime and Punishment" explore?
a) Love and friendship
b) Human nature, morality, guilt, and consequences of actions
c) Adventure and travel
d) Political intrigue

14. How does Raskolnikov's mental state change throughout the story?
a) He becomes more stable and confident
b) He becomes increasingly troubled and unstable
c) He becomes indifferent to his actions
d) He becomes a criminal mastermind

15. What is the overall impact of "Crime and Punishment" as a work of literature?
a) It is a light-hearted comedy
b) It is a timeless and powerful exploration of human nature
c) It is a simple love story
d) It is a fantasy novel

[Grammar Check-up]

1. The story follows the life of Rodion Raskolnikov, an (impoverished, impoverishing) former student.

2. (Overwhelming, Overwhelmed by) poverty and his nihilistic beliefs, Raskolnikov develops a theory (what, that) extraordinary individuals are above (traditional, tradition) moral laws and can commit crimes for the greater good.

3. He decides to test this theory (to murder, by murdering) Alyona Ivanovna, an elderly pawnbroker, and her innocent sister, Lizaveta, for their money.

4. Raskolnikov believes that he will use the (stolen, stealing) money to help others and prove his superiority.

5. After committing the double murder, Raskolnikov becomes overwhelmed with guilt and fear of (catching, being caught).

6. He becomes (mentally, mental) unstable and struggles to cope with the consequences of his actions.

7. Meanwhile, the (investigated, investigating) magistrate, Porfiry Petrovich, becomes suspicious of Raskolnikov and begins to closely monitor his movements.

8. Raskolnikov befriends Marmeladov, a drunkard and the father of Sonya, a young woman (who turns, turns) to prostitution to support her family.

9. Sonya's unwavering faith and self-sacrifice deeply (effect, affect) Raskolnikov, and he starts to see the possibility of redemption for his crimes.

10. As Raskolnikov's mental state continues to deteriorate, he (haunts, is haunted by) hallucinations and visions, (particularly, particular) of a malevolent figure named Mephistopheles.

11. He (confessions, confesses) his crime to Sonya, who becomes his confidante and moral compass.

12. Raskolnikov becomes increasingly (torn, tearing) between the idea of confessing to the police and maintaining his theory of superiority.

13. During the investigation, Porfiry Petrovich (is clever, cleverly) manipulates Raskolnikov, trying to lead him into a confession.

14. They have been (receiving, received) financial support from a wealthy suitor, Luzhin, but Dounia rejects him after learning about his vile intentions.

15. He (brings, is brought) to the police station, (which, where) he admits to the murders and is subsequently (sentenced, sentencing) to exile in Siberia.

[Writing Practice]

1. _____, Raskolnikov develops a theory

     가난과 허무주의적 신념에 압도되어 (분사구)

that extraordinary individuals are above traditional moral laws and can commit

crimes for the greater good.

2. He _____ Alyona Ivanovna, and her innocent sister.

  ~를 살해함으로써 이 이론을 시험하기로 결심하다

3. Raskolnikov believes that _____ and prove his superiority.

          그는 다른 사람들을 돕기 위해 훔친 돈을 사용할 것이다

4. He _____ and struggles to cope with the consequences of

his actions. 정신적으로 불안정해 지다

5. Porfiry Petrovich becomes suspicious of Raskolnikov and _____

_____. 그의 움직임을 면밀히 관찰하기 시작한다

6. As Raskolnikov's mental state continues to deteriorate, _____,

_____ particularly of a malevolent figure named Mephistopheles.

그는 환각(ha~)과 환영(vi~)에 사로잡혀 있다

7. During the investigation, Porfiry Petrovich cleverly manipulates Raskolnikov, _____

_____. 그를 자백으로 이끌기 위해 노력하면서 (분사구)

8. They _____ a wealthy suitor but Dounia rejects him

  ~로부터 재정적인 지원을 받아왔다 (현재완료)   after learning about his vile intentions.

9. He is brought to the police station, where he admits to the murders and

_____ in Siberia.

     그 후(su~) 추방형(exile)을 선고 받다

[Word Quiz]

1. Which word describes someone who is very poor and lacks financial resources?
a) Impoverished   b) Extraordinary   c) Consequences   d) Commit

2. What term refers to the belief that life is meaningless and devoid of purpose?
a) Nihilistic   b) Unwavering   c) Confess   d) Magistrate

3. What word means exceptionally remarkable or outstanding?
a) Extraordinary   b) Hallucinations   c) Investigation   d) Manipulate

4. What is the result or outcome of a particular action or event?
a) Consequences   b) Prostitution   c) Deteriorate   d) Redemption

5. What verb means to carry out or perform a wrongdoing or illegal act?
a) Commit   b) Emotional   c) Guilt   d) Exile

6. What is the process of a thorough examination or inquiry?
a) Investigation   b) Authorities   c) Epilogue   d) Repentance

7. Who is a government official responsible for upholding the law and administering justice?
a) Magistrate   b) Confession   c) Philosophical   d) Transformation

8. What term refers to engaging in sexual activity for payment?
a) Prostitution   b) Unwavering   c) Deteriorate   d) Exploration

9. Which word means showing firm determination and commitment?
a) Unwavering   b) Remorse   c) Financial   d) Malevolent

10. What is the act of being saved from sin, error, or suffering?
a) Redemption   b) Subsequently   c) Confront   d) Emotional

11. What word describes the process of gradually becoming worse or declining in quality?
a) Deteriorate   b) Profound   c) Confess   d) Epilogue

12. What term refers to perceptions of objects or events that do not actually exist?
a) Hallucinations   b) Philosophical   c) Extraordinary   d) Guilt

13. What adjective describes something having evil intent or wishing harm to others?
a) Malevolent   b) Exploration   c) Psychological   d) Impoverished

14. What is the act of admitting or acknowledging one's wrongdoing or guilt?
a) Confess   b) Timeless   c) Transformation   d) Exile

15. What verb means to influence or control someone cleverly and unfairly?
a) Manipulate   b) Nihilistic   c) Consequences   d) Commit

16. What word refers to matters related to money and finances?
a) Financial   b) Unwavering   c) Epilogue   d) Redemption

17. What is the act of facing someone or something in opposition or challenge?
a) Confront   b) Emotional   c) Investigation   d) Prostitution

18. What adjective describes strong feelings and emotions?
a) Emotional   b) Magistrate   c) Guilt   d) Exploration

19. Who are the people in charge of enforcing laws and regulations in a particular area?
a) Authorities   b) Remorse   c) Commit   d) Confession

20. What is the act of being forced to live in a foreign country away from one's homeland?
a) Exile   b) Philosophical   c) Repentance   d) Redemption

Unit 27: War and Peace (1869)

"War and Peace" is a classic novel written by the Russian author Leo Tolstoy. It is considered one of the greatest works of world literature and was published in serialized form between 1865 and 1869. The novel is set against the backdrop of Napoleon's invasion of Russia in 1812 and explores themes of war, love, society, and the human condition. The story is vast and intricate, featuring a wide array of characters and subplots. Here is a detailed summary of the plot of "War and Peace":

The novel opens in Saint Petersburg, Russia, in 1805. We are introduced to the aristocratic Bolkonsky family, particularly Prince Andrei Bolkonsky, who is unhappy in his marriage to the beautiful but shallow Liza. Andrei becomes enamored with the idea of military service and decides to join the army to fight against Napoleon. His departure leaves Liza devastated. We are also introduced to the Rostov family, specifically Countess Rostova and her children, Natasha, Petya, and Nicholas. The Rostovs are a loving and close-knit family, and Natasha is known for her beauty and vivacity.

Prince Andrei arrives at a military encampment in Austria, where he meets several fellow officers, including the cynical Anatole Kuragin and the idealistic Pierre Bezukhov. Pierre is the illegitimate son of Count Bezukhov and is uncertain about his place in society. Back in Russia, Natasha Rostova is introduced to society and becomes the center of attention. She forms a close friendship with Princess Sonya, her cousin, and attracts the interest of several suitors, including the dashing but fickle Anatole Kuragin.

The novel shifts to 1808, and we see the characters dealing with various personal and societal issues. Pierre marries the beautiful but unfaithful Helene Kuragin, Anatole's sister, and becomes embroiled in a messy marriage. Meanwhile, Prince Andrei's wife, Liza, dies in childbirth, and he is left feeling lost and disillusioned. He becomes a close friend of Pierre and begins to question the meaning of life and his place in the world.

The year is now 1810, and the characters' lives continue to evolve. Natasha Rostova is courted by Prince Andrei, and they fall deeply in love. They plan to marry, but Natasha's youthful impulsiveness almost derails their relationship when she briefly becomes infatuated with Anatole Kuragin. Pierre, in his search for meaning, joins the Freemasons and becomes more introspective and spiritual.

By 1812, Napoleon's army is advancing on Russia, and Prince Andrei, Pierre, and many other characters are called to serve in the war. The Russian aristocracy faces the upheaval and chaos of the impending invasion. The Battle of Borodino takes place, and the Russian army, led by General Kutuzov, faces off against Napoleon's forces. The battle is a devastating and bloody encounter, and both sides suffer heavy losses.

After the Battle of Borodino, Pierre is taken prisoner by the French but is eventually released. He returns to Moscow to find it in ruins, set ablaze by the retreating Russians to deny Napoleon resources. Pierre experiences a spiritual awakening and seeks to live a more meaningful life. Natasha and the Rostov family, who had taken refuge in Moscow, are forced to flee the burning city. Their journey is arduous and harrowing.

The novel's conclusion explores the aftermath of the war and the fates of the main characters. Napoleon's retreat from Russia marks a turning point in his fortunes, and the Russian army pursues him. Prince Andrei, who was gravely wounded at Borodino, reconciles with Natasha, and they marry. Pierre also finds happiness in a new life.

The novel ends with reflections on history, fate, and the enduring spirit of the Russian people. "War and Peace" is a rich and complex novel that delves into the lives of its characters against the backdrop of historic events. It explores profound philosophical and existential themes and is considered a masterpiece of Russian literature.

[Vocabulary]

literary 문학적인 summarized 요약된 aristocratic 귀족적인 primarily 주로 illegitimate 불법의/사생아 philosophical 철학적인 spiritual 영적인 ambitious 야심있는 disillusioned 환멸을 느끼는 vivacious 활기찬 engaged 약혼한 dramatic 극적인 explore 탐구하다 personal 개인적인 delve 탐구하다 historical 역사적인 chaotic 혼돈의 skillfully 능숙하게 portray 묘사하다 existence 존재 profound 심오한 panoramic 파노라마적인 exploration 탐구 meditation 명상 essence 본질 battlefield 전쟁터

[본문 해석] 전쟁과 평화

"전쟁과 평화"는 러시아 작가 레오 톨스토이에 의해 쓰여 진 고전 소설입니다. 그것은 세계 문학의 가장 위대한 작품 중의 하나로 여겨지며 1865년에서 1869년 사이에 연재되었습니다. 이 소설은 나폴레옹의 러시아 침략을 배경으로 전쟁, 사랑, 사회, 그리고 인간의 상태를 탐구합니다. 이야기는 방대하고 복잡하며, 다양한 등장인물과 하위 줄거리를 가지고 있습니다:

이 소설은 1805년 러시아 상트 페테르부르크에서 시작됩니다. 귀족적인 볼콘스키 가문, 특히 아름답지만 고상하지 못한 리자와의 결혼에서 불행한 안드레이 볼콘스키 왕자가 나옵니다. 안드레이는 군복무에 대한 생각에 매료되어 나폴레옹에 맞서 싸우기로 결심합니다. 그의 (전쟁터로의) 출발은 리자를 망연자실케 합니다. 또한 로스토프 가문, 특히 로스토바 백작부인과 그녀의 자녀들인 나타샤, 페티아, 니콜라스가 등장합니다. 로스토프 가문은 애정이 많고 친밀한 가문이며, 나타샤는 그녀의 아름다움과 활기로 알려져 있습니다.

안드레이 왕자는 오스트리아의 한 군사 캠프에 도착하여 냉소적인 아나톨 쿠라긴과 이상주의

자인 피에르 베주코프를 포함한 몇몇 동료 장교들을 만나게 됩니다. 피에르는 베주코프 백작의 사생아로 사회에서 그의 위치에 대해 확신이 없습니다. 배경은 다시 러시아로 돌아가서, 나타샤 로스토바는 사교계에 입문하고 관심의 중심에 섭니다. 그녀는 그녀의 사촌인 소냐 공주와 긴밀한 우정을 형성하고, 늠름하지만 변덕스러운 아나톨 쿠라긴을 포함한 몇몇 구혼자들의 관심을 끕니다.

소설은 1808년으로 옮겨가고, 우리는 등장인물들이 다양한 개인적, 사회적 문제를 다루는 것을 보게 됩니다. 피에르는 아름답지만 불성실한 아나톨의 여동생인 헬레네 쿠라긴과 결혼하여 지저분한 결혼생활에 휘말리게 휘말리게 됩니다. 한편, 안드레이 왕자의 아내 리자(Liza)는 출산으로 사망하자, 그는 상실감을 느끼고 각성하게 됩니다. 그는 피에르와 가까운 친구가 되고, 삶의 의미와 세상에서 자신이 차지하는 위치에 대해 질문하기 시작합니다.

이제 1810년이 되었고, 등장인물들의 삶은 계속 발전합니다. 나타샤 로스토바는 안드레이 왕자의 구애를 받고, 그들은 깊은 사랑에 빠집니다. 그들은 결혼을 계획하고 있지만, 나타샤가 혈기 왕성한 충동으로 아나톨 쿠라긴에게 잠시 매료되자 그들의 관계는 거의 파경에 이릅니다. 삶의 의미를 찾는 피에르는 프리메이슨 가족과 합류하여 더욱 자기 반성적이고 영적으로 변합니다.

1812년 무렵, 나폴레옹의 군대는 러시아로 진격하고 있고, 안드레이 왕자, 피에르, 그리고 다른 많은 인물들이 전쟁에 참전하기 위해 소집됩니다. 러시아 귀족들은 임박한 침략으로 인한 격변과 혼란에 직면합니다. 보로디노 전투가 일어나고, 쿠투조프 장군이 이끄는 러시아 군대는 나폴레옹 군대와 맞서 싸웁니다. 전투는 파괴적이고 피비린내 나는 대결입니다. 그리고 양측 모두 큰 손실을 입습니다.

보로디노 전투 이후, 피에르는 프랑스군에게 포로로 잡히지만 결국 풀려납니다. 그는 모스크바로 돌아오지만, 나폴레옹 군대에게 자원을 제공하지 않기 위해 러시아 군에 의해 그곳이 불태워져 폐허가 되었다는 것을 알게 됩니다. 피에르는 정신적인 각성을 경험하고 더 의미 있는 삶을 살고자 합니다. 모스크바로 피신한 나타샤와 로스토프 가족은 어쩔수 없이 불타는 도시를 떠나게 됩니다. 그들의 여정은 고되고 참혹합니다.

소설의 결론은 전쟁의 여파와 주인공들의 운명을 탐구합니다. 나폴레옹의 러시아로부터의 퇴각은 그의 운명의 전환점을 의미하고 러시아 군대는 그를 추격합니다. 보로디노에서 심각한 부상을 입은 안드레이 왕자는 나타샤와 화해하고 그들은 결혼합니다. 피에르는 또한 새로운 삶에서 행복을 발견합니다.

그 소설은 역사, 운명, 그리고 러시아 사람들의 영원한 정신에 대한 성찰로 끝을 맺습니다. "전쟁과 평화"는 역사적 사건을 배경으로 등장인물들의 삶을 파헤치는 풍부하고 복잡한 소설입니다. 그것은 심오한 철학적이고 실존적인 주제들을 탐구하고 러시아 문학의 걸작으로 여겨집니다.

[Reading Comprehension]

1. When was "War and Peace" published?

a) 1865-1869   b) 1805-1812   c) 1810-1812   d) 1812-1815

2. Where does the novel open?

a) Moscow, Russia   b) Saint Petersburg, Russia

c) Paris, France   d) Vienna, Austria

3. Who among the following characters becomes enamored with military service and decides to join the army to fight against Napoleon?

a) Natasha Rostova   b) Pierre Bezukhov

c) Prince Andrei Bolkonsky   d) Countess Rostova

4. Which character briefly becomes infatuated with Anatole Kuragin?

a) Natasha Rostova   b) Princess Sonya

c) Liza Bolkonsky   d) Helene Kuragin

5. What event leads Prince Andrei to feel lost and disillusioned?

a) The death of his father   b) The birth of his son

c) The death of his wife   d) The loss of his wealth

6. Who becomes embroiled in a messy marriage with Helene Kuragin?

a) Pierre Bezukhov

b) Anatole Kuragin

c) Prince Andrei Bolkonsky

d) Nicholas Rostov

7. In what year does the Battle of Borodino take place?

a) 1805   b) 1808   c) 1810   d) 1812

8. Who leads the Russian army in the Battle of Borodino?

a) General Kutuzov

b) Prince Andrei Bolkonsky

c) Pierre Bezukhov

d) Anatole Kuragin

9. What happens to Pierre after the Battle of Borodino?

a) He is taken prisoner by the Russians.

b) He joins Napoleon's army.

c) He is taken prisoner by the French.

d) He becomes a spy for the Russian army.

10. What is the fate of Moscow after the Battle of Borodino?

a) It is captured by the French.

b) It remains untouched.

c) It is set ablaze by the retreating Russians.

d) It becomes the capital of Napoleon's empire.

11. Who experiences a spiritual awakening after the Battle of Borodino?

a) Natasha Rostova   b) Princess Sonya

c) Pierre Bezukhov   d) Prince Andrei Bolkonsky

12. Who marries Prince Andrei at the end of the novel?

a) Natasha Rostova   b) Princess Sonya

c) Helene Kuragin   d) Liza Bolkonsky

13. What philosophical and existential themes does "War and Peace" explore?

a) Love and betrayal   b) Society and politics

c) History and fate   d) Wealth and power

14. What is considered the backdrop of "War and Peace"?

a) The French Revolution

b) Napoleon's invasion of Russia

c) The Industrial Revolution

d) The American Civil War

15. Which literary movement is "War and Peace" often associated with?

a) Romanticism

b) Realism

c) Naturalism

d) Surrealism

[Grammar Check-up]

1. "War and Peace" is a novel written by Leo Tolstoy and (considers, is considered) one of the greatest literary (work, works) in history.
2. It was first (published, publishment) in 1869.
3. The plot of "War and Peace" is vast and complex, (covering, covers) several years and multiple characters.
4. The story (primary, primarily) follows three main characters: Pierre Bezukhov, Prince Andrei Bolkonsky, and Natasha Rostova.
5. Pierre Bezukhov is a (socially, social) awkward and illegitimate son of a wealthy nobleman.
6. Pierre seeks meaning in life and goes through various philosophical and spiritual (struggle, struggles).
7. Prince Andrei Bolkonsky is a young and ambitious military officer (married, marries) to the charming and manipulative Princess Lise.
8. He (disillusions, is disillusioned) with his life and seeks glory on the battlefield.
9. Natasha Rostova is a vivacious and young girl, (filled, full) of life and energy.
10. She is (engaging, engaged) to Prince Andrei but (fallen, falls) in love with Anatole Kuragin, a scoundrel who is already married.
11. This love triangle (leading, leads) to a series of dramatic events that impact the lives of all (involve, involved).
12. As the story progresses, Tolstoy weaves in and out of the lives of (these, this) characters and their families, (exploring, explores) their personal struggles, ambitions, and relationships.
13. Amidst the personal dramas, the novel delves into the historical events of the Napoleonic Wars, (particularly, particular) the French invasion of Russia in 1812.
14. The characters' lives are profoundly (effected, affected) by the chaos of war, love, loss, and self-discovery.
15. Tolstoy (skillfully, skillful) portrays the human experience in times of peace and war, delving into themes of fate, free will, and the nature of human existence.
16. "War and Peace" is not just a (historically, historical) novel; it is a profound philosophical exploration of life, society, and the human condition.
17. Tolstoy's epic masterpiece (provides, offers) readers a panoramic view of Russian society and a profound meditation on the essence of life and death.

[Writing Practice]

1. "War and Peace" is a novel written by Leo Tolstoy and _____
in history.   가장 위대한 문학 작품 중의 하나로 간주된다

2. Pierre Bezukhov is _____ a wealthy nobleman.
                              사회적으로 서툰 사생아이다   *illegitimate

3. He _____ *a central figure* in Moscow's high society.
         그의 아버지의 재산을 상속받아 *중심인물이* 된다

4. Pierre seeks meaning in life and _____ struggles.
                         다양한 철학적 그리고 정신적인 어려움을 겪는다

5. He _____ and seeks glory on the battlefield.
         그의 삶의 환상에서 벗어난다 *동사: disillusion

6. Natasha Rostova is a vivacious and young girl, _____.
                                                            생명과 에너지로 충만한

7. She _____ Prince Andrei but _____ Anatole Kuragin,
            ~와 약혼하다   ~와 사랑에 빠지다
a scoundrel who is already married.

8. This love triangle leads to a series of dramatic events _____.
                         연관된 모든 사람들의 삶에 영향을 미치는 사건 (관계사)

9. Amidst the personal dramas, the novel _____ of the Napoleonic
Wars, particularly the French invasion of Russia in 1812. 역사적인 사건들을 탐구 한다

10. The characters' lives _____ the chaos of war, love, loss,
and self-discovery.   ~에 의해서 심오하게 영향을 받는다

11. Tolstoy's epic masterpiece _____ Russian society and a
                      독자들에게 ~의 파노라마적 풍경을 제공한다
profound meditation on the essence of life and death.

[Word Quiz]

1. Choose the word that means "related to literature or writing":
a) Literary   b) Philosophical   c) Historical   d) Chaotic

2. Select the word that is synonymous with "briefly explained" or "condensed":
a) Disillusioned   b) Summarized   c) Vivacious   d) Engaged

3. Which word describes someone belonging to the highest social class or nobility?
a) Primarily   b) Aristocratic   c) Ambitious   d) Delve

4. Identify the word that means "mainly" or "chiefly":
a) Illegitimate   b) Spiritual   c) Primarily   d) Dramatic

5. What word refers to something that is not considered lawful or legitimate?
a) Vivacious   b) Philosophical   c) Illegitimate   d) Engaged

6. Select the word that is related to the study of fundamental questions about existence, knowledge, and reality:
a) Philosophical   b) Disillusioned   c) Exploration   d) Panoramic

7. Which word describes a person who is eager to achieve success or power?
a) Ambitious   b) Skillfully   c) Portray   d) Chaotic

8. Identify the word that means "disenchanted".
a) Engaged   b) Disillusioned   c) Vivacious   d) Explore

9. Choose the word that means "lively" or "full of energy":
a) Dramatic   b) Vivacious   c) Meditation   d) Battlefield

10. What word refers to actively participating or being involved in something?
a) Summarized   b) Engaged   c) Personal   d) Historical

11. Select the word that means "related to history" or "based on past events":
a) Delve   b) Philosophical   c) Historical   d) Spiritual

12. Identify the word that means "to examine or investigate thoroughly":

a) Chaotic   b) Explore   c) Ambitious   d) Profound

13. Choose the word that means "relating to individual experiences or feelings":

a) Skillfully   b) Personal   c) Battlefield   d) Illegitimate

14. What word refers to skillfully representing or describing something?

a) Portray   b) Existence   c) Essence   d) Dramatic

15. Select the word that means "the state of being or being actual":

a) Historical   b) Summarized   c) Exploration   d) Existence

16. Identify the word that means "deep" or "intense":

a) Profound   b) Vivacious   c) Meditation   d) Aristocratic

17. Choose the word that means "capturing a wide view" or "all-encompassing":

a) Panoramic   b) Engaged   c) Disillusioned   d) Spiritual

18. What word refers to the act of exploring or investigating something, often for discovery or learning?

a) Battlefield   b) Exploration   c) Ambitious   d) Philosophical

19. Select the word that means "deep contemplation or reflection":

a) Delve   b) Primarily   c) Chaotic   d) Meditation

20. Identify the word that means "the most essential or fundamental part of something":

a) Essence   b) Summarized   c) Dramatic   d) Vivacious

Unit 28: 20,000 Leagues Under the Sea (1870)

"20,000 Leagues Under the Sea" is an adventure novel written by Jules Verne and published in 1870. The story follows Professor Pierre Aronnax, a French marine biologist, and his companions as they embark on an extraordinary undersea journey aboard the enigmatic submarine known as the Nautilus, commanded by the mysterious Captain Nemo.

The narrative begins with numerous sightings of a sea monster that is causing havoc in the oceans. Professor Aronnax, along with his loyal servant Conseil and a Canadian harpooner named Ned Land, join an expedition to investigate and potentially capture the creature. During their pursuit, their ship is attacked, and the trio is thrown overboard.

To their surprise, they discover that the "monster" is, in fact, the Nautilus, a highly advanced submarine created by Captain Nemo. They are taken aboard the vessel, which serves as a self-sustaining world beneath the waves. The

Nautilus is equipped with innovative technology, including powerful engines, electricity, and various scientific instruments.

As the Nautilus journeys through the oceans, Aronnax and his companions are exposed to breathtaking underwater landscapes and encounter various marine creatures. They witness the wonders of the deep sea, such as coral reefs, underwater forests, and even an encounter with a giant squid. Captain Nemo, a complex and enigmatic character, shares his knowledge and philosophies with them while maintaining an air of secrecy about his past and motives.

However, tensions arise when the group becomes conflicted with Nemo's actions, which include attacking and sinking warships. Aronnax and his companions find themselves torn between fascination with the oceanic wonders they experience and the moral implications of Nemo's aggressive actions.

Eventually, the group manages to escape from the Nautilus, thanks to a series of events that include a deep-sea burial and a daring escape attempt. They are rescued by a passing ship, leaving behind the submarine and its enigmatic captain. The story ends with Professor Aronnax reflecting on the incredible journey and the enduring mystery of Captain Nemo.

"20,000 Leagues Under the Sea" explores themes of exploration, the wonders of the natural world, the ethics of science and technology, and the consequences of human actions on the environment. It remains a classic adventure novel that captivates readers with its imaginative depiction of the undersea world and the enigmatic character of Captain Nemo.

[Vocabulary]

Adventure 모험 Embark 탑승하다/시작하다 Extraordinary 비범한 Enigmatic 수수께끼의 Submarine 잠수함 Self-sustaining 자체 유지되는 Innovative 혁신적인 Breathtaking 아름다운 Coral reefs 산호초 Enounter 마주치다 Consequence 결과 Environmental 환경의 Exploration 탐험 Ethic 윤리 Ingenious 기발한 Marine 해양의 Elusive 잡기 어려운 Sophisticated 세련된 Sophistication 세련됨 Investigate 조사하다 Discrepancy 불일치 Subsequent 그 후의 Expedition 원정 Extensive 광범위한 Elaborate 정교한 Profound 심오한 Implication 함축 Aggressive 공격적인 Enduring 영속하는 Impression 인상 Exposition 밝힘/설명 Enthusiasm 열정 Reflection 반사/숙고 Captivate 매혹시키다 Captivating 매혹적인

[본문 해석] 해저 2만리

　"해저 20,000리"는 쥘 베른에 의해 쓰여 져 1870년에 출판된 모험 소설입니다. 프랑스 해양 생물학자인 피에르 아론낙스 교수와 그의 동료들이 신비로운 니모 선장에 의해 지휘되는 노틸러스로 알려진 신비로운 잠수함을 타고 놀라운 해저 여행을 시작하면서 이야기가 전개됩니다.

　이야기는 바다에서 큰 혼란을 일으키고 있는 바다 괴물의 수많은 목격으로 시작합니다. 아론낙스 교수는 그의 충실한 하인 콘세일과 네드 랜드라는 이름의 캐나다인 작살잡이와 함께 그 바다 생물을 조사하고 잠재적으로 포획하기 위해 탐험에 참가합니다. 그들의 추적 동안, 그들의 배는 공격을 받고, 세 사람은 배 밖으로 던져집니다.

　놀랍게도, 그들은 "괴물"이 사실 니모 선장에 의해 만들어진 매우 진보된 잠수함인 노틸러스라는 것을 발견합니다. 그들은 파도 아래에서 자생적인 세계의 역할을 하는 배에 실려 갑니다. 노틸러스는 강력한 엔진, 전기, 그리고 다양한 과학적인 도구들을 포함하여 혁신적인 기술을 갖추고 있습니다.

　노틸러스호가 바다를 여행하면서, 아론낙스와 그의 동료들은 숨 막히는 수중 풍경에 노출되고 다양한 해양 생물들과 마주칩니다. 그들은 산호초, 수중 숲, 그리고 심지어 거대한 오징어와의 만남과 같은 심해의 경이로움을 목격합니다. 복잡하고 수수께끼 같은 등장인물인 니모 선장은 그의 과거와 동기에 대해 비밀스러운 태도를 유지하면서 그의 지식과 철학을 그들과 공유합니다.

　하지만, 이 세 사람은 군함을 공격하고 침몰시키는 니모 선장의 행동과 충돌하게 되면서 긴장이 발생합니다. 아론낙스와 그의 동료들은 그들이 경험하는 해양 경이로움에 대한 매료와 니모 선장의 공격적인 행동의 도덕적인 영향 사이에서 고민하게 됩니다.

　마침내, 심해 매장과 대담한 탈출 시도를 포함한 일련의 사건들 덕분에, 이 세 사람은 노틸러스호에서 탈출하는데 성공합니다. 잠수함과 불가사의한 선장을 뒤로 한 채, 그들은 지나가는 배에 의해 구조됩니다. 이야기는 아론낙스 교수가 그가 겪은 믿을 수 없는 여행과 니모 선장의 지속되는 미스터리를 되새겨 보는 것으로 끝이 납니다.

　"해저 20,000리"는 탐험의 주제들, 자연계의 경이로움, 과학과 기술의 윤리, 그리고 인간의 행동이 환경에 미치는 결과들을 탐구합니다. 그것은 해저 세계에 대한 상상적인 묘사와 니모 선장의 수수께끼 같은 등장인물로 독자들을 사로잡는 고전적인 모험 소설로 남아 있습니다.

[Reading Comprehension]

1. "20,000 Leagues Under the Sea" is an adventure novel written by whom?
a) Jules Verne
b) Captain Nemo
c) Pierre Aronnax
d) Ned Land

2. What is the name of the enigmatic submarine in the novel?
a) Nautilus   b) Atlantis   c) Poseidon   d) Leviathan

3. Professor Pierre Aronnax is described as a marine biologist from which country?
a) France
b) England
c) Spain
d) Germany

4. What leads Professor Aronnax and his companions to embark on an undersea journey?
a) Investigating a sea monster
b) Treasure hunting
c) Underwater exploration for scientific research
d) Searching for lost artifacts

5. What innovative technology equips the Nautilus?
a) Wind-powered engines
b) Steam engines
c) Powerful engines
d) Solar-powered engines

6. What breathtaking underwater landscapes do Aronnax and his companions encounter?
a) Volcanoes
b) Coral reefs
c) Mountain ranges
d) Icebergs

7. What is the main cause of tension between Aronnax's group and Captain Nemo?

a) Disagreements about marine creatures

b) Disputes over the route of the journey

c) Captain Nemo's aggressive actions, attacking warships

d) Issues with the submarine's technology

8. How do Aronnax and his companions manage to escape from the Nautilus?

a) They defeat Captain Nemo in a battle

b) They sabotage the submarine's engines

c) They are rescued by a passing ship

d) They use a hidden escape pod

9. What themes does "20,000 Leagues Under the Sea" explore?

a) War and peace

b) Science and ethics

c) Love and betrayal

d) Time travel and alternate realities

10. What captivates readers in the novel?

a) The undersea world and Captain Nemo's character

b) The historical events during the expedition

c) The treasure hunt for a lost artifact

d) The romance between characters

[Grammar Check-up]

1. The story (following, follows) Professor Pierre Aronnax, a French marine biologist, and his companions as they embark on an (extraordinary, extraordinarily) undersea journey aboard the enigmatic submarine known as the Nautilus, (commanding, commanded by) the mysterious Captain Nemo.

2. The narrative begins with numerous sightings of a sea monster that is (caused, causing) havoc in the oceans.

3. Professor Aronnax, along with his loyal servant Conseil and a Canadian harpooner (named, naming) Ned Land, join an expedition to investigate and (potential, potentially) capture the creature.

4. During their pursuit, their ship (attacks, is attacked), and the trio is thrown overboard.

5. To their (surprise, surprising), they discover that the "monster" is, in fact, the Nautilus, a highly (advanced, advancing) submarine created by Captain Nemo.

6. They (take, are taken) aboard the vessel, which (is served, serves) as a self-sustaining world beneath the waves.

7. The Nautilus (is equipped, equips) with innovative technology, including powerful engines, electricity, and various scientific (instrument, instruments).

8. As the Nautilus journeys through the oceans, Aronnax and his companions (expose, are exposed) to breathtaking underwater landscapes and encounter various marine (creature, creatures).

9. They (witness, are witnessed) the wonders of the deep sea, such as coral reefs, underwater forests, and even an encounter with a giant squid.

10. Captain Nemo, a complex and enigmatic character, shares his knowledge and philosophies with them while (maintenance, maintaining) an air of secrecy about his past and motives.

11. However, tensions (rises, arise) when the group becomes conflicted with Nemo's actions, which (includes, include) attacking and sinking warships.

12. Aronnax and his companions find themselves torn between fascination with the oceanic wonders they experience (as well as, and) the moral implications of Nemo's aggressive actions.

13. Eventually, the group manages to escape from the Nautilus, thanks (for, to) a series of events that (include, including) a deep-sea burial and a daring escape attempt.

14. They are rescued by a passing ship, (left, leaving) behind the submarine and its enigmatic captain.

15. The story ends with Professor Aronnax (reflecting, reflects) on the incredible journey and the enduring mystery of Captain Nemo.

16. It remains a classic adventure novel that (is captivated, captivates) readers with its imaginative depiction of the undersea world and the enigmatic character of Captain Nemo.

[Writing Practice]

1. They _____ aboard the enigmatic submarine.
　　　　특별한(ex~) 해저 여행을 시작한다(em~)

2. The submarine is known as the Nautilus, _____.
Captain Nemo.　　　　　　　　　불가사의한 *Nemo 선장*에 의해 명령을 받는 (분사구)

3. The narrative begins with numerous sightings of *a sea monster* _____
_____ 바다에서 혼란(havoc)을 일으키고 있는 *바다 괴물* (관계사)

4. Professor Aronnax and other two men _____
the creature.　　　　　　　　~를 조사하고 잠정적으로 포획하기 위한 탐험에 합류하다

5. _____, and the trio is thrown overboard.
　　　그들이 추격하는 동안, 그들의 배가 공격을 당한다

6. _____, they discover that the "monster" is, in fact, the Nautilus,
　　　놀랍게도　　　　　　　　_____ *Captain Nemo.*
　　　　　　　　　*Nemo 선장*에 의해서 만들어진 매우 발달된 잠수함

7. The Nautilus _____, including powerful engines,
electricity, and various scientific instruments. 혁신적인 기술을 갖추고 있다

8. As the Nautilus journeys through the oceans, Aronnax and his companions _____
_____ and encounter various marine creatures.
　숨막히게 아름다운 해저의 경치에 노출되다

9. However, _____ *Nemo's actions,*
　　　그 그룹이 *니모의 행동과* 의견충돌(갈등)을 겪자, 긴장감이 발생하다

10. Aronnax and his companions find themselves torn _____
_____ and the moral implications of Nemo's aggressive actions.
그들이 경험하는 바다의 경이로운 것들에 대한 매혹과 ~사이에서

[Word Quiz]

1. What is the term for a thrilling or exciting experience?
a) Adventure   b) Submarine   c) Encounter   d) Impression

2. Which word means to start or begin a journey or activity?
a) Embark   b) Extraordinary   c) Exploration   d) Elaborate

3. What does "Enigmatic" mean?
a) Sophistication   b) Elusive   c) Breathtaking   d) Mysterious

4. What is a vessel designed to travel and operate underwater?
a) Undersea   b) Submarine   c) Enduring   d) Expedition

5. What is a word that describes something that is unique, remarkable, or exceptional?
a) Enigmatic   b) Self-sustaining   c) Extraordinary   d) Ethic

6. What is a self-sufficient system capable of maintaining itself without external influence?
a) Self-sustaining   b) Innovative   c) Elaborate   d) Ingenious

7. Which term refers to something so beautiful or awe-inspiring that it takes one's breath away?
a) Embark   b) Breathtaking   c) Implication   d) Sophistication

8. What is the word for anything located or occurring below the surface of the water?
a) Underwater   b) Exploration   c) Captivating   d) Enduring

9. What are the structures formed by corals in the ocean?
a) Coral reefs   b) Coral pink   c) Coral tree   d) Coral exposition

10. Which term means to come across or meet unexpectedly?
a) Subsequent   b) Encounter   c) Aggressive   d) Captivate

11. What is the result or effect of a particular action or situation?

a) Consequence   b) Ingenious   c) Impression   d) Environmental

12. Which word relates to the natural surroundings or conditions of a place?

a) Marine   b) Investigate   c) Embark   d) Submarine

13. What does "Elusive" mean?

a) Sophisticated   b) Captivating   c) Difficult to find or catch   d) Implication

14. What is a term for something refined, elegant, or cultured?

a) Sophistication   b) Ethic   c) Exploration   d) Reflection

15. What does "Investigate" mean?

a) Self-sustaining   b) Undersea
c) Explore or examine thoroughly   d) Elaborate

16. What word refers to something that follows or comes after something else in time or order?

a) Implication   b) Subsequent   c) Discrepancy   d) Expedition

17. Which term means a journey or voyage undertaken for a particular purpose?

a) Elusive   b) Captivating   c) Enduring   d) Expedition

18. What word means comprehensive or wide-ranging in scope, extent, or effect?

a) Extensive   b) Enigmatic   c) Innovative   d) Embark

19. Which word means to add details, clarify, or explain further?

a) Elaborate   b) Exploration   c) Impression   d) Sophistication

20. What is the term for something having deep insight or great depth of knowledge?

a) Ethic   b) Elusive   c) Profound   d) Enthusiasm

Unit 29: Anna Karenina (1877)

"Anna Karenina" is a novel written by Leo Tolstoy, first published in 1877. It is considered one of the greatest works of world literature. The story is set in 19th-century Russia and revolves around the lives of several characters, but the central focus is on the tragic heroine, Anna Karenina.

The novel begins with the introduction of the Oblonsky family, particularly Prince Stepan(Stiva) Oblonsky, who has been unfaithful to his wife, Princess Darya(Dolly) Alexandrovna Oblonskaya. Dolly discovers the affair and is devastated. Stiva's sister, Princess Ekaterina(Kitty) Alexandrovna Shcherbatskaya, is also introduced, and she is in love with the wealthy Count Alexei Kirillovich Vronsky.

At a ball, Kitty expects Vronsky to propose to her, but instead, he becomes infatuated with Anna Karenina, the beautiful and sophisticated wife of government official Alexei Karenin. Anna is initially resistant to Vronsky's advances, as she is married and has a young son, Sergei. However, she eventually succumbs to her feelings for Vronsky and begins a passionate affair with him, risking her reputation and social standing.

As the affair becomes public knowledge, Anna faces judgment and isolation from Russian high society. She is torn between her love for Vronsky and her duty as a wife and mother. Meanwhile, Kitty, heartbroken by Vronsky's rejection, goes through a period of deep sadness and self-discovery.

The novel also follows the life of Konstantin(Kostya) Dmitrievich Levin, a landowner and friend of Stiva. Levin is deeply in love with Kitty and proposes to her after her breakup with Vronsky. They eventually marry and move to Levin's estate in the countryside.

Throughout the novel, Tolstoy weaves themes of love, family, morality, and social norms. Anna's struggle with societal expectations and her desire for love and freedom lead her into a spiral of emotional turmoil. She faces a difficult decision between her family and her lover, and her internal conflict takes a toll on her mental and emotional health.

As the story progresses, Anna's situation becomes more desperate, and she becomes increasingly isolated and depressed. Vronsky is torn between his love for Anna and his desire to maintain his social status. He becomes frustrated with Anna's emotional instability and her jealousy.

Meanwhile, Levin grapples with philosophical and spiritual questions about life, work, and the meaning of existence. He seeks solace and answers in nature and his relationship with Kitty.

As the novel reaches its climax, Anna's mental state deteriorates further, and she becomes increasingly paranoid and delusional. In a moment of despair, she tragically throws herself under a train and dies.

The novel concludes with Levin's epiphany about the importance of faith, love, and the simple joys of life. He embraces his role as a husband, father, and landowner, finding meaning and fulfillment in his connection to the land and his family.

"Anna Karenina" is a sweeping and complex work that delves into the depths of human emotions and relationships. It is a timeless exploration of love, morality, and the human condition, making it a classic of world literature.

[본문 해석] 안나 카레니나

"안나 카레니나"는 1877년에 처음 출판된 레오 톨스토이에 의해 쓰여 진 소설입니다. 그것은 세계 문학의 가장 위대한 작품 중 하나로 여겨집니다. 이야기는 19 세기 러시아를 배경으로 하고 여러 등장인물들의 삶을 중심으로 전개되지만, 중심은 비극적인 여주인공인 안나 카레니나에 있습니다.

소설은 오블론스키 가족, 특히 그의 아내인 다리야 알렉산드로브나 오블론스카야 공주에게 불성실했던 스테판 오블론스키 왕자의 소개로 시작합니다. 다리아는 남편의 불륜을 발견하고 망연자실합니다. 스티바의 여동생 에카테리나(키티) 알렉산드로브나 슈체르바츠카야 공주 또한 소개됩니다. 그리고 그녀는 부유한 알렉세이 키릴로비치 브론스키 백작과 사랑에 빠집니다.

무도회에서, 키티는 브론스키가 그녀에게 청혼하기를 기대하지만, 대신 그는 정부 관리 알렉세이 카레닌의 아름답고 세련된 아내인 안나 카레니나에게 푹 빠지게 됩니다. 안나는 결혼했고 어린 아들 세르게이가 있기 때문에 처음에는 브론스키의 접근에 저항합니다. 하지만, 그녀는 결국 브론스키에 대한 그녀의 감정에 굴복하고 그녀의 명성과 사회적 지위를 무릅쓰며 그와 열정적인 관계를 시작합니다.

이 일이 대중에게 알려지면서 안나는 러시아 상류사회로부터 심판과 고립에 직면하게 됩니다. 그녀는 브론스키에 대한 사랑과 아내와 엄마로서의 의무 사이에서 갈등합니다. 한편, 브론스키의 거부로 상심한 키티는 깊은 슬픔과 자아 발견의 시기를 겪습니다.

소설은 또한 토지 소유주이자 스티바의 친구인 콘스탄틴 "코스티야" 드미트리에비치 레빈의 삶도 뒤이어 이야기 합니다. 레빈은 키티와 깊은 사랑에 빠졌고, 그녀가 브론스키와 헤어진 후 그녀에게 청혼합니다. 그들은 결국 결혼하고 시골에 있는 레빈의 사유지로 이사합니다.

소설 전체에 걸쳐 톨스토이는 사랑, 가족, 도덕 및 사회적 규범의 주제를 엮습니다. 사회적 기대와의 투쟁과 사랑과 자유에 대한 안나 카레니나의 열망은 그녀를 감정적 혼란의 소용돌이로 이끌었습니다. 그녀는 가족과 연인 사이에서 어려운 결정에 직면하고, 그녀의 내적 갈등은 그녀의 정신적 및 감정적 건강에 타격을 입힙니다.

이야기가 진행될수록 안나의 상황은 더욱 절박해지고 점점 고립되고 우울해집니다. 브론스키는 안나에 대한 사랑과 사회적 지위를 유지하려는 자신의 욕구 사이에서 갈등합니다. 그는 안나의 정서적 불안정과 그녀의 질투로 인해 좌절하게 됩니다. 한편, 레빈은 삶, 일, 존재의 의미에 대한 철학적이고 영적인 질문들을 고심합니다. 그는 자연과 키티와의 관계에서 위안과 대답을 추구합니다.

소설이 극에 달하면서 안나의 정신 상태는 더욱 악화되고, 점점 편집증적이고 망상적으로 변합니다. 절망의 순간에 안나는 비극적으로 열차 아래로 몸을 던져 죽게 됩니다.

소설은 믿음과 사랑의 중요성, 삶의 단순한 기쁨에 대한 레빈의 깨달음으로 마무리됩니다. 그는 남편, 아버지, 지주로서의 역할을 받아들이며, 땅과 그의 가족과의 관계에서 의미와 성취감을 발견합니다. '안나 카레니나'는 인간의 감정과 관계의 깊이를 파헤치는 포괄적이고 복잡한 작품으로, 사랑과 도덕, 인간의 상태에 대한 시대를 초월한 탐구로 인해 세계 문학의 고전이 되었습니다.

[Vocabulary]

be considered 간주되다 literature 문학 revolve around ~주위를 돌다 heroine 여자 주인공 introduction 소개 unfaithful 불성실한 devastated 파괴된 sophisticated 세련된 advances 진보 reputation 평판 judgment 판결 isolation 고립 heartbroken 비탄에 잠긴 philosophical 철학적인 spiritual 영적인 solace 위로 climax 정점/절정 deteriorate 악화되다 paranoid 편집증적인 despair 절망 fulfillment 충족/성취 connection 연결 spiral 나선 emotional 감정적인 jealousy 질투 existence 존재 timeless 영원한 exploration 탐구 humanity 인간성 morality 도덕 complexity 복잡함 relationship 관계 conclusion 결말 significance 중요성 sweeping 광범위한

[Reading Comprehension]

1. Who is the author of the novel "Anna Karenina"?
a) Leo Tolstoy b) Fyodor Dostoevsky c) Anton Chekhov d) Vladimir Nabokov

2. When was "Anna Karenina" first published?
a) 1777 b) 1877 c) 1977 d) 1871

3. In which country is the story of "Anna Karenina" set?
a) France b) England c) Russia d) Germany

4. Who is the central focus of the story in "Anna Karenina"?
a) Konstantin Levin b) Alexei Karenin c) Kitty Shcherbatskaya d) Anna Karenina

5. What is the relationship between Prince Stepan Oblonsky and Princess Darya Oblonskaya?
a) Siblings b) Cousins c) Husband and wife d) Friends

6. Who does Kitty Shcherbatskaya fall in love with at the ball?
a) Konstantin Levin
b) Alexei Karenin
c) Anna Karenina
d) Count Alexei Vronsky

7. What is Anna Karenina's initial response to Vronsky's advances?
a) She accepts his proposal immediately.
b) She rejects him politely.
c) She becomes infatuated with him.
d) She is hesitant due to her marriage.

8. What risks does Anna take by having an affair with Vronsky?
a) Her social standing and reputation
b) Her friendship with Kitty
c) Her financial stability
d) Her relationship with other women

9. What themes are woven throughout the novel?
a) Love, family, morality, and social norms
b) Adventure, mystery, and suspense
c) Politics, economics, and technology
d) Science, art, and culture

10. How does Anna's situation progress as the story unfolds?
a) She becomes happier and more content.
b) She becomes isolated and depressed.
c) She gains more social status and popularity.
d) She becomes more successful in her career.

11. What is Vronsky torn between?
a) His duty to his family and his love for Anna
b) His love for Kitty and his friendship with Levin
c) His desire for fame and his desire for love
d) His political career and his desire for adventure

12. What does Levin seek solace and answers in?
a) Nature and his relationship with Kitty
b) Philosophy books
c) Social gatherings
d) His job and career

13. How does the novel "Anna Karenina" end for the character Anna?
a) She lives happily ever after with Vronsky.
b) She becomes successful in her career.
c) She tragically dies by throwing herself under a train.
d) She leaves Russia to start a new life.

14. What is Levin's epiphany at the conclusion of the novel?
a) The importance of faith, love, and the simple joys of life
b) The pursuit of wealth and power
c) The meaning of existence in the modern world
d) The importance of social status and reputation

15. What is "Anna Karenina" considered in the world of literature?
a) A timeless exploration of love, morality, and the human condition
b) A thrilling adventure novel set in 19th-century Russia
c) A historical biography of a tragic heroine
d) A philosophical treatise on the meaning of life

[Grammar Check-up]

1. "Anna Karenina" is a novel _____ by Leo Tolstoy.
a) written b) writing c) wrote d) write

2. The novel "Anna Karenina" was _____ in 1877.
a) published b) publishing c) publish d) publishes

3. The story of "Anna Karenina" is set in _____ Russia.
a) nineteenth   b) nineteenth-century
c) nineteenth centuries   d) nineteen-century's

4. The central focus of the novel is on the tragic _____, Anna Karenina.
a) heroine b) heroines c) heroin d) hero

5. Dolly discovers the affair and is _____.
a) devastate b) devastated c) devastating d) devastates

6. Princess Ekaterina(Kitty) Alexandrovna Shcherbatskaya is in love with the _____
Count Alexei Kirillovich Vronsky.
a) wealthy b) wealth c) healthy d) wealthily

7. Anna is initially resistant to Vronsky's advances because she is _____ and has
a young son.
a) married b) marrying c) marries d) marriage

8. Anna eventually succumbs to her feelings for Vronsky and begins a passionate
affair, risking her _____ and social standing.
a) reputating b) reputational c) reputation d) reputably

9. As the affair becomes public knowledge, Anna faces judgment and _____ from
Russian high society.
a) isolate b) isolated c) isolation d) isolating

10. Anna is torn between her love for Vronsky and her _____ as a wife and
mother.
a) duties b) dutiful c) dutifully d) duty

11. Kitty goes through a period of deep sadness and self-_____.
a) discovery b) discover c) discovering d) discovered

12. Levin proposes to Kitty after her breakup with Vronsky, and they eventually _____.
a) marry b) marries c) marrying d) marriage

13. Throughout the novel, Tolstoy weaves themes of love, family, morality, and _____ norms.
a) socially b) social c) society d) societies

14. Anna's struggle with societal expectations leads her into a spiral of _____ turmoil.
a) emotionally b) emotional c) emotion d) emotions

15. As the story progresses, Anna becomes increasingly isolated and _____.
a) depression b) depress c) depressed d) depressing

16. Vronsky is torn between his love for Anna and his desire to maintain his social _____.
a) status b) statue c) statues d) stating

17. Levin grapples with philosophical and spiritual questions about life, work, and the _____ of existence.
a) mean b) means c) meaning d) meanings

18. Anna's mental state deteriorates further, and she becomes increasingly paranoid and _____.
a) delusional b) delusions c) delude d) deluding

19. The novel concludes with Levin's _____ about the importance of faith, love, and the simple joys of life.
a) epiphany b) epitaph c) epigram d) episode

20. "Anna Karenina" is a sweeping and complex work that delves into the _____ of human emotions and relationships.
a) deepen b) depths c) deep d) deeply

[Writing Practice]

1. The novel begins with the introduction of the Oblonsky family, particularly Prince Stepan "Stiva" *Oblonsky*, _____

오랫동안 그의 아내에게 불성실해왔던 *Oblonsky* (관계사)

2. Anna _____ Vronsky's advances, as she is married and

처음에는 ~에 저항한다   has a young son, Sergei.

3. However, _____ for Vronsky and begins a passionate affair with him. 그녀는 마침내 그녀의 감정에 굴복한다

4. She _____ as a wife and mother.

Vronsky를 향한 그녀의 사랑과 그녀의 의무 사이에서 갈등한다(tear)

5. Levin is deeply in love with Kitty and _____

Vronsky와 헤어진 후에 그녀에게 청혼한다

6. She _____.

그녀의 가족과 그녀의 연인 사이에서 어려운 결정에 직면한다

7. She _____

그녀는 점점 더 고립되고 우울해진다

8. He _____

그는 Anna의 감정적 불안정과 질투에 좌절하게 된다

9. He _____

그는 자연과 Kitty와의 관계에서 위안과 해답을 찾는다

10. _____, she _____

절망의 순간에,   그녀는 비극적으로 열차 아래로 몸을 던져 죽는다.

[Word Quiz]

1. What is the term used to describe the evaluation of someone or something based on their actions or qualities?
a) Philosophy   b) Judgment   c) Morality   d) Significance

2. In literature, what is the turning point or highest point of tension in a story called?
a) Climax   b) Existence   c) Fulfillment   d) Jealousy

3. Which word refers to a feeling of intense sadness and hopelessness?
a) Paranoid   b) Despair   c) Sophisticated   d) Connection

4. What do we call a woman who is the main character of a story or play?
a) Heroine   b) Humanity   c) Relationship   d) Isolation

5. Which term signifies the quality of being disloyal?
a) Timeless   b) Unfaithful   c) Spiritual   d) Exploration

6. What is the term for a complex and intricate situation or idea?
a) Deteriorate   b) Philosophy   c) Complexity   d) Introduction

7. What is the process of gradually getting worse or declining?
a) Jealousy   b) Solace   c) Deteriorate   d) Conclusion

8. What is the name for a person's or thing's state of being set apart from others?
a) Connection   b) Isolation   c) Heartbroken   d) Humanity

9. Which word describes a person who is calm, composed, and refined in their manner?
a) Spiritual   b) Sophisticated   c) Literature   d) Climax

10. In philosophical terms, what encompasses the concept of being alive or in being?
a) Revolve around   b) Fulfillment   c) Existence   d) Despair

11. What is the term for a feeling of comfort or consolation during a difficult time?
a) Significance   b) Solace   c) Emotional   d) Connection

12. Which term is used for actions or developments that promote progress and improvement?
a) Humanity   b) Advances   c) Sweeping   d) Timeless

13. What do we call the process of gradually breaking down or worsening over time?
a) Conclusion   b) Unfaithful   c) Deteriorate   d) Relationship

14. What term describes a feeling of being suspicious and distrustful of others?
a) Paranoid   b) Isolation   c) Heroine   d) Judgment

15. Which word refers to a deep and profound exploration of the innermost essence or nature of a person?
a) Exploration   b) Spiritual   c) Jealousy   d) Philosophy

16. In literature, what is the beginning part of a story that introduces the characters and setting?
a) Fulfillment   b) Climax   c) Introduction   d) Complexity

17. What term describes the state of deep emotional pain or distress?
a) Delight   b) Heartbroken   c) Connection   d) Humanity

18. Which term signifies a connection or link between different things or people?
a) Sweeping   b) Relationship   c) Significance   d) Timeless

19. What word describes something that is not limited by time and exists eternally?
a) Timeless   b) Revolve around   c) Spiritual   d) Conclusion

20. What is the term for a wide-ranging and extensive impact on various aspects?
a) Isolation   b) Sweeping   c) Morality   d) Devastated

Unit 30: Treasure Island (1883)

"Treasure Island" is an adventure novel written by Robert Louis Stevenson, first published in 1883. The story follows young Jim Hawkins as he becomes involved in a thrilling quest for buried treasure on a mysterious island.

The story begins at the Admiral Benbow Inn, run by Jim Hawkins' father, in the late 18th century. A mysterious old seaman named Billy Bones arrives at the inn, seeking refuge from his past and carrying a treasure map. Jim befriends Billy, but soon, a band of pirates led by the sinister Blind Pew comes looking for the map. Billy dies of a stroke during the confrontation, leaving the map in Jim's possession. Realizing its value, Jim shows the map to a local squire, Dr. Livesey, and the honorable but unscrupulous Captain Smollett.

Jim, Dr. Livesey, and Captain Smollett decide to embark on an expedition to find the buried treasure described in the map. They hire a crew for the Hispaniola, a ship, including the one-legged Long John Silver, who becomes the ship's cook and seems friendly and trustworthy. Unknown to the others, Long John Silver is secretly the quartermaster and leader of a band of pirates planning a mutiny to seize the treasure for themselves.

As the Hispaniola sails toward Treasure Island, Long John Silver gradually reveals his true nature to Jim, who is caught in a moral dilemma, unsure of whom to trust. Meanwhile, the ship's crew becomes increasingly divided between the loyal sailors and the plotting mutineers. Jim discovers the mutineers' plans and informs Captain Smollett and Dr. Livesey, leading to a tense standoff on the island.

Upon arriving at Treasure Island, Jim manages to escape from the pirates and hides in the wilderness. There, he befriends a marooned former pirate named Ben Gunn, who knows the island well. With Ben's help, Jim finds the hidden treasure cache and retrieves some of the treasure before the pirates locate him. He narrowly escapes capture and rejoins Captain Smollett and the loyal crew.

A fierce battle ensues between the mutineers and the loyal crew for control of the treasure. Jim plays a crucial role in the fight, showing courage and resourcefulness. Long John Silver, despite his treachery, eventually sides with the loyal crew, feeling a sense of loyalty to Jim and Dr. Livesey.

The surviving crew, including Long John Silver, returns to England on the Hispaniola with their hard-won treasure. Jim reflects on the adventure and the moral complexities he faced, and he is forever changed by the experience. In the end, Long John Silver escapes capture and goes on to live a life of freedom and adventure, while Jim and his friends return to their normal lives.

"Treasure Island" is a classic tale of pirates, treasure hunts, and moral dilemmas, and it remains one of the most beloved and influential adventure stories in literature.

[Vocabulary]

Admiral 해군사령관 Seaman 선원 Refuge 피난처 Confrontation 대면 Possession 소유 Expedition 원정 Buried treasure 묻힌 보물 Quartermaster 보좌관 Mutiny 반란 Tense standoff 긴장된 대치 Wilderness 황무지 Marooned 적막한 Hidden treasure 숨겨진 보물 Treachery 배반 Fierce battle 치열한 전투 Courage 용기 Resourcefulness 기민함/지략 Loyalty 충성심 Hard-won 힘들게 얻은 Adventure 모험 Reflect 반영하다 Complexities 복잡성 Influence 영향력 Sinister 사악한 Unscrupulous 부도덕한 Embark 탑승하다 Confrontation 대립 Loyal 충실한 Sails 돛 Gradually 점차적으로 Morality 도덕성 Dilemma 딜레마 Retrieve 회수하다 Narrowly 간신히 Surviving 생존하는 Crucial 결정적인 Influential 영향력 있는 Expeditions 원정 Treasure hunts 보물찾기 Rejoin 다시 합류하다

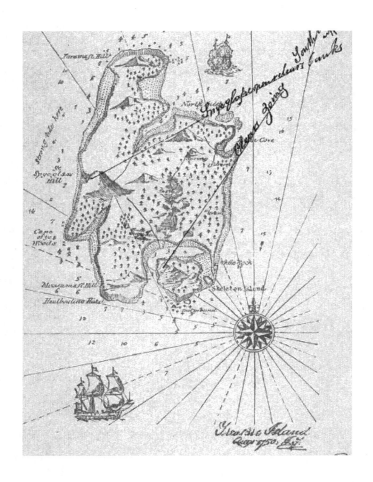

[본문 해석] 보물섬

"보물섬"은 로버트 루이스 스티븐슨이 쓴 모험 소설로, 1883년에 처음 출판되었습니다. 이 이야기는 어린 짐 호킨스가 신비한 섬에 묻힌 보물을 찾기 위한 스릴 넘치는 탐색에 참여하면서 전개됩니다.

이야기는 18 세기 후반 짐 호킨스의 아버지가 운영하는 제독 벤보우 여관에서 시작됩니다. 빌리 본즈라는 이름의 미스터리한 늙은 선원이 보물지도를 들고 그의 과거로부터 피난처를 찾아 그 여관에 도착합니다. 짐은 빌리와 친구가 되지만, 곧, 사악한 블라인드 퓨가 이끄는 해적 무리가 지도를 찾으러 옵니다. 빌리는 지도를 짐의 손에 맡기고 그들과 대치하는 동안 뇌졸중으로 사망합니다. 그 지도의 가치를 깨닫고, 짐은 그조것을 지역의 대지주인 리버시 박사와 명예는 있지만 부도덕한 스몰렛 선장에게 보여줍니다.

짐, 리버시 박사, 스몰렛 선장은 지도에 묘사된 묻혀있는 보물을 찾기 위한 탐험을 시작하기로 결정합니다. 그들은 히스패니올라 호를 위해 선원을 고용하는데, 그 중에 그 배의 요리사가 되고 친근하고 신뢰할 수 있어 보이는 외다리 롱 존 실버가 포함됩니다. 다른 사람들에게는 알려지지 않았지만, 롱 존 실버는 자신들이 그 보물을 차지하기 위해 비밀스럽게 반란을 계획하고 있는 해적 무리의 조타수이자 리더입니다.

히스파니올라호가 보물섬을 향해 항해하면서 롱 존 실버는 누구를 믿어야 할지 확신하지 못한 도덕적 딜레마에 빠져 있는 짐에게 점차 자신의 본성을 드러냅니다. 한편, 배의 승무원들은 충성스러운 선원들과 음모를 꾸미는 반란자들 사이에서 점점 더 분열됩니다. 짐은 반란자들의 계획을 발견하고 스몰렛 선장과 리버시 박사에게 알리자 섬에서 팽팽한 대치 상황에 이릅니다.

보물섬에 도착하자마자, 짐은 해적들로부터 탈출하여 황야에 몸을 숨깁니다. 그곳에서, 그는 섬을 잘 아는 벤 건이라는 이름의 고립된 전 해적과 친구가 됩니다. 벤의 도움으로, 짐은 숨겨진 보물 창고를 찾아내고 해적들이 그의 위치를 찾기 전에 보물 중 일부를 되찾습니다. 그는 간신히 탈출하여 스몰렛 선장과 충성스러운 선원들과 다시 합류합니다.

보물을 관리하기 위해 반란자들과 충성스러운 승무원들 사이에 치열한 전투가 이어집니다. 짐은 용기와 지략을 보여주며 싸움에서 중요한 역할을 합니다. 롱 존 실버는 그의 배신에도 불구하고, 짐과 리버시 박사에 대한 충성심을 느끼며 결국 충성스러운 승무원의 편이 됩니다.

롱 존 실버를 포함한 살아남은 선원들은 어렵게 얻은 보물을 가지고 히스파니올라호를 타고 영국으로 돌아옵니다. 짐은 모험과 그가 직면했던 도덕적 복잡성을 되새기며, 그 경험으로 인해 그는 끊임없이 변합니다. 결국, 롱 존 실버도 탈출하여 자유와 모험의 삶을 살고, 짐과 그의 친구들은 평범한 삶으로 돌아옵니다.

"보물섬"은 해적, 보물찾기, 도덕적 딜레마에 대한 고전적인 이야기이며, 문학에서 가장 사랑받고 영향력 있는 모험 이야기 중 하나로 남아 있습니다.

[Reading Comprehension]

1. Who is the author of "Treasure Island"?
a) Charles Dickens   b) Mark Twain   c) Robert Louis Stevenson   d) Jules Verne

2. What is the main quest in "Treasure Island"?
a) Hunting for mythical creatures
b) Searching for a hidden city
c) Seeking buried treasure on an island
d) Exploring ancient ruins

3. At the beginning of the story, where does the action take place?
a) The Treasure Island   b) The Hispaniola ship
c) The Admiral Benbow Inn   d) Dr. Livesey's house

4. What is the name of the old seaman who arrives at the inn carrying a treasure map?
a) Captain Smollett   b) Ben Gunn   c) Jim Hawkins   d) Billy Bones

5. How does Billy Bones die?
a) He is killed by Jim Hawkins
b) He has a stroke during a confrontation
c) He falls off a cliff on Treasure Island
d) He succumbs to a tropical disease

6. Who becomes the ship's cook on the Hispaniola?
a) Dr. Livesey   b) Long John Silver   c) Blind Pew   d) Captain Smollett

7. What is Long John Silver's secret role on the ship?
a) Quartermaster and pirate leader
b) Navigator and map reader
c) Ship's doctor and medic
d) Spy for the British Navy

8. Why is Jim Hawkins caught in a moral dilemma?
a) He is torn between joining the pirates and the loyal crew
b) He doesn't know which treasure map is the real one
c) He is unsure if he should trust Long John Silver or Captain Smollett
d) He wants to keep the treasure for himself

9. Who helps Jim find the hidden treasure cache on Treasure Island?
a) Blind Pew b) Captain Smollett c) Long John Silver d) Ben Gunn

10. What role does Long John Silver eventually play in the battle for the treasure?
a) He betrays the loyal crew and joins the mutineers
b) He remains neutral and doesn't take part in the fight
c) He sides with the loyal crew and fights against the mutineers
d) He takes the treasure and escapes on his own

11. Where do the surviving crew members return with the treasure?
a) To Treasure Island
b) To England on the Hispaniola
c) To a nearby island for safekeeping
d) They bury the treasure on an uninhabited island

12. How is Long John Silver's fate at the end of the story?
a) He is captured and hanged for his treachery
b) He escapes capture and continues his life of adventure
c) He becomes the captain of the Hispaniola
d) He settles down on Treasure Island with the treasure

13. What is the genre of "Treasure Island"?
a) Romance
b) Mystery
c) Adventure
d) Science Fiction

14. What does Jim Hawkins learn from the experience on Treasure Island?
a) He becomes a pirate and joins Long John Silver's crew
b) He loses all interest in treasure hunting and adventures
c) He gains courage and resourcefulness
d) He becomes a treasure hunter, searching for more riches

15. What is the significance of the character Ben Gunn in the story?
a) He is the main antagonist and opposes Jim Hawkins
b) He reveals the true identity of Long John Silver
c) He helps Jim find the hidden treasure cache
d) He becomes the new captain of the Hispaniola

[Grammar Check-up]

1. The story follows young Jim Hawkins as he (involves in, becomes involved in) a (thrilling, thrilled) quest for buried treasure on a mysterious island.

2. The story begins at the Admiral Benbow Inn, (run, running) by Jim Hawkins' father, in the late 18th century.

3. A mysterious old seaman named Billy Bones (is arrived, arrives) at the inn, seeking refuge from his past and (carries, carrying) a treasure map.

4. Jim befriends Billy, but soon, a band of pirates (leading, led by) the sinister Blind Pew comes looking for the map.

5. Billy dies of a stroke during the confrontation, (is left, leaving) the map in Jim's possession.

6. (Realized, Realizing) its value, Jim shows the map to a local squire, Dr. Livesey, and the honorable but unscrupulous Captain Smollett.

7. Jim, Dr. Livesey, and Captain Smollett decide (to embark, embarking) on an expedition (finding, to find) the buried treasure described in the map.

8. They hire a crew for the Hispaniola, a ship, (includes, including) the one-legged Long John Silver, (where, who) becomes the ship's cook and seems friendly and trustworthy.

9. Unknown to the others, Long John Silver is (secretly, secret) the quartermaster and leader of a band of pirates (who planning, planning) a mutiny to seize the treasure for themselves.

10. As the Hispaniola sails toward Treasure Island, Long John Silver (gradually, gradual) reveals his true nature to Jim, who (caught, is caught) in a moral dilemma, unsure of (whom, who) to trust.

11. Meanwhile, the ship's crew becomes (increasingly, increasing) divided between the loyal sailors and the plotting mutineers.

12. Jim discovers the mutineers' plans and (informing, informs) Captain Smollett and Dr. Livesey, (who leading, leading) to a tense standoff on the island.

13. (For, Upon) arriving at Treasure Island, Jim manages to escape from the pirates and hides in the wilderness.

14. There, he befriends a marooned former pirate named Ben Gunn, (who knows, knows) the island well.

15. With Ben's help, Jim finds the hidden treasure cache and (is retrieved, retrieves) some of the treasure before the pirates locate him.

16. He (narrow, narrowly) escapes capture and rejoins Captain Smollett and the loyal crew.

17. A fierce battle (is ensued, ensues) between the mutineers and the loyal crew for control of the treasure.

18. Jim plays a crucial role in the fight, (showing, shows) courage and resourcefulness.

19. Long John Silver, despite his treachery, (eventual, eventually) sides with the loyal crew, feeling a sense of loyalty to Jim and Dr. Livesey.

20. The surviving crew, including Long John Silver, returns to England on the Hispaniola with their (hard-winning, hard-won) treasure.

[Writing Practice]

1. The story follows young Jim Hawkins as he becomes involved in _____
_____ 신비한 섬에 있는 묻혀있는 보물을 위한 떨리는 탐색

2. A mysterious old seaman named Billy Bones arrives at the inn, _____
_____ 그의 과거로부터의 은신처를 *찾아서* 보물지도를 들고 (*분사구*)

3. Jim is caught in a moral dilemma, _____.
                                        누구를 믿어야 할지에 대해 확신하지 못하고 (분사구)

4. Meanwhile, the ship's crew _____ the loyal sailors
and the plotting mutineers.   ~간에 점점 더 사이가 갈라진다

5. _____, Jim manages to escape from the pirates and
    보물섬에 도착하자마자   hides in the wilderness.

6. With Ben's help, Jim finds the hidden treasure cache and _____
_____ before the pirates locate him.   보물 중의 일부를 회수한다

7. He _____ Captain Smollett and the loyal crew.
        간신히 생포에서 탈출하여 ~와 합류한다

8. _____ between the mutineers and the loyal crew for
    ~ 간에 치열한 전투가 뒤따른다(en~)   control of the treasure.

9. Long John Silver, despite his treachery, _____, feeling
a sense of loyalty to Jim and Dr. Livesey.   결국 충실한 선원들의 편에 선다

10. The surviving crew, including Long John Silver, returns to England on the
Hispaniola _____. 힘들게 얻은 보물을 가지고

[Word Quiz]

1. What word means a high-ranking naval officer?
a) Seaman b) Marooned c) Admiral d) Mutiny

2. Which term refers to an uncovered valuable object, often sought after in stories?
a) Adventure b) Sinister c) Hidden treasure d) Wilderness

3. What is the synonym for "bravery in the face of danger"?
a) Loyalty b) Courage c) Treachery d) Embark

4. Which word means "a difficult decision between two morally challenging options"?
a) Confrontation b) Dilemma c) Possession d) Influence

5. What is the opposite of "honest and honorable"?
a) Loyal b) Unscrupulous c) Gradually d) Retrieve

6. Which term refers to a group of people traveling for a specific purpose?
a) Wilderness b) Expedition c) Reflect d) Tense standoff

7. What is the synonym for "a betrayal of trust"?
a) Resourcefulness b) Tense standoff c) Treachery d) Survival

8. Which word means "the act of encountering someone or something"?
a) Seaman b) Confrontation c) Embark d) Influence

9. What term describes a person who works on a ship's crew?
a) Seaman b) Loyal c) Confrontation d) Possession

10. What word means "to start a journey or activity"?
a) Confrontation b) Embark c) Reflect d) Refuge

11. Which term refers to a situation where two opposing sides face each other with hostility?
a) Gradually b) Tense standoff c) Treasure hunts d) Influence

12. What term describes something that is perceived as ominous?
a) Sinister b) Adventure c) Loyalty d) Expeditions

13. What term describes a person who assists the captain and manages the ship's supplies?
a) Sails b) Quartermaster c) Treasure hunts d) Marooned

14. Which word means "something that is owned"?
a) Hidden treasure b) Buried treasure c) Possession d) Courage

15. What is the synonym for "a complicated and intricate situation"?
a) Retrieve b) Resourcefulness c) Complexities d) Adventure

16. Which term refers to a situation of intense struggle and conflict?
a) Fierce battle b) Rejoin c) Morality d) Survival

17. What word means "to set out on a journey"?
a) Reflect b) Embark c) Quartermaster d) Treachery

18. What is the synonym for "having a strong impact or effect"?
a) Crucial b) Influence c) Gradually d) Retrieve

19. Which term describes a strong sense of commitment, allegiance, or faithfulness to someone or something?
a) Loyalty b) Possession c) Expedition d) Unscrupulous

20. What word refers to the act of obtaining or recovering something that was lost, misplaced, or inaccessible?
a) Retrieve b) Reflect c) Morality d) Influence

Unit 31: What Men Live By (1885)

"What Men Live By" is a short story written by Leo Tolstoy. It was first published in 1885 as part of a collection of stories titled "Where Love Is, God Is." The story revolves around themes of love, compassion, and the true meaning of life. Here is a brief summary of the plot:

The story begins with a mysterious event where an angel named Michael is sent down to Earth by God. As a punishment for a past transgression, Michael is condemned to live on Earth as a human being until he learns the answer to the question: "What do men live by?"

In his human form, Michael is found naked and half-dead in the snow by a kindhearted cobbler named Simon. Simon takes him into his home, provides him with clothing and shelter, and nurses him back to health. Michael, still unaware of his angelic identity, becomes grateful for Simon's kindness and decides to stay and work with the cobbler and his family.

Over time, Michael becomes an integral part of Simon's household, assisting with various tasks and bringing a sense of peace and harmony. He develops a strong bond with the cobbler's family, especially with Simon's wife, Matryona, and their young orphans whom they have adopted.

As the story progresses, Michael's angelic nature becomes more apparent through his actions and words. He possesses extraordinary insights and compassion, helping those in need and offering guidance to those who seek it. However, the mystery of his true identity remains unknown to Simon and his family.

One day, an unexpected visitor arrives at Simon's home - a wealthy and cruel landowner named Ivan, who is infamous for mistreating his workers. Ivan seeks refuge at Simon's house to escape a snowstorm, but his cold and selfish demeanor clashes with the warm and loving atmosphere of the cobbler's home.

During Ivan's stay, a series of events unfold that test the characters' virtues and reveal the true nature of each individual. The central question, "What do men live by?" becomes the underlying theme of these events.

In a poignant and heartwarming conclusion, it is revealed that Michael's true mission on Earth was to learn the answer to the question he was tasked with. It becomes clear that "What Men Live By" is not material possessions, wealth, or power, but rather the values of love, compassion, and selflessness that Simon and Matryona exemplify in their lives.

The story emphasizes the importance of kindness and empathy towards others, regardless of their social status or past mistakes. It shows that true fulfillment in life comes from embracing love and understanding, and it is through these virtues that human beings find purpose and happiness. The tale of "What Men Live By" serves as a beautiful parable that transcends time and continues to resonate with readers as a reminder of the essence of being truly human.

[Vocabulary]

Collection 집합/모음 Themes 주제/테마 Compassion 동정심 Meaning 의미 Mysterious 신비로운 Punishment 처벌 Transgression 위반/범죄 Condemn 비난하다 Human being 인간 Identity 정체성 Kindhearted 친절한 Cobbler 구두수선공 Shelter 숨을 곳/보호 Grateful 감사하는 Integral 불가분의/필수적인 Orphans 고아/고아원 Adopt 입양하다 Angelic 천사 같은 Insights 통찰력 Seek 찾다/추구하다 Virtues 덕목, 미덕 Material possessions 유산/재산 Wealth 재산/부 Selflessness 이타심 Atmosphere 분위기 Cruel 잔혹한 Demeanor 행동/태도 Fulfillment 성취 Embrace 포옹하다/받아들이다

[본문 해석] 인간은 무엇으로 사는가?

"인간은 무엇으로 사는가?"은 레오 톨스토이가 쓴 단편 소설입니다. 이 소설은 1885년 처음 출판되었으며 "사랑이 있는 곳에 하나님이 계신다"라는 이야기 모음집에 포함되었습니다. 이 소설은 사랑, 동정심, 그리고 삶의 진정한 의미를 주제로 합니다. 다음은 이 소설의 간단한 줄거리입니다:

이 소설은 천사인 미카엘이 하나님에 의해 지구로 내려오는 신비로운 사건으로 시작합니다. 과거에 저지른 죄로 미카엘은 "인간은 무엇으로 사는가?"라는 질문에 대한 답을 배울 때까지 인간으로 지구에서 살아야 하는 형벌을 받았습니다.

인간의 모습으로, 미카엘은 벌거벗은 채로 눈 속에서 반쯤 죽은 상태에서 사이먼이라는 친절한 구두장이에게 발견됩니다. 사이먼은 그를 그의 집으로 데려가서, 그에게 옷과 쉼터를 제공하고, 그를 돌봐주어 건강을 되찾게 합니다. 여전히 그의 천사의 정체성을 알지 못하는 미카엘은 사이먼의 친절에 감사하게 되고, 구두장이와 그의 가족과 함께 머물며 일하기로 결정합니다.

시간이 지나면서 미카엘은 사이먼의 가정에서 필수적인 부분이 되어 다양한 일을 돕고 평화와 조화를 가져옵니다. 그는 구두장이의 가족, 특히 사이먼의 아내 마트료나와 그들이 입양한 어린 고아들과 강한 유대감을 형성합니다.

이야기가 진행될수록 미카엘의 천사 같은 본성은 그의 행동과 말을 통해 더욱 분명해집니다. 그는 도움이 필요한 사람들을 돕고 그것을 추구하는 사람들에게 길잡이를 제공하는 특별한 통찰력과 연민을 가지고 있습니다. 그러나 그의 진짜 정체에 대한 신비는 사이먼과 그의 가족에게 알려지지 않은 채로 남아 있습니다.

어느 날, 뜻하지 않은 방문객이 사이먼의 집에 도착합니다. 이반은 눈보라를 피하기 위해 사이먼의 집으로 피신하지만, 그의 차갑고 이기적인 태도는 구두장이 집의 따뜻하고 사랑스러운 분위기와 충돌합니다. 이반이 머무는 동안 인물들의 덕목을 시험하고 각 개인의 실체를 드러내는 일련의 사건들이 전개됩니다. 중심이 되는 질문인 "인간은 무엇으로 사는가?"가 이 사건들의 근본 주제가 됩니다.

가슴 아프지만 마음을 따뜻하게 하는 결론으로, 미카엘의 지구상에서의 진정한 사명은 그가 맡은 질문에 대한 답을 배우는 것이었음이 밝혀집니다. "인간은 무엇으로 사는가?"는 물질적 소유, 부, 권력이 아니라 사이먼과 마트료나가 삶에서 예시한 사랑, 연민, 무아의 가치라는 것이 분명해집니다.

이야기는 사회적 지위나 과거의 잘못을 떠나 타인에 대한 친절과 공감의 중요성을 강조합니다. 삶의 진정한 성취는 사랑과 이해를 포용하는 데서 비롯되며, 인간이 목적과 행복을 찾는 것은 이러한 덕목을 통해서임을 보여줍니다. "인간은 무엇으로 사는가?"란 이야기는 시간을 초월한 아름다운 비유로써의 역할을 하며, 진정한 인간임의 본질을 일깨워주는 책으로써 독자들의 공감을 계속 이어갑니다.

[Reading Comprehension]

1. "What Men Live By" is a short story that revolves around themes of:
a) Power and wealth
b) Love, compassion, and the true meaning of life
c) Revenge and justice
d) Mystery and suspense

2. Why is the angel Michael sent down to Earth?
a) To find a new home
b) To learn the true meaning of life
c) To punish humans for their mistakes
d) To seek redemption for his past actions

3. How does Simon first encounter Michael in his human form?
a) Michael visits him in a dream
b) Michael appears as a stranger at his doorstep
c) Michael is found naked and half-dead in the snow
d) Michael falls from the sky during a storm

4. What does Michael feel towards Simon after the cobbler takes him in and cares for him?
a) Gratefulness
b) Indifference
c) Anger
d) Suspicion

5. What does Michael develop with Simon's family during his stay with them?
a) A strong bond
b) A sense of competition
c) A feeling of jealousy
d) A desire to leave

6. What becomes the underlying theme of the events that unfold during Ivan's stay at Simon's home?
a) Wealth and power
b) True identity of Michael
c) The central question, "What do men live by?"
d) The weather and snowstorm

7. What is the conclusion of the story regarding the true mission of Michael on Earth?
a) To seek revenge on God's behalf
b) To gain material possessions and wealth
c) To learn the answer to the question, "What do men live by?"
d) To become a human permanently

8. What values are exemplified by Simon and Matryona in their lives?
a) Love, compassion, and selflessness
b) Greed, selfishness, and deceit
c) Ambition, power, and dominance
d) Indifference, cruelty, and dishonesty

9. According to the story, where does true fulfillment in life come from?
a) Embracing love and understanding
b) Accumulating material possessions
c) Seeking revenge on those who wronged us
d) Attaining social status and power

10. The tale of "What Men Live By" serves as a beautiful parable that emphasizes the importance of:
a) Ambition and success
b) Kindness and empathy towards others
c) Mysteries and enigmas
d) Avoiding social interactions

[Grammar Check-up]

1. It was first published in 1885 as part of a collection of stories (are titled, titled) "Where Love Is, God Is."

2. The story begins with a mysterious event (which, where) an angel named Michael is sent down to Earth by God.

3. As a punishment for a past transgression, Michael (condemns, is condemned) to live on Earth (for, as) a human being until he learns the answer to the question: "What do men live by?"

4. In his human form, Michael (finds, is found) naked and half-dead in the snow by a kindhearted cobbler (named, naming) Simon.

5. Simon takes him into his home, provides him with clothing and shelter, and (nursing, nurses) him back to health.

6. Michael, still unaware of his angelic identity, becomes grateful for Simon's kindness and decides (staying, to stay) and work with the cobbler and his family.

7. Over time, Michael becomes an integral part of Simon's household, (assisting, assists) with various tasks and bringing a sense of peace and harmony.

8. He develops a strong bond with the cobbler's family, especially with Simon's wife, Matryona, and their young orphans whom they have (been adopted, adopted).

9. As the story progresses, Michael's angelic nature becomes more (apparent, apparently) through his actions and words.

10. He possesses (extraordinary, extraordinarily) insights and compassion, helping those in need and offering guidance to those who (seeks, seek) it.

11. However, the mystery of his true identity remains (unknowing, unknown) to Simon and his family.

12. One day, an (unexpected, unexpecting) visitor arrives at Simon's home - a wealthy and cruel landowner named Ivan, who (are, is) infamous for mistreating his workers.

13. Ivan seeks refuge at Simon's house (escaping, to escape) a snowstorm, but his cold and selfish demeanor clashes with the warm and loving atmosphere of the cobbler's home.

14. During Ivan's stay, a series of events unfold that (tests, test) the characters' virtues and reveal the true nature of each individual.

15. The central question, "What do men live by?" becomes the (underlying, underlie) theme of these events.

16. In a poignant and heartwarming conclusion, it (reveals, is revealed) that Michael's true mission on Earth was to learn the answer to the question he was tasked with.

17. The story emphasizes the importance of kindness and empathy towards others, (regarding, regardless) of their social status or past mistakes.

[Writing Practice]

1. The story begins with a mysterious event where _____
down to Earth by God.   Michael이라고 불리는 천사가 지상으로 보내진다

2. As a punishment for a past transgression, Michael _____
                          인간으로서 지구에 살도록 선고를 받는다(condemn)
until he learns the answer to the question: "What do men live by?"

3. In his human form, Michael _____ in the snow by a
kindhearted cobbler named Simon. 벌거벗고 반쯤 죽은 상태로 발견된다

4. Simon takes him into his home, _____, and nurses
him back to health.   그에게 옷과 집을 제공한다

5. Michael, still unaware of his angelic identity, _____
                          Simon의 친절에 감사하게 되고 ~하기로 결심한다
stay and work with the cobbler and his family.

6. Over time, Michael becomes an integral part of Simon's household,
_____
다양한 작업을 돕고 평화와 조화를 가져오면서 (분사구)

7. He _____ the cobbler's family, especially with
     구장장이의 가족과 강한 유대를 발전시킨다
Simon's wife, Matryona, and their young orphans whom they have adopted.

8. As the story progresses, Michael's angelic nature _____.
                          그의 행동과 말을 통해 더욱 명확해 진다

9. He possesses extraordinary insights, _____
                          그리고 그것을 구하는 자들에게 지침을 제공한다 (분사구)

10. One day, an _____ Simon's home, who is infamous for
mistreating his workers. 예상치 못한 방문객이 ~에 도착한다

[Word Quiz]

1. What term refers to a central or recurring idea, motif, or subject matter?
a) Compassion   b) Identity   c) Theme   d) Shelter

2. Which word means showing kindness and empathy towards others' suffering?
a) Mysterious   b) Punishment   c) Transgression   d) Compassion

3. What term refers to something that is necessary for completeness or wholeness?
a) Grateful   b) Fulfillment   c) Insights   d) Integral

4. A person who works as a shoemaker is called a/an:
a) Cobbler   b) Orphan   c) Seeker   d) Angelic

5. Choose the word that means a place of safety and protection:
a) Collection   b) Material possessions   c) Shelter   d) Atmosphere

6. The act of legally taking another person's child as one's own is called:
a) Adopt   b) Condemn   c) Embrace   d) Virtues

7. "Mysterious" means:
a) Easy to understand   b) Cruel   c) Full of wonder and intrigue   d) Selflessness

8. When someone violates a law or rule, it is called a:
a) Demeanor   b) Identity   c) Transgression   d) Wealth

9. What is the definition of "Condemn"?
a) Praise   b) Blame   c) Seek   d) Embrace

10. "Kindhearted" refers to someone who is:
a) Cruel   b) Integral   c) Grateful   d) Compassionate

11. A person's sense of self and individuality is known as:
a) Insights   b) Identity   c) Themes   d) Angelic

12. "Seek" means to:

a) Reject   b) Embrace   c) Adopt   d) Look for or search

13. What do we call the moral principles and qualities of a person?

a) Virtues   b) Atmosphere   c) Orphans   d) Human beings

14. Choose the word that means a group of items gathered together:

a) Collection   b) Wealth   c) Punishment   d) Embrace

15. What does "Grateful" mean?

a) Unthankful   b) Full of wonder

c) Showing appreciation and thankfulness   d) Cruel

16. Which word means to accept and support someone wholeheartedly?

a) Fulfillment   b) Material possessions   c) Embrace   d) Seek

17. "Wealth" is best defined as:

a) Selflessness   b) Atmosphere

c) Riches and abundance of resources   d) Compassion

18. A person's outward behavior and conduct are referred to as:

a) Demeanor   b) Transgression   c) Meaning   d) Integral

19. The understanding gained through observation and contemplation is called:

a) Insights   b) Shelter   c) Collection   d) Orphans

20. The atmosphere or feeling in a particular environment is known as:

a) Identity   b) Themes   c) Compassion   d) Atmosphere

Unit 32: The Brothers Karamazov (1880)

"The Brothers Karamazov" is a complex and multi-layered novel written by the Russian author Fyodor Dostoevsky, published in 1880. The story revolves around the lives of the Karamazov family and explores themes such as faith, morality, and the human condition. Here is a summary of the novel:

The novel begins with the introduction of Fyodor Pavlovich Karamazov, a wealthy and immoral landowner. He has three sons: Dmitri, Ivan, and Alexei (Alyosha). Each son has a distinct personality and a complicated relationship with their father.

Dmitri, the oldest son, returns to his hometown after being away for some time. He is passionately in love with Grushenka, a beautiful and seductive woman, who is also involved with his father. The tension between Dmitri and his father escalates as they clash over inheritance and Grushenka's affections. Dmitri becomes a prime suspect in his father's murder, adding further complexities to the family dynamics.

Ivan, the second son, is an intellectual and tormented by moral dilemmas. He engages in deep philosophical discussions with Alyosha, the youngest son who is gentle and deeply religious. Ivan wrestles with the concepts of God, the existence of evil, and the nature of human suffering.

Alyosha becomes involved in the life of a local monastery and befriends a wise and humble elder, Father Zosima. Father Zosima serves as a spiritual guide for Alyosha and others in the town, offering profound insights into human nature and the path to spiritual redemption.

The plot further explores the relationships between the brothers and the people around them, including the intriguing character of Grushenka and other townspeople. The novel delves into their personal struggles, desires, and the consequences of their actions.

The story takes a dramatic turn when Fyodor Karamazov is found murdered, and Dmitri is accused of the crime. The ensuing trial exposes the depths of human nature, the struggle between good and evil, and the complexities of justice and morality. The trial also brings to light the various motives and conflicts within the Karamazov family.

Throughout the novel, the characters grapple with their inner demons, ethical choices, and the search for meaning in a turbulent world. Each brother represents a different aspect of the human psyche and presents a unique philosophical perspective.

"The Brothers Karamazov" is not just a murder mystery but a profound exploration of the human soul, moral dilemmas, and the complexities of human relationships. The novel concludes with the characters coming to terms with their actions and their roles in the Karamazov family saga. It leaves the readers with profound questions about life, faith, and the nature of humanity. The novel remains a timeless classic in world literature, celebrated for its psychological depth and philosophical richness.

[Vocabulary]

complex 복잡한 multi-layered 다층적인 revolve 중심을 돌다 explore 탐구하다 theme 주제 morality 도덕 introduction 소개 landowner 땅주인 relationship 관계 passionately 열렬히 seductive 매혹적인 tension 긴장 clash 충돌하다 inheritance 상속 suspect 용의자 intellectual 지성적인 philosophical 철학적인 discussions 대화 profound 깊은 insights 통찰 explore 탐구하다 intriguing 흥미로운 delve 파헤치다 consequences 결과 dramatic 극적인 accused 고발당한 ensuing 이어지는 expose 드러내다 struggle 투쟁 justice 정의 conflicts 갈등 throughout 내내 grapple 씨름하다 ethical 윤리적인 turbulent 혼란스러운 psychological 심리적인 philosophical 철학적인

[본문 해석] 카라마조프가의 형제들

"카라마조프가의 형제들"은 러시아 작가 표도르 도스토예프스키가 쓴 복잡하고 다층적인 소설로, 1880년에 출판되었습니다. 이 소설은 카라마조프 가족의 삶을 중심으로 하며, 믿음, 도덕, 인간 본성과 같은 주제들을 탐구합니다. 다음은 이 소설의 개요입니다:

이 소설은 부유하고 비도덕적인 땅주인인 표도르 파블로비치 카라마조프의 소개로 시작합니다. 그는 드미트리, 이반, 알렉세이(알료샤)라는 세 아들을 두고 있습니다. 각 아들은 매우 다른 성격을 가지고 있으며, 아버지와의 관계도 복잡합니다.

드미트리는 장자로 오랜 시간 외지에 있다가 고향으로 돌아옵니다. 그는 아버지와도 관련된 여인 아름다운 그루센카를 열렬히 사랑하고 있습니다. 드미트리와 아버지 사이의 긴장은 상속과 그루센카의 애정을 두고 충돌하면서 고조됩니다. 드미트리는 아버지 살인의 주요 용의자로 의심받게 되어 가족 간의 관계가 더욱 복잡해집니다.

이반은 둘째 아들로 지성적이고 도덕적인 딜레마에 시달립니다. 그는 부드럽고 신앙심이 깊은 막내인 알료샤와 깊은 철학적인 대화를 나눕니다. 이반은 신의 존재, 악의 존재, 그리고 인간 고통의 본성에 대한 개념들과 씨름합니다.

알료샤는 지역 수도원의 생활에 참여하고 현자이자 겸손한 장로인 조시마와 친분을 맺습니다. 조시마 장로는 알료샤와 다른 사람들에게 인간 본성과 영적인 구원의 길에 대한 깊은 통찰을 제공합니다.

줄거리는 또한 형제들과 주변 사람들 간의 관계를 탐구하며, 흥미로운 그루센카와 다른 마을 주민들의 캐릭터를 포함합니다. 이 소설은 그들의 개인적인 갈등, 욕망, 그리고 행동의 결과들을 자세히 파헤칩니다.

이야기는 표도르 카라마조프가 살해된 사건을 기점으로 급격한 전환을 겪게 됩니다. 그리고 드미트리는 살인범으로 의혹을 받게 됩니다. 이어지는 재판은 인간 본성의 깊이, 선과 악 사이의 투쟁, 그리고 정의와 도덕의 복잡성을 드러냅니다. 재판은 또한 카라마조프 가족 내의 다양한 동기와 갈등을 드러내게 됩니다.

소설 전반에서 등장인물들은 내면의 악마와 윤리적 선택, 그리고 혼란스러운 세상에서의 의미를 탐색합니다. 각 형제는 인간의 심리의 다른 면을 대표하며 독특한 철학적 시각을 제시합니다.

"카라마조프가의 형제들"은 단순한 살인 미스터리뿐만 아니라 인간의 영혼, 도덕적 딜레마, 그리고 인간관계의 복잡성을 깊이 탐구한 뛰어난 소설입니다. 이 소설은 등장인물들이 자신들의 행동과 카라마조프 가족 이야기에서의 역할에 대해 이해하고 받아들이는 부분으로 마무리됩니다. 독자들에게 삶, 믿음, 그리고 인간 본성에 대한 깊은 질문을 남기며, 심리적 깊이와 철학적인 풍부함으로 인해 세계 문학의 희소성을 누리는 무궁한 걸작으로 평가받고 있습니다.

[Reading Comprehension]

1. What is the main theme explored in "The Brothers Karamazov"?
a) Adventure and exploration
b) Family dynamics and relationships
c) Political intrigue and power struggles
d) Science and technology

2. Who is the author of "The Brothers Karamazov"?
a) Leo Tolstoy
b) Fyodor Dostoevsky
c) Anton Chekhov
d) Alexander Pushkin

3. How many sons does Fyodor Pavlovich Karamazov have?
a) One b) Two c) Three d) Four

4. What is the name of the oldest son who returns to his hometown and becomes entangled in a complex love triangle?
a) Alexei b) Ivan c) Dmitri d) Grushenka

5. What philosophical themes does Ivan, the second son, grapple with?
a) The nature of faith and devotion
b) The pursuit of wealth and success
c) The existence of evil and human suffering
d) The importance of physical strength

6. Who serves as a spiritual guide for Alyosha, the youngest son?
a) Dmitri Karamazov b) Father Zosima c) Grushenka d) Fyodor Pavlovich

7. What is the role of Father Zosima in Alyosha's life?
a) He is a romantic interest
b) He is a mentor and spiritual guide
c) He is a rival for Grushenka's affections
d) He is a prosecutor in Dmitri's trial

8. Who is suspected to be his father's murder?
a) Alexei b) Ivan c) Dmitri d) Grushenka

9. What is the main focus of the trial in the novel?

a) Political corruption

b) Family inheritance disputes

c) Fyodor Karamazov's murder

d) Religious ceremonies

10. Which son engages in deep philosophical discussions with Ivan?

a) Alexei b) Dmitri c) Fyodor Pavlovich   d) Alyosha

11. How does the novel conclude?

a) With a dramatic battle scene

b) With the capture of a criminal mastermind

c) With the characters reflecting on their actions and roles

d) With a sudden and unresolved ending

12. What is the significance of Grushenka's role in the story?

a) She is a detective investigating the murder

b) She is a key witness in the trial

c) She represents the seductive and alluring aspects of life

d) She is a lawyer defending Dmitri in court

13. What is the novel's exploration of justice and morality primarily centered around?

a) An international conflict

b) A court case and trial

c) A medical breakthrough

d) A family reunion

14. What is the ultimate impact of "The Brothers Karamazov" on readers?

a) It leaves them with no questions unanswered

b) It challenges their understanding of human nature

c) It offers a light-hearted and comedic view of life

d) It provides a guide to successful living

15. How is "The Brothers Karamazov" described in terms of its literary significance?

a) A forgotten and irrelevant work

b) A shallow exploration of simple themes

c) A timeless classic with psychological depth and philosophical richness

d) A predictable and formulaic mystery novel

[Grammar Check-up]

1. "The Brothers Karamazov" is a complex and (multi-layered, multi-layering) novel written by the Russian author Fyodor Dostoevsky, published in 1880.
2. The story revolves around the lives of the Karamazov family and (is explored, explores) themes such as faith, morality, and the human condition.
3. Dmitri, the oldest son, (returning, returns) to his hometown after being away for some time.
4. He is (passionate, passionately) in love with Grushenka, a beautiful and seductive woman, who is also (involved, involving) with his father.
5. The tension between Dmitri and his father (escalate, escalates) as they clash over inheritance and Grushenka's affections.
6. Dmitri becomes a prime suspect in his father's murder, adding (farther, further) complexities to the family dynamics.
7. He engages in deep philosophical discussions with Alyosha, the youngest son who is gentle and (deep, deeply) religious.
8. Ivan wrestles with the concepts of God, the (existing, existence) of evil, and the nature of human suffering.
9. Alyosha becomes (involved, involving) in the life of a local monastery and befriends a wise and humble elder, Father Zosima.
10. Father Zosima serves as a spiritual guide for Alyosha and (other, others) in the town, (offering, offers) profound insights into human nature and the path to spiritual redemption.
11. The plot further explores the relationships between the brothers and the people around them, (include, including) the intriguing character of Grushenka and other townspeople.
12. The novel (is delved, delves) into their personal struggles, desires, and the consequences of their actions.
13. The story takes a dramatic turn (where, when) Fyodor Karamazov is found murdered, and Dmitri (accuses, is accused) of the crime.
14. The (ensued, ensuing) trial exposes the depths of human nature, the struggle between good and evil, and the complexities of justice and (moral, morality).
15. The trial also (brings, is brought) to light the various motives and conflicts within the Karamazov family.
16. Throughout the novel, the characters grapple with their inner demons, ethical choices, and the search for meaning in a (turbulent, turbulently) world.
17. Each (brother, brothers) represents a different aspect of the human psyche and presents a unique philosophical perspective.
18. The novel (leaves, is left) the readers with profound questions about life, faith, and the nature of humanity.

[Writing Practice]

1. Dmitri, the oldest son, returns to his hometown _____.
_____ 얼마 동안 집에서 멀리 떨어져 있은 후에 (전치사구)

2. He _____ Grushenka, a beautiful and seductive woman,
열정적으로 ~와 사랑에 빠진다 who is also (involved, involving) with his father.

3. Dmitri becomes a prime suspect in his father's murder, _____
the family dynamics. ~에 더 많은 복잡함을 추가한다 (분사구)

4. He _____ Alyosha, the youngest son who is gentle
~와 깊은 철학적 토론들을 한다(engage) and deeply religious.

5. Father Zosima serves as a spiritual guide for Alyosha and others in the town,
_____ and the path to spiritual redemption.
인간 본성에 대한 심오한 통찰력을 제공하면서 (분사구)

6. The story takes a dramatic turn when Fyodor Karamazov is found murdered, and
_____. Dritri는 그 범죄에 대해 기소당한다

7. _____, the struggle between good and evil.
그 후의(ensue~) 재판은 인간 본성의 깊이를 드러낸다

8. The trial _____ the Karamazov family.
또한 ~내의 다양한 동기와 갈등을 밝혀준다(bring, light)

9. _____ _____ the human psyche and presents a unique
각각의 형제는 ~의 다른 양상을 나타낸다 philosophical perspective.

10. The novel _____ life, faith, and the nature
of humanity. 독자들에게 ~에 관한 심오한 의문을 남긴다

- 332 -

[Word Quiz]

1. What term refers to something intricate and difficult to understand?
a) Complex   b) Revolve   c) Explore   d) Theme

2. Which word refers to something that has various levels, aspects, or dimensions?
a) Multi-layered   b) Intellectual   c) Dramatic   d) Morality

3. What does it mean when something is said to "revolve"?
a) To explore deeply
b) To have conflicting opinions
c) To rotate around a central point
d) To discuss philosophically

4. Which term refers to the act of investigating or examining thoroughly?
a) Explore   b) Seductive   c) Tension   d) Clash

5. What is the central idea or message of a piece of art or literature called?
a) Introduction   b) Morality   c) Theme   d) Landowner

6. Which word describes principles of right and wrong behavior?
a) Morality   b) Relationship   c) Tension   d) Passionately

7. What term refers to the beginning or opening part of something?
a) Landowner   b) Introduction   c) Intellectual   d) Seductive

8. Who is the owner of a piece of land called?
a) Relationship   b) Inheritance   c) Landowner   d) Suspect

9. What is the connection or association between people called?
a) Introduction   b) Relationship   c) Justice   d) Tension

10. Which term describes doing something with intense emotion or fervor?
a) Passionately   b) Revolve   c) Expose   d) Grapple

11. What word describes something that attracts or entices?

a) Intellectual   b) Seductive   c) Clash   d) Ethical

12. What term refers to a state of strain or unease?

a) Tension   b) Inheritance   c) Conflict   d) Dramatic

13. What happens when opposing ideas or interests collide?

a) Delve   b) Suspect   c) Clash   d) Grapple

14. What is received from a predecessor, typically as a legal right or title?

a) Revolve   b) Inheritance   c) Expose   d) Struggle

15. Who is someone believed to be guilty of a crime or offense?

a) Intellectual   b) Accused   c) Ethical   d) Intriguing

16. Which term refers to exchanges of ideas?

a) Intellectual   b) Philosophical   c) Discussions   d) Consequences

17. What term describes having deep insight or understanding?

a) Profound   b) Ethical   c) Expose   d) Struggle

18. What does it mean to investigate or examine something thoroughly?

a) Exclude   b) Intriguing   c) Delve   d) Ensue

19. What term describes something fascinating or captivating?

a) Consequences   b) Dramatic   c) Accused   d) Intriguing

20. What is the result or outcome of an action or event?

a) Struggle   b) Justice   c) Conflicts   d) Consequences

Unit 33: Thus Spoke Zarathustra (1883)

"Thus Spoke Zarathustra" is a philosophical novel written by Friedrich Nietzsche, published in multiple parts between 1883 and 1885. It presents the ideas and teachings of the fictional character Zarathustra, a prophet who descends from his solitude in the mountains to share his wisdom with humanity.

The book is structured in four parts, each containing a series of discourses and encounters. Zarathustra begins by announcing the "death of God" and urging humanity to embrace the concept of the "overman" or "superman"—a liberated individual who embraces life's challenges and creates their own values.

In Part One, Zarathustra delivers a series of speeches to the people, critiquing conventional morality and religion. He advocates for the "will to power," the inherent drive within individuals to exert their strength and create meaning in their lives. Zarathustra encourages the rejection of herd mentality and the pursuit of personal greatness.

Part Two focuses on Zarathustra's encounters with various individuals, including a king, a dwarf, and an old woman. Through these encounters, Zarathustra emphasizes the importance of individuality, self-overcoming, and embracing suffering as a means of personal growth.

In Part Three, Zarathustra engages in dialogues with a group of ascetics, who reject worldly pleasures in pursuit of spiritual enlightenment. Zarathustra challenges their beliefs, arguing for a life-affirming approach that embraces joy, sensuality, and the fullness of earthly existence.

In the final part, Zarathustra undergoes a transformation and retreats to a cave. There, he experiences solitude, self-reflection, and a confrontation with his own limitations. He emerges from his seclusion with a renewed understanding of the eternal recurrence, the idea that life repeats itself in an endless cycle. Zarathustra imparts this wisdom to his disciples and bids farewell, urging them to carry on his teachings and continue the search for self-realization.

"Thus Spoke Zarathustra" explores themes of individualism, the rejection of traditional values, the quest for personal meaning, and the overcoming of adversity. It challenges established moral and religious frameworks and calls for the creation of new values based on personal will and self-mastery. Nietzsche's work remains highly influential in philosophical and literary circles, provoking critical examination of human existence and the possibilities of personal transformation.

[Vocabulary]

philosophical 철학적인 prophet 예언자 solitude 고독 overman 극복인/위버멘쉬 wisdom 지혜 humanity 인류 liberated 해방된 conventional morality 관습적 도덕 religion 종교 will to power 힘에의 의지 inherent drive 타고난 추구 herd mentality 무리 정신 encounter 만남 individuality 개성 self-overcoming 자기극복 ascetics 금욕주의자 worldly pleasures 세속적 쾌락 pursuit 추구 spiritual enlightenment 영적 깨달음 life-affirming approach 생활을 긍정하는 방법 sensuality 감각적 쾌락 earthly existence 세속적 존재 transformation 변화 retreat 은둔 self-reflection 자기반성 confrontation 대립 limitation 한계 eternal recurrence 영원 회귀 critical examination 비판적 조사 personal transformation 개인적 변화

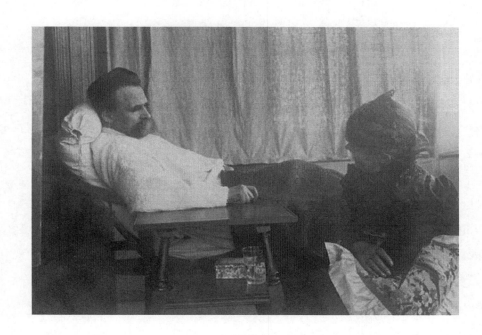

[본문 해석] 차라투스트라는 이렇게 말했다

　"차라투스트라는 이렇게 말했다"는 프리드리히 니체가 1883년부터 1885년까지 여러 파트로 출간한 철학 소설입니다. 이 소설은 허구의 캐릭터인 예언자 차라투스트라의 이념과 가르침을 담고 있으며, 차라투스트라는 산속의 고독에서 내려와 인류와 자신의 지혜를 나누기 위해 헤쳐 나가는 이야기를 전합니다.

　이 책은 네 개의 파트로 구성되어 있으며, 각 파트에는 연설과 만남의 연속이 담겨 있습니다. 차라투스트라는 먼저 "신의 죽음"을 선언하고 인류에게 "극복인" 또는 "위버맨쉬"의 개념을 받아들이도록 권유합니다. 위버맨쉬는 삶의 도전을 받아들이고 자신만의 가치를 창출하는 자유로운 개인입니다.

　제 1부에서 차라투스트라는 대중들에게 연설을 통해 전통적 도덕과 종교를 비판합니다. 그는 "힘에의 의지"를 옹호하며 개인의 내재적인 힘을 발휘하여 삶에 의미를 부여하도록 권장합니다. 차라투스트라는 대중 마인드의 거부와 개인적 위대함의 추구를 촉구합니다.

　제 2부에서는 차라투스트라가 여러 인물들과 만나는 상황을 그립니다. 이 인물들에는 왕, 난쟁이, 노년 여성 등이 포함되며, 이를 통해 차라투스트라는 개인주의, 자기 극복, 그리고 고통을 받아들여 개인적인 성장을 장려합니다.

　제 3부에서는 차라투스트라가 성도들과 대화합니다. 성도들은 세속적 기쁨을 거절하고 영적 깨달음을 추구합니다. 차라투스트라는 그들의 믿음에 도전하며 기쁨과 감각적인 삶, 그리고 대지의 존재의 풍요로움을 옹호합니다.

　마지막 파트에서 차라투스트라는 변화를 겪고 동굴로 은둔합니다. 거기서 그는 고독과 자기반성, 그리고 자신의 한계와의 대면을 경험합니다. 그는 영원한 반복의 개념, 인생이 끊임없이 순환하는 아이디어(영원회귀)를 깨닫고 은둔에서 벗어납니다. 차라투스트라는 이 지혜를 그의 제자들에게 전달하고 작별을 고하며 그들에게 자신의 가르침을 계승하고 자기실현을 위한 탐구를 계속하도록 권합니다.

　"차라투스트라는 이렇게 말했다"는 개인주의, 전통적 가치의 거부, 개인적인 의미를 찾는 탐구, 그리고 역경 극복에 대한 주제들을 탐구합니다. 이 책은 형성된 도덕과 종교적 틀에 도전하며 개인적 의지와 자기 통제를 기반으로 새로운 가치를 창조하도록 호소합니다. 니체의 작품은 철학적이고 문학적인 분야에서 여전히 큰 영향력을 미치며, 인간의 존재와 개인적 변화의 가능성에 대한 비판적인 고찰을 자극합니다.

[Reading Comprehension]

1. What is the main focus of "Thus Spoke Zarathustra" by Friedrich Nietzsche?

a) The history of Zarathustra's mountain retreat

b) The fictional life of a king and his encounters

c) The teachings and ideas of the character Zarathustra

d) The challenges of writing a philosophical novel

2. How is the book "Thus Spoke Zarathustra" structured?

a) It consists of a single long narrative.

b) It is divided into four parts with discourses and encounters.

c) It follows the life of a dwarf and his struggles.

d) It contains various unrelated philosophical essays.

3. Who is Zarathustra in the context of the novel?

a) A historical figure from ancient Persia

b) A prophet descending from a mountain

c) The author of the book

d) A king ruling over a kingdom

4. What concept does Zarathustra urge humanity to embrace?

a) Conventional morality   b) The rejection of individuality

c) The "overman" or "superman"   d) Asceticism and self-denial

5. In Part One, what does Zarathustra critique and advocate for?

a) He critiques the rejection of herd mentality.

b) He advocates for the pursuit of worldly pleasures.

c) He critiques conventional morality and religion.

d) He advocates for embracing suffering without growth.

6. What does "will to power" refer to in the novel?

a) The power of religious institutions

b) The inherent drive to exert strength and create meaning

c) The rejection of personal values

d) The power of conventional morality

7. What is the central message Zarathustra conveys to the ascetics in Part Three?

a) He encourages them to reject spiritual enlightenment.

b) He challenges their beliefs and advocates for joy and sensuality.

c) He advises them to embrace herd mentality.

d) He supports their pursuit of conventional values.

8. What is the focus of Part Four of the novel?

a) Zarathustra's transformation during his seclusion

b) Zarathustra's encounters with various animals

c) Zarathustra's return to the mountains

d) Zarathustra's dialogues with other philosophers

9. What does Zarathustra learn during his retreat in Part Four?

a) He confronts his limitations and rejects eternal recurrence.

b) He engages in debates with ascetics.

c) He experiences solitude and self-reflection.

d) He learns the importance of worldly pleasures.

10. What is the "eternal recurrence" as mentioned in the passage?

a) A concept of multiple lifetimes

b) The belief in an afterlife

c) The idea that life repeats in an endless cycle

d) A process of spiritual enlightenment

11. What themes does "Thus Spoke Zarathustra" explore?

a) Traditional values and religious dogma

b) The rejection of personal growth and transformation

c) The importance of material wealth

d) Individualism, self-overcoming, and personal meaning

12. How does Zarathustra's philosophy challenge established norms?

a) By advocating for conventional morality

b) By rejecting personal will and self-mastery

c) By calling for the creation of new values

d) By emphasizing the pursuit of herd mentality

13. What effect has "Thus Spoke Zarathustra" had on philosophical and literary circles?
a) It has been forgotten over time.
b) It has led to the rejection of critical examination.
c) It has provoked discussions about personal transformation.
d) It has discouraged the exploration of human existence.

14. What does Zarathustra urge his disciples to do at the end of the novel?
a) To abandon his teachings
b) To carry on his teachings and search for self-realization
c) To reject personal transformation
d) To continue conventional beliefs

15. What is the significance of the character Zarathustra in the novel?
a) He is a historical figure from ancient Persia.
b) He represents the author's personal experiences.
c) He embodies the teachings and ideas of Nietzsche.
d) He is a fictional king ruling over a kingdom.

[Grammar Check-up]

1. "Thus Spoke Zarathustra" is a philosophical novel (which writes, written) by Friedrich Nietzsche, published in multiple parts.
2. It presents the ideas and teachings of the fictional character Zarathustra, a prophet (who, which) descends from his solitude in the mountains (for, to) share his wisdom with humanity.
3. The book (structures, is structured) in four parts, each (containing, contains) a series of discourses and encounters.
4. Zarathustra (is begun, begins) by announcing the "death of God" and urging humanity to embrace the concept of the "overman" or "superman"—a liberated individual who (is embraced, embraces) life's challenges and creates their own values.
5. In Part One, Zarathustra delivers a series of (speeches, speech) to the people, (critiquing, critique) conventional morality and religion.

6. He advocates (for, against) the "will to power," the inherent drive within individuals to exert their strength and create meaning in their lives.

7. Zarathustra encourages the (rejection, reject) of herd mentality and the pursuit of personal greatness.

8. Part Two focuses on Zarathustra's encounters with (variety, various) individuals, including a king, a dwarf, and an old woman.

9. Through (this, these) encounters, Zarathustra emphasizes the importance of individuality, self-overcoming, and (embrace, embracing) suffering as a (mean, means) of personal growth.

10. In Part Three, Zarathustra engages in dialogues with a group of ascetics, who (rejects, reject) worldly pleasures in pursuit of spiritual enlightenment.

11. Zarathustra challenges their beliefs, (arguing, argues) for a life-affirming approach that (embracing, embraces) joy, sensuality, and the fullness of earthly existence.

12. In the final part, Zarathustra (undergoes, undergoing) a transformation and retreats to a cave.

13. He (is emerged, emerges) from his seclusion with a renewed understanding of the eternal recurrence, the idea (which, that) life repeats itself in an endless cycle.

14. Zarathustra imparts this wisdom to his disciples and (bids, bidding) farewell, urging them to carry on his teachings and continue the search for self-realization.

15. "Thus Spoke Zarathustra" explores themes of individualism, the (rejection, reject) of traditional values, the quest for personal meaning, and the (overcoming, overcome) of adversity.

16. Nietzsche's work remains (high, highly) influential in philosophical and literary circles, (provoking, provokes) critical examination of human existence and the possibilities of personal transformation.

[Writing Practice]

1. It presents the ideas and teachings of the fictional character Zarathustra, a prophet who descends from his solitude in the mountains _____

_____ 인간들과 그의 지혜를 공유하기 위해서

2. The book _____, each containing a series of discourses and encounters. 4 부분으로 구성되어 있다

3. Zarathustra _____ the "death of God" and urging humanity to
   선포함으로써 시작한다   embrace the concept of the "overman."

4. In Part One, Zarathustra _____, critiquing conventional morality and religion.   사람들에게 일련의 연설을 한다(deliver)

5. He _____ the inherent drive within individuals to exert
   힘에의 의지에 대해서 옹호한다   their strength and create meaning in their lives.

6. Zarathustra _____ and the pursuit of personal greatness.
   군중 심리의 거절을 고무하다

7. _____ Zarathustra's encounters with various individuals,
   2부는 ~에 초점을 둔다   including a king, a dwarf, and an old woman.

8. _____, Zarathustra emphasizes the importance of individuality,
   이러한 만남들을 통해   self-overcoming, and embracing suffering.

9. In Part Three, Zarathustra _____ a group of ascetics,
   who reject worldly pleasures.   ~와 대화를 시작한다(engage)

10. In the final part, Zarathustra _____ a cave.
    변화를 겪고 동굴로 은둔한다(retreat)

11. He _____ a renewed understanding of the eternal recurrence.
    ~를 지니고 그의 은둔에서 벗어난다

12. Zarathustra imparts this wisdom to his disciples and bids farewell,
_____ the search for self-realization.
그들에게 그의 가르침을 지니고 ~~~ 를 계속하라고 촉구한다 (분사구)

[Word Quiz]

1. What term describes the study or inquiry into fundamental truths and principles?
a) Prophet   b) Solitude   c) Philosophical   d) Overman

2. Who is someone believed to have the ability to foretell the future?
a) Wisdom   b) Prophet   c) Humanity   d) Liberation

3. What word refers to the state of being alone or isolated from others?
a) Conventional Morality   b) Solitude   c) Religion   d) Pursuit

4. What concept, introduced by Friedrich Nietzsche, describes a person who rises above conventional morality to create their own values?
a) Wisdom   b) Overman   c) Humanity   d) Ascetics

5. Which term denotes the quality of having knowledge and experience to make sound judgments?
a) Wisdom   b) Liberated   c) Herd Mentality   d) Encounter

6. What term refers to the collective aspects of human life and culture?
a) Humanity   b) Will to Power   c) Ascetics   d) Sensuality

7. What word describes being freed from constraints or restrictions?
a) Liberation   b) Conventional Morality   c) Eternal Recurrence   d) Herd Mentality

8. Which term refers to the traditional or commonly accepted principles of right and wrong behavior?
a) Religion   b) Will to Power   c) Inherent Drive   d) Conventional Morality

9. What concept represents the belief in and worship of a higher power or powers?
a) Liberation   b) Religion   c) Transformation   d) Retreat

10. What term is characterized by a lack of independent thinking and a willingness to follow the crowd?
a) Inherent Drive   b) Herd Mentality   c) Wisdom   d) Spiritual Enlightenment

11. Which phrase refers to an instinctive urge or motivation that is fundamental to one's nature?
a) Encounter   b) Individuality   c) Inherent Drive   d) Worldly Pleasures

12. What term refers to individuals who practice self-discipline, self-denial, and austerity
a) Encounter   b) Herd Mentality   c) Individuality   d) Ascetics

13. What word refers to a meeting or interaction with someone or something?
a) Retreat   b) Confrontation   c) Limitation   d) Eternal Recurrence

14. What term denotes the quality of being unique or distinct from others?
a) Liberation   b) Individuality   c) Ascetics   d) Pursuit

15. Which term describes the process of overcoming one's limitations or weaknesses?
a) Self-Reflection   b) Self-Overcoming   c) Sensuality   d) Transformation

16. What term refers to a significant change, alteration, or conversion in form, nature, and appearance?
a) Worldly Pleasures   b) Transformation   c) Philosophical   d) Solitude

17. What term refers to the quality which involves a heightened appreciation or enjoyment of the physical senses?
a) Sensuality   b) Worldly Pleasures
c) Spiritual Enlightenment   d) Earthly Existence

18. What term describes the act of actively seeking or striving for something?
a) Pursuit   b) Transformation   c) Encounter   d) Limitation

19. What concept involves attaining a higher level of understanding or awareness beyond the physical realm?
a) Earthly Existence   b) Pursuit   c) Spiritual Enlightenment   d) Liberation

20. What term describes an approach to life that embraces the positive aspects and affirms existence?
a) Life-Affirming Approach   b) Critical Examination   c) Individuality   d) Pursuit

Unit 34: Dr. Jekyll and Mr. Hyde (1886)

"Dr. Jekyll and Mr. Hyde" is a novella written by Scottish author Robert Louis Stevenson, first published in 1886. The story follows the life of Dr. Henry Jekyll, a respected and kind-hearted scientist and physician in Victorian London. Dr. Jekyll becomes increasingly intrigued by the concept of dual personalities, the coexistence of good and evil in one person. He believes that every individual has both virtuous and wicked tendencies.

Driven by a desire to separate his darker nature from his virtuous self, Dr. Jekyll conducts a series of experiments to create a potion that can transform him into a completely different person, who he later names Edward Hyde. The potion's effect is shocking: when he drinks it, Dr. Jekyll transforms into Mr. Hyde, a cruel, immoral, and violent man. Hyde represents the embodiment of Jekyll's darkest impulses and desires, acting without restraint or conscience.

At first, Dr. Jekyll is fascinated by his newfound ability to switch between his two distinct personas. He enjoys the freedom that Mr. Hyde's uninhibited nature brings him. However, as time passes, he begins to lose control over his transformations. Mr. Hyde becomes increasingly dominant, and Jekyll's ability to revert to his original self becomes more challenging.

The situation worsens when Mr. Hyde commits a series of heinous crimes, including the murder of Sir Danvers Carew, a respected member of society. Dr. Jekyll is horrified by Hyde's actions but finds himself unable to stop the transformations. He realizes that he has unwittingly created a monster, and his experiment has gone terribly wrong.

The story unfolds through the perspective of Dr. Jekyll's friend and lawyer, Gabriel John Utterson, who becomes suspicious of Mr. Hyde's relationship with Jekyll. Utterson investigates the strange occurrences and discovers that Jekyll and Hyde are the same person.

As the novella reaches its climax, Jekyll writes a confession letter revealing the truth behind his dual identity. He explains that he can no longer control his transformations, and Hyde is now taking over completely. Fearing the consequences of his actions, Dr. Jekyll decides to end his life and avoid harming others through Hyde's actions.

In the end, Dr. Jekyll commits suicide to prevent Hyde from causing further harm. The novella concludes with Utterson and Jekyll's butler breaking into Jekyll's laboratory and finding the confession letter and evidence of his tragic experiments.

"Dr. Jekyll and Mr. Hyde" is a classic tale of duality, the struggle between good and evil within oneself, and the consequences of unchecked desires. Stevenson's novella continues to be a compelling exploration of human nature and the dark complexities of the human psyche, making it one of the most enduring and influential works in English literature.

[Vocabulary]

Novella 소설 Respected 존경받는 Victorian 빅토리아 시대의 Intrigue 흥미를 끌다 Coexistence 공존 Virtuous 덕 있는 Wicked 악한 Tendency 경향 Desires 욕망 Inhibited 억제된 Conscience 양심 Dominant 우세한 Revert 되돌아가다 Heinous 극악한 Confession 고백 Identity 정체성 Unchecked 억제되지 않은 Consequences 결과 Tragic 비극적인 Exploration 탐구 Complexity 복잡함 Enduring 지속적인 Influential 영향력 있는 Physician 의사 Dual 이중의 Transformations 변화 Reveal 드러내다 Fearing 두려워하는 Laboratory 실험실 Relationship 관계 Butcher 도살업자/도살하다 Experimental 실험적인

[본문 해석] 지킬박사와 하이드

"지킬박사와 하이드"는 스코틀랜드 작가 로버트 루이스 스티븐슨에 의해 쓰인 소설로, 1886년 처음 출판되었습니다. 이 이야기는 빅토리아 시대 런던에서 존경받고 따뜻한 마음의 과학자이자 의사인 헨리 지킬 박사의 삶을 따릅니다. 지킬 박사는 이중성격의 개념에 더욱 호기심을 가지며 한 사람 안에서 선과 악의 공존을 연구합니다. 그는 모든 개인이 선하고 사악한 성향을 갖고 있다고 믿습니다.

더 어두운 본성과 선한 자아를 구분하고 싶어 하는 욕망에 이끌려 지킬 박사는 자신을 완전히 다른 사람으로 변모시킬 수 있는 물약을 만들기 위해 일련의 실험을 진행합니다. 이 변모 물약의 영향은 충격적입니다. 지킬 박사가 물약을 마시면, 잔인하고 비도덕적이며 폭력적인 남자인 하이드로 변모합니다. 하이드는 지킬 박사의 어두운 충동과 욕망의 상징으로서 억제나 양심 없이 행동합니다.

처음에는 지킬 박사는 두 가지 독특한 인격 사이를 자유롭게 전환하는 능력에 황홀해합니다. 그는 하이드의 억제되지 않은 본성이 가져다주는 자유를 즐깁니다. 그러나 시간이 지남에 따라 그는 변모를 통제하는 것을 잃어가고, 하이드가 지킬 박사를 본래의 자아로 돌아가게 하는 능력이 더 어려워집니다.

상황은 하이드가 사회에서 존경받는 댄버스 커루 경의 살해를 비롯한 일련의 악행을 저지르면서 악화됩니다. 지킬 박사는 하이드의 행동에 경악하지만, 변모를 멈출 수 없다는 것을 깨닫게 됩니다. 그는 뜻하지 않게 괴물을 만들어냈다는 사실을 깨닫고, 그의 실험이 끔찍하게 잘못되었다는 것을 깨닫게 됩니다.

이 이야기는 지킬 박사의 친구이자 변호사인 가브리엘 존 어터슨의 시각을 통해 펼쳐집니다. 어터슨은 이상한 사건들을 조사하고 지킬과 하이드가 같은 사람임을 발견합니다.

소설이 절정에 이를 때, 지킬 박사는 이중성격의 진실을 드러내는 자백서를 씁니다. 그는 이제 더 이상 변모를 통제할 수 없으며, 하이드가 완전히 지배하고 있다고 설명합니다. 자신의 행동의 결과를 두려워한 지킬 박사는 하이드의 행동을 통해 다른 사람들을 해치지 않기 위해 자신의 삶을 끝내기로 결정합니다.

결국 지킬 박사는 하이드가 더 큰 해를 끼치는 것을 막기 위해 자살을 합니다. 이 소설은 자신 안의 선과 악의 투쟁, 그리고 억제되지 않은 욕망의 결과를 다룬 이중성에 관한 고전적인 이야기로, 스티븐슨의 소설은 인간의 본성과 어둠 속의 복잡성을 탐구하는 흥미진진한 작품으로서 영어 문학에서 가장 오래 지속되고 영향력 있는 작품 중 하나입니다.

[Reading Comprehension]

1. What is the title of the novella written by Robert Louis Stevenson?
a) Strange Case of Dr. Hyde and Mr. Jekyll b) Dr. Jekyll and Mr. Hyde
c) The Dual Nature of Man   d) The Scottish Scientist

2. What is the profession of the main character, Dr. Henry Jekyll?
a) Lawyer b) Scientist and Physician c) Detective d) Artist

3. What intrigues Dr. Jekyll about human nature?
a) The concept of coexistence of animals and humans
b) The duality of personalities, good and evil within one person
c) The struggle between social classes
d) The relationship between science and spirituality

4. Why does Dr. Jekyll conduct a series of experiments?
a) To find a cure for his illness
b) To prove the existence of supernatural beings
c) To create a potion that can transform him into a monster
d) To separate his darker nature from his virtuous self

5. What does the potion created by Dr. Jekyll do?
a) It cures physical ailments
b) It transforms him into a cruel and immoral person
c) It turns him into a vampire
d) It grants him eternal life

6. What is the effect of the potion on Dr. Jekyll?
a) It enhances his physical strength
b) It allows him to time travel
c) It gives him the ability to fly
d) It transforms him into Mr. Hyde, a violent and immoral man

7. How does Dr. Jekyll feel about his transformations at first?
a) He is horrified and disgusted
b) He enjoys the freedom and power it brings
c) He becomes depressed and isolated
d) He regrets conducting the experiments

8. What happens to Dr. Jekyll's control over the transformations?
a) He gains complete control over them

b) He loses control as Mr. Hyde becomes dominant

c) He transforms into a completely different person

d) He decides to never transform again

9. What crimes does Mr. Hyde commit?

a) Theft of valuable artifacts
b) Forgery of legal documents

c) Series of heinous crimes, including murder
d) Acts of kindness and charity

10. How does Gabriel John Utterson, the lawyer, become involved in the story?

a) He is a close friend of Mr. Hyde

b) He investigates Dr. Jekyll's laboratory

c) He becomes Mr. Hyde's accomplice

d) He becomes suspicious of Mr. Hyde's relationship with Dr. Jekyll

11. What does Dr. Jekyll reveal in his confession letter?

a) His love for literature and art

b) His plans to travel the world

c) The truth behind his dual identity and inability to control transformations

d) His desire to become a famous scientist

12. Why does Dr. Jekyll decide to end his life?

a) He is tired of living
b) He fears the consequences of Hyde's actions

c) He wants to escape from the law
d) He is in love with another woman

13. What is the conclusion of the novella regarding Dr. Jekyll?

a) He lives a long and happy life

b) He continues to transform into Mr. Hyde

c) He commits suicide to prevent further harm

d) He escapes to another country

14. What does "Dr. Jekyll and Mr. Hyde" explore?

a) The relationship between two brothers

b) The journey of a detective solving a mystery

c) The duality of human nature and consequences of unchecked desires

d) The adventures of a time traveler

15. Why is Robert Louis Stevenson's novella considered influential?

a) It is a romance novel with a happy ending

b) It explores the supernatural world of vampires and werewolves

c) It delves into human nature and the complexities of the human psyche

d) It is a biography of a famous scientist

[Grammar Check-up]

1. "Dr. Jekyll and Mr. Hyde" was _____ by Scottish author Robert Louis Stevenson.
a) writing   b) written   c) wrote   d) write

2. The novella _____ in 1886.
a) published   b) publishing   c) publish   d) was published

3. The story _____ the life of Dr. Henry Jekyll.
a) follows   b) following   c) followed   d) will follow

4. Dr. Jekyll becomes _____ interested by the concept of dual personalities.
a) increasing   b) increased   c) increases   d) increasingly

5. He believes that every individual has _____ virtuous and wicked tendencies.
a) both   b) either   c) neither   d) every

6. Driven by a desire to separate his darker nature from his virtuous self, Dr. Jekyll _____ a series of experiments.
a) conduct   b) conducting   c) conducted   d) conduction

7. The potion's effect is _____.
a) shock   b) shocking   c) shocked   d) shocks

8. Dr. Jekyll transforms _____ Mr. Hyde when he drinks the potion.
a) at   b) into   c) on   d) with

9. Mr. Hyde represents the embodiment of Jekyll's _____ impulses and desires.
a) darkly   b) darkest   c) brightly   d) bright

10. At first, Dr. Jekyll is _____ by his newfound ability to switch between personas.
a) fascinating   b) fascinated   c) fascinate   d) fascinates

11. He enjoys the freedom that Mr. Hyde's _____ nature brings him.
a) uninhibited   b) uninhibit   c) uninhibiting   d) uninhibits

12. However, as time passes, he begins to lose _____ over his transformations.
a) controls   b) controlling   c) controlled   d) control

13. The situation _____ when Mr. Hyde commits heinous crimes.
a) worsen   b) worsens   c) worse   d) worsening

14. Dr. Jekyll is _____ by Hyde's actions.
a) horrify   b) horrified   c) horrifies   d) horrifying

15. He realizes that he has _____ created a monster.
a) unwittingly   b) unwitting   c) witness   d) witnessing

16. The story unfolds through _____ of Dr. Jekyll's friend and lawyer, Gabriel John Utterson.
a) respective   b) perspective   c) perspectively   d) respectively

17. Utterson investigates _____ strange occurrences.
a) the   b) an   c) a   d) that

18. As the novella reaches its climax, Jekyll writes a confession letter.
a) For   b) Though   c) Despite   d) As

19. He explains that he can no longer _____ his transformations.
a) controlling   b) control   c) controlled   d) controls

20. Stevenson's novella continues to be _____ exploration of human nature.
a) compelling   b) compelled   c) compels   d) compel

[Writing Practice]

1. "Dr. Jekyll and Mr. Hyde" _____ Scottish author Robert Louis Stevenson.
                            ~에 의해 쓰여 졌다

2. The novella _____ 1886. 1886년에 출판 되었다.

3. Dr. Jekyll _____ the concept of dual personalities.
              점점 ~에 흥미를 느끼게 된다

4. He believes that _____ tendencies.
              모든 개인은 미덕의 경향과 사악한 경향을 둘 다 지니고 있다

5. _____ his darker nature from his virtuous self,
   ~을 분리하고자 하는 욕망에 이끌려 (drive) Dr. Jekyll conducts a series of experiments.

6. Dr. Jekyll _____ Mr. Hyde when he drinks the potion.
          ~로 변신한다

7. *Mr. Hyde* _____ Jekyll's dark impulses and desires.
      미스터 하이드는 ~의 구체화를 표현한다

8. Dr. Jekyll _____ switch between personas.
     지킬 박사는 ~할 수 있는 새롭게 발견한 자신의 능력에 매료됩니다.

9. However, as time passes, he _____ *his transformations*.
           그는 *자신의 변화*에 대한 통제력을 잃기 시작합니다.

10. *He explains* that _____.
          그는 더 이상 자신의 변화를 통제할 수 없다고 *설명합니다.*

[Word Quiz]

1. What is the term for a short novel or a long short story?
a) Novella   b) Respected   c) Victorian   d) Intrigue

2. Which word refers to a predisposition or inclination towards a particular behavior, action, or outcome?
a) Coexistence   b) Virtuous   c) Wicked   d) Tendency

3. Which word relates to the period in English history during the reign of Queen Victoria?
a) Desires   b) Inhibited   c) Victorian   d) Conscience

4. What term describes a mysterious or fascinating quality?
a) Dominant   b) Revert   c) Heinous   d) Intrigue

5. Which word signifies the state of being together peacefully?
a) Confession   b) Identity   c) Coexistence   d) Unchecked

6. Which term refers to having high moral standards or principles?
a) Tragic   b) Virtuous   c) Exploration   d) Complexity

7. What is the opposite of morally good or righteous?
a) Enduring   b) Wicked   c) Influential   d) Physician

8. What term refers to a complete shift from one state or condition to another?
a) Tendency   b) Dual   c) Transformation   d) Reveal

9. What term describes strong wants or cravings?
a) Desires   b) Fearing   c) Laboratory   d) Relationship

10. Which word means restricted or held back?
a) Inhibited   b) Butcher   c) Experimental   d) Consequences

11. What is the inner sense of what is right or wrong in one's conduct?
a) Conscience   b) Dominant   c) Heinous   d) Unchecked

12. Which word signifies having control or power over others?
a) Influential   b) Novella   c) Complexity   d) Tragic

13. What is the term for going back to a previous state or condition?
a) Revert   b) Confession   c) Identity   d) Laboratory

14. Which word describes something extremely evil or wicked?
a) Heinous   b) Relationship   c) Enduring   d) Intrigue

15. What term refers to admitting one's sins or wrongdoings?
a) Confession   b) Identity   c) Dual   d) Transformations

16. Which word indicates the qualities, beliefs, personality, looks, and/or expressions that make a person or group?
a) Identity   b) Unchecked   c) Consequences   d) Experimental

17. What is the term for not controlled or restrained?
a) Unchecked   b) Coexistence   c) Intrigue   d) Butcher

18. Which word denotes the outcomes or results of an action or decision?
a) Consequences   b) Virtuous   c) Fearing   d) Physician

19. What is the term for causing extreme sorrow or distress?
a) Tragic   b) Complexity   c) Reveal   d) Dominant

20. Which word refers to the act of investigating, studying, or examining something thoroughly?
a) Exploration   b) Tendency   c) Respected   d) Heinous

Unit 35: Resurrection (1899)

"Resurrection" is a classic novel written by Leo Tolstoy, first published in 1899. The story revolves around the themes of love, redemption, and the search for meaning and purpose in life. Here's a detailed plot summary of "Resurrection":

The novel opens in the 1870s in the Russian city of St. Petersburg. Prince Dmitri Ivanovich Nekhlyudov, a young aristocrat and nobleman, is attending the trial of a group of political prisoners. To his shock, he recognizes one of the prisoners, a woman named Katerina Maslova, as someone he had once known in his youth. Nekhlyudov is haunted by guilt and regret for his past actions toward Maslova, as he realizes that he played a significant role in her downfall.

The narrative shifts back to the past, where Nekhlyudov's army regiment is stationed in a provincial town. There, he meets and falls in love with a young and innocent woman named Ekaterina (Katyusha) Ivanovna, who is the daughter of a merchant. Nekhlyudov spends time with Katyusha, promising her love and marriage. However, his love for her remains superficial and selfish.

As Nekhlyudov leaves town to return to St. Petersburg, he forgets about Katyusha and his promises to her. Meanwhile, Katyusha, who has fallen deeply in love with him, is heartbroken and desperate. Left with no financial support, she turns to a life of prostitution in an attempt to survive.

As the novel returns to the present, Nekhlyudov becomes determined to make amends for his past actions and seeks to help Katerina Maslova. He attends the trial and learns that Maslova has been falsely accused of poisoning a client in a brothel and is facing a possible death sentence. Nekhlyudov is appointed as a juror for the trial, and as the evidence unfolds, he becomes convinced of her innocence.

Despite Nekhlyudov's efforts to convince the other jurors of Maslova's innocence, she is found guilty and sentenced to hard labor in Siberia. Nekhlyudov is devastated by the outcome and decides to follow her to Siberia to seek redemption for his past actions.

Nekhlyudov travels to Siberia and visits Maslova in prison. He confesses his past relationship with her and his role in her downfall. Maslova is initially resentful and bitter towards him but eventually forgives him. As Nekhlyudov spends time with her and witnesses the harsh conditions of the prison system, he becomes increasingly aware of the social injustices and inequalities in Russia.

Determined to make a difference, Nekhlyudov dedicates himself to social reform and fighting for the rights of prisoners. He uses his wealth and influence to improve prison conditions and provide support to Maslova and other inmates. Throughout his journey, he undergoes a spiritual transformation and finds redemption through selfless actions and service to others.

As the novel concludes, Nekhlyudov decides to dedicate his life to the pursuit of justice and social equality. He chooses to live a simple life and devotes himself to helping the less fortunate. Maslova, inspired by Nekhlyudov's transformation, begins to find solace and redemption in her own life, seeking forgiveness for her past mistakes. The novel ends on a hopeful note, emphasizing the potential for human beings to change and find redemption through love and compassion.

"Resurrection" explores profound themes of human nature, social responsibility, and the search for meaning in life. It remains a powerful and thought-provoking novel that continues to resonate with readers to this day.

[Vocabulary]

Resurrection 부활 Redemption 구원 Search 탐구 Purpose 목적 Detailed 상세한 Plot 줄거리 aristocrat 귀족 Nobleman 귀족 Attend 참석하다 Trial 재판 Political prisoners 정치 수감자들 Recognize 알아차리다 Guilt 죄책감 Regret 후회 Significant role 중요한 역할 Downfall 몰락 Narrative 이야기 Shif 변화하다 Provincial town 지방 도시 Innocent 순진한 Superficial 표면적인 Financial support 재정적 지원 Prostitution 매춘 False accusation 잘못된 고발 death sentence 사형 선고 Juror 배심원 Devastated 곤혹스러운 Spiritual 영적인 transformation 변화 reform 개혁 Inequalities 불평등

[본문 해석] 부활

"부활"은 톨스토이가 1899년에 처음 출판한 고전 소설입니다. 이 소설은 사랑, 구원, 삶의 의미와 목적을 중심으로 이야기가 전개됩니다. "부활"의 자세한 줄거리는 다음과 같습니다:

소설은 1870년대 러시아의 상트페테르부르크에서 시작됩니다. 양반이자 귀족인 데미트리 이바노비치 네플류도프 공작은 정치 수감자들의 재판을 참석하러 갑니다. 충격적이게도, 그는 그곳에서 어린 시절 알고 지낸 여자인 카테리나 마슬로바가 수감자 중 한 명이라는 것을 알게 됩니다. 그녀의 몰락에서 자신이 중요한 역할을 한 것을 깨닫고, 네플류도프는 마슬로바에 대한 자신의 과거 행동으로 인한 죄책감과 후회에 시달리게 됩니다.

이야기는 네플류도프의 군 연대가 지방 도시에 주둔하던 과거로 돌아갑니다. 거기서 그는 상인의 딸인 어리고 순수한 여자인 카추샤와 만나 사랑에 빠집니다. 네플류도프는 카테리나와 시간을 보내며 사랑과 결혼을 약속합니다. 그러나 그녀에 대한 그의 사랑은 표면적이고 이기적인 것으로 남게 됩니다.

네플류도프는 상트페테르부르크로 돌아가면서 카테리나와 한 그의 약속을 잊게 됩니다. 한편, 그를 깊이 사랑하게 된 카테리나는 상심하고 절망합니다. 재정적인 지원도 받지 못한 채, 그녀는 생존을 위해 매춘부의 삶으로 눈을 돌립니다.

소설은 다시 현재로 돌아와 네플류도프가 자신의 과거 행동에 대한 보상을 하기로 결심하고 카테리나 마슬로바를 돕기 위해 노력하는 모습을 보여줍니다. 그는 재판에 참석하고, 마슬로바가 매춘굴에서 한 손님을 독살한 죄로 잘못 기소되어 사형에 직면하고 있음을 알게 됩니다. 네플류도프는 재판의 배심원으로 임명되며, 증거가 드러남에 따라 그녀의 무죄를 믿게 됩니다.

네플류도프의 노력에도 불구하고, 그녀의 무죄를 다른 배심원들에게 설득하지 못해 그녀는 유죄 판결을 받고 시베리아의 고단한 노동으로 처벌받게 됩니다. 네플류도프는 이 결과에 큰 상심을 느끼고, 자신의 과거 행동을 보상하기 위해 그녀를 따라 시베리아로 향하게 됩니다.

네플류도프는 시베리아로 여행하여 감옥에 있는 마슬로바를 만나러 갑니다. 그는 그녀와의 과거 관계와 자신이 그녀의 몰락에 기여한 역할을 고백합니다. 마슬로바는 처음에는 그를 원망하고 괴로워하지만 결국 그를 용서합니다. 네플류도프는 그녀와 함께 시간을 보내고 감옥 시스템의 가혹한 상황을 목격하면서 러시아의 사회적 불평등과 불평등에 대해 점점 더 인식하게 됩니다.

네플류도프는 사회개혁과 수감자들의 권리를 위해 자신을 바치기로 결심합니다. 그는 자신의 부와 영향력을 이용하여 감옥 조건을 개선하고 마슬로바와 다른 수감자들에게 지원을 제공합니다. 그의 여정을 통해 그는 영적으로 변화하고 이타적인 행동과 다른 사람들을 위한 봉사를 통해 구원을 찾아가게 됩니다.

소설이 끝날 때에는 네플류도프가 정의와 사회평등을 위한 삶을 바치기로 결심합니다. 그는 단순한 삶을 선택하고 불우한 이들을 돕기 위해 헌신합니다. 네플류도프의 변화에 영감 받은 마슬로바는 자신의 과거 실수에 대해 용서를 구하며 자신의 삶에서 위로와 구원을 찾기 시작합니다. 소설은 사람들이 사랑과 동정을 통해 변화하고 구원을 찾을 수 있는 잠재력을 강조하여 희망적으로 끝납니다.

[Reading Comprehension]

1. What is the main theme of "Resurrection"?
a) Revenge
b) Adventure
c) Love, redemption, and the search for meaning
d) Power struggles

2. Who is Prince Dmitri Ivanovich Nekhlyudov?
a) A political prisoner
b) A young aristocrat and nobleman
c) A merchant's daughter
d) A juror in the trial

3. What is the name of the woman recognized by Nekhlyudov at the trial?
a) Katyusha
b) Ekaterina Ivanovna
c) Katerina Maslova
d) Ekaterina Nekhlyudova

4. Why does Nekhlyudov feel guilty and regretful toward Katerina Maslova?
a) He had betrayed her sister in their past relationship.
b) He had falsely accused her of a crime.
c) He had abandoned her after promising love and marriage.
d) He had stolen from her.

5. In which city does the novel open?
a) Moscow   b) St. Petersburg   c) Siberia   d) A provincial town

6. What does Katerina Maslova resort to in order to survive?
a) Seeking employment as a maid
b) Joining a political movement
c) A life of prostitution
d) Becoming a lawyer

7. What is Katerina Maslova accused of?
a) Theft
b) Treason
c) Murder
d) Kidnapping

8. How does Nekhlyudov initially react to being appointed as a juror for Maslova's trial?
a) He is apathetic and uninterested.
b) He is determined to find her guilty.
c) He is relieved to have the opportunity to serve.
d) He is shocked and overwhelmed.

9. Despite Nekhlyudov's efforts, what is the outcome of Maslova's trial?

a) She is acquitted and set free.

b) She is sentenced to hard labor in Siberia.

c) She is given a lenient punishment.

d) Her case is dismissed due to lack of evidence.

10. What prompts Nekhlyudov to travel to Siberia?

a) A business opportunity

b) A desire for adventure

c) His sense of guilt and need for redemption

d) A political mission

11. How does Maslova initially react to Nekhlyudov's visit to her in prison?

a) She is grateful and forgiving.

b) She is angry and resentful.

c) She is indifferent and unresponsive.

d) She is fearful and apologetic.

12. What does Nekhlyudov dedicate himself to after visiting Maslova in prison?

a) Pursuing a political career

b) Seeking revenge against his enemies

c) Social reform and helping prisoners

d) Becoming a lawyer

13. What does Nekhlyudov's transformation entail?

a) Becoming a criminal

b) Seeking wealth and power

c) Devoting himself to self-interest

d) Spiritual growth and selflessness

14. How does the novel conclude for Nekhlyudov?

a) He becomes a hermit in the mountains.

b) He becomes a wealthy businessman.

c) He dedicates his life to justice and social equality.

d) He returns to his life of aristocratic luxury.

15. What is the overall message conveyed in "Resurrection"?

a) Revenge is the ultimate justice.

b) Love and compassion can change lives.

c) Social inequality is inevitable.

d) Wealth and power bring happiness.

[Grammar Check-up]

1. Here's a (detailed, detail) plot summary of "Resurrection."

2. Prince Dmitri Ivanovich Nekhlyudov, a young aristocrat and nobleman, (are, is) attending the trial of a group of political prisoners.

3. To (him, his) shock, he recognizes one of the (prisoners, prisoner), a woman named Katerina Maslova.

4. Nekhlyudov (haunts, is haunted by) guilt and regret for his past actions toward Maslova, as he realizes (that, what) he played a significant role in her downfall.

5. The narrative shifts back to the past, (which, where) Nekhlyudov's army regiment (stations, is stationed) in a provincial town.

6. There, he meets and falls in love with a young and (innocent, innocence) woman named Ekaterina Ivanovna, (who is, is) the daughter of a merchant.

7. Nekhlyudov spends time with Katyusha, (promises, promising) her love and marriage.

8. However, his love for her (is remained, remains) superficial and selfish.

9. Meanwhile, Katyusha, who has fallen deeply in love with him, is (heartbroken, heartbreaking) and desperate.

10. (Left, Leaving) with no financial support, she turns to a life of prostitution in an attempt to survive.

11. As the novel returns to the present, Nekhlyudov becomes (determining, determined) to make amends for his past actions and seeks to help Katerina Maslova.

12. He (attends to, attends) the trial and learns that Maslova has been falsely accused of (poisoning, poison) a client in a brothel.

13. Nekhlyudov (appoints, is appointed) as a juror for the trial, and as the evidence unfolds, he becomes (convincing, convinced) of her innocence.

14. (Even though, Despite) Nekhlyudov's efforts to convince the other jurors of Maslova's (innocent, innocence), she is found (guilty, guilt) and sentenced to hard labor in Siberia.

15. Nekhlyudov is (devastating, devastated by) the outcome and decides to follow her to Siberia to seek redemption for his past actions.

16. Maslova is (initial, **initially**) resentful and bitter towards him but eventually forgives him.

17. As Nekhlyudov (is spent, **spends**) time with her and witnesses the harsh conditions of the prison system, he becomes (**increasingly**, increasing) aware of the social injustices and inequalities in Russia.

18. (Determining, **Determined**) to make a difference, Nekhlyudov dedicates himself to social reform and (fight, **fighting**) for the rights of prisoners.

19. He (**uses**, is used) his wealth and influence to improve prison conditions and provide support to Maslova and other (inmate, **inmates**).

20. Throughout his journey, he (is undergone, **undergoes**) a spiritual transformation and finds redemption through (**selfless**, selfish) actions and service to others.

21. As the novel concludes, Nekhlyudov decides (dedicating, **to dedicate**) his life to the pursuit of justice and social equality.

22. He chooses (living, **to live**) a simple life and devotes himself to (help, **helping**) the less fortunate.

23. Maslova, (inspiring, **inspired by**) Nekhlyudov's transformation, begins to find solace and redemption in her own life, (seeks, **seeking**) forgiveness for her past mistakes.

24. The novel ends on a hopeful note, (emphasizes, **emphasizing**) the potential for human beings to change and find redemption through love and compassion.

25. "Resurrection" explores (profound, **profoundly**) themes of human nature, social responsibility, and the search for meaning in life.

26. It remains a powerful and (**thought-provoking**, thought-provoked) novel that continues to resonate with readers to this day.

[Writing Practice]

1. Nekhlyudov _____, and as the evidence unfolds, he becomes convinced of her innocence. 재판을 위한 배심원으로서 임명된다

2. _____ Maslova's innocence, ~에 대해서 다른 배심원들을 납득시키려는 그의 노력에도 불구하고
she is found guilty and sentenced to hard labor in Siberia.

3. He _____ the social injustices and inequalities in Russia.
　　　점점 ~에 대해서 인식하게 된다

4. _____, Nekhlyudov dedicates himself to social
　　　변화(di~)를 만들어 내기로 결심하고   reform and fighting for the rights of prisoners.

5. Throughout his journey, he undergoes a spiritual transformation and _____
_____ and service to others.
　　　이타적인 행동들을 통해 구원을 찾다

6. As the novel concludes, Nekhlyudov _____ of justice and social equality.　　　　　　　　그의 삶을 ~의 추구에 바치기로 결심하다

7. He chooses to live a simple life and _____.
　　　　　　　　　　　　　　　자신을 덜 운이 좋은 자들을 돕는데 바치다

8. Maslova begins to find solace and redemption in her own life, _____
_____. 그녀의 과거의 실수들에 대해서 용서를 구하면서 (분사구)

9. "Resurrection" _____, social responsibility, and the search for meaning in life. 인간 본성이라는 심오한 주제를 탐구한다

10. It _____ that continues to resonate with

강력하고 <u>시사하는 바가 많은</u>(thought~) 소설로 남아있다   readers to this day.

11. _____, she turns to a life of prostitution in an attempt to survive.

어떠한 재정적 지원도 없이 남겨져 (분사구)

12. He _____ that Maslova has been falsely accused of

          재판에 참석하여 ~를 알게 된다   poisoning a client in a brothel.

[Word Quiz]

1. What term refers to the act of coming back to life after death?

a) Redemption   b) Search   c) Resurrection   d) Purpose

2. What term describes the act of making up for past mistakes or wrongdoings?

a) Guilt   b) Downfall   c) Regret   d) Redemption

3. What word indicates the act of looking for something or someone?

a) Purpose   b) Detailed   c) Search   d) Narrative

4. What term represents the reason or aim behind an action or existence?

a) Plot   b) Purpose   c) Attend   d) Trial

5. What word suggests a thorough and comprehensive examination or description?

a) Detailed   b) Plot   c) Trial   d) Recognize

6. Which term refers to being present at an event or gathering?

a) Attend   b) Trial   c) Purpose   d) Narrative

7. What word describes a legal proceeding where evidence is presented to determine
guilt or innocence?

a) Devastated   b) False accusation   c) Trial   d) Plot

8. What term means to identify or remember someone or something from the past?

a) Recognize   b) Guilt   c) Regret   d) Downfall

9. What word signifies a feeling of responsibility or remorse for a wrongdoing?
a) False accusation   b) Guilt   c) Redemption   d) Devastated

10. Which term indicates feeling sorry for something that has been done?
a) False accusation   b) Recognize   c) Guilt   d) Regret

11. What expression describes an important or influential part in a situation?
a) Significant role   b) Spiritual transformation   c) Detailed   d) Innocent

12. What word refers to a sudden decline or failure?
a) Guilt   b) False accusation   c) Downfall   d) Redemption

13. What term denotes the way a story is told or recounted?
a) Plot   b) Narrative   c) Resurrection   d) Reform

14. What term indicates a change or shift from one thing to another?
a) Shelter   b) Devastated   c) Purpose   d) Transformation

15. What term represents a town or city located outside a major urban area?
a) Provincial town   b) Spiritual transformation   c) Redemption   d) Narrative

16. What word describes someone who is not guilty of a crime?
a) False accusation   b) Devastated   c) Innocent   d) Resurrection

17. What term describes something appearing to be lacking true depth?
a) Purpose   b) Innocent   c) Superficial   d) Guilt

18. Which term involves activities such as managing, investing, or budgeting?
a) Purpose   b) Financial   c) False accusation   d) Trial

19. What term indicates a wrong claim or assertion about someone?
a) Innocent   b) False accusation   c) Devastated   d) Resurrection

20. What term signifies a punishment of death imposed by a court of law?
a) Guilt   b) Regret   c) Death sentence   d) Trial

아레테 고전 2
명작으로 영어 도장깨기
정답지

Unit 1: The Iliad

[Reading Comprehension]

1. d) Homer 2. c) The Trojan War 3. c) Agamemnon's betrayal 4. d) Agamemnon 5. d) He rejoins the battle seeking revenge. 6. d) Grief and a thirst for revenge 7. a) Achilles 8. b) He desecrates it and leaves it on the battlefield. 9. c) He sneaks into the Greek camp to plead with Achilles. 10. c) Compassion 11. b) "The Odyssey" 12. c) Heroism, honor, pride, and the futility of war 13. d) She is Achilles' war prize. 14. b) It boosts the Greeks' morale. 15. d) He displays exceptional strength and courage.

[Grammar Check-up]

1. (attributing, -attributed) 2. (-significant, significance) 3. (fights, -is fought) (-particularly, particular) 4. (-covers, is covered) 5. (war, -warrior) 6. (is named, -named) 7. (is withdrawn, -withdraws) (-causing, causes) 8. (gains, -gain) 9. (-convinces, is convinced) (hoped, -hoping) 10. (devastating, -devastates) 11. (driving, -driven) (seeks, -seeking) 12. (-regain, regaining) 13. (confront, -confronts) 14. (desecrates, -desecrating) 15. (pleading, -pleads) 16. (-Touched by, Touching) 17. (-where, who) 18. (In spite, -Despite) (narrate, -are narrated)

[Writing Practice]

1. one of the most significant works of Western literature
2. which is fought between
3. a great warrior and hero of the Greeks
4. causing significant losses for the Greeks
5. With Achilles refusing to fight
6. convinces Achilles to let him lead
7. Hearing about Patroclus' death and driven by grief and rage
8. Touched by the old king's grief
9. the poem does not cover

[Word Quiz]

1. C) Old 2. D) be attributed to 3. A) significance 4. C) literature 5. C) main plot 6. D) sequel 7. D) conflict 8. C) devastated 9. C) morale 10. C) vengeance 11. D) fierce 12. D) mercy 13. C) desecrate 14. B) proper funeral 15. D) mourn 16. A) heroism 17. B) honor 18. B) futility 19. B) delve into 20. D) compassion

Unit 2: The Odyssey

[Reading Comprehension]

1. d) Homer 2. d) The Iliad 3. c) Odysseus 4. b) 20 years 5. c) Odysseus' son 6. b) To search for his father 7. c) Athena 8. d) Ogygia 9. d) Hermes 10. b) Alcinous 11. c) The unfavorable winds are released, leading them astray. 12. c) The prophet Tiresias 13. c) Thrinacia 14. b) Athena disguises him as a beggar. 15. b) Athena intervenes to restore peace.

[Grammar Check-up]

1. (attributes, -attributed) 2. (-the other, another) 3. (is told, -tells) 4. (-encompasses, is

encompassed) (is faced, -faces) 5. (which, -who) 6. (which, -that) 7. (-feeling, felt) 8. (-assembly, assemble) (-declares, is declared) 9. (Inspiring, -Inspired) 10. (for, -during) 11. (offering, -offers) 12. (-is being held, is holding) 13. (which, -where) (held, -holding) 14. (sends, -is sent by) 15. (Reluctant, -Reluctantly) 16. (offers, -offer) 17. (is recounted, -recounts) 18. (offering, -offers) 19. (are hosted, -host) 20. (brings, -bringing) 21. (organizes, -organize) 22. (for, -with) 23. (narration, -to narrate) 24. (where, -whom) 25. (-describing, describes) (give, -gives) 26. (releases, -releasing) 27. (which, -where) (-deceased, deceasing) 28. (which, -where) (incurs, -incurring) 29. (-bring, brings) 30. (them, -they) 31. (-disguises, disguising) 32. (welcoming, -welcomes) 33. (advices, -advises) 34. (hide, -hides) 35. (disguising, -disguised) 36. (-reveals, is revealed) 37. (-suggesting, suggestion) (whom, -who) 38. (-is exposed, exposes) 39. (defeat, -defeats) 40. (execute, -are executed)

[Writing Practice]

1. that Odysseus faces during his ten-year voyage
2. has been away for twenty years
3. feeling frustrated by the suitors
4. Odysseus is being held captive by
5. to command Calypso to release Odysseus
6. who offer him hospitality
7. tells them of his desire to return home
8. where he meets the spirit of
9. where his men eat the sacred cattle of
10. disguises Odysseus as an old beggar

[Word Quiz]

1. c) Old 2. b) Epic 3. c) Include 4. a) Excursions 5. a) Challenges 6. c) Unwillingly 7. b) Imprisonment 8. a) Mythical creatures 9. c) Conflict 10. c) Prowess 11. c) Recount 12. d) Welcoming behavior 13. c) Captivity 14. b) Challenges 15. d) Native land 16. c) Involvement 17. c) Perseverance 18. c) Anger 19. b) Deception 20. a) Conclusion

Unit 3: The Three Kingdoms

[Reading Comprehension]

1. a) Luo Guanzhong 2. b) Ming Dynasty 3. b) Three Kingdoms 4. c) Han 5. b) Battle of Chibi (Red Cliffs) 6. c) Liu Bei 7. b) Battle of Chibi (Red Cliffs) 8. c) Zhuge Liang 9. d) Guan Yu and Zhang Fei 10. a) Shu 11. c) Cao Pi 12. b) Jin 13. c) Rise of the Jin Dynasty 14. d) Luo Guanzhong 15. b) Power struggles among warlords

[Grammar Check-up]

1. (-attributed, attributing) 2. (Novel, -Novels) (writing, -written) 3. (-tumultuous, tumultuously) 4. (primary, -primarily) (shaping, -shape) 5. (-ruled, been ruled) 6. (effective, -ineffective) 7. (raise, -rise) 8. (-prominent, prominently) 9. (-establishes, establishing) 10. (is found, -founds) 11. (are, -is) (-where, which) 12. (-solidifies, solidifying) 13. (-sworn, swearing) (not only, -as well as) 14. (-faces, is faced) 15. (ambitious, -ambitions) 16. (are, -is) 17. (-instrumental, instrument) 18. (are known, -known) 19. (legend, -legendary) 20. (are met, -meet) 21. (success,

-succeeds) 22. (-leads, leading) (limiting, -limited) 23. (fells, -falls) 24. (internally, -internal) (-eventually, eventual) 25. (-rise, arise)

[Writing Practice]

1. historical novel attributed to
2. during the Ming Dynasty in the 14th century
3. It primarily follows the lives and adventures of
4. which had ruled China for centuries
5. is fraught/filled with corruption and internal strife
6. Various warlords rise to prominence
7. One of the most famous episodes in the novel is
8. is renowned for his intelligence and strategic acumen
9. succeeds him as the ruler of
10. In an attempt to unify the land

[Word Quiz]

1. a) Sprawling 2. c) Tumultuous 3. a) Charismatic 4. a) Unify 5. d) Strategist 6. a) Solidify 7. a) Power struggles 8. b) Martial prowess 9. a) Regent 10. c) Logistical 11. a) Defeated 12. a) Solidify 13. d) Narrative 14. a) Enduring 15. c) Adaptations 16. a) Ineffective 17. b) Imperial court 18. c) Fractured 19. d) Ambitious 20. a) Military campaigns

Unit 4: The Divine Comedy (1320)

[Reading Comprehension]

1. b) Dante Alighieri 2. c) Three 3. a) Inferno 4. c) Virgil 5. c) Nine 6. c) A place where souls are cleansed 7. b) Beatrice 8. c) Souls being cleansed and purified 9. c) Paradiso 10. b) Beatrice 11. d) A vision of God's infinite love and wisdom 12. c) Sin, redemption, and divine justice 13. b) Personal experiences and political allegory 14. d) A search for union with the divine 15. c) It delves into themes of sin, redemption, and divine love

[Grammar Check-up]

1. (-14th, 14) 2. (-considered, considers) (work, -works) 3. (-consists, is consisted) (describes, -describing) 4. (-depicts, depicting) 5. (-Guided, Guiding) (encounters, -encountering) 6. (All, -Each) (progress, -progressing) 7. (as long as, -as) 8. (-portrays, portraying) 9. (clean, -cleansed) 10. (guides, -is guided) (-where, which) (becoming, -becomes) 11. (witnessing, -witnesses) 12. (narrating, -narrates) 13. (-saints, saint) (soul, -souls) (-impart, imparts) 14. (which, -where) 15. (-Throughout, Though) 16. (is combined, -combines) 17. (-remains, is remained)

[Writing Practice]

1. is an epic poem written by
2. is widely considered one of the greatest works
3. consists of three parts
4. Guided by the ancient Roman poet
5. Each circle represents a different sin

6. as well as contemporary individuals/people
7. are cleansed of their sins and prepared for
8. where the spirit of Beatrice becomes his guide
9. encounters various saints and other blessed souls
10. explores themes of sin, redemption

[Word Quiz]

1. a) Afterlife 2. b) Inferno 3. c) Purgatorio 4. d) Paradiso 5. a) Journey 6. b) Concentric 7. c) Sinners 8. d) Punishment 9. a) Contemporary 10. b) Ascent up 11. c) Divine 12. d) Penitent 13. a) Celestial 14. c) Ultimate 15. a) Theological 16. b) Mythology 17. c) Allegory 18. d) Redemption 19. a) Symbolism 20. c) Metaphysical

Unit 5: Decameron (1353)

[Reading Comprehension]

1. b) Giovanni Boccaccio 2. c) 100 3. c) To flee from the Black Death 4. c) The Black Death epidemic 5. c) 10 6. b) To choose the theme for the storytelling 7. d) Various genres including romance, comedy, tragedy, and satire 8. d) They use wit and intelligence to navigate challenges 9. c) The complexities of human relationships 10. c) He critiques the church, nobility, and societal norms 11. c) Solace and escape from reality 12. c) 10 13. c) They enrich the listeners' understanding of human nature and the world 14. c) Its resilience and vitality even in challenging circumstances 15. c) Its artistry, humor, and insightful commentary

[Grammar Check-up]

1. a) written 2. a) narrated 3. d) is considered 4. b) during 5. a) coming 6. c) taking 7. b) narrating 8. c) exploring 9. a) navigate 10. a) the power 11. a) and 12. a) societal 13. b) in 14. c) which 15. b) imaginative 16. a) to 17. b) as 18. d) showcases 19. b) for 20. b) their

[Writing Practice]

1. is a collection of novellas written by
2. consists of 100 tales narrated by
3. is considered a masterpiece of
4. come from different social backgrounds
5. To pass the time and distract themselves from
6. take turns narrating/telling a story that fits the chosen theme
7. explore various aspects of human nature
8. while others are more serious and thought-provoking
9. even in the face of adversity
10. allows the characters to escape from their immediate reality

[Word Quiz]

1. c) An introduction or forerunner 2. a) Narrative 3. a) Diverse 4. b) To cause confusion or diversion 5. a) Plague 6. a) Genres 7. c) To critique and ridicule human flaws 8. a) Morality 9. a) Protagonists 10. c) To find a solution or explore through difficulties 11. a) Lighthearted 12. d)

Imagination 13. c) To express insightful commentary 14. a) Nobility 15. d) Widely accepted customs and behaviors 16. a) Resilience 17. d) Difficulties and misfortune 18. c) To provide comfort and consolation 19. d) Imaginative 20. a) Insightful

Unit 6: Canterbury Tales (1390)

[Reading Comprehension]
1. d) The diverse society and its stories 2. c) 29 3. d) Harry Bailey, the host of the inn 4. b) A chivalric romance about love and honor 5. d) All of the above 6. c) The Reeve 7. a) Greed and deception 8. b) Engage in lively discussions and debates 9. d) 120 10. c) The Tabard Inn in Southwark 11. b) The Nun's Priest 12. b) Medieval English society and its various classes, customs, and values 13. a) The Miller 14. a) Abruptly with the pilgrims still on their way to Canterbury 15. a) Its keen observations of human nature and society

[Grammar Check-up]
1. b) began 2. b) vivid 3. a) wide 4. a) allegory 5. a) viewpoints 6. c) with 7. c) who 8. a) vivid 9. a) is 10. a) humorous 11. a) take 12. b) narrating 13. b) enjoyed 14. b) observation 15. a) tell 16. b) include 17. a) representing 18. a) deep 19. a) covering 20. a) curious

[Writing Practice]
1. who are traveling together from London to
2. each representing a different social class and profession
3. each pilgrim should tell two tales on their way to
4. take turns telling their tales
5. Each tale reflects the personality and interests of the storyteller
6. Other memorable tales include
7. revealing their differing/different viewpoints and world views
8. These interactions provide insights into the social and religious issues.
9. the work remains unfinished
10. with the pilgrims still on their way to Canterbury

[Word Quiz]
1. c) A variety of items gathered together 2. c) A challenge to win or achieve something 3. c) Travelers on a religious journey 4. d) A place of worship 5. c) A religious building of significance 6. c) Different and varied 7. c) A hierarchy based on economic or social status 8. c) A skilled trade or occupation 9. d) People of high social rank 10. c) To lead religious services 11. d) Traders who buy and sell goods 12. d) Practicing skilled handicraft or trades 13. c) People of lower social rank 14. d) A person who provides hospitality 15. c) An idea or plan suggested for consideration 16. b) A form of pilgrimage 17. b) The distinctive qualities that define an individual 18. c) Related to knights and their code of conduct 19. b) Clever and skillful actions used to deceive 20. c) Principles concerning right and wrong conduct

Unit 7: Romeo and Juliet (1597)

[Reading Comprehension]

1. b) Around 1597 2. c) Verona 3. b) A feud between two families 4. d) Romeo and Juliet 5. b) At a masked ball 6. a) Friar Laurence 7. b) His involvement in a brawl 8. a) By challenging Tybalt to a duel 9. c) To fake her own death 10. c) He gives Juliet a potion to make her appear dead 11. a) Friar John, tasked with delivering the message to Romeo, is unable to do so 12. c) He dies by Juliet's side 13. a) She stabs herself with Romeo's dagger 14. c) Their families reconcile and end their feud 15. c) With the Prince's speech about love and conflict

[Grammar Check-up]

1. (are belonging, -belong) 2. (leading, -leads) 3. (-between, both) 4. (attends to, -attends) (hosts, -hosted) (which, -where) 5. (Aware, -Unaware) (-secretly, secret) 6. (worsening, -worsens) 7. (-to fight, fighting) 8. (is avenged, -avenges) 9. (-is banished, banishes) 10. (-is pressured, pressures) 11. (-devises, is devised) 12. (what, -that) 13. (apparently, -apparent) 14. (-Heartbroken, Heartbreaking) (lifelessness, -lifeless) 15. (Consuming, -Consumed) 16. (-lifeless, lifelessness) (able, -unable) 17. (senseless, -senselessness) (-has, is) 18. (delivers, -delivering) (highlights, -highlighting)

[Writing Practice]

1. who belong to feuding families
2. that ultimately *leads to* their untimely deaths *causes
3. begins with a longstanding conflict between
4. attends a masked ball hosted by
5. *Unaware of* each other's family backgrounds *Not knowing
6. The situation worsens when
7. As a result, he is banished from
8. Meanwhile, Juliet is pressured by
9. who devises a plan to reunite
10. that will make her appear dead temporarily
11. unable to bear living without him
12. *highlighting* the power of love to end hatred *emphasizing

[Word Quiz]

1. b) Sad and sorrowful 2. c) It rotates or orbits 3. b) A triggering event or agent 4. c) Unexpectedly early 5. b) A struggle or disagreement 6. d) A festive dance event 7. b) Deep and thoughtful 8. c) A link or relationship 9. b) In a concealed or hidden manner 10. b) A state of despair and urgency 11. b) To create or invent a plan 12. b) They meet again after being apart 13. c) To eat or use up 14. b) Sorrow and sadness 15. d) To be forced to leave a place

Unit 8: Hamlet (1599)

[Reading Comprehension]

1. b) 1599-1601 2. c) Denmark 3. d) Horatio 4. c) To reveal his murderer and seek revenge 5. b) He pretends to be mad 6. d) A play reenacting the murder 7. b) "To be or not to be, that is the question." 8. b) Polonius 9. c) To avoid Hamlet's threats 10. b) She drowns in water 11. a) Revenge for his father's murder 12. b) Laertes stabs Hamlet with a poisoned sword 13. b) Hamlet 14. d) He stabs him with a poisoned sword 15. c) Tell his story to others

[Grammar Check-up]

1. (believing, -believed) 2. (confronts, -is confronted) 3. (reveals, -revealing) (murdered, -was murdered) (whom, -who) 4. (Driving, -Driven) (embarking, -embarks) 5. (plagues, -is plagued) (-explore, explores) 6. (-increasingly, increasing) (-surrounding, surrounded) 7. (another, -other) (manipulates, -is manipulated) 8. (is featured, -features) (is served, -serves) 9. (Since, -As) 10. (delaying, -to delay) 11. (leads, -leading) (-including, includes) 12. (finally, -final) (is confronted, -confronts) 13. (lays, lies) 14. (symbolizes, -symbolizing) 15. (-remains, is remained)

[Writing Practice]

1. is *believed* to have been written between *thought
2. revealing that he was murdered by
3. embarks on a mission to avenge
4. that/which explore the nature of life, death, and the human condition
5. becomes increasingly unstable as he struggles to
6. who is manipulated by
7. by staging a play reenacting his father's murder
8. decides to delay his revenge
9. *leading to* the tragic demise/death of *causing=resulting in
10. remains one of his most celebrated/famous works

[Word Quiz]

1. c) To seek revenge for a wrongdoing 2. c) Deceiving or being disloyal to someone's trust 3. b) Carefully considering options 4. b) A close and trusted friend 5. c) Disagreements or disputes 6. d) You face a challenge directly 7. c) Careful thought and consideration 8. c) A person in the royal court or social circle 9. c) Manipulative and dishonest actions 10. c) A tragic death or downfall 11. d) To create or invent a plan 12. c) A difficult choice between two options 13. c) A serious fight or conflict between two individuals 14. d) You start a new journey or undertaking 15. c) To place trust or responsibility in someone's care 16. a) A philosophical belief that emphasizes individual existence, freedom, and choice 17. c) Resulting in death or disaster 18. c) A state of confusion and inability to choose 19. c) The quality of being unavoidable 20. c) Occurring within oneself

Unit 9: Othello (1603)

[Reading Comprehension]

1. c) Othello 2. b) Trust and betrayal 3. c) Venice 4. b) He feels deep-seated resentment towards Othello involving promotion 5. b) By using insidious suggestions and planted evidence 6. b) He commits suicide 7. b) Emilia 8. a) The consequences of their actions 9. b) Racism, trust, and unchecked jealousy 10. c) By revealing the inner thoughts and emotions of characters

[Grammar Check-up]

1. (tragedy, -tragic) 2. (-Set, Setting) 3. (explore, -explores) (-suspicion, suspicious) 4. (-respected, respecting) 5. (angry, -angers) (who, whose) 6. (-manipulating, manipulate) 7. (-cunningly, cunning) (-using, used) 8. (consuming, -consumed) 9. (Although, -Despite) (seeking, -to seek) revenge 10. (-characters, character) (included, -including) 11. (leads, -leading) 12. (is suffocated, -suffocates) 13. (-discovers, discovering) 14. (Realized, -Realizing) (is killed, -kills) 15. (-subsequent, subsequently) 16. (-remaining, remained) 17. (destruction, -destructive) 18. (raise, -arise)

[Writing Practice]

1. Set primarily in the city-state of
2. a highly respected military leader
3. who harbors deep-seated resentment towards
4. seeking to destroy Othello's life and reputation
5. using planted/planned evidence and insidious suggestions
6. becomes consumed by jealousy and suspicion
7. becomes determined to seek revenge
8. leading Othello to the brink of madness
9. believing he is justified in his actions
10. The characters remaining alive are left to

[Word Quiz]

1. a) Planted 2. b) evidence 3. c) Discover 4. b) Manipulative 5. b) Justified 6. b) Innocence 7. b) Secret 8. d) consumed 9. c) Manipulative 10. c) Progress 11. a) Cunning 12. a) Scheming 13. c) Suspicion 14. a) Remorse 15. a) Reputation 16. a) Convince 17. c) Progress 18. a) Manipulative 19. d) Protestation 20. d) Madness

Unit 10: King Lear (1605)

[Reading Comprehension]

1. d) King Lear 2. b) Power, Betrayal, Madness 3. c) Based on their flattery of him 4. a) She is disowned by Lear 5. d) Edmund 6. a) They mistreat him and reduce his retinue of servants 7. a) Fool and Edgar 8. b) She is hanged 9. b) Lear dies holding Cordelia's lifeless body 10. c) Gloucester's manipulation by Edmund mirrors Lear's betrayal by his daughters

[Grammar Check-up]

1. (decide, -decides) (base, -based) 2. (exploring, -explores) 3. (-to express, expressing) 4. (driving, -driven) (exaggerating, -exaggerated) (engaging, -to engage) 5. (-divides, is divided) 6. (-gradually, gradual) (abuses, -abuse) 7. (reducing, -reduce) 8. (-wandering, wanders) 9. (-involves, is involved) 10. (fueling, -fueled) 11. (forces, -is forced) 12. (-dethroned, dethroning) 13. (which, -when) 14. (Although, -Despite) (-remains, is remained) 15. (hangs, -is hanged) 16. (leading, -lead) 17. (leave, -are left)

[Writing Practice]

1. who decides to divide his kingdom among
2. explores themes of power, betrayal, madness,
3. wanting to retire from the responsibilities of ruling
4. refuses to engage in such empty praise
5. who quickly abuse their newfound power
6. feeling betrayed and abandoned
7. (Being) Parallel to Lear's story
8. manipulates his father into believing
9. unjustly accused
10. Eventually, they are reconciled

[Word Quiz]

1. a) Ancient 2. d) Kingdom 3. d) Flattery 4. c) Declaration 5. a) Refuse 6. a) Engage 7. a) Grief 8. b) Disown 9. a) Deteriorate 10. a) Despair 11. a) Exploration 12. b) Unchecked 13. a) Betrayal 14. a) Exaggerate 15. a) Subplot 16. a) Reconcile 17. a) Dethrone 18. c) Deteriorate 19. a) Grief 20. a) Inevitability

Unit 11: Macbeth (1623)

[Reading Comprehension]

1. b) Ambition and power 2. c) Three witches 3. b) He will become the Thane of Cawdor and the King of Scotland 4. b) He is appointed by King Duncan 5. a) She encourages and persuades him to carry out the murder 6. c) They leave Scotland to seek refuge in a neighboring country 7. b) He becomes terrified and confesses his crimes 8. a) He should beware of Macduff 9. c) He hires assassins to murder Macduff's family 10. c) She is haunted by guilt and descends into madness 11. a) Macduff and Malcolm 12. c) He is defeated in battle by Macduff 13. b) The danger of excessive ambition and unchecked power 14. d) He is defeated and killed in battle 15. c) By illustrating how uncontrolled ambition can lead to ruin and destruction

[Grammar Check-up]

1. (performs, -performed) 2. (-revolves, is revolved) 3. (to know, -known) (prophet, -prophesy) 4. (intriguing, -intrigued) 5. (-receives, is received) (naming, -named) 6. (For, -Upon) (claiming, -to claim) 7. (encourage, -encouragement) (-while, whereas) 8. (see, -sees) 9. (suspicion, -suspicious) (hiring, -hired) 10. (reveals, -revealing) 11. (-further, farther) 12. (-to eliminate, eliminating) 13. (reveals, -revealing) 14. (-nobles, noble) 15. (is faced, -faces) (tells, -is told) 16.

(fulfills, fulfilling) 17. (proclaims, -is proclaimed)

[Writing Practice]

1. who prophesy that Macbeth will become
2. are intrigued by their prophecies
3. that he has been named/appointed
4. Upon hearing the witches' prediction
5. decides to carry out the murder of
6. to eliminate anyone he sees as a threat to his throne
7. becomes suspicious of
8. in an attempt to eliminate any opposition
9. revealing the horrors of their actions
10. is told that he cannot be killed by

[Word Quiz]

1. c) Ambitious 2. c) Prediction 3. a) Ambition 4. b) Contemplate 5. b) Throne 6. b) Encouragement 7. c) Assassination 8. c) Eliminate 9. a) Paranoid 10. a) Prophecy 11. a) Opposition 12. b) Proclaim 13. c) Consequence 14. b) Frequently 15. c) Explore 16. b) Tyrant 17. b) Battle 18. c) Revealing 19. a) Destructive 20. b) Overthrow

Unit 12: Don Quixote (1605)

[Reading Comprehension]

1. d) Alonso Quixano 2. b) His obsession with books about knights 3. b) Dulcinea 4. a) Windmills 5. c) Sancho Panza 6. a) Defeat in confrontations with various characters 7. c) They find amusement in his delusions 8. d) Sanson Carrasco 9. b) Governor 10. c) Altisidora 11. d) The battle with the Knight of the Mirrors 12. c) Don Quixote renounces his knighthood and passes away 13. c) The power of imagination and the complexities of human folly 14. Don Quixote renounces his knighthood and returns to his true identity 15. b) It is the first modern novel and explores various themes

[Grammar Check-up]

1. (-obsessed, obsessing) (is lost, loses) 2. (particular, -particularly) 3. (because, -Due to) (-obsessed, obsessing) 4. (adopting, -to adopt) 5. (be dubbed, -dub) 6. (delusion, -delusional) 7. (-named, who names) 8. (are, -is) (of, -for) 9. (-is thrown, throws) 10. (-transported, transporting) 11. (be undertaken, -undertake) 12. (-situations, situation) 13. (is, -are) 14. (-valiantly, valiant) 15. (-tells, is told) 16. (is involved, -involves) 17. (-pretending, pretends) 18. (-believing, believes) 19. (recognizes, -is recognized) (is, -are) 20. (-to give up, giving up) 21. (-Despite, Even thought) (deciding, -decides) (accompanying, -accompanied) 22. (-have, has) 23. (-faces, is faced) (which, -who) 24. (-to govern, governing) 25. (who, -which) 26. (-is convinced, convinces) (-different, differently) 27. (is faced, -faces) (-ultimately, ultimate) 28. (-where, which) 29. (-seriously, serious) 30. (is regarded, -regarded)

[Writing Practice]

1. a two-part novel published in
2. who became so obsessed with *tales of chivalry* that he lost touch with
3. Due to his excessive reading
4. persuades an innkeeper to dub/call him a knight
5. He falls in love with a peasant woman named
6. One of the most famous episodes in the novel
7. prisoners (who are) being transported
8. who he believes are oppressing
9. involves a beautiful woman named
10. try to persuade him to give up
11. Despite the pleas of his friends

[Word Quiz]

1. a) Adventures 2. c) Obsessed 3. a) Chivalry 4. a) Knights-errant 5. a) Reality 6. a) Transform 7. a) Self-proclaimed 8. a) Quest 9. a) Revive 10. a) Defend 11. a) Obscene 12. a) Valiantly 13. a) Excessive 14. a) Sanity 15. a) Adopt 16. a) Delusion 17. a) Declaration 18. a) Peasant 19. a) Imagination 20. a) Antagonize

Unit 13: The Pilgrim's Progress (1678)

[Reading Comprehension]

1. a) A journey from the City of Destruction to the Celestial City 2. b) It symbolizes the weight of sins and challenges of the spiritual life. 3. b) The Bible 4. a) Evangelist 5. a) Salvation 6. b) The Interpreter's House 7. d) Obstacles 8. c) Help 9. c) The Palace Beautiful 10. b) The weight of sins and spiritual challenges 11. c) He meets Help, who rescues him. 12. b) Shepherds offering guidance and comfort 13. b) The air induces forgetfulness of their purpose. 14. b) Peace and rest 15. a) They cross the River of Death with the help of angels.

[Grammar Check-up]

1. a) making 2. a) living 3. b) which 4. a) directs 5. b) while 6. a) illustrating 7. d) guiding 8. b) of 9. a) consequently 10. c) as well as 11. b) captured 12. a) unlocking 13. a) offering 14. c) sleepy 15. b) finding 16. d) carry 17. a) and 18. a) similar 19. c) who 20. d) challenges

[Writing Practice]

1. is considered one of the most significant works of religious literature
2. a man named Christian living in the City of Destruction
3. his city will be destroyed due to its sinful nature
4. that tells him to flee from
5. who directs him to a narrow gate
6. Evangelist encourages Christian to begin his journey immediately.
7. he finds the gate and enters the straight and narrow path
8. where he sees various allegorical visions illustrating different aspects of
9. faces challenges and trials
10. where he is welcomed by the inhabitants

[Word Quiz]
1. a) Allegorical 2. a) Significant 3. a) Religious 4. a) Literature 5. a) Spiritual 6. a) Pilgrimage 7. a) Impending 8. a) Distractions 9. a) Temptations 10. a) Interpreter 11. a) Challenges 12. a) Obstacles 13. a) Inhabitants 14. a) Despair 15. a) Imprisoned 16. a) Enchanted 17. a) Forgetfulness 18. a) Reunite 19. a) Devoted 20. a) Allegory

Unit 14: Robinson Crusoe (1719)

[Reading Comprehension]
1. c) Daniel Defoe 2. d) Stable profession 3. b) 1651 4. d) Caribbean Island 5. c) He uses his wits and skills to hunt and farm 6. b) Wooden walls 7. d) A native named Friday 8. b) Friday rescues him from captivity 9. c) English language and Christianity 10. c) Mutineers 11. d) He returns thanks to the help of a Portuguese captain 12. c) Survival, isolation, and the human spirit 13. b) He learns to be self-sufficient 14. d) Bond of friendship and loyalty 15. c) It explores themes of survival, self-discovery, and resilience

[Grammar Check-up]
1. (dreaming, -dreams) 2. (-Ignoring, Ignore) 3. (-Initially, Initial) (striking, -strikes) 4. (Stranding, -Stranded) (-unforgiving, unforgiven) 5. (salvaging, -to salvage) 6. (-proficient, proficiently) (able, -enables) 7. (between, -both) (grappling, -grapples) 8. (absently, -absent) 9. (is found, -finds) 10. (-years, year) (-indicating, indicates) 11. (potentially, -potential) 12. (-his, him) (does, -do) 13. (-natives, native) 14. (fosters, -fostering) 15. (task, -tasks) 16. (arrive, -arriving) 17. (rescuing, -to rescue) 18. (-is, are) 19. (Although, -Despite)

[Writing Practice]
1. much to the dismay of his family
2. Ignoring his father's wishes to pursue a more stable profession
3. as he embarks on his third sea journey
4. Stranded and alone on the island
5. he manages to salvage supplies
6. which enables him to sustain himself
7. While he enjoys the solitude
8. the decisions that led him to this predicament
9. After several years of isolation
10. Fearing that it may belong to cannibals
11. who do not pose any immediate danger to him
12. rescues one of the natives from his enemies

[Word Quiz]
1. b) Exciting experiences 2. d) Investigation 3. c) A feeling of shock or distress 4. c) Follow 5. c) An occupation or career 6. a) Unfavorable circumstances 7. c) Long journeys, often by sea or air 8. b) Success 9. b) Embark 10. c) A strong, destructive weather event 11. c) The remains of something that has been destroyed 12. a) Stuck or left in a difficult situation 13. c) To overcome difficulties and stay alive 14. b) A harsh and relentless setting 15. c) To save or recover something from wreckage 16. c) A temporary and improvised place of refuge 17. c) To be skilled

or competent 18. b) To make possible or provide the means for something 19. c) Being alone or separated from others 20. c) A negative consequence or bad luck

Unit 15: Gulliver's Travels (1726)

[Reading Comprehension]
1. c) Jonathan Swift 2. c) Four 3. c) Lilliput 4. a) Six inches tall 5. c) Their flaws, including vanity, greed, and corruption 6. d) Final voyage 7. b) Music and mathematics 8. d) Houyhnhnms 9. b) Human nature 10. a) Human nature 11. c) Satire 12. b) Ship's surgeon 13. b) Intellectuals 14. b) Second voyage 15. a) Humanity's base instincts

[Grammar Check-up]
1. (at, -on) (-unique, uniquely) 2. (-shipwrecked, shipwrecking) 3. (is encountered, -encounters) 4. (Even though, -Despite) 5. (embroiling, -embroiled) 6. (-extreme, extremely) 7. (-is, are) 8. (-faces, facing) 9. (Despite, -Through) (included, -including) 10. (-inhabited, inhabiting) (detach, -are detached) 11. (preoccupying, -preoccupied) (-neglecting, neglect) 12. (-absurd, -absurdity) 13. (-reaches, reaches to) 14. (-a, an) (which, -where) 15. (is encountered, -encounters) 16. (contrast, -contrasting) 17. (Thought, -Throughout) 18. (-becomes disillusioned, disillusions) 19. (what, -that) 20. (-uses, is used) (aspect, -aspects)

[Writing Practice]
1. who embarks on four remarkable voyages to
2. finds himself shipwrecked
3. (who are) no more than six inches tall
4. possess a complex society and engage in
5. discovers the opposite extreme
6. are preoccupied with abstract theories
7. reaches the land of
8. becomes disillusioned with
9. that combines adventure, satire,
10. to criticize and satirize various aspects of society

[Word Quiz]
1. b) Satirical 2. a) Inhabitants 3. c) Remarkable 4. a) Customs 5. c) Shipwrecked 6. b) Petty 7. b) Internal 8. a) Engage 9. d) Intrigue 10. a) Gigantic 11. c) Preoccupied 12. d) Intellectualism 13. c) Detached 14. b) Satirize 15. d) Practical 16. b) Encounter 17. a) Base 18. b) Contrasting 19. d) Disillusioned 20. c) Institutions

Unit 16: Faust (1808)

[Reading Comprehension]
1. D) 60 years 2. D) Faust's potential salvation or damnation 3. C) True fulfillment and understanding 4. B) "Thou art so fair" 5. C) Her mother dies 6. C) Her social rejection and incidents in her life 7. C) Through her faith in God 8. B) To achieve a utopian society 9. C) Destruction and chaos ensue 10. D) Through her faith and forgiveness 11. B) The

consequences of unchecked ambition 12. D) Tragedy, philosophy, spirituality, and social commentary 13. B) Scholar 14. B) Salvation through God's grace 15. C) Creation of a utopian society

[Grammar Check-up]

1. (was published, -published) 2. (is dissatisfied, -dissatisfied) 3. (disillusions, -is disillusioned) 4. (-offering, offered) 5. (tempts, -tempting) 6. (divides, -is divided) 7. (engaging, -engages) 8. (-lead, leading) 9. (where, -which) (-subsequent, subsequently) 10. (for, -on) 11. (involving, -involved) (seeks, -seeking) 12. (assist, -assistance) (-amassing, amass) 13. (endeavor, -endeavors) (leads, -lead) 14. (-constantly, constant) 15. (-deep, deeply) 16. (finally, -final) (selflessness, -selfless) 17. (rewarded, -are rewarded) 18. (unchecking, -unchecked) 19. (is remained, -remains)

[Writing Practice]

1. who is dissatisfied with his life and thirsting for knowledge
2. is disillusioned with
3. offering his soul in exchange for
4. tempting him with / tempting him to do
5. is divided into several significant
6. engages in a romantic relationship with
7. becomes tragic as
8. gives birth to Faust's child, which *leads to *causes=results in*
9. embarks on a series of ambitious ventures
10. becomes involved in
11. engages in grand projects such as
12. these endeavors ultimately lead to

[Word Quiz]

1. D) To extend across a period of time 2. A) Revise 3. A) Posthumous 4. B) Despair 5. C) Instinct 6. C) Lost or off the right path 7. B) Obscure 8. C) Aspiration 9. B) Influence 10. B) To make pregnant 11. C) Without being married 12. D) Cast out by society 13. B) Being alone and separated 14. A) Execute 15. C) Remorse 16. C) Proposal 17. A) Imaginative or visionary, usually describing an ideal society 18. B) Embark on 19. C) Unfulfilled 20. C) The outcome or result of an action

Unit 17: Pride and Prejudice (1813)

[Reading Comprehension]

1. c) Pride and Prejudice 2. b) Rural England 3. d) Elizabeth Bennet 4. c) Haughty and proud 5. b) Pride and prejudice 6. b) Social commentary 7. b) Its witty humor 8. b) A tapestry of social commentary 9. d) All of the above 10. b) It has remained popular and celebrated as a great work of English literature.

[Grammar Check-up]

1. (what, -that) 2. (-follows, following) 3. (are, -is) 4. (determines, -is determined) 5. (arriving,

-arrival) 6. (-well-received, well-receiving) 7. (is accompanied, -accompanies) 8. (-complicated, complicating) 9. (Initial, -Initially) (form, -to form) 10. (is undergone, -undergo) 11. (-depicting, depicts) 12. (is satirized, -satirizes) 13. (their, -its) 14. (being seen, -seeing) 15. (-skillfully, skillful) (-imposed, imposing) 16. (-timeless, timelessly) 17. (is remained, -has remained) (work, -works)

[Writing Practice]

1. who is one of five sisters
2. is determined to marry them off to
3. begins with the arrival of
4. one of her daughters will win his affections
5. revolves around the complicated relationship between
6. lead them to form negative opinions of each other.
7. as they come to know and understand each other better
8. depicting/describing the lives and aspirations of the various characters
9. is renowned for its sharp wit
10. the limitations imposed on women

[Word Quiz]

1. c) Pride 2. c) Prejudice 3. b) Impact 4. a) Impression 5. b) Rural 6. b) Protagonist 7. b) Independent-minded 8. a) Determined 8. b) Bachelor 10. a) Neighbor 11. c) Undergo 12. b) Narrative 13. c) Tapestry 14. b) Depict 15. c) Celebrated 16. a) Engaging 17. b) Explore 18. c) Complicated and intricate aspects or factors 19. c) Limitations 20. a) Social dynamics

Unit 18: Frankenstein (1818)

[Reading Comprehension]

1. c) Frankenstein 2. b) Margaret 3. a) He witnesses a lightning strike that destroys a tree. 4. b) He is horrified by its appearance and abandons it. 5. b) To create a companion for him 6. b) The rejection and shunning by society 7. d) His "Creator" 8. c) He murders several of Victor's loved ones. 9. d) The Arctic 10. a) The dangers of unrestrained ambition and obsession. 11. b) His actions and the death of his creator 12. d) Walton decides to abandon his quest for the North Pole. 13. a) Ambition, responsibility, and compassion 14. c) The creature 15. a) Monster

[Grammar Check-up]

1. (-obsessed, obsession) 2. (detail, -detailed) 3. (stranding, -stranded) 4. (within, -with) 5. (-interest, interested) 6. (-that, what) (harness, -harnessing) 7. (an, -a) (for, -with) 8. (to study, -studying) 9. (-abandons, is abandoned) 10. (-abandoned, abandoning) 11. (rejects, -is rejected) 12. (is filled, -fills) (-refers, is referred) 13. (creates, -create) 14. (untelling, -untold) 15. (feels, -feeling) 16. (-newlywed, newly wedding) 17. (which, -where) 18. (-mutual, mutually) 19. (determines, -is determined) 20. (-Weakened, Weaken) 21. (restrained, -unrestrained) 22. (-appears, is appeared) 23. (to immolate, -by immolating) 24. (checked, -unchecked) 25. (-understanding, understands)

[Writing Practice]

1. who becomes obsessed with the idea of creating life.
2. agrees to share his story with
3. grows up with a strong interest in
4. spends years studying and experimenting
5. fills the creature with anger and bitterness toward
6. demands that he create a companion for him
7. Despite Victor's pleas to destroy the creature
8. warns Walton of the dangers of
9. the consequences of unchecked ambition
10. decides to abandon his quest for

[Word Quiz]

1. b) Exploration 2. c) Warning 3. b) Responsibility 4. a) Companionship 5. d) Resembling a monster 6. d) Resolve 7. c) Intense preoccupation 8. d) Enchantment 9. b) Electricity 10. c) Phenomenon 11. b) Companionship 12. d) Chasing or seeking 13. c) Transformation 14. b) Tragedy 15. b) Eternal or undying 16. c) Investigation 17. a) Responsibility 18. c) Aspiration 19. c) Melancholy 20. c) To sacrifice by fire

Unit 19: Oliver Twist (1838)

[Reading Comprehension]

1. b) 1838 2. c) Workhouse 3. b) Mr. Bumble 4. c) 9 5. c) Artful Dodger 6. b) Gang of pickpockets and thieves 7. b) Artful Dodger 8. c) Darker aspects 9. c) He is wrongly accused. 10. b) Mr. Brownlow 11. c) To prevent Oliver from revealing their secrets 12. b) Nancy 13. c) Bill Sikes 14. b) Murder Nancy 15. d) Oliver finds happiness with Mr. Brownlow and Rose Maylie.

[Grammar Check-up]

1. b) written 2. a) was born 3. a) known 4. d) decide 5. a) who 6. c) who is 7. b) into 8. b) who 9. a) who 10. a) who 11. c) feeling 12. d) including 13. a) a kind-hearted 14. b) murders 15. b) ensues 16. c) discovers 17. b) fates 18. c) shines 19. a) resilience 20. c) which

[Writing Practice]

1. was known for its harsh treatment of the children.
2. Due to the mistreatment and cruelty he faces
3. who introduces Oliver to the criminal world
4. is wrongly accused of stealing by Mr. Brownlow
5. The truth about Oliver's parentage is revealed
6. feeling for her role in Oliver's abduction
7. Nancy's plan to save Oliver is discovered by Bill Sikes
8. where he discovers *his newfound happiness* *happiness that he newly finds*
9. throughout the novel
10. who flees London with Oliver as his hostage

[Word Quiz]

1. b) Navigate 2. b) Orphan 3. c) Cruel 4. a) Workhouse 5. a) Childbirth 6. b) Orphanage 7. b) Apprentice 8. c) Undertaker 9. a) Mistreatment 10. b) Charismatic 11. c) Mischievous 12. a) Cunning 13. a) The elderly 14. c) Pickpocket 15. c) Unwittingly 16. a) Innocence 17. b) Dangerous 18. a) Brutal 19. a) Encounter 20. b) Ruthless

Unit 20: The Count of Monte Cristo (1844)

[Reading Comprehension]

1. b) Betrayal, revenge, and forgiveness 2. b) He was falsely accused of treason 3. b) Abbé Faria 4. a) The existence of a hidden treasure on Monte Cristo 5. c) He uses Abbé Faria's corpse to fake his own death 6. c) The Count of Monte Cristo 7. b) To seek revenge against his enemies 8. d) Fernand Mondego 9. b) Blackmail and extortion 10. b) The impact of his actions on the innocent 11. a) Mercédès 12. b) That justice cannot be achieved through revenge alone 13. d) All of the above 14. a) It has been turned into numerous films, plays, and television series 15. b) Love and happiness

[Grammar Check-up]

1. (-accused, accusing) 2. (who is, -is) 3. (-falsely accused, false accuse) 4. (imprison, -imprisoned) 5. (While, -During) (-another, other) (becomes, -who becomes) 6. (is revealed, -reveals) 7. (is used, -using) 8. (is acquired, -acquires) 9. (newfind, -newfound) (-who, which) 10. (-systematically, systenatical) 11. (is exposed, -exposes) 12. (-Throughout, Thought) 13. (moral, -morality) 14. (-had on, had) 15. (-be achieved, achieve) 16. (forgiving, -to forgive) 17. (-abandoning, abandon) 18, (-betrayal, betray)

[Writing Practice]

1. who is unjustly accused of treason and imprisoned
2. is about to marry
3. when he is betrayed by his friends and falsely accused of
4. befriends another inmate named
5, reveals the existence of a hidden treasure
6. manages to escape from prison
7. transforms himself into the enigmatic and wealthy Count
8. exposes their secrets, manipulates their lives
9. the impact his actions have had on the innocent
10. learns to forgive and finds redemption through

[Word Quiz]

1. c) Unfairly 2. c) Treason 3. a) Imprisoned 4. a) Drastic 5. c) Conspirator 6. a) Betrayed 7. c) Untruthfully 8. a) Mentor 9. c) Enigmatic 10. c) Orchestrate 11. b) Diverse 12. c) Dishonest 13. b) Pursuit 14. a) Redemption 15. c) Vengeance 16. c) Reunite 17. b) Impact 18. a) Justice 19. a) Conclude 20. c) Triumph

Unit 21: Jane Eyre (1847)

[Reading Comprehension]

1. A) Charlotte Brontë 2. A) Lowood Institution 3. D) Helen Burns 4. A) He is already married to Bertha. 5. B) In the attic 6. B) Mr. Rivers 7. D) Because Mr. Rochester is already married 8. A) It is burned down by Bertha's actions. 9. B) Trying to save Bertha from a fire 10. B) Love, independence, morality, and social class 11. B) Teacher 12. C) Teacher and student 13. B) A loving family 14. D) St. John Rivers 15. B) With Jane narrating her contented life as Mrs. Rochester

[Grammar Check-up]

1. (rosen, -raised) 2. (sends, -is sent) 3. (-are, is) (is friends, -befriends) (teach, -teaches) 4. (leaves, -leaving) 5. (As long as, -As) 6. (-receives, is received) 7. (-develops, is developed) (fallen, -falls) 8. (deeps, -deepens) (despite of, -despite) 9. (-add, adds) 10. (-mentally, mental) (-locked, locking) 11. (heartbreaking, -heartbroken) 12. (takes, -take) 13. (-becomes, become) (asks, -asking) 14. (is realized, -realizes) 15. (Due to, -Despite) 16. (-other, another) (to call, -calling) 17. (burning, -burned) 18. (impairing, -impaired)

[Writing Practice]

1. who is raised by
2. is sent away to
3. who teaches her the value of endurance
4. receives an offer from, to be the governess for
5. develops a strong bond with
6. They become close despite their differences in social status.
7. Distraught and heartbroken *Confused and brokenhearted
8. who take her in and help her find work
9. asking her to accompany him
10. Despite her strong feelings for

[Word Quiz]

1. c) Protagonist 2. b) Orphan 3. b) Abuse 4. a) Orphanage 5. a) Endurance 6. b) Piety 7. c) Governess 8. c) Mysterious 9. d) Brooding 10. a) Relationship 11. c) Social status 12. b) Occurrences 13. a) Eerie 14. b) Attic 15. a) Heartbroken 16. b) Embark 17. c) Contemplate 18. b) Realization 19. b) Recovery 20. c) Confess

Unit 22: Wuthering Heights (1847)

[Reading Comprehension]

1. b) Emily Brontë 2. a) 1847 3. b) Yorkshire, England 4. c) Wuthering Heights and Thrushcross Grange 5. d) Mr. Lockwood 6. a) Marry Edgar Linton 7. c) "I am Heathcliff." 8. a) To exact revenge on Hindley and Edgar 9. b) Isabella Linton 10. b) Her health deteriorates rapidly, and she dies. 11. b) Edgar Linton 12. b) He descends into madness and darkness. 13. c) His reunion with Catherine in death 14. d) Cathy and Hareton 15. b) With Heathcliff's death and hope for the future

[Grammar Check-up]

1. (span, -spans) 2. (-city-dwelled, -city-dwelling) 3. (-where, which) 4. (inhabits, -inhabitants) 5. (-late, lately) (is named, -names) 6. (presents, -resents) 7. (-turns, is turned) 8. (-to become, becoming) 9. (tears, -is torn) 10. (leads, -leading) 11. (-sophisticated, sophisticating) 12. (determining, -determined) 13. (now marries, -is now married) 14. (-marries, is married) 15. (rapid, -rapidly) 16. (obsess, -obsession) 17. (Tormenting, -Tormented by) 18. (wane, -wanes)

[Writing Practice]

1. that spans several generations
2. Intrigued by his landlord's mysterious personality
3. In the late 18th century
4. resents the boy's presence
5. turns into a passionate and intense love
6. leads her to become close to
7. Despite her love for
8. After a three-year absence
9. gives birth to a daughter, deteriorates rapidly
10. His grief and obsession with

[Word Quiz]

1. c) Complicated 2. b) Scary 3. b) A group of people born at the same time 4. c) Retaliation 5. a) Creative 6. b) Love 7. c) Deserted 8. d) Marshy and boggy areas 9. c) Nearby 10. a) Large properties or landholdings 11. b) Puzzling 12. b) Inner thoughts and feelings 13. c) A story or account of events 14. b) Change 15. d) Negative experiences 16. b) Overwhelming 17. c) Conflicting opinions 18. b) Indecisive 19. c) A famous saying or expression 20. d) When they want to express their emotions openly

Unit 23: Moby-Dick (1851)

[Reading Comprehension]

1. c) Herman Melville 2. c) A giant white whale named Moby Dick 3. c) Through the perspective of Ishmael, a young sailor 4. a) Pequod 5. b) Ahab's lost leg due to an encounter with the whale 6. c) A Polynesian harpooner and Ishmael's close friend 7. b) The ship's first mate 8. c) He becomes increasingly detached and consumed by madness 9. c) It faces dangerous encounters and destruction 10. d) A coffin 11. d) Ishmael 12. b) Themes of obsession, fate, human nature, and the struggle between man and nature 13. c) There is a constant struggle and tension between man and nature 14. d) The Pequod is destroyed and most of the crew dies 15. b) Ishmael reflects on the tragic events and is rescued

[Grammar Check-up]

1. (-obsessively, -obsessive) (is known, -known) 2. (obsessive, -obsession) 3. (-who. which) (commanding, -commanded) 4. (determining, -determined) 5. (-consisting, consisted) 6. (-provides, providing) 7. (intersperses, -is interspersed) (-serving, serves) 8. (For, -During) (-other, another) 9. (-These, this) 10. (are included, -include) 11. (-increasingly, increasing) 12. (-pursuit, pursue) (culminates, -culminating) 13. (-formidable, formidably) 14. (clinging, -clings)

(ponders, -pondering) 15. (-its, their) 16. (-destructive, destruction) 17. (-is considered, considers)

[Writing Practice]

1. obsessive quest for revenge against
2. the struggle between man and nature
3. commanded by the enigmatic and vengeful
4. is determined to find and kill the whale
5. consisting of a diverse group of sailors
6. provides vivid descriptions of
7. becomes increasingly detached from
8. The pursuit of the elusive whale
9. proves to be a formidable force of nature
10. clings to a coffin and is rescued by
11. is renowned for its rich symbolism
12. is considered a masterpiece of American literature

[Word Quiz]

1. a) Revenge 2. a) Whale 3. a) Themes 4. a) Obsession 5. a) Fate 6. a) Human nature 7. a) Struggle 8. a) Narrate 9. a) Whaling ship 10. a) Enigmatic 11. a) Vengeful 12. a) Vendetta 13. a) Camaraderie 14. a) Philosophical musings 15. a) Interspersed 16. a) Informative interludes 17. a) Metaphorical reflections 18. a) Encounters 19. a) Perspectives 20. a) Harpooner

Unit 24: Walden (1854)

[Reading Comprehension]

1. a) 1854 2. a) Thoreau's reflections on living in a cabin 3. d) All of the above 4. a) To find a deeper connection to nature 5. c) People should live authentically 6. a) Civil disobedience 7. b) Society values material possessions too much 8. c) Two years 9. a) A testament to the importance of simplicity and self-reliance 10. c) American literature

[Grammar Check-up]

1. a) written 2. b) daily 3. a) connection 4. a) simple 5. b) settled 6. a) spiritual 7. b) exploring 8. a) authentically 9. b) importance 10. b) commentary 11. a) role 12. a) unjust 13. c) society 14. a) interdependence 15. b) an end 16. d) return 17. c) importance 18. b) work 19. b) meaningful 20. d) testament

[Writing Practice]

1. seeking to find a deeper connection to nature
2. wanted to escape the distractions of modern society
3. settled there to observe nature and learn from it
4. which he finds to be a source of deep spiritual and intellectual insight
5. spends his time exploring the woods, fishing, and cultivating
6. recognizing the interdependence of humans and the natural world
7. people *to live* authentically and not be governed by societal norms *who live

8. not being consumed by the pursuit of wealth and status

9. carries *with him* the lessons and insights he gained from his experience. *맨 뒤도 가능

10. for those seeking to live a more meaningful and deliberate life.

[Word Quiz]

1. a) Reflection 2. a) Embark on 3. d) Simplicity 4. a) Deliberately 5. b) Essentials
6. a) Distractions 7. a) Settle 8. b) Observe 9. b) Spiritual 10. d) Intellectual 11. b) Insight 12. c)
Explore 13. b) Interdependence 14. a) Self-reliance 15. b) Individuality 16. c) Authenticity 17. a)
Be governed 18. b) Commentary 19. a) Legitimacy 20. b) Advocate

Unit 25: Great Expectations (1861)

[Reading Comprehension]

1. c) Philip Pirrip (Pip) 2. c) The marshes of Kent, England 3. a) A convict named Abel
Magwitch 4. c) Miss Havisham 5. a) He wants to become a gentleman like her 6. b) He has
inherited a fortune from a wealthy relative 7. c) Abel Magwitch 8. c) She caused damage to
Estella 9. a) He is devastated 10. b) She dies in a fire at Satis House 11. c) Joe Gargery 12. b)
He becomes more appreciative of their love and care 13. b) An abusive marriage 14. b)
Identity, social class, love, and forgiveness 15. c) Bildungsroman (coming-of-age novel)

[Grammar Check-up]

1. (and, -to) 2. (who live, -living) 3. (deceasing, -deceased) (humbly, -humble) 4. (visit,
-visiting) (who names, -named) (threatening, -threatens) 5. (invites, -is invited) (wearing,
-wears) 6. (-adopted, adopting) 7. (-ignited, igniting) 8. (is received, -receives) (mean, -means)
9. (-assumes, is assumed) 10. I(tutoring, -tutored by) 11. (-ashame, -ashamed) 12. (is spent,
-spends) 13. (have, -has) 14. (-distant, distantly) 15. (and, -but) 16. (-returns, returning) 17.
(-devastated by, devastating) 18. (particular, -particularly) 19. (-accidentally, accidental) 20. (-to
reevaluate, reevaluate) 21. (nursing, -nursed) 22. (While, -During) 23. (genuinely, -genuine) 24.
(-anew, new) 25. (risen, -raised) 26. (was made, -made) 27. (-uncertain, uncertainly) 28.
(exploring, -explores) 29. (self-discover, -self-discovery) (work, -works).

[Writing Practice]

1. while visiting the graves of his parents
2. is invited to the grand and decaying Satis House
3. asks Pip to play with her adopted daughter
4. his desire to become a gentleman is ignited
5. has provided him with the *means* to become *ways
6. becomes ashamed of his humble background
7. who has always *cared for* him. *taken care of
8. She is accidentally killed in a fire
9. they offered him throughout his life.
10. who was raised to be heartless

[Word Quiz]

1. c) Cruel and harmful 2. a) Deceased 3. c) To meet or come across unexpectedly 4. c) Convict

5. d) To express intent to harm or cause fear 6. c) Chains or restraints on someone's wrists or ankles 7. d) Impressive and magnificent 8. d) In a state of rot or deterioration 9. b) Eccentric 10. c) Expressing scorn or contempt 11. c) A person who offers help or financial aid 12. d) Cultured and polished 13. c) An intense but short-lived passion or admiration 14. c) An accidental discovery 15. c) A state of extreme destruction and ruin 16. d) A feeling of regret and guilt for past actions 17. c) By chance or without intention 18. c) A moment of significant change or decision in a story 19. c) To restore friendly relations after a disagreement 20. a) Unable to see

Unit 26: Crime and Punishment (1866)

[Reading Comprehension]

1. b) Crime and Punishment 2. b) St. Petersburg 3. c) Rodion Raskolnikov 4. b) To test his theory of superiority 5. a) They are above the law 6. c) Sonya 7. b) He becomes mentally unstable and overwhelmed with guilt 8. c) He is the investigating magistrate 9. c) Sonya 10. c) Confess his crime to the authorities 11. d) Siberia 12. c) Raskolnikov's life in Siberia 13. b) Human nature, morality, guilt, and consequences of actions 14. b) He becomes increasingly troubled and unstable 15. b) It is a timeless and powerful exploration of human nature

[Grammar Check-up]

1. (-impoverished, impoverishing) 2. (Overwhelming, -Overwhelmed by) (what, -that) (-traditional, tradition) 3. (to murder, -by murdering) 4. (-stolen, stealing) 5. (catching, -being caught) 6. (-mentally, mental) 7. (investigated, -investigating) 8. (-who turns, turns) 9. (effect, -affect) 10. (haunts, -is haunted by) (-particularly, particular) 11. (confessions, -confesses) 12. (-torn, tearing) 13. (is clever, -cleverly) 14. (-receiving, received) 15. (brings, -is brought) (which, -where) (-sentenced, sentencing)

[Writing Practice]

1. Overwhelmed by poverty and his nihilistic beliefs
2. decides to test this theory by murdering
3. he will use the stolen money to help others
4. becomes mentally unstable
5. begins to closely *monitor* his movements *examine
6. he is haunted by hallucinations and visions
7. trying to lead him into a confession
8. have been receiving financial support from
9. is subsequently sentenced to exile

[Word Quiz]

1. a) Impoverished 2. a) Nihilistic 3. a) Extraordinary 4. a) Consequences 5. a) Commit 6. a) Investigation 7. a) Magistrate 8. a) Prostitution 9. a) Unwavering 10. a) Redemption 11. a) Deteriorate 12. a) Hallucinations 13. a) Malevolent 14. a) Confess 15. a) Manipulate 16. a) Financial 17. a) Confront 18. a) Emotional 19. a) Authorities 20. a) Exile

Unit 27: War and Peace (1869)

[Reading Comprehension]

1. a) 1865-1869 2. b) Saint Petersburg, Russia 3. c) Prince Andrei Bolkonsky 4. a) Natasha Rostova 5. c) The death of his wife 6. a) Pierre Bezukhov 7. d) 1812 8. a) General Kutuzov 9. c) He is taken prisoner by the French. 10. c) It is set ablaze by the retreating Russians. 11. c) Pierre Bezukhov 12. a) Natasha Rostova 13. c) History and fate 14. b) Napoleon's invasion of Russia 15. b) Realism

[Grammar Check-up]

1. (considers, -is considered) (work, -works) 2. (-published, publishment) 3. (-covering, covers) 4. (primary, -primarily) 5. (-socially, social) 6. (struggle, -struggles) 7. (-married, marries) 8. (disillusions, -is disillusioned) 9. (filled, -full) 10. (engaging, -engaged) (fallen, -falls) 11. (leading, -leads) (involve, -involved) 12. (-these, this) (-exploring, explores) 13. (-particularly, particular) 14. (effected, -affected) 15. (-skillfully, skillful) 16. (historically, -historical) 17. (provides, -offers)

[Writing Practice]

1. is considered one of the greatest literary works
2. a socially awkward and illegitimate son of
3. inherits his father's fortune and becomes
4. goes through various philosophical and spiritual
5. is disillusioned with his life
6. full of life and energy
7. is engaged to, falls in love with
8. that impact the lives of all (the people who are) involved
9. delves into the historical events
10. are profoundly affected by
11. offers readers a panoramic view of

[Word Quiz]

1. a) Literary 2. b) Summarized 3. b) Aristocratic 4. c) Primarily 5. c) Illegitimate 6. a) Philosophical 7. a) Ambitious 8. b) Disillusioned 9. b) Vivacious 10. b) Engaged 11. c) Historical 12. b) Explore 13. b) Personal 14. a) Portray 15. d) Existence 16. a) Profound 17. a) Panoramic 18. b) Exploration 19. d) Meditation 20. a) Essence

Unit 28: 20,000 Leagues Under the Sea (1870)

[Reading Comprehension]

1. a) Jules Verne 2. a) Nautilus 3. a) France 4. a) Investigating a sea monster 5. c) Powerful engines 6. b) Coral reefs 7. c) Captain Nemo's aggressive actions, attacking warships 8. c) They are rescued by a passing ship 9. b) Science and ethics 10. a) The undersea world and Captain Nemo's character

[Grammar Check-up]
1. (following, -follows) (-extraordinary, extraordinarily) (commanding, -commanded by) 2. (caused, -causing) 3. (-named, naming) (potential, -potentially) 4. (attacks, -is attacked) 5. (-surprise, surprising) (-advanced, advancing) 6. (take, -are taken) (is served, -serves) 7. (-is equipped, equips) (instrument, -instruments) 8. (expose, -are exposed) (creature, -creatures) 9. (-witness, are witnessed) 10. (maintenance, -maintaining) 11. (rises, -arise) (includes, -include) 12. (as well as, -and) 13. (for, -to) (-include, including) 14. (left, -leaving) 15. (-reflecting, reflects) 16. (is captivated, -captivates)

[Writing Practice]
1. embark on an extraordinary undersea journey
2. commanded by the mysterious Captain Nemo
3. that is causing havoc in the oceans.
4. join an expedition to investigate and potentially capture
5. During their pursuit, their ship is attacked
6. To their surprise, a highly advanced submarine *created* by *made*
7. is equipped with innovative technology
8. are exposed to breathtaking underwater landscapes
9. tensions arise when the group becomes conflicted with
10. between fascination with the oceanic wonders they experience

[Word Quiz]
1. a) Adventure 2. a) Embark 3. d) Mysterious 4. b) Submarine 5. c) Extraordinary 6. a) Self-sustaining 7. b) Breathtaking 8. a) Underwater 9. a) Coral reefs 10. b) Encounter 11. a) Consequence 12. a) Marine 13. c) Difficult to find or catch 14. a) Sophistication 15. c) Explore or examine thoroughly 16. b) Subsequent 17. d) Expedition 18. a) Extensive 19. a) Elaborate 20. c) Profound

Unit 29: Anna Karenina (1877)

[Reading Comprehension]
1. a) Leo Tolstoy 2. b) 1877 3. c) Russia 4. d) Anna Karenina 5. c) Husband and wife 6. d) Count Alexei Vronsky 7. d) She is hesitant due to her marriage. 8. a) Her social standing and reputation 9. a) Love, family, morality, and social norms 10. b) She becomes isolated and depressed. 11. a) His duty to his family and his love for Anna 12. a) Nature and his relationship with Kitty 13. c) She tragically dies by throwing herself under a train. 14. a) The importance of faith, love, and the simple joys of life 15. a) A timeless exploration of love, morality, and the human condition

[Grammar Check-up]
1. a) written 2. a) published 3. b) nineteenth-century 4. a) heroine 5. b) devastated 6. a) wealthy 7. a) married 8. c) reputation 9. c) isolation 10. d) duty 11. a) discovery 12. a) marry 13. b) social 14. b) emotional 15. c) depressed 16. a) status 17. c) meaning 18. a) delusional 19. a) epiphany 20. b) depths

[Writing Practice]

1. who has been unfaithful to his wife for a long time
2. is initially resistant to
3. she eventually succumbs to her feelings
4. is torn between her love for Vronsky and her duty
5. proposes to her after her breakup with Vronsky
6. faces a difficult decision between her family and her lover
7. she becomes increasingly isolated and depressed.
8. becomes frustrated with Anna's emotional instability and her jealousy.
9. seeks solace and answers in nature and his relationship with Kitty.
10. In a moment of despair, she tragically throws herself under a train and dies.

[Word Quiz]

1. b) Judgment 2. a) Climax 3. b) Despair 4. a) Heroine 5. b) Unfaithful 6. c) Complexity 7. c) Deteriorate 8. b) Isolation 9. b) Sophisticated 10. c) Existence 11. b) Solace 12. b) Advances 13. c) Deteriorate 14. a) Paranoid 15. b) Spiritual 16. c) Introduction 17. b) Heartbroken 18. b) Relationship 19. a) Timeless 20. b) Sweeping

Unit 30: Treasure Island (1883)

[Reading Comprehension]

1. c) Robert Louis Stevenson 2. c) Seeking buried treasure on an island 3. c) The Admiral Benbow Inn 4. d) Billy Bones 5. b) He has a stroke during a confrontation 6. b) Long John Silver 7. a) Quartermaster and pirate leader 8. c) He is unsure if he should trust Long John Silver or Captain Smollett 9. d) Ben Gunn 10. c) He sides with the loyal crew and fights against the mutineers 11. b) To England on the Hispaniola 12. b) He escapes capture and continues his life of adventure 13. c) Adventure 14. c) He gains courage and resourcefulness 15. c) He helps Jim find the hidden treasure cache

[Grammar Check-up]

1, (involves in, -becomes involved in) (-thrilling, thrilled) 2. (-run, running) 3. (is arrived, -arrives) (carries, -carrying) 4. (leading, -led by) 5. (is left, -leaving) 6. (Realized, -Realizing) 7. (-to embark, embarking) (finding, -to find) 8. (includes, -including) (where, -who) 9. (-secretly, secret) (who planning, -planning) 10. (-gradually, gradual) (caught, -is caught) (-whom, who) 11. (-increasingly, increasing) 12. (informing, -informs) (who leading, -leading) 13. (For, -Upon) 14. (-who knows, knows) 15. (is retrieved, -retrieves) 16. (narrow, -narrowly) 17. (is ensued, -ensues) 18. (-showing, shows) 19. (eventual, -eventually) 20. (hard-winning, -hard-won)

[Writing Practice]

1. a thrilling quest for buried treasure on a mysterious island
2. seeking refuge from his past and carrying a treasure map.
3. unsure of whom *to trust* *whom *he should trust*
4. becomes increasingly divided between
5. Upon arriving at Treasure Island
6. retrieves some of the treasure

7. narrowly escapes capture and rejoins
8. A fierce battle ensues
9. eventually sides with the loyal crew
10. with their hard-won treasure

[Word Quiz]

1. c) Admiral 2. c) Hidden treasure 3. b) Courage 4. b) Dilemma 5. b) Unscrupulous 6. b) Expedition 7. c) Treachery 8. b) Confrontation 9. a) Seaman 10. b) Embark 11. b) Tense standoff 12. a) Sinister 13. b) Quartermaster 14. c) Possession 15. c) Complexities 16. a) Fierce battle 17. b) Embark 18. b) Influence 19. a) Loyalty 20. a) Retrieve

Unit 31: What Men Live By (1885)

[Reading Comprehension]

1. b) Love, compassion, and the true meaning of life 2. b) To learn the true meaning of life 3. c) Michael is found naked and half-dead in the snow 4. a) Gratefulness 5. a) A strong bond 6. c) The central question, "What do men live by?" 7. c) To learn the answer to the question, "What do men live by?" 8. a) Love, compassion, and selflessness 9. a) Embracing love and understanding 10. b) Kindness and empathy towards others

[Grammar Check-up]

1. (are titled, -titled) 2. (which, -where) 3. (condemns, -is condemned) (for, -as) 4. (finds, -is found) (-named, naming) 5. (nursing, -nurses) 6. (staying, -to stay) 7. (-assisting, assists) 8. (been adopted, -adopted) 9. (-apparent, apparently) 10. (-extraordinary, extraordinarily) (seeks, -seek) 11. (unknowing, -unknown) 12. (-unexpected, unexpecting) (are, -is) 13. (escaping, -to escape) 14. (tests, -test) 15. (-underlying, underlie) 16. (reveals, -is revealed) 17. (regarding, -regardless)

[Writing Practice]

1. an angel named Michael is sent
2. is condemned to live on Earth as a human being
3. is found naked and half-dead
4. provides him with clothing and shelter
5. becomes grateful for Simon's kindness and decides to
6. assisting with various tasks and bringing (a sense of) peace and harmony
7. develops a strong bond with
8. becomes more apparent through his actions and words
9. offering guidance to those who seek help
10. unexpected visitor arrives at

[Word Quiz]

1. c) Theme 2. d) Compassion 3. d) Integral 4. a) Cobbler 5. c) Shelter 6. a) Adopt 7. c) Full of wonder and intrigue 8. c) Transgression 9. b) Blame 10. d) Compassionate 11. b) Identity 12. d) Look for or search 13. a) Virtues 14. a) Collection 15. c) Showing appreciation and thankfulness 16. c) Embrace 17. c) Riches and abundance of resources 18. a) Demeanor 19. a) Insights 20. d) Atmosphere

Unit 32: The Brothers Karamazov (1880)

[Reading Comprehension]

1. b) Family dynamics and relationships 2. b) Fyodor Dostoevsky 3. c) Three 4. c) Dmitri 5. c) The existence of evil and human suffering 6. b) Father Zosima 7. b) He is a mentor and spiritual guide 8. c) Dmitri 9. c) Fyodor Karamazov's murder 10. d) Alyosha 11. c) With the characters reflecting on their actions and roles 12. c) She represents the seductive and alluring aspects of life 13. b) A court case and trial 14. b) It challenges their understanding of human nature 15. c) A timeless classic with psychological depth and philosophical richness

[Grammar Check-up]

1. (-multi-layered, multi-layering) 2. (is explored, -explores) 3. (returning, -returns) 4. (passionate, -passionately) (-involved, involving) 5. (escalate, -escalates) 6. (farther, -further) 7. (deep, -deeply) 8. (existing, -existence) 9. (-involved, involving) 10. (other, -others) (-offering, offers) 11. (include, -including) 12. (is delved, -delves) 13. (where, -when) (accuses, -is accused) 14. (ensued, -ensuing) (moral, -morality) 15. (-brings, is brought) 16. (-turbulent, turbulently) 17. (-brother, brothers) 18. (-leaves, is left)

[Writing Practice]

1. after being away for some time from home
2. is passionately in love with
3. adding further complexities to
4. engages in deep philosophical discussions with
5. offering profound insights into human nature
6. Dmitri is accused of the crime
7. The ensuing trial exposes the depths of human nature
8. also brings to light the various motives and conflicts within
9. Each brother represents a different aspect of
10. leaves the readers with profound questions about

[Word Quiz]

1. a) Complex 2. a) Multi-layered 3. c) To rotate around a central point 4. a) Explore
5. c) Theme 6. a) Morality 7. b) Introduction 8. c) Landowner 9. b) Relationship 10. a) Passionately 11. b) Seductive 12. a) Tension 13. c) Clash 14. b) Inheritance 15. b) Accused 16. c) Discussions 17. a) Profound 18. c) Delve 19. d) Intriguing 20. d) Consequences

Unit 33: Thus Spoke Zarathustra (1883)

[Reading Comprehension]

1. c) The teachings and ideas of the character Zarathustra 2. b) It is divided into four parts with discourses and encounters 3. b) A prophet descending from a mountain 4. c) The "overman" or "superman" 5. c) He critiques conventional morality and religion 6. b) The inherent drive to exert strength and create meaning 7. b) He challenges their beliefs and advocates for joy and sensuality 8. a) Zarathustra's transformation during his seclusion 9. c) He experiences solitude and self-reflection 10. c) The idea that life repeats in an endless cycle

11. d) Individualism, self-overcoming, and personal meaning 12. c) By calling for the creation of new values 13. c) It has provoked discussions about personal transformation 14. b) To carry on his teachings and search for self-realization 15. c) He embodies the teachings and ideas of Nietzsche

[Grammar Check-up]

1. (which writes, -written) 2. (-who, which) (for, -to) 3. (-containing, contains) 4. (is begun, -begins) 5. (-speeches, speech) (-critiquing, critique) 6. (-for, against) 7. (-rejection, reject) 8. (variety, -various) 9. (this, -these) (embrace, -embracing) (mean, -means) 10. (rejects, -reject) 11. (-arguing, argues) (embracing, -embraces) 12. (-undergoes, undergoing) 13. (is emerged, -emerges) (which, -that) 14. (-bids, bidding) 15. (-rejection, reject) (-overcoming, overcome) 16. (high, -highly) (-provoking, provokes)

[Writing Practice]

1. to share his wisdom with humanity.
2. is structured in four parts
3. begins by announcing
4. delivers a series of speeches to the people
5. advocates for the "will to power"
6. encourages the rejection of herd mentality
7. Part Two focuses on
8. Through these encounters
9. engages in dialogues with
10. undergoes a transformation and retreats to a cave
11. emerges from his seclusion with
12. urging them to carry on his teachings and continue

[Word Quiz]

1. c) Philosophical 2. b) Prophet 3. b) Solitude 4. b) Overman 5. a) Wisdom 6. a) Humanity 7. a) Liberation 8. d) Conventional Morality 9. b) Religion 10. b) Herd Mentality 11. c) Inherent Drive 12. d) Ascetics 13. b) Confrontation 14. b) Individuality 15. b) Self-Overcoming 16. b) Transformation 17. a) Sensuality 18. a) Pursuit 19. c) Spiritual Enlightenment 20. a) Life-Affirming Approach

Unit 34: Dr. Jekyll and Mr. Hyde (1886)

[Reading Comprehension]

1. b) Dr. Jekyll and Mr. Hyde 2. b) Scientist and Physician 3. b) The duality of personalities, good and evil within one person 4. d) To separate his darker nature from his virtuous self 5. b) It transforms him into a cruel and immoral person 6. d) It transforms him into Mr. Hyde, a violent and immoral man 7. b) He enjoys the freedom and power it brings 8. b) He loses control as Mr. Hyde becomes dominant 9. c) Series of heinous crimes, including murder 10. d) He becomes suspicious of Mr. Hyde's relationship with Dr. Jekyll 11. c) The truth behind his dual identity and inability to control transformations 12. b) He fears the consequences of Hyde's actions 13. c) He commits suicide to prevent further harm 14. c) The duality of human

nature and consequences of unchecked desires 15. c) It delves into human nature and the complexities of the human psyche

[Grammar Check-up]

1. b) written 2. d) was published 3. a) follows 4. d) increasingly 5. a) both 6. c) conducted 7. b) shocking 8. b) into 9. b) darkest 10. b) fascinated 11. a) uninhibited 12. d) control 13. b) worsens 14. b) horrified 15. a) unwittingly 16. b) perspective 17. a) the 18. d) As 19. b) control 20. a) compelling

[Writing Practice]

1. was written by
2. was published in
3. becomes increasingly interested in
4. every individual has both virtuous and wicked
5. Driven by a desire to separate
6. transforms into
7. represents the embodiment of
8. is fascinated by his newfound ability to
9. begins to lose control over
10. he can no longer control his transformations

[Word Quiz]

1. a) Novella 2. d) Tendency 3. c) Victorian 4. d) Intrigue 5. c) Coexistence 6. b) Virtuous 7. b) Wicked 8. c) Transformation 9. a) Desires 10. a) Inhibited 11. a) Conscience 12. a) Influential 13. a) Revert 14. a) Heinous 15. a) Confession 16. a) Identity 17. a) Unchecked 18. a) Consequences 19. a) Tragic 20. a) Exploration

Unit 35: Resurrection (1899)

[Reading Comprehension]

1. c) Love, redemption, and the search for meaning 2. b) A young aristocrat and nobleman 3. c) Katerina Maslova 4. c) He had abandoned her after promising love and marriage 5. b) St. Petersburg 6. c) A life of prostitution 7. c) Murder 8. d) He is shocked and overwhelmed 9. b) She is sentenced to hard labor in Siberia 10. c) His sense of guilt and need for redemption 11. b) She is angry and resentful 12. c) Social reform and helping prisoners 13. d) Spiritual growth and selflessness 14. c) He dedicates his life to justice and social equality 15. b) Love and compassion can change lives

[Grammar Check-up]

1. (-detailed, detail) 2. (are, -is) 3. (him, -his) (-prisoners, prisoner) 4. (haunts, -is haunted by) (-that, what) 5. (which, -where) (stations, -is stationed) 6. (-innocent, innocence) (-who is, is) 7. (promises, -promising) 8. (is remained, -remains) 9. (-heartbroken, heartbreaking) 10. (-Left, Leaving) 11. (determining, -determined) 12. (attends to, -attends) (-poisoning, poison) 13. (appoints, -is appointed) (convincing, -convinced) 14. (Even though, -Despite) (innocent, -innocence) (-guilty, guilt) 15. (devastating, -devastated by) 16. (initial, -initially) 17. (is spent,

-spends) (-increasingly, increasing) 18. (Determining, -Determined) (fight, -fighting) 19. (-uses, is used) (inmate, -inmates) 20. (is undergone, -undergoes) (-selfless, selfish) 21. (dedicating, -to dedicate) 22. (living, -to live) (help, -helping) 23. (inspiring, -inspired by) (seeks, -seeking) 24. (emphasizes, -emphasizing) 25. (-profound, profoundly) 26. (-thought-provoking, thought-provoked)

[Writing Practice]

1. is appointed as a juror for the trial
2. Despite his efforts to convince the other jurors of
3. becomes increasingly aware of
4. Determined to make a difference
5. finds redemption through selfless actions
6. decides to dedicate his life to the pursuit
7. devotes himself to helping the less fortunate
8. seeking forgiveness for her past mistakes
9. explores profound themes of human nature
10. remains a powerful and thought-provoking novel
11. Left with no financial support
12. attends the trial and learns

[Word Quiz]

1. c) Resurrection 2. d) Redemption 3. c) Search 4. b) Purpose 5. a) Detailed 6. a) Attend 7. c) Trial 8. a) Recognize 9. b) Guilt 10. d) Regret 11. a) Significant role 12. c) Downfall 13. b) Narrative 14. d) Transformation 15. a) Provincial town 16. c) Innocent 17. c) Superficial 18. b) Financial 19. b) False accusation 20. c) Death sentence